Some Poets, Artists
&
'A Reference for Mellors'

Some Poets, Artists & 'A Reference for Mellors'

Anthony Powell

First published in the UK in 2005 by
Timewell Press Limited
10 Porchester Terrace, London W2 3TL

A catalogue record for this title is available from the
British Library.

ISBN 1 85725 210 1

Typeset by TW Typesetting, Plymouth, Devon
Printed and bound in the UK by Biddles Ltd, King's Lynn

For John Bayley

CONTENTS

PART TWO
The Artists

ACKNOWLEDGEMENTS

The pieces that follow were published in *Apollo*, the *Daily Telegraph* (by far the most of them), *Punch*, the *Times Literary Supplement*, *Encounter*, *Sotheby's Preview Magazine* and 'A Reference for Mellors' in *The New Savoy*.* I am grateful to editors and publishers of these for permission to reprint them here; also to Tessa Davies, Roland Glasser, David Higham Associates and Violet Powell for more photocopies when necessary.

Anthony Powell
1990

Thanks are also due to Michael Meredith, Eton College librarian, for extensive assistance with the final preparation of the manuscript, to George Lilley for the use of his *Anthony Powell: A Bibliography*, and to both Georgia Powell and Sarah Legge of *Apollo* magazine for further photocopies.

John Powell
2005

---

*Also as a private limited edition by Moorhouse and Sørensen in 1994.

INTRODUCTION

This volume of criticism covers the same ground, 1946–1990, as *Miscellaneous Verdicts* and *Under Review*, but some of the pieces are about artists not writers. I first planned to call the book *Some Poets, Painters and 'A Reference for Mellors'*, thinking that a few sculptors could be included with the Painters without needing special mention. When examining what was collected together I found that all sorts of people connected with painting and sculpture, who were not themselves painters or sculptors, were included, for example Augustus Hare or Bernard Berenson (who would have enjoyed being included under Artists). So although *Painters* rather than *Artists* is my preferred title (artists having a much wider implication) *Artists* seemed to offer a way out.

Most of what is written is biographical about the Artists, rather than strictly speaking critical: the same is true of the Poets. I was often given books I wanted to review by well-disposed literary editors. But in the last resort I had to take what was going. In other words, Poets vary from Chaucer to W. S. Gilbert, with one or two Frenchmen and Americans as well; the Artists from van Dyck to the obscure eighteenth-century romantic James Barry. Many famous names are omitted in both categories, simply because books about them did not appear, or at any rate I was not given them to review. It is, I'm afraid, no use grumbling at the account. There is something to be said for reconsidering John Skelton or William Davenant, Wenceslaus Hollar or Félix Fénéon, rather than the well-known figures. One is again struck by how many books on writers and artists were published between the 1960s and the 1980s compared with today.

'A Reference for Mellors' is another matter, being a parody written in 1946 for a 'little magazine' called *The New Savoy*, edited by Mara Meulen and Francis Wyndham; one number only appeared. The story envisages someone visiting Lady Chatterley to obtain a reference for the redoubtable gamekeeper. It subsequently appeared in several publications and as a very limited private edition on both sides of the Atlantic and should, of course, have come at the end of several pieces about D. H. Lawrence in *Under Review*. I forgot about it, and someone pointed out that 'Mellors', which had shown itself as reasonably popular, ought to be available between hard covers. In the course of various appearances I polished up the parody in minor ways. For example, in his first version Lawrence had given the name Parkin to the gamekeeper (which explains Lady Chatterley's uncertainty about his identity), and the apparently unconventional sexual relations of the Mellors family appeared later.

Anthony Powell

PART ONE

The Poets

GEOFFREY CHAUCER

I

It would be hard to imagine a more suitable figure than Geoffrey Chaucer (b. about 1340) to start the ball of English literature rolling. All kinds of poets might have appeared at that moment to produce an undeniably great book who had, purely personally, little or no relation to the main stream of English life.

Chaucer covers the ground in this respect in an extraordinary manner, while as a writer he runs only second to Dante, and first when it comes to treating the essential aspects of life in a humorous manner.

To begin with, in his own background and career Chaucer straddles an exceptional social span. His family, now known for four generations, were always connected with the leather and wine trades, owning land in Ipswich and London. They belonged to the prosperous middle class. Chaucer appears to have been brought up as a page in the household of the wife of Lionel, Duke of Clarence, third son of Henry IV.

One imagines that was a pretty good start in life, but not one which by any means forecast the fact that Chaucer would end as brother-in-law of John of Gaunt, Duke of Lancaster, Edward III's fourth son and the father of Henry IV.

Chaucer was just about the same age as John of Gaunt, whose dominating personality, perhaps chiefly due to Shakespeare, still makes something of an echo down the ages. Chaucer's wife's sister was 'time-honoured Lancaster's' mistress. After marrying a Plantagenet cousin and a Spanish princess, John of Gaunt took her as his third wife.

It must have been a lively family connection to possess, and is a good illustration of how variegated English social life has always been. There were advantages to be derived from it. Chaucer was given various civil service jobs, which included two diplomatic visits to Italy, where he may have met Petrarch and certainly came across the work of Boccaccio with obvious importance to him in the light of *The Canterbury Tales*.

A certain amount of the duties for Chaucer's official appointments was farmed out, and one is relieved to find that, although he must have been highly regarded as a suitable man for secret missions, his qualities were not wholly those of a civil servant, at times even indicating a certain vagueness and dislike for business.

In 1380 there was some trouble about a young woman with the attractive name of Cecilia Chaumpaigne, who had brought a case against Chaucer for rape. It must be remembered that this charge may have been a technical one involving some sort of abduction in relation, say, to a runaway marriage. On the other hand, it may have meant the real thing. Opinions differ.

All these facts are well set out in Albert C. Baugh's *Chaucer's Major Poetry*, which includes everything Chaucer wrote in verse, except *The Romaunt of the Rose* and a few miscellaneous fragments. A feature of this edition is a good deal of annotation on the page itself, which is a help in dealing with Chaucer's language, in general perfectly understandable provided the occasional out-of-date word or phrase is explained at the foot of the page.

The Canterbury Tales is, of course, Chaucer's most famous work, but *Troilus and Criseyde* perhaps represents the peak of his achievement. It is really a kind of early novel in verse and its subtleties have, incidentally, been well examined in John Bayley's *The Character of Love*. This ability to indicate individual character with a phrase is particularly characteristic of Chaucer, making him almost one of the great novelists as well as a great poet.

Chaucer in His Time, aimed at the non-specialist, gives a very readable account of the period always keeping Chaucer in view, but relating him to what was happening in history.

Derek Brewer makes a number of good points, for example, the unexpected way in which, by the fourteenth century, the Middle Ages had taken on King Arthur as a national hero. The general view of Arthur now – as opposed to that of the nineteenth century – is that he was a historical character, but, if so, he had fought against the Anglo-Saxons. It is strange that at the period when the Anglo-Saxon fusion with the Normans was at last complete King Arthur, a purely 'Celtic' figure, should be superimposed on the whole edifice.

Dr Brewer deals, too, with Chaucer's association with the 'Lollard knights'. Historical views of the Lollards have varied in recent times. At one moment they were regarded as forerunners of the Reformation; then that perspective went out of fashion. Dr Brewer shows that there is much to be said for reconsidering it, because, even if the descent of Lollard opinion was not direct in England (being driven underground), the Lollards had a strong effect on Huss and Luther, who, in their turn, greatly influenced the subsequent Reformation in this country.

When Chaucer got into his trouble with Cecilia Chaumpaigne, one of the witnesses of the document of settlement was a Lollard knight called Sir Jon Clanvowe, who probably wrote the Chaucerian poem 'The Cuckoo and the Nightingale'. Dr Brewer calls him a 'Herefordshire man', but he is perhaps more correctly described as Welsh, as he was descended from a Welsh prince, and his family were associated with what is now Radnorshire.

This seems of interest in regard to Chaucer's appointment in 1390 as a subforester in North Petherton, Somerset, allegedly by Roger Mortimer, Earl of March. That Chaucer owed this job to Mortimer has been questioned. It is at least worth remembering – if I may put this forward – that Clanvowe, apparently a close friend of Chaucer's, came from the heart of Mortimer's fief, and was, one imagines, his tenant. This was in Chaucer's later years, when he suffered considerable financial worries.

Chaucer's Major Poetry, edited by Albert C. Baugh, Routledge.

Chaucer in His Time, Derek Brewer, Nelson.

1964
Daily Telegraph

II

There is perhaps no more time-honoured quotation in the language than 'He was a verray, parfit gentil knyght' – particularly old favourite for striking the deeper note in obituaries while remaining the right side of pomposity.

Chaucer's Knight, as we are all aware, was one of the Canterbury Pilgrims, but not everyone will know that for some decades now certain cracks have been noted in what had hitherto been taken to be his unassailable surface. Terry Jones (more popularly known in television as a member of *Monty Python's Flying Circus*) now comes along with a scholarly – but exceedingly entertaining – book, which sets out the reasons for thinking that, far from presenting the Knight as a kind of Colonel Newcome, Chaucer was being savagely satirical at the expense of a figure who was wholly on the make, and probably wasn't a knight at all.

In the fourteenth century there was a great deal more 'social mobility' than is generally supposed, and one of the ways of going up in the world was becoming a professional soldier.

Falstaff's broken-down levies, with whom he declared he would not march through Gloucester, were being given a chance, albeit a slender one, of winning fame and fortune. For instance, Sir John Hawkwood, the renowned *condottiere*, had begun life as an English tailor's apprentice, and appears to have been an impressed archer at the start of his military career.

To Chaucer's contemporary readers the irony of certain statements made about the Knight would have been immediately apparent, says Mr Jones, and his arguments are convincing. The Knight had fought in Egypt,

Prussia, Lithuania, Russia, Spain, Morocco, Turkey, for Spanish, German, Cypriot, Turkish and Moorish masters. One of the few countries he had never fought for was England.

In short the Knight was a mercenary, one of a class that had then grown up comparatively recently, and was causing much shaking of heads. In the past men-at-arms had been attached to their feudal lords, or indentured for life at an early age to some magnate. They were not like Sir John Hawkwood (of whose knighthood no record exists), who would sometimes be fighting for the Pope against the Visconti; sometimes for the Visconti against the Pope.

Chaucer's Knight's down-at-heel appearance and lack of armorial bearings, far from being signs of modesty (as modern commentators have supposed), would immediately have aroused suspicions among his own contemporaries. Mr Jones shows that the Knight was wearing the absolute minimum of knightly equipment (laid down by law), in order to avoid being regarded as a rich booty to be ransomed and worth capturing in time of war.

To the contemporary reader the epithet 'gentil' applied to the Knight would have meant well-born, but the concept 'noble is as noble does' was already a flourishing one, so that not only does the Knight appear to have had no coat-of-arms (not an absolute sine qua non of gentility at the period, though certainly usual), but the war service mentioned includes some of history's most appalling massacres and in general unbelievably savage conflicts. Nor, so far as the moral meaning of 'gentil' is concerned, does the Knight appear to have been at all keen on 'largesse', that is generosity in money matters.

The Knight's story (all the Pilgrims told one in the hope of winning a free supper) concerns Theseus, who emerges as a pitiless tyrant. In the course of this tale the Temple of Venus is described which, instead of being concerned with courtly love in the style of Boccaccio, presents a scene which a fourteenth-century audience would have found intensely funny, appropriate not to the love-vision of the poet but to the rapes and brothels of a freebooting life.

When tournaments are mentioned by the Knight he makes a point of emphasising that he had killed his opponent, something that was extremely badly regarded, like glorying in football hooliganism or throwing beer-cans at cricket. One way and another the Knight had disposed of at least eighteen men.

In short the Knight is an ominous figure in Chaucer's picture of the world round him, with its Lollards, peasant revolts, bands of mercenaries, the last in certain cases exceeding in size a medieval national army. Chaucer knew what he was talking about because he had actually visited Italy, and negotiated with Sir John Hawkwood in person, prototype of the successful mercenary, who was at least reputed to honour his contracts.

Mr Jones's book, well indexed and documented, is full of interesting material about the period

Chaucer's Knight:
The Portrait of a Medieval Mercenary,
Terry Jones, Weidenfeld.

1980
Daily Telegraph

THE WYATTS, FATHER AND SON

The two Sir Thomas Wyatts are, it must be admitted, rather confusing. Sir Thomas Wyatt the father (*c.* 1503–1542) was the poet and diplomatist; Sir Thomas Wyatt the son (*c.* 1521–1554), leader of the rebellion against Bloody Mary.

A difficult situation in this respect is not improved by Patricia Thomson's book, which is about Wyatt the Elder, giving on the jacket a picture that Eric N. Simon's book captions as a portrait of Wyatt the Younger. I am on Miss Thomson's side in this difference of opinion, and think the portrait is that of Wyatt the Elder; although it certainly looks rather like another portrait of Wyatt the Younger.

Miss Thomson is a lecturer in English at London University. Her book, *Sir Thomas Wyatt and his Background*, is a scholarly study of the elder Wyatt's career and poetry. This necessitates investigation of various other aspects of Henry VIII's reign and there is much interesting historical information concentrated here. Miss Thomson is sometimes rather diffuse in arrangement of her material. Anyone interested in the period will enjoy her specialised angle on its personalities.

Mr Simon's book, *The Queen and the Rebel*, is of a totally different sort. It is a jolly, slangy, popular account of Wyatt the Younger's rebellion. It rattles along and gives a good idea of what happened, without overdoing the politics or psychology. It can also be recommended to those interested in Kent, where the early stages of the rising took place.

The Wyatts came from Yorkshire. The poet-diplomat's father, Sir Henry Wyatt, had backed Henry VII – rather exceptionally for a squire of the county. He survived being put on the rack and made to drink a lot of 'mustard and vinegar' by Richard III, becoming a rich man and moving to Allington Castle, Kent, when the Tudor dynasty took over.

Sir Henry's son, Thomas Wyatt the Elder, went to Court and performed various diplomatic missions for Henry VIII, including one to the Pope – then assailed on all sides by hostile armies – in 1527, when a papal official brought two of the choicest courtesans to the English embassy with 'a plenary dispensation verbal'.

Wyatt the Elder was also involved with Anne Boleyn. Was he her lover? Was any of the five men executed for adultery with her in fact her lover? The Spanish ambassador, delighted by her removal, at the same time thought not.

One has the picture of the lively, flirtatious queen, determined that all men who came in contact with her should fall. No doubt some did. On the whole, it probably ended there. Yet there is a suggestion in what remains of the evidence that Wyatt was more than casually attracted by Anne. He was arrested as being on too good terms with her, but later released.

The greater part of Miss Thomson's study deals in a highly technical manner with Wyatt's verse, its value and derivations. Wyatt was, indeed, with Lord Surrey, practically the only English poet of any standing since Chaucer. There had been no individual or school of poets in fifteenth-century England contemporary with Villon, though Wales had Lewis Glyn Cothi. Wyatt's fame as a poet rests, of course, on:

> They flee from me that sometime did me seek
> With naked foot stalking in my chamber.
> I have seen them gentle, tame and meek
> That now are wild and do not remember . . .

Miss Thomson truly remarks that this wonderful poem has had no objectors, therefore needs no defence; but on the whole Wyatt is now regarded by critics – by Miss Thomson herself – as producing little more than the verses to be expected from a distinguished civil servant.

Miss Thomson is at times a little doctrinaire on this subject, and some may disagree with her in apparently assuming that 'They' (in the poem quoted above) include friends and business associates, as well as the lady who

> . . . caught me in her arms long and small;
> Therewithall sweetly did me kiss,
> And softly said, dear heart, how like you this?

Surely, whatever grumbling Wyatt indulged in about the way his friends behaved, in this particular poem he speaks only of other mistresses.

Turning to Sir Thomas Wyatt the Younger, the pattern remains of great interest. This Wyatt was, roughly speaking, a professional soldier, not primarily involved in politics. He had been brought up a Roman Catholic.

When Queen Mary Tudor decided, in the face of almost total opposition from her counsellors, that she would marry Philip of Spain, the country was in an uproar. This is the sort of popular history that we keep vaguely in the back of the mind, perhaps feeling that modern research presents rather a different picture.

On the contrary, there seems abundant evidence, that the Spanish match was detested almost as much by Roman Catholics, as by Protestants. The Inquisition and the prospect of foreign rule roused a national spirit that is hardly imaginable a century before. When a Spanish mission arrived to arrange the marriage, they were snowballed by the London crowds.

Others felt that even stronger measures were required, and the conspiracy of which, almost by chance, Wyatt the Younger became the head, had ramifications all over the country. Paradoxically enough, the royal troops who opposed him were commanded by Lord Pembroke, a Calvinist, though one – as we learn from Aubrey – prepared to turn his coat fairly easily.

Things went against Wyatt: false allies, the weather, perhaps a certain indecision in his own character. He was captured, racked like his grandfather, and executed. The rebellion was put down with considerable savagery. Lady Jane Grey and her husband were among the victims.

The question was: would the future Queen Elizabeth also be regarded as inculpated? Wyatt seems to have written her letters. Probably, under torture, he said that she was implicated, but later denied it. There seems every reason to believe that Elizabeth was in no way part of the conspiracy, although it is likely she would have been put on the throne had it succeeded, which might easily have happened.

In his speech from the scaffold Wyatt declared that Princess Elizabeth was entirely innocent. The priest attending him at his end interrupted this statement and shouted that it was untrue. As at communist trials, the authorities thought the prisoner completely reduced. He was nearly, but not quite. There is much in *The Queen and the Rebel*, (including an extraordinary parallel to a post-Eichmann incident) that has a curiously modern ring.

Sir Thomas Wyatt and his Background, 1965
Patricia Thomson, Routledge. *Daily Telegraph*

The Queen and the Rebel:
Mary Tudor and Wyatt the Younger,
Eric N. Simons, Muller.

JOHN SKELTON

It would be reasonable to assume that most people, even if they have heard of the poetry of John Skelton (*c.* 1460–1529), do not know much about him. This was once far from the case. He was a famous name. In this excellent biography by Maurice Pollet (smoothly translated from the French by John Warrington), Skelton's talent and odd, aggressive personality are acutely examined.

As a poet, Skelton stands between what verse meant to Chaucer, and the emerging poetry of the Renaissance, exemplified by Surrey and Wyatt. Here is an example of Skelton:

> Merry Margaret,
>   As midsummer flower,
> Gentle as falcon
> Or hawk of the tower:
> With solace and gladness,
> Much mirth and no madness,
> All good and no badness . . .

Skelton's family origins have been argued. It now seems fairly certain that he came from Yorkshire. He appears to have been marked down for success early, made poet-laureate at Cambridge, and later Oxford, found employment at court, was praised by Erasmus, and took religious orders when he was thirty-eight.

He was tutor to Prince Henry (later Henry VIII) while his elder brother Arthur, Prince of Wales, was alive, but when Arthur died, and Henry became heir apparent, Skelton was replaced. His career in the world of Churchly politics was not dazzling. He was given the living of Diss in Norfolk, but there promotion rested.

One imagines him too eccentric, not enough of a down-to-earth politician to make that sort of a career. This was not due to any backwardness on his own part to join the hurly-burly, be ambitious, violent and offensive. He might be very keen on his status as poet (signing 'laureat' when he witnessed a will), but he was also far from being the sort of poet who concerned himself only with poetry.

Pope called him 'beastly Skelton'. Pope's feelings were probably due to an aspect of Skelton's legend which is carefully investigated by M. Pollet, that of Skelton as a famous comic figure of his period. This is worth a word, because it has bearing on biographical writing even to this day.

Skelton's verses to ladies, even allowing for conventional phrasing, suggest that he found them attractive. His 'The Tunnyng of Elynour Rummynge' (a repulsive harridan who keeps a pub), a poem popular in the 1920s when reprinted and illustrated, also shows his familiarity with the seamy side of sex and drinking.

Admitting this, also admitting a contemporary reputation for wit and eccentricity, we find a mild anecdote about Skelton included during his own lifetime in one of those collections of jokes popular at the time, *A Hundred Merry Tales*. Shakespeare took some of his funny stories from this particular anthology.

So far so good, but hardly was Skelton in his coffin before further stories began to pour out about him, in which he was confused with a friend of Chaucer's called Scoggin – also, as it happened, a poet and royal tutor – who had lived about a hundred years earlier.

That was bad enough, but worse was to come. Scoggin, as has been said, was an earlier personality, but one who, from his career, might be judged to possess a somewhat similar line of wit to Skelton's. Unfortunately, on this already muddled situation descended an avalanche of chestnuts, many of a bawdy sort, told about another Scoggin, who almost certainly never existed, but was said to have been court fool to Henry VII.

Simply as regards confusion of identity, it was rather as if a story told about Evelyn Waugh was then said to refer to P. G. Wodehouse, and, as a result, not only were Waugh and Wodehouse anecdotes impossible to sort out, but they could also not be distinguished from those about Bertie Wooster, believed by many to be a real man. As a consequence of this misunderstanding, Skelton in due course became notorious for having lived a life of the most disreputable sort – which there is not a shred of evidence to suggest is true.

M. Pollet – head of the English Department in the University of Dakar, Senegal, and, like Skelton himself, former tutor to a royal prince, the late King Feisal II – also points out that Skelton's political approach has often been misunderstood. Because of his opposition to Wolsey, some of his invective was later useful to supporters of the Reformed Church, but Skelton was, in fact, a strong adherent of papal power; also, to some extent, of the feudal aristocracy against the centralising Tudors. A surprising amount of material remains about Skelton, an interesting figure of whom one would like to know even more.

John Skelton: Poet of Tudor England, 1971
Maurice Pollet, Dent. *Daily Telegraph*

WILLIAM SHAKESPEARE

I

This book contains the text of Shakespeare's Sonnets, essays on them by Edward Hubler, Northrop Frye, Leslie A. Fielder, Stephen Spender and R. P. Blackmur, together with Oscar Wilde's short story on the same subject, 'The Portrait of Mr W. H.'. It is a volume that investigates the enigma of the Sonnets very thoroughly in a manageable and entertaining manner.

In recent years books, articles and essays about Shakespeare have increased in spate to what seems like three a day. In so wide a field, of which the Sonnets offer not least of the material, the problems are not easy to boil down to simple terms. However, an effort must by made.

The Sonnets are some hundred and fifty poems, probably written when Shakespeare was about thirty, in 1593, but not published until sixteen years later. Of these 126 are addressed to a young man: twenty-five to a woman. It has been suggested that the young man was Lord Pembroke or Lord Southampton. The woman has come to be known as the 'Dark Lady'. A 'Rival Poet' is also mentioned, for whose identity various Elizabethan writers have been canvassed.

The question, broadly speaking, is whether Shakespeare was writing about imaginary situations or 'real people'; and, if 'real people', who they were and what was the involved story of which the Sonnets give us a glimpse.

Much scholarship has been expended in the former view, that the Sonnets are no more than a poetic exercise. On the whole Mr Hubler, Mr Frye and Mr Fiedler seem to lean towards this explanation. They are all worth reading, although one feels that scholarship and theory sometimes obscure the simple fact. Mr Blackmur also has good things to say, but I am less certain of his conclusions.

For the side that opposes a 'true story', it must be admitted that there cannot be a novelist, from Petronius onwards, who has not been repeatedly forced to explain that characters in a novel are something on their own. They do not stand or fall by whether or not they are 'meant to be' existing persons.

On the other hand, a poem is not a novel, and many, probably most, commentators on Shakespeare's Sonnets have felt that he is dealing with figures very close to him, rather than writing a sequence of 'imaginary' poems.

So far, so good: scholars are of two opinions; one chooses whichever one prefers. For my own part, I think the likelihood overwhelming that Shakespeare was speaking of himself and his own immediate emotions. However, there's the rub.

The Sonnets to the young man are written in terms of passionate love. The question has therefore to be faced: was Shakespeare homosexual; or, at least, ambi-sexual, for the 'Dark Lady' (who appears to have seduced the young man) is specifically described as the poet's mistress. This tricky problem has been approached in various ways, chiefly by the traditional British method, when such questions arise, of pretending it does not exist.

For example, *The Oxford Companion to English Literature* says of the Sonnets:

> Most of them trace the course of the writer's affection for a young patron of rank and beauty . . . Other characters are alluded to, who evidently played a real part in Shakespeare's life . . .

It would be hard to imagine more of an understatement of the manner in which the young man is addressed; while it might be added that, although there are reasons for supposing he could be a patron, that status is by no means settled.

For sheer silliness, indeed deliberate misleading statements, as to this uncomfortable aspect of the Sonnets, Bernard Shaw (quoted by Mr Spender) takes the palm:

> the language of the sonnets addressed to Pembroke, extravagant as it now seems, is the language of compliment and fashion . . . unmistakable for anything else than the expression of a friendship delicate enough to be wounded, and a manly loyalty deep enough to be outraged.

To check this I looked for a comparable dedication and found one to some sonnets (1602) by Samuel Daniel (tipped by some as the Rival Poet) to his patron, Sir Edward Dymoke. You could say that the language is that 'of compliment and fashion'; it bears not the smallest resemblance to, say, Shakespeare's Sonnet 20. A book like John Buxton's *Sir Philip Sidney and the English Renaissance*, which particularly deals with writers and their patrons, shows nothing in the least resembling Shakespeare's language, which far outruns 'manly loyalty'.

Accordingly, it is not surprising to find Shakespeare acclaimed as one of the great homosexuals of literature. But, if that were so, one would certainly expect to find the subject dealt with in his plays. On the contrary, it is scarcely mentioned. There is no reason why it should not have been touched upon, as Marlowe touched upon it in *Edward II*. Not a bit of it. In *Richard II*, a parallel case, Shakespeare obviously feels no tendency at all to approach the story with such an emphasis.

What then is the answer? I think Mr Spender, after giving an excellent sketch of the probable character of the young man depicted, suggests it. He takes the view – also that of Mr Martin Seymour Smith, quoted here in an as yet unpublished introduction to the Sonnets – that Shakespeare was a normal man who for several months, or even years, was obsessed by a boy.

It is perfectly clear that the world Shakespeare depicts in his plays is a normal one. His characters of women in them are essentially women seen by a normal man. At the same time, it may well be that the heightened sensibilities that produced a writer like Shakespeare also produced a self-knowledge which a lesser mind of that period would not have possessed. Shakespeare knew what was happening and bitterly resented it.

Finally, there is Wilde's story, 'The Portrait of Mr W. H.', in which the theory is put forward that 'Mr W. H.' of the dedication was a boy actor called Will Hughes. On the whole, the dedication, famous as it is, gets rather peremptory treatment by commentators. It is often suggested that 'Mr W. H.' was merely put in by the publisher for some quite unimportant reason.

The fact remains that throughout the Sonnets puns about 'hews' and 'use' are too numerous to list, while Sonnet 135 seems to state categorically that 'Will' was the young man's name as well as Shakespeare's:

> Whoever hath her wish, though as thy *Will*,
> And *Will* to boot, and *Will* in over-plus;
> More than enough am I that vex thee still,
> To thy sweet will making addition thus,

Even if the case for him being an actor is a thin one, can 'Will Hughes' be altogether dismissed? Was he in fact a different person from the young man of the earlier Sonnets advised to marry and get a son?

It is an extraordinarily enjoyable experience to re-read the Sonnets, but it is the way madness lies.

The Riddle of Shakespeare's Sonnets, 1962
Stephen Spender et al., Routledge. *Daily Telegraph*

II

One of the legends about Shakespeare is that little or nothing is known of his life. This is altogether untrue. A large amount of material exists, compared with other dramatists of his period. Perhaps the reverse seems to be the case simply because Shakespeare's personality was not of the apparently clear-cut sort that Ben Jonson has transmitted.

The rather unmanageably sized volume, *William Shakespeare: A Documentary Life*, contains all the documents that refer to Shakespeare, reproduced in facsimile, with a commentary by S. Schoenbaum. For those who enjoy first-hand sources this is a very useful and interesting collection. Mr Schoenbaum is occasionally a trifle arch, but his observations are always tolerant, matter-of-fact, and informed by historical sense.

The documentation gives a particularly clear picture of John Shakespeare, the Bard's father. John Shakespeare seems to have been a glover; though he probably also engaged in other commercial dealings. He was coming up in the world, becoming in due course Bailiff and JP of Stratford.

Owing apparently to an economic recession that hit others in the town, John Shakespeare fell into depressed circumstances, but even at the end of his life he could put up £10 (say, half the annual income of a vicar or schoolmaster) as a surety for someone he knew.

Since John Shakespeare always signed with an elaborate mark, it has been suggested that he was illiterate, but many known literates signed with a mark, and it is most unlikely that he would have held the appointments he did had he been unable to write – though often great noblemen of the period could not do so. John Shakespeare put in for a grant of a coat-of-arms in 1568 (when his son was only a small child) and, by the terms of reference of the Heralds, held just the sort of offices envisaged for making such a grant. The fact that he suffered financial losses perfectly explains why he never went forward with a proceeding that all sorts of men of his position were engaged in.

Mr Schoenbaum is kinder about the deer-stealing legend than perhaps it deserves, but gives the arguments against: that the Lucys of Charlecote did not have a park for deer at that period; that whipping was not a punishment for poaching; that Shakespeare is complimentary when he mentions the Lucy family; that 'luces' were represented on several other family arms as well as the Lucys of Charlecote's. Those others included the arms of one Gardiner, with whom Shakespeare is known to have had a row and to whom the jokes about 'louses' in *Henry IV* are more likely to refer. There was, in fact, a well-known deer-poaching case at Charlecote before Star Chamber in 1610, which may have been the root of the legend.

Just how much Shakespeare made from his plays when the going was good is hard to estimate. Mr Schoenbaum puts forward figures that suggest about £200 and £300 a year: that could, in a sense, be compared with the £500 a year of a squire at the lower end of the recognised upper landed class, but the squire would probably be able to put his hand on less ready money than Shakespeare. Certainly when New Place was assessed at ten hearths (usually approximated for the size of the house rather than actually counted) Shakespeare was living in a rich man's mansion.

Aubrey wrote down some conversation of an old actor called Beeston, who had known Shakespeare. These jottings were, in Aubrey's usual manner, scattered all over the page. Mr Schoenbaum says that 'later authorities' (later than Aubrey's editor Andrew Clarke) have shown that the remarks about 'not a company keeper . . . wouldn't be debauched, etc.' refer to Shakespeare, not to Beeston. They may; but it is not as certain as all that. If the MS is examined, the meaning can be seen as anybody's guess.

But one is entirely on Mr Schoenbaum's side in discarding the supposed symbolism of the 'second-best bed'. If Shakespeare's will is notable for anything, it is for the extreme conventionality of its terms among wills of the period. Edmond Malone, the eighteenth-century Shakespearian critic, started off this particular hare; one of the many examples of how completely the eighteenth-century was out of touch with the ways of the early seventeenth-century. The wills of the earlier century habitually take a great deal for read (the wife, for example, getting automatically a third of the property), and, if any old scores are paid off, they are likely to be specifically mentioned. It is more probable that, so far from being insulting, the bed was a nice one that the testator did not want the family to bicker over.

In short, the whole of this collection, reproduced in its original form, suggests the almost humdrum nature of Shakespeare's exterior life. That there was another side, no one would doubt. Mr Schoenbaum produces of course, the famous dedication of the Sonnets and lists the more prominent 'fair young men' candidates for 'Mr W. H.'. As an adherent of Hotson's choice, William Hatcliffe, I must point out that Hatcliffe was not a 'Lancashire man', but came from Lincolnshire; quite a different matter. I admit that, if Hotson's dating is right, this means that Shakespeare was writing some of his best poetry at the same time as far less good stuff; but, socially and psychologically, I feel Hatcliffe fits the bill.

Sir Gelly Meyrick (preferable to Mr Schoenbaum's less usual 'Sir Gilly Meyrick'), one of the Essex conspirators, arranged for a special performance of Shakespeare's *Richard III* on the eve of the rebellion. In Gamini Salgado's interesting *Eyewitnesses of Shakespeare*, the Essex trial is quoted as one of the earliest mentions of a Shakespearian performance. Mr Salgado records that the eighteenth-century actor Betterton, 'naturally ruddy and sanguine', was said, as Hamlet seeing the ghost, to have been able to turn white. In 1809, a performance of *Hamlet* was given by a troupe of dogs at the Royal Circus.

William Shakespeare: A Documentary Life,
S. Schoenbaum, OUP/Clarendon Press
with the Scholar Press.

1975
Daily Telegraph

Eyewitnesses of Shakespeare:
First Hand Accounts of Performances, 1590–1890,
Gamini Salgado, Chatto for Sussex University Press.

III

It is not easy to write (or review) sanely about Shakespeare. Peter Levi manages to keep a level head. He is scholarly without being ponderous (in fact, often extremely amusing), and confines his own quirks to the Appendix.

There he puts his recently much-discussed claim to have established certain formal verses written for a private party at the Earl of Huntington's house at Ashby-de-la-Zouch, Leicestershire, as by Shakespeare. The initialled signature has at the same moment been amended, and is therefore enigmatic. It has been suggested as referring to a Leicestershire neighbour, Sir William Skipwith. But, Shakespeare or not, the poem is an essentially minor work, its chief interest, even if Shakespearean, to strengthen the likelihood of Shakespeare having worked for Lord Strange's men.

Mr Levi begins with a close look at the Stratford background, giving useful pedigrees of family connections. As in every local community of the period there was an immense amount of inter-relationship, some of this most revealing. Clearly the dominating experience of Shakespeare's boyhood must have been his father's rapid ascent in business, then equally rapid decline.

Mr Levi has an interesting theory about this. John Shakespeare, describing himself as a glover, was (not altogether legally) involved in the wool trade, and several other commercial enterprises. He seems to have been one of those able businessmen always taking just too much risk. Mr Levi thinks he was a Roman Catholic, but not at all enthusiastically. John Shakespeare's home does not figure on Recusant lists; his non-appearances at church were apparently due to fear of writs of debt.

None the less, these circumstances do not quite explain the efforts of the Stratford authorities to make John Shakespeare's ominously rickety position as easy as possible and his simultaneous persecution – not only by creditors, but by a disreputable professional informer. Mr Levi thinks this was all part of a much larger Warwickshire feud between the old and powerful family of Arden (of which John Shakespeare's wife was a ramification) against the upstart Lord Leicester's supporters; polemics comparable to rows Aubrey records between the Longs, old established in Wiltshire, and the locally parvenu Welsh Herberts.

Mr Levi accepts Aubrey's story of Shakespeare as a young man 'killing a calf in high style'. He does not mention that this was perhaps a mummer's routine performance, nor Hamlet referring to killing a calf when he rags Polonius for boasting of former skill as an amateur actor. Incidentally, when interviewing the old actor Beeston, Aubrey's words are quoted: 'Lived in Shoreditch . . . if invited to court ['court' is omitted here for some reason], writ he was in pain'. The manuscript certainly looks as if Aubrey (in an insertion) meant Beeston, rather than Shakespeare, lived in Shoreditch, and so on. Aubrey's best editor, Clark, thought that.

Mr Levi backs Southampton as the Young Man of the Sonnets. The exhortation to marry fits Southampton (even then, 'Get married, stop bitching about' may have been meant for someone else), but I don't think Shakespeare would have talked of his patron's 'budding name' or said he had been 'one hour mine', or mentioned Southampton's private parts. The Young Man was undoubtedly a social superior, but (in my view) not so far above the poet as a great nobleman like Southampton. If Shakespeare was prepared to include a sonnet (145) about Ann Hathaway in the sequence, he may well have started with Southampton (marriage, mother) and continued with another young man (possibly William Hatcliffe). Anyway, what about Will, what about Hew?

Having dealt with Shakespeare's early life, Mr Levi runs through the plays (his believed chronology), linking them when possible with the life. He usually has something acute to say about each. I share his dislike for *Much Ado*, but not his fancy for Desdemona. One suspects Desdemona was a bit of an *allumeuse*. If Cassio couldn't carry his drink he had no place on Othello's staff. As the general said to Evelyn Waugh, 'I can't have an ADC who gets foxed.'

By the time Shakespeare wrote *Twelfth Night* there are signs of fatigue, Mr Levi thinks. He had been pouring out work of high quality with unparalleled speed. The result of this comparative exhaustion was to complicate the mood in writing comedy. *Twelfth Night* begins with resounding gaiety, but, however unpleasant Malvolio may have been, his tormenting later becomes a shade unpleasant.

Mr Levi says his favourite character is Caliban. I think mine is Shallow, but we come together in taste for Abhorson, the executioner in *Measure for Measure*, Mr Levi being in the happy position of actually having met a professional hangman whose conversation turned out exactly like Abhorson's.

Among the points Mr Levi makes is that Shakespeare had the reputation of a bright fellow very early on. That does not always make for ease in earning a living. It is, however, something to bear in mind. If he did indeed hold horses outside a theatre, that seems to have taken the form (if true) of, say, a young temporary employee who totally reorganises an inconvenient car park.

Some critics are fond of saying Shakespeare was only concerned with being a poet and scarcely at all interested in his plays' survival. This is here shown to be incorrect by the manner in which Shakespeare would sometimes quite radically revise the text of plays, work with the printer, etc., though no doubt, like most writers, fail to be in complete control of what he wrote all the time when either acted or published.

Contrary to many conjectures, Mr Levi takes the view that Shakespeare was happily married and devoted – indeed perhaps rather over-devoted –

to his children. The various minor scandals about his kin after he died are typical of the sort of thing that abounds in local records of the period. They should not be taken too seriously. Shakespeare ended up, although by different means, very much as he might have done had his father not failed in the business. He was a typically upward mobile figure of his time. Mr Levi thinks the memorial bust shows an intelligent head. It might be added that A. C. Benson, no bad critic of such things, borrowed a ladder from the verger, from which eminence he felt confident the features were taken from a death mask.

The Life and Times of William Shakespeare, 1988
Peter Levi, Macmillan. *Daily Telegraph*

IV

The idea that Shakespeare may have served for a time in the army is not, in itself, a new one; and, among the various theories regarding the poet – ranging from overwhelming probability to fantastic imaginings of the wildest sort – the possibility of a short military career might be said to hold a good outside place. Sir Duff Cooper approaches the problem from the standpoint of a general reader who also happens to have seen as much of the world as could reasonably be expected of a man; including service with troops that was far from undistinguished. He does not rely on elaborate scholarship so much as common sense; and his thesis certainly strengthens the case for Shakespeare the Soldier.

'Sergeant Shakespeare' (surely 'sejeant' is, in fact, more correct military usage, even in these days) takes its title from the author's theory that Shakespeare's rank was that of an NCO; and here, at once, we touch on problems from which pedantry can scarcely be excluded. According to Mr C. G. Cruickshank's *Elizabeth's Army* there were three sorts of recruits: gentlemen volunteers, ordinary volunteers and pressed men. The former of these probably joined with a view to an eventual captaincy. Sir Duff Cooper speaks of 'an age when deep divisions were set between the classes'; but we do not feel convinced that Shakespeare (whose background appears to have been at times decidedly prosperous) might not have passed himself off in the first category. A reader thinks, for example, of the case of Donne in the army: though the latter's ironmonger father was no doubt richer than John Shakespeare. At least Sir Duff Cooper seems rather determined to make the Bard an NCO of the First World War – almost with a waxed moustache – whereas, we suggest, a volunteer who could read (and, after all, did not write at all badly though, apparently, in a somewhat crabbed hand) might well have joined for promotion. At any rate, if he were a sergeant, he is to be thought of far more in terms of the

Second World War, when such a rank was held from time to time by all kinds of unlikely persons.

We make this point because Sir Duff Cooper insists that Shakespeare's experience of war was viewed essentially from an NCO's point of view; although in an army of under ten thousand men the two sergeants in a company of a hundred or two hundred, officered only by a captain, a lieutenant and an ensign, must have seen a good deal of the game – even admitting the validity of the contention that regimental troops know little or nothing of the higher command. A possibility not examined here, perhaps not to be dismissed too lightly, is that Shakespeare might have been 'the clerk' – an important administrative official in the company.

If we might advance an argument in the other direction, we should say that the scene in *Antony and Cleopatra*, when the generals carouse on the ship, goes some way to indicate that the writer was familiar with such high-level jollifications, though no doubt viewed in a subordinate capacity. There are also passages in the historical plays that might be quoted to support a view that he had attended a staff conference or two. The evidence in Dr Leslie Hotson's *Shakespeare versus Shallow* might be used to prove that, if it was worth someone's while to try and guarantee legally that Shakespeare would not assault them, the poet was a man to be reckoned with physically and would have made some showing in the forces.

Sir Duff Cooper's suggestion that Iago was mad with rage simply and solely because he had been passed over for promotion is convincing, though the reader is less confident that Othello was so definitely 'not that sort of man'. There seems no reason why anyone should be 'shocked' at Shakespeare accepting Jeanne d'Arc as a witch; after all, she was very generally so regarded by contemporaries; and, though no doubt controversial, modern research has produced a good deal of evidence that points to the fact that she might have belonged to the witch-cult. William Beeston, not 'William Burton', was responsible for the story that Shakespeare had been a schoolmaster; and it is doubtful whether Leicester 'was probably the only man in the country who could give protection against the law of the land' in the case of the poaching legend – which rests on the slenderest and most unconvincing authority. A glance through, say, Star Chamber Proceedings would show that such playing about with the law was happening all the time in the sixteenth century. These are small points, however, and they do not take away from the stimulating quality of the book, with its good, straightforward arguments.

Sergeant Shakespeare, 1949
Duff Cooper, Hart-Davis. *Daily Telegraph*

V

So far as I am aware Hamlet is never played with a beard other than by Alec Guinness and certainly not by the author's father, Paul Scofield, though Hamlet himself says that no one 'plucks off my beard and blows it in my face'. Perhaps he had merely worn a beard during a hippie phase at Wittenberg University.

The only reason for reflecting on this small point is that every other aspect of Hamlet has been investigated so closely that the possibility of a beard, its effects for good or ill, might have been examined too.

Martin Scofield examines what Mallarmé, Laforgue, Eliot, Joyce, Lawrence, Kierkegaard, Claudel, Valéry and Kafka thought about the play, ending the book with some views of his own. This last section seemed the clearest and best, with emphasis on the 'authority' of the Ghost, the extent to which Hamlet felt justified in doing the spectre's bidding.

It would be interesting to know how many of the French writers cited by Mr Scofield read *Hamlet* with a real knowledge of English, Shakespearian English at that. French translations of Shakespeare can sound fairly odd. We have only to remember that 'Wormwood, wormwood' is changed into 'Absinthe, absinthe' to be convinced of the difficulties of translation.

Mallarmé (who possessed one of Manet's illustrations to *Hamlet*) looked upon the Prince as a hero of the spirit, seeking truth and order. The play to him is Shakespeare's 'central meditation on the problem of action', says Mr Scofield.

Claudel, on the other hand, thought Hamlet was doing no more than play a role. He had lost his sense of the world about him. Like Claudel, Valéry saw the modern intellect in all its verity in Hamlet, but with the additional twist of 'its mixture of fragments of past culture'; a point of view that looks forward to T. S. Eliot and the borrowed invocations of *The Waste Land*.

Kierkegaard felt Hamlet to be an example of the 'dread' that plays such a part in this author's writings, but religion is not tackled sufficiently in the play to make Hamlet's doubt unambiguously religious – and if it had, drama might not have been the best way of dealing with such a theme. Kierkegaard had the additional problem of being a Dane himself in ruminating on Hamlet's circumstances.

Kafka was naturally keen on Hamlet's relationship with his father and the feelings of sexual disgust. On the whole the goings-on between Hamlet and Ophelia take a comparatively minor place in Mr Scofield's book compared with the Ghost and Claudius. It always seems to me that a side of Hamlet's disgruntlement which sometimes receives insufficient attention is the fact that, quite apart from his mother's dubious behaviour, Hamlet himself had been done out of the throne without a shadow of justice.

Broadly speaking Eliot was not well disposed to the play. He saw Hamlet as partly heroic, partly the fool. We get the contrast with Prufrock.

Eliot well appreciated the many comic moments in the play, which Mr Scofield seems almost apologetic about admitting.

James Joyce's Stephen Dedalus is seen by Mr Scofield as a kind of self-righteous Hamlet. Stephen was certainly self-righteous, but Hamlet undeniably had his self-righteous schoolmasterish side too. So for that matter did Ophelia, and Mr Scofield observes that someone has remarked that her soliloquy beginning 'O what a noble mind is here o'erthrown' sounds like a *Times* obituary. Joyce, who held the unusual theory that Shakespeare had been cuckolded by his brother, obviously knew the play extremely well, as is displayed in *Ulysses*.

D. H. Lawrence (who does not wear well as a critic) found the Ghost 'trivial'. He held the strange view that sensual consciousness in Europe suffered a decline after the Renaissance owing to the introduction of syphilis from the New World.

My impression is that the transatlantic arrival of syphilis is now regarded as at best doubtful, but even had that been true, as Mr Scofield points out, fear of sex and hatred of the body had been perhaps the most prominent feature of medieval asceticism. Renaissance pictures and sculpture loudly proclaim absolutely contrary sentiments. Lawrence was in general uneasy with the play and the divided nature of Hamlet himself.

The Ghosts of Hamlet: The Play and Modern Writers, Martin Scofield, Cambridge UP. — 1981 *Daily Telegraph*

VI

The late William Empson was an acute, scholarly, above all amusing critic, who enjoyed nothing better than pulling the legs of fellow academics. It is no chance that he speaks more than once with approval in these essays of remarks made about Shakespeare by Hugh Kingsmill, one of the least academic men to be imagined.

Essays on Shakespeare includes a long piece on the structure of the Globe Theatre (which raises a number of points about the production of Shakespeare's plays); Shakespeare's narrative poems; the rate of motion of the Fairies in *A Midsummer Night's Dream* (about the same velocity as Major Gagarin's space journey). There is also an examination of the contemporary passion for supposing that everything Shakespeare – or for that matter any other writer – put down was 'symbolic'. The three most striking essays, however, are those on Falstaff, Hamlet and Macbeth.

Empson, in examining the character of Falstaff, disregards the shadowy figure, who (as Falstolfe) is branded as a coward in the *Henry VI* plays, also the farcical Falstaff of *The Merry Wives*, concentrating on what we are told in the two *Henry IV*'s and *Henry V*, where Falstaff's death is so movingly described.

In these three plays many must have felt that Prince Hal, notwithstanding his heroic leadership at Agincourt, emerges as an odious figure. In fact John Bayley has even compared him with Stavrogin in Dostoevsky's *The Devils*. Prince Hal is, indeed, an excellent example of Shakespeare's grasp of the essential contradictions in human character.

To begin with, Empson asks, in what did Prince Hal's 'wildness' actually consist? It does not seem to have been sex or drunkenness. Dover Wilson thought the Prince did not even envisage robbery, but when he says: 'Where shall we take a purse tomorrow, Jack?' it certainly looks as if he and Falstaff were old partners in crime. On the other hand, when Poins appears, Hal says: 'Who, I rob? I a thief? Not I, by my faith.'

Of course Shakespeare had to be careful not to libel royalty, and, as Empson points out, the text remains on a razor's edge in that aspect. Then, when Hal waylays Falstaff and takes his stolen plunder from him, does Falstaff really recognise him?

Falstaff's cowardice also remains an undecided point. Obviously there must have been occasions in his life with he could hardly have avoided showing a certain amount of spirit, and by now he was over seventy (he had broken Scogan's head fifty-five years before). Falstaff was perfectly prepared to drive Pistol out of the pub when the latter was being a nuisance.

My own feeling is that Falstaff would probably have put up quite a good show if he absolutely had to, but hoped to avoid all danger, if that could be done without too much loss of face.

In favour of Prince Hal when he became Henry V (although he had allowed Falstaff no hint that he was going to round on him when that happened), Empson points out that Falstaff might easily have become a genuinely sinister figure behind the throne. What resulted from the Falstaff connection, as things turned out, was that Prince Hal had made some very useful contacts in low life, which, helping to keep the common touch, in fact stood him in good stead when he became king.

Empson even goes so far as to suggest that in the relations between Falstaff and Prince Hal there may have been something of Shakespeare and his humiliation by the Fair Young Man of the Sonnets.

Moving on to Hamlet the question of identification arises much more acutely. To what extent, as some suppose, was Hamlet a self-portrait? Empson thinks that Hamlet represents chiefly (perhaps only) Shakespeare's 'theatricality' of temperament.

It might be added that when Hamlet interviews the Players one seems to hear the actual tone of Shakespeare the actor-manager. It is interesting to reflect that Hamlet's character has been regarded as enigmatic only during the last hundred and fifty years or so. To Samuel Johnson it presented no particular problem.

Had Hamlet been to bed with Ophelia? Empson is certain he had not. Others – Madariaga, for example – think he had. Undoubtedly some of the songs suggest the latter. Empson's view is that her father and brother were really playing for her to become queen. Their suggestion that she was looking too high was eye-wash. At the same time Polonius and Laertes did not want her to give herself to Hamlet. That might well have prejudiced her chances.

After all, the Queen spoke of Ophelia as a potential daughter-in-law, Empson also thinks that Hamlet would not have made his brutally coarse remarks to Ophelia if they had been physically lovers. That would have been regarded by the audience as 'unprincely'; something that should never be forgotten in the play, where a Prince as villain-hero was expected.

Macbeth, so Empson thinks, was already brooding on murder by the time he met the Witches. People make fun of the sort of criticism that asks how many children had Lady Macbeth, but Empson shows this to be an important matter. Macbeth was particularly irked by the Witches' prophecy that his line would not inherit. His preoccupation with the succession would have been of additional interest had the Macbeths been till then childless. I hope I have said enough to suggest the stimulating nature of Empson's essays.

Essays on Shakespeare, 1986
William Empson, *Daily Telegraph*
edited by David B. Pirie, CUP.

VII

The main purpose of this book is described by the publishers as 'to afford readers of the plays and producers for stage and screen, information which will enable them to see more clearly the picture Shakespeare conjures up' when he speaks of heraldic matters. The historical plays are taken in chronological sequence and their various heraldic aspects examined; while a chapter is also devoted to the subject of the grant of arms made to John Shakespeare, the poet's father.

A study of this sort can hardly avoid being a little disjointed as the questions it raises, although apparently similar, often resemble each other only superficially. For example, when Ophelia says 'Oh, you must wear your rue with a difference,' the supposition that she may refer to an armorial 'difference' – that is to say, a mark placed on the shield of a younger son – has little in common with the practical consideration of whether or not Falstaff should be represented wearing the insignia of the Falstaff family.

The whole business of Shakespeare's own coat-of-arms is well set out. This is a subject often approached in a sadly anachronistic manner. It cannot be insisted too often that the granting of a coat-of-arms by the

College of Arms was never a kind of patent of nobility in the continental sense. When a man reached a certain state of wealth and eminence, as in the case of John Shakespeare, it would be perfectly normal for him to apply for a grant of arms; though obviously some relatively rich and eminent persons did not bother to do so: while others used arms and did not apply for a grant as may be seen from lists of 'disclaimers'.

John Shakespeare is described as a Justice of the Peace and Bailiff of Stratford, and was a typical applicant. Indeed, it could easily be shown that bailiffs of such towns were often drawn from local families, already armigerous. In Mr Scott-Giles's clear statement of the known facts there seems little reason to disbelieve the assertion made in the existing application that John Shakespeare had applied twenty years before, when his son, the poet, was still a child. Quite naturally, he took no further steps during his period of financial embarrassment; and finally proceeded with the matter on the strength of his son's fortune. If William Shakespeare had remained unknown and made his money by, say, a voyage to the Indies, the whole affair of the grant would have aroused no possible comment; and to talk about Shakespeare's 'snobbishness' suggests an utter lack of appreciation of the Elizabethan scene and Shakespeare's position in it. Mr Scott-Giles outlines all this; though he is, perhaps, a trifle inclined to accept too absolutely what might be called the Heralds' point of view which naturally emphasized the 'necessity' of arms for a 'gentleman' and assumed the regulation of arms-bearing to be governed with complete efficiency.

It is less easy to agree with the author in the matter of Shallow being a supposed caricature of Sir Thomas Lucy of Charlecote. In this connexion it is really remarkable how determinedly the poaching legend has survived. It rests on the slenderest evidence, a century later than the supposed offence, to which the penalty of whipping was in any case not attached. It might have been thought that Dr Leslie Hotson's *Shakespeare versus Shallow* had (in so much as it is possible to identify a figure in fiction with one in real life) incontrovertibly marked down William Gardiner as Shallow's prototype. Mr Scott-Giles mentions this as 'an alternative theory' which seems an altogether inadequate phrase; while he adds that the Shallow-Gardiner attribution is 'from the heraldic point of view' not well founded, as the pun regarding 'Lucys' and 'louses' refers only to Gardiner's mother's arms. The fact remains that Gardiner quartered this maternal coat (e.g., on the Communion Cup of St Mary Magdalene, Bermondsey, illustrated in Dr Hotson's book) and the obliquity of the reference may have made it appear less deliberately 'libellous' from Shakespeare's point of view; though it is true that Shakespeare may first have encountered the Lucy-lousy joke in Warwickshire.

In dealing with the battle of Agincourt, as it appears in the light of Shakespeare's *King Henry V,* Mr Scott-Giles writes: '"Sir Richard Ketly,

Davy Gam esquire" who were also among the slain, cannot be identified . . . There is a Welsh family of Gam or Gamme, bearing *Argent, three cocks gules, with gold combs.*' But David Gam is given a column and-a-half in the DNB. It has even been suggested that he may have been the original of Shakespeare's Fluellen: while the arms quoted are the well-known coat attributed to the Welsh chieftain Eineon Sais, borne by various families, to one of which Davydd ap Llewelyn ap Hywel, called ' Gam' ('squinting'), who was killed at Agincourt, belonged. However, in general, *Shakespeare's Heraldry* should be of great assistance to producers of the plays: and a number of interesting heraldic points are raised.

Shakespeare's Heraldry,
C. W. Scott-Giles,
Dent.

1950
Times Literary Supplement

WILLIAM DAVENANT

William Davenant (1606–1668), although Poet Laureate, cannot be said to have survived very well as a poet, except, perhaps for 'Beauty Retire' (which Pepys set to music), or the occasional line like 'The Lark now leaves his wat'ry Nest'. This has not prevented Mary Edmond from writing in the Revels Plays Companion Library series an absorbing book about him scholarly, funny, with new material, which no one interested in the seventeenth century should miss.

The Davenants (D'Avenant was a piece of nonsense on the poet's part) came from the Essex/Suffolk border, but for several generations had belonged to that substantial London mercantile society, Merchant Adventurers (with strong associations with the Merchant Taylors' School), families with coats-of-arms, to whom England owed a great deal of her wealth. It is utterly misleading to look down on this background (as previous American academic Davenant biographers have done), accepting snobbish unhistorical nineteenth-century detractions of 'trade'. Miss Edmond puts this right.

Davenant's father and grandfather had been vintners, his father finally keeping a tavern (wine, no accommodation, as opposed to an inn, beer, rooms to let) in Oxford. Davenant *père* had wide intellectual and social connections (his wife was daughter of the King's Perfumer). Shakespeare, on his way to Stratford via Oxford, used to stay with the Davenants. It should be noted that (as taverns, unlike inns, were not hotels), the Bard must have been put up as a friend.

William Davenant was Shakespeare's godson, no doubt owing his first name to that fact. After a few drinks (says Aubrey, who devotes a long 'Brief Life' to Davenant), he used to say that it must be agreed he himself wrote very like Shakespeare, implying that the relationship was a good deal closer than godson.

Mrs Davenant was a beautiful and intelligent woman. All one can say is that Faithorne's portrait of Davenant is not entirely unlike the Droeshout engraving of Shakespeare, which appears in the First Folio.

There was, however, a feature, or rather lack of feature, that makes the faces hard to compare. In his early twenties Davenant (says Aubrey) 'gott a terrible clap of a black handsome wench that lay in Axeyard Westminster' (where Pepys lived in his early married life). This mishap caused Davenant to lose most of his nose. His second wife (he had three, as well as many children) was widow of the doctor who appears to have cured his syphilis, so she at least must have known what she was in for.

When his father died Davenant was sent to London to become an apprentice, but, much too adroit to do anything of the sort, found a job first with the Duchess of Richmond, then with the poet Fulke Greville Lord Brooke. The courtiers Endymion Porter and Lord Jermyn were also Davenant's patrons, bringing him into the entourage of Queen Henrietta Maria. He was soon not only well known as a poet, but regarded as an unusually able man.

During the Civil War Davenant became a Cavalier general (when he was knighted). He was apparently an efficient organiser, who introduced the use of carrier pigeons (earlier mentioned in one of his plays as the medium used by lovers to exchange messages). On two occasions Davenant came extremely near to being executed by the Cromwellians, one of these when he was captured on his way to America, where he had been appointed by the King in exile to the Council of Virginia.

Having managed to save his head, Davenant now set about earning a living, no easy matter during the Interregnum, when no plays were allowed. He conceived the extremely ingenious idea of what amounted to the establishment of opera (using that term) in London. When the Restoration came Davenant (who seems to have run by far the more successful company) divided what was more or less a monopoly of putting on plays with Sir William Killigrew.

The modern Theatre Royal, Drury Lane (Killigrew's), and the Royal Opera House, Covent Garden (Davenant's), are the only two theatres to derive their rights, not from the Lord Chamberlain or local authorities, but by direct grant from the Crown. Incidentally, actors nowadays are fond of boasting that until recently they were looked on as 'rogues and vagabonds'. A good many actors occur in legal documents in this book, where they are invariably described as 'Gent.'.

Miss Edmond has been extremely ingenious in digging out material about Davenant (including minor Shakespearian connections); in fact one is staggered by her research, which proves the point that scholarly biography is by far the most entertaining kind. Davenant, as might be expected, was not very good at paying his tailor, who sued him (though Davenant continued to have his clothes made there), which leads to a lot of relevant information. The previous generation of Davenant's family had made use of the quack doctor and astrologer Simon Forman, whose diary has so often proved an invaluable source of Shakespearian material.

Davenant, as a manager, of course knew the actor William Beeston, from whom Aubrey acquired his notes on Shakespeare. Miss Edmond grasps – something which some writers on Shakespeare have misunderstood – that the remark 'he was not a company keeper' seems (from its place on the page) to apply to Beeston, not Shakespeare, but her 'invited to writt' was read by Aubrey's editor Clarke as 'invited to court'. I confess I thought it was 'court', when years ago I looked at Aubrey's manuscript; perhaps wrongly.

'*o rare Sr Will; Davenant*' was put on his grave in Westminster Abbey in conscious imitation of Ben Jonson. It was well deserved.

Rare Sir William Davenant, 1987
Mary Edmond, Manchester UP. *Daily Telegraph*

JOHN MILTON

Milton took a pretty sever hammering from T. S. Eliot within living memory, and, although a handsome withdrawal followed, things were never again quite on their nineteenth-century basis, the Victorians liking all sorts of aspects of the poet that seem less sympathetic nowadays.

This is therefore a good moment for a new biography. A. N. Wilson (whose *The Laird of Abbotsford* gave an admirable account of Sir Walter Scott) was just the man to do it. He is deeply interested in religion, unsqueamish, aware that to write a serious book is likely to require being unserious some of the time.

Like several of the major poets John Milton (1608–1674) was recognised from the start as possessing altogether exceptional gifts. The question was where best these should be used. He himself felt objections to the obvious pull of the Church, in the first instance choosing what was becoming an increasingly, old-fashioned, support for a writer of poetry, that of aristocratic patronage. In this field, Mr Wilson draws attention to a truly extraordinary juxtaposition, which disturbs any grave Victorian picture of Milton's life.

An early patron of the poet was Alice, daughter of Sir John Spencer of Althorp (ancestor of the Princess of Wales), who married first the fifth Earl of Derby, then Sir Thomas Egerton, though she is always known by the former title. Lady Derby had only daughters by her first husband, one of whom married the second Earl of Castlehaven; another, her mother's stepson, the second Earl of Bridgewater. Lord Bridgewater was a wholly reputable figure, but Lord Castlehaven became involved in one of the most hair-raising sex scandals of the age, in which homosexuality, rape, paedophilia, mass orgies, were the order of the day. This took place at, of all places, Fonthill, where Beckford was to indulge his own fantasies, such as they were, two centuries later.

Lord Bridgewater was appointed Lord Lieutenant of Wales and the Marches. To celebrate this Milton wrote *Comus*, performed at Ludlow Castle by the Bridgewater children on Michaelmas Day, 1631. Lord Bridgewater's brother-in-law Lord Castlehaven had been executed for his sinister goings-on. It will be remembered that Milton's masque describes how Comus, god of Revelry, waylays three young travellers, and some of Milton's lines appear to have been cut as unsuitable for the Bridgewater children to speak in the light of what had recently been happening to their first cousin. What could have been Milton's thoughts in relation to all this?

Mr Wilson deals soberly with Milton's marital troubles with his first wife, Mary Powell, daughter of a rather feckless Oxfordshire squire, a Cavalier in politics. Mary Powell, although she was to return to him later and bear three children, left her husband after a few weeks, feeling lonely in Milton's small London house after her lively family life, and upset by his beating his nephews, whom he was educating. Mr Wilson has reservations about believing Aubrey in noting this last fact. But Aubrey knew the two nephews personally in later life. I really see no reason why he should not be speaking the truth. Indeed, Mr Wilson himself relents to the extent of admitting that it would be hard to inculcate Oppian's 'Cynegetica' and 'Haleutica' without recourse to blows.

In connection with this temporary disruption of Milton's first marriage it should be remembered that something similar had happened in the Pepys marriage (a real marriage if ever there was one) before the *Diary* opens. The dangers of the Civil War then beginning to take shape also undoubtedly played a part in Milton's wife not rejoining her husband at that moment in London.

Mr Wilson is well aware of the essential point about the Civil Wars that – in spite of what Marxists and near-Marxists may try and prove to the contrary – they were religious wars. Milton's great intellectual experience had been his period in Italy as a young man, where he first found himself looked upon as a person of consequence as a poet. He met Galileo, and became convinced that Laud's High Anglicanism offered imminent threat by the establishment of something not much short of the Inquisition in England. The Italian trip formed Milton's public approach.

His views were often to change, in the end finding disillusion in Cromwell's absolutism as much as the King's. Mr Wilson has interesting things to say about Milton's earlier personal regard for Cromwell, seeing in it not at all the idealisation of a revolutionary figure but the confidence Milton always felt in territorial magnates. Mr Wilson also emphasises that the disposal of Charles I was for Milton essentially a religious rather than political matter; either the King was a martyr or he had transgressed God's command and must be slain.

Milton's extraordinary command of languages, his powerful if somewhat uncontrolled prose style, made him an important civil servant under the Commonwealth in his position as Secretary of Languages. When the Restoration took place things could have gone badly notwithstanding his blindness. After all, he had written a pamphlet saying that to kill a king might be justified.

It speaks well for the mildness of the returned regime that inconveniences were not more severe. There appears even to have been a tentative offer of re-employment later on, which the poet, rightly one feels, refused.

There is much else to Milton's story in addition to matters touched on above. On the whole Mr Wilson's absorbing book avoids literary criticism, while giving useful comments on the major works. Again and again these startle with sentences that have now become everyday phrases. He was a great man but the portrait on the wrapper (attributed to Faithorne) gives a hint of why one does not feel more drawn to him personally.

The Life of John Milton,
A. N. Wilson, OUP.

1983
Daily Telegraph

SAMUEL BUTLER

Samuel Butler (1612–1680), author of *Hudibras* is not to be confused with Samuel Butler (1835–1902), author of *Erewhon* and *The Way of all Flesh.*

Oddly enough, they were both satirists, and, although one imagines them infinitely different in character, each in his very individual way set out to draw attention to the characteristic hypocrisies and follies of his own time.

Hudibras, admirably introduced and annotated in a new edition by John Wilders, is a remarkable mock-heroic poem of some 12,000 lines. Written when Butler was nearly fifty, it appeared in the early years of Charles II's Restoration. The poem was an instant success, but never managed to lift its author out of the rut of devilling – probably largely legal odd jobs – for rich patrons.

Butler's target was Puritanism – the drab Cromwellian years – at one end of the scale tyrannical repression, at the other crazy fanaticism. In Butler, as Mr Wilders points out, we have the beginnings of the Augustans, a classical 'rational' view of life that saw men's natures as to some extent capable of being controlled by good sense, but not, in the final resort, to be improved by religion or laws.

Butler's method of presenting his views is worth examining. The story of *Hudibras,* it has to be admitted, tails off at the end – it seems probable that a Fourth Part was intended – but the technique employed for including all the author's dislikes is extraordinarily ingenious.

The narrative – with touches of Rabelais – consciously follows the story of Don Quixote, but Hudibras, instead of being an amiable romantic, is a pompous, pedantic, conceited Presbyterian knight who goes out 'a-colonelling'; his squire is an Independent with Anabaptist leanings, despising book-learning, self-satisfied as his master on the grounds of having been endowed with a natural revelation of the truth; and Hudibras's Dulcinea is a rich widow, whose fortune he covets.

Butler, in this manner, rags not only the Puritans, but also the romantic tales of the past and Caroline love-poetry of his own time:

> The Sun and Day shall sooner part,
> Than love, or you, shake off my heart,
> The Sun that shall not more dispence
> His own, but your bright influence;

I'll carve your name on Barks of Trees,
With true-loves knots and flourishes;
That shall infuse eternal spring,
And ever-lasting flourishing.

In order to get help in softening up the heart of the Widow, Hudibras consults Sidrophel, apparently a mixture of the astrologer Lilly and the scientist Sir Paul Neal, F.R.S. Here again the aim is to kill two birds with one stone, for Sidrophel represents not only bogus fortune-telling, but also the experimental science of the period – in Butler's eyes too cocksure.

To what extent real persons are satirised by Butler is in doubt. He admitted that Hudibras himself was founded on a West Country knight, though his hero is usually – though one would say doubtfully – taken to be a certain Sir Samuel Luke, for whom Butler is supposed to have worked.

Butler denied in a letter that the minor characters who appear in the poem are intended to represent actual people, but he may have been speaking ironically, for the very reason that identification was so obvious to contemporaries.

It is tempting to try to transpose the setting of *Hudibras* to our own times, of which one is constantly reminded by Butler's barbed wit. An enormous amount of its point has inevitably been lost by the contemporary nature of the jokes – run to earth often with great brilliance by Mr Wilders – but what remains has in some ways a remarkably up-to-date ring.

Perhaps one might conceive a modern version in form like the romantic Leftist poems of the 1930s (thereby giving an antique setting), in which, say, a Left-wing MP, one of the party's intellectuals, travels, and quarrels with a Trade Union boss. Who the Widow would be whose fortune they both seek can only be surmised – perhaps merely the electorate – but Sidrophel might well appear as offering advice, on the one hand about psychiatry, on the other about technology.

That is roughly how *Hudibras* must have appeared to contemporaries, and the energy of the writing carried all before it. As Mr Wilders says:

> His [Butler's] originality lies partly in the fact that he composed a satire that was simultaneously a criticism of contemporary public morality and outmoded ways of thinking, and a parody of what . . . he regarded as an outmoded literary form.

As one reads *Hudibras* the ear is struck by two things; first, phrases that Butler, if he did not invent, has at least been responsible for carrying into life today, such as 'he knew what's what' or 'have a care of the main chance'; secondly, the influence on the poets who followed him.

The Dunciad, though far more precise, owes a lot to Butler. Byron is perpetually recalled, and, in rather another manner, Scott. Kipling has echoes and, of course deliberately, so has Roy Campbell. The mention of the 1930s poets is not without a direct connection, for they too owe something to lines like:

> Not by your Individual Whiskers,
> But by your Dialect and Discourse.

Of Butler himself very little is known. He seems to have been offered preferments at the height of his success, but none he considered good enough for him. As a result, it is thought that he died in poverty. This, one would say, was the character to be expected of him; knowing his own worth, but preferring to be given nothing, rather than something he did not want.

'I saw the famous old Mr Butler,' wrote a contemporary (not John Aubrey, also a friend and chronicler of Butler's), 'an old paralytick claret drinker, a morose surly man, except elevated with claret, when he becomes very brisk and incomparable company.'

One cannot with honesty recommend the general reader to sit down and read *Hudibras* from cover to cover, but there will be few who take it up who will not find something to laugh over even to this day.

Hudibras,
Samuel Butler,
edited by John Wilders
Clarendon Press/OUP.

1968
Daily Telegraph

LORD ROCHESTER

Probably few men over sixty (even younger perhaps) can feel quite immune to the pull of Rochester's 'Song of a Young Lady to her Ancient Lover' that begins:

> Ancient Person, for whom I,
> All the flatt'ring Youth defy;
> Long be it ere thou grow old,
> Aching, shaking, crazy, cold;
> But still continue as thou art,
> Ancient Person of my Heart.

Cyril Connolly wrote somewhere that Rochester represents a frontline almost too hot to hold by apologists for pleasure, one which has to be abandoned in favour of more defendable positions. Certainly even if Rochester's reputation is in some respects not altogether justified, his behaviour accommodated bisexuality, prolonged intoxication (five years on end), general racketyness which might make the average Hell's Angel or Punk pause for thought.

John Wilmot, second Earl of Rochester (1648–1680), son of a distinguished and eccentric Cavalier who had accompanied Charles II on his escape from Worcester field, came into a comparatively modest inheritance as a boy. At the age of eighteen he attempted to abduct the heiress he subsequently married, was sent to the Tower, and emerged volunteering for the Navy, where he served with bravery.

As well as being a poet, Rochester was an accomplished scholar, attracted by the philosophy of Hobbes, and a sceptic prepared to listen to contemporary arguments about religion. He did not take long to establish himself at Court, where in spite of frequent banishments he was always after a time indispensable to the King. He died at the age of thirty-one, reconciled with the Broad Church views of Bishop Burnet, though not precisely in the sudden death-bed repentance depicted in legend.

Aubrey's reported saying of Rochester that the Devil came into him on approaching London and never left him till he returned to the country, carries complete conviction. At home he was a good landlord, and (within the ample terms of reference) an affectionate husband. His *Letters*, impeccably edited by Jeremy Treglown, present a vivid picture of his marriage, and one can only regret Lady Rochester's own letters do not survive as she was obviously an engaging figure.

There is a striking 'modernness' about Rochester's poems, in which he will introduce a colloquial word (not seldom a four-letter one) in the midst of quite other phrases; a characteristic equally to be seen in the *Letters*, where Rochester's are enormously more readable than those of other Wits (including Dryden) also reproduced here.

The contributors to Mr Treglown's *Spirit of Wit: Reconsiderations of Rochester* are himself, Barbara Everett, John Wilder, Peter Porter, Basil Greenslade, David Trotter, Sarah Wintle, Pat Rogers and Raman Selden. They write of the various sides of Rochester, and all are worth reading. Among them Barbara Everett's essay brilliantly stands out as making Rochester a far more definite figure among his Restoration gang (who must be admitted to be rather difficult to sort out where personality is concerned), and doing that in a very amusing manner.

She begins by invoking Henry James's fascination with English society, so well illustrated in Max Beerbohm's cartoon where James stoops to examine the mixed pairs of shoes outside the bedroom doors of some hotel or house party. She compares this with Rochester allegedly bribing the footman to tell him who was sleeping with whom at Court. She adds of Rochester that 'he inhabited, he half invented, that social world where James was never much more than a wonderful life-long tourist'.

Peter Porter is rather starry-eyed in an old-fashioned Whig manner about the joys of Cromwell's (theatreless) dictatorship, and he must have been wrongly informed to suppose there was 'little sequestration of property' (see HMSO publications on the subject), but he has some good comments on Rochester's development as a poet. David Trotter draws attention to the Latitudinarian's emphasis on the language of everyday speech to heal the wounds of the Civil War – an interesting parallel to today's frequent squeamishness about calling things by their true names. In this area Rochester was often himself under attack.

Mr Treglown's edition of the *Letters* shows several portraits of Rochester, but not that by David Loggan used on the wrapper of *Spirit of Wit*. These pictures all hold the attention in different ways. That by an unknown artist (property of Lord Bathurst), painted perhaps not long after Rochester's naval service, suggests a faint retention of the shyness from which he was said to have suffered when first at Court.

The best-known one, however, is that in the National Portrait Gallery (after Huysmans): Rochester with his monkey. This is the Court Wit as he would wish to be painted. Finally there is the Loggan drawing (British

Museum), executed with characteristic delicacy – a sad, uncertain, deeply intelligent, rather tortured face. The Loggan, one feels, is a good likeness.

Spirit of Wit: Reconsiderations of Rochester, 1982
edited by Jeremy Treglown, Blackwell. *Daily Telegraph*

The Letters of John Wilmot, Earl of Rochester,
edited and with introduction by Jeremy Treglown,
Blackwell.

CHRISTOPHER SMART

Christopher Smart – to sound an echo from the lecture room – is the poet who links Dryden with Blake, the Augustans with the Romantics. His story is one of the saddest in what are, on the whole, the sad lives of poets. Fr Christopher Devlin in *Poor Kit Smart* recounts it with skill, sympathy and an urbanity at times almost overwhelming.

Smart was born in 1722, of a Durham family of some distinction. His mother was a Welsh woman from Radnor, a fact of which he was always very conscious, feeling this ancestry gave him a link with a remote Romano-British past.

At an early age he showed an extraordinary facility for writing poetry. He also possessed what one of his critics (at whom Fr Devlin cocks an amused eyebrow) calls 'a voluptuousness of mind somewhat startling in a thirteen-year-old boy'. This was instanced by such lines as 'To Ethelinda – on her doing my lines the honour of wearing them in her bosom'.

> Oft thro' my eyes my soul has flown
> And wanton'd on that ivory throne:
> There with extatic transport burn'd
> And thought it was to heav'n return'd.
> Tell me, is the omen true
> Shall the body follow too?

However, be that as it may, Smart made in general a good impression as a boy, and the Duchess of Cleveland paid for him to go up to Cambridge. The fact that he had not much money did not prevent him from liking to have a good time and a lot to drink. Heads were wagged when he was an undergraduate: the situation did not improve when he became a fellow.

The poet Gray was a Cambridge don at the same time as Smart. The two of them did not get on well together, in spite of their poetic gifts and a common interest in 'Welch-ness'. Smart left Cambridge in due course to earn his living by freelance writing.

To Smart's taste for drinking and parties, he added a strong tendency in the direction of religious mania. This is the side of his life which Fr Devlin sets out to examine, coming to the very reasonable conclusion that, so far as his poetry is concerned, there is nothing mad about him at all.

Whether or not Smart's poetry was mad affects, of course, only one side of the picture. There was ordinary existence to be coped with; a living to be earned; debtors to be appeased; all of which was difficult for a man who decided to take literally the Biblical injunction to pray 'without ceasing'.

Just how impossible things became is hard to judge. Dr Johnson, a friend of Smart's, at one moment appears to have thought it necessary to confine him; at another, that he could well have been allowed at large. Whichever was true, Smart spent long years in lunatic asylums; it can only be hoped – and appears, in fact, to have been so – not the most terrible madhouses of that terrible period for the insane.

Fr Devlin deals at some length with an aspect of Smart's life that has, up to date, been largely unemphasised – that is to say that his wife, Anna-Maria, was a devout Roman Catholic. It seems not impossible that Smart's clandestine marriage (university fellows had to be celibate) was, in fact, a Roman Catholic one.

Smart himself was what would now be called a High Anglican. He remained throughout his life far from well disposed to the Roman Church. The complicated emotional, intellectual and religious states in which his own situation involved him are often referred to in his extraordinary poem written in the madhouse, *Jubilate Agno*.

Fr Devlin deals with all this involved and controversial material with the greatest competence and good humour. At the same time he does seem to me to weigh the balance in favour of Smart's wife, Anna-Maria, when, in truth, no judgement can be made.

One of the obsessive themes in Smart's verse was cuckoldry. Now, there is no evidence that his wife was unfaithful to him, and, whether or not he was strictly speaking mad, it certainly cannot be denied that he might have developed such a form of persecution mania without the smallest reason.

At the same time, the fact remains that Mrs Smart did finally abandon her husband and retire to earn a living in Dublin. That she had had appalling trials to endure – that we are not in a position to judge her – I would certainly agree. All the same, Smart *was* her husband, and she *did* leave him; so that, in fairness to Smart, I do not think Fr Devlin has quite the right to say, 'What poor Anna-Maria thought or said about the false and disgusting hints against her fidelity we do not know.' It seems to me to be simply one of those situations where blame cannot be attributed. This happens in contemporary life; how much more so at a distance of two hundred years! I do not attack Mrs Smart, I simply put in a word for Smart. The fact that he continued to speak well of her in other respects proves nothing.

Often uneven as a poet, Smart at his best has a peculiar charm. His 'Hymn to the Nativity' shows him at his most magical:

Where is this stupendous stranger,
  Swains of Solyma, advise,
Lead me to my Master's manger
  Show me where my Saviour lies? . . .

Spinks and ouzles sing sublimely,
  'We too have a Saviour born.'
Whiter blossoms burst untimely
  On the blest Mosaic thorn.

God all-bounteous, all-creative,
  Whom no ills from good dissuade,
Is incarnate, and a native
  Of the very world he made.

Smart died in a debtors' prison in 1771. There really was no answer to all his problems. A great part of his life had been devoted to a metrical version of the Psalms, which did not meet with the approbation of the critics or of the Established Church.

A final word should be said of Smart's fondness for animals, especially cats. 'My cat Jeoffry', his solace in the madhouse – to whom he wrote a very beautiful sequence in *Jubilate Agno* – must, as Fr Devlin says, be one of the most famous cats of history. I myself have often pondered the line in the same poem: 'Let Powell, house of Powell rejoice with Synochitis a precious stone abused by sorcerers.'

Poor Kit Smart, 1961
Christopher Devlin, Hart-Davis *Daily Telegraph*

FORGOTTEN BEST-SELLERS

The whole question of the 'best-seller' is an interesting one. By the phrase, I do not mean the books of authors who have gradually built up large sales, or even first books that sell well by an author who continues to be very popular with his subsequent writings. The works I have in mind are those by known or unknown writers which suddenly enjoy a freak success.

It is to such that Robert Birley turns his attention in *Sunk Without Trace*. These are the six Clark Lectures that the headmaster of Eton delivered at Cambridge. They deal with William Warner's *Albion's England*, Nathaniel Lee's *The Rival Queens*, Edward Young's *Night Thoughts*, William Robertson's *Charles V*, Moore's *Lalla Rookh*, P. J. Bailey's *Festus*.

Speaking for myself, when confronted with the list, I knew Young's *Night Thoughts* well by name and could remember having a copy in my hands. *Lalla Rookh* I possess and have dipped into more than once. I was aware that *Festus* was a Victorian epic poem of immense length.

Of the other three I was ignorant, although the title *Albion's England* was faintly familiar. This turned out also to be an epic poem by a contemporary of Shakespeare's. Its author was once called 'our English Homer'. The poem contains some enjoyable passages, greatly inferior to Drayton's *Poly-Olbion*, but somewhat in that manner.

The Rival Queens is Restoration tragedy: as Mr Birley truly comments, 'of all the great traditions of English literature, the one that is most disliked'. It is undeniably *heavy* going, and contains lines that changes in language have wrecked, such as when one of the Queens says of Alexander: 'Then he would talk, good Gods, how he would talk!'

William Robertson's *History of the Reign of Charles V* belongs to rather a different category. Although Mr Birley has much that is of interest to say of this book, I am not sure that it should have been included. Robertson was a competent, highly respectable historian, who has simply been superseded by subsequent historical material and improved technique. It is, of course, true to say that nothing supersedes Gibbon, who himself greatly admired Robertson.

However, Robertson has nothing in common with Young, who hit off one of those fantastic literary successes with his *Night Thoughts*, not only here but also in France and Germany. Mr Birley laughs at Young's lines on the Resurrection, but they are not without a surrealist charm:

Now charnels rattle; scatter'd limbs, and all
The various bones, obsequious to the call,
Self-mov'd, advance, the neck perhaps to meet
The distant head, the distant legs the feet.
Dreadful to view, see through the dusky sky
Fragments of bodies in confusion fly.

In 1755 a friend wrote to the poet Gray that he had met a formidable blue-stocking in Hamburg:

> She asked me who was the famous poet that writ the Nitt toats. I replied Doctor Yonge. She begged leave to drink his health in a glass of sweet wine adding that he was her favourite English Author . . . I asked if she had ever read La Petite Elegie dans la Cœmeterie Rustique, C'est Beaucoup Jolie je vous Assure! . . . Oui. Monsieur (she replied) Je lu, & elle est bien Jolie & Melancholique mais elle ne touché point La Cœur comme mes tres chers Nitt toats.

With Thomas Moore and his *Lalla Rookh* we are on less unfamiliar ground. Moore had a notable gift for the drawing-room ballad style of verse, even if he were not a great poet. One feels it must have been rather fun in 1822 when the Grand Duke Nicholas (later Tsar) visited Berlin and took part, with other royalties and a hundred and fifty members of the Court, in Tableaux Vivants and songs from *Lalla Rookh.*

That was just what it was intended for, and at least the lines 'I never nurs'd a dear gazelle . . . but it was sure to die' have survived.

Festus is another matter. Mr Birley has high claims to be the only man who has ever unravelled its plot. The epic began as a mere eight thousand lines, but by the time it had run to innumerable editions, these had gradually increased to forty thousand.

Bailey produced other books of verse, which were never a success. The brilliant idea struck him of incorporating chunks of these unsaleable works into his ever saleable epic. He lived to a great age, becoming of such an appallingly venerable appearance that Edmund Gosse confessed himself to have been positively irritated by the sight of him.

Is there something to be learnt about public taste from all this? I think there is, although it is hard to express with lucidity what precisely the message is. Perhaps 'best-selling' has something to do with the presentation of a new literary fashion of thought and feeling in already outdated technical forms. Yet that does not explain why Stendhal read *Lalla Rookh* five times or Tennyson proclaimed the greatness of *Festus.* If you like literary curiosities, they can be examined at leisure in the headmaster of Eton's book.

Sunk Without Trace: 1962
Some Forgotten Masterpieces Reconsidered, *Daily Telegraph*
Robert Birley, Hart-Davis.

WILLIAM WORDSWORTH

The bicentenary year of the French Revolution has been more notable, anyway in this country, for reminders of the horrors that took place during that event, and the wars that followed Bonaparte's consequent seizure of power, than for any feeling that it would have been bliss to have been alive and young in that dawn.

In short, history seems to have endorsed Wordsworth's change of mind about the Revolution, which, after all, everyone has the right to do on any subject; though perhaps later to be against Roman Catholic Emancipation and the Reform Bill of 1832 was going rather far in the other direction.

All the same, the circumstances of the political upheaval building up in France had an important effect on the life of William Wordsworth (1770–1850). He had gone there first in 1790, scarcely aware that revolution was taking place, to do an austere Grand Tour with a Welsh fellow-undergraduate:

> Jones! as from Calais southward you and I
> Went pacing side by side.

He returned to France two years later, having no doubt polished up his schoolboy French (though there is no reason to suppose he ever spoke the language at all fluently), full of enthusiasm for what was happening round him.

Then Wordsworth was involved in what seems an extraordinary affair. He was in rooms at Orléans, where he had a few introductions, 'knew two or three officers in the Cavalry' and a 'very agreeable family'. The last were probably the Vallons – the widow of a surgeon, remarried to another surgeon, two sons also of the medical profession, a third son who was a lawyer's clerk, and a daughter called Annette.

In a matter of two months Annette was pregnant by Wordsworth and she subsequently gave birth to a daughter, Caroline, while Wordsworth (who had made comparatively high-level political contact in Paris) returned to England.

Stephen Gill, in his thorough scholarly biography, is chiefly concerned with the poetry and the fact that when Wordsworth went to live in the Lake District, in spite of a hard time so far as money was concerned, he established a proper grip on his work, which he had not managed before.

This, of course, is what matters, and in any case absolutely nothing is known about the mechanics of the Annette incident.

All the same, anyone at all familiar with the works of Stendhal and Balzac cannot fail to find it fascinating. Was this seduction due to the revolutionary effect on bourgeois morals? But the Vallons were Royalist, on the edge, it would appear, of *petite noblesse.* There seems no doubt whatever that Annette expected to marry Wordsworth, but he did nothing to further that, nor, later on, much to contribute financial help. True he was always broke. Nevertheless, when he married Mary Hutchinson in 1802, they went to France and met Annette, with Wordsworth's daughter. There appears to have been remarkably little ill feeling, though again one knows nothing truly to the purpose.

Mary Hutchinson was almost literally the girl next door. She and Wordsworth had been at school together. She was all that a difficult poet could hope for in the way of a wife, which in Wordsworth's case included putting up with his sister Dorothy, who was, it is not too much to say, passionately in love with her brother. This brother-and-sister relationship included occasionally going off on jaunts together, leaving Mary Wordsworth to cope with domestic problems, always thick on the ground, in the Wordsworth home. Mary seems finally to have objected to that, though Dorothy remained an appalling burden for five years after her brother's death, out of her mind and bedridden.

One is apt to forget the extraordinary savagery with which Wordsworth was attacked for his poetry, quite apart from Byron, Shelley & Co objecting to his change of political sides: 'Puerile . . . namby-pamby . . . paradigm of silliness and affectation . . . unintelligible, contemptible effusions . . . wilderness of sublimity, tenderness, bombast and absurdity'. So far as the man himself was concerned, Southey claimed that Wordsworth's 'entire and intense selfishness' was 'so pure and unmixed a passion in him that Ben Jonson would have had him in a play had he been a contemporary'.

Mr Gill well expresses the view of Wordsworth which took the place of this earlier abuse, when he calls him 'pre-eminently the celebrant of unregarded lives'. When Wordsworth was given an honorary degree at Oxford the panegyric was spoken by Keble, the poet himself awarding the Newdigate Prize to the twenty-year-old John Ruskin.

The latter years imposed on Wordsworth the canonisation with which the Victorians liked to envelop their poets, ending with the Laureateship. When Wordsworth went to a Court ball in that capacity he borrowed Samuel Rogers' court dress and Sir Humphry Davy's sword. The American minister's wife burst into tears when she saw the grey-haired poet kneel before the young queen.

Mr Gill tells whatever is to be known, but Wordsworth remains a figure hard to imagine in the flesh. His early friend Coleridge, whose goings-on in due course made him less than popular with the Wordsworth family, is only too easy to picture. Wordsworth remains enigmatic. His unapproachableness, on one side, is countered by friendly chats with peasants (missing all that was sinister in the village, according to Harriet Martineau) or his close companionship with a man as genial as Sir Walter Scott.

Incidentally, Wordsworth himself did not see the solitary Highland lass: he read an account of her written by his friend Thomas Wilkinson.

William Wordsworth: A Life, 1989
Stephen Gill, OUP Clarendon Press. *Daily Telegraph*

BYRON

I

Few literary revivals of the last thirty years have been more remarkable than the renewed interest in Byron. He had reached a very low ebb, critically speaking, at the time when Peter Quennell and others began to turn their attention to him.

Bryon's particular qualities – except perhaps his professional anti-Establishmentism – are on the whole not at all those favoured by the fashionable pundits of the period in which this change has come to pass.

As a matter of fact, Byron as an opponent of 'the Establishment' does not bear too close investigation. He was not above making a row about his own social precedence, for example, and in many ways he would not fit with the views of people now anxious to be regarded as progressive.

Moreover Byron's writing is often frivolous, sometimes slipshod. He is just the sort of poet who might be expected to have been relegated to the darkest end of the bookcase.

M. K. Joseph, himself a poet and novelist, Professor of English in New Zealand, now comes forward with a full-length study of Byron's major poems. These are still often neglected, and Byron's reputation as a poet is spoken of as if it rested on a few nostalgic short poems like:

> So, we'll go no more a roving
> So late into the night,
> Though the heart be still as loving,
> And the moon be still as bright.

Professor Joseph deals at length with the dramas, the satires and the epics. Most of all he deals with *Don Juan.*

It so happens that I read the whole of Byron's *Don Juan* within the last year, so that I can bear out from personal experience the extraordinary liveliness and amusing qualities of that poem. It is long, certainly – over two thousand stanzas; but it has some of the qualities of a novel in verse, and entirely justifies Professor Joseph's praise.

Byron's poem has, of course, little or nothing to do with the legendary Don Juan. The Don Juan of tradition, though he takes various forms, was in general a cold-blooded pursuer of women, interested in their conquest more as the satisfaction of power than for sensual motives. Byron's hero bears scarcely any resemblance to that, except that he is very attractive to women. He is in some ways an innocent, the victim of the world round him.

Don Juan is, of course, partly a self-portrait. At the same time the poet himself enters the narrative as well as a commentator. This is one of the poem's most entertaining and effective sides. Byron had begun writing *Don Juan* in Venice in 1818, when he was thirty, and, as Professor Joseph points out, it was the Italian romantic epic that made him realise his own potentialities in that line.

Byron's discovery was that he had no need to amalgamate the two sides of him – his romanticism and his taste for satire. He could, so to speak, run them both separately in the same poem. This he did in *Don Juan* with immense success. There are all kinds of shrewd, biting comments on his own time there, and also much romantic verse of the kind at which he was so adept: this, too, has its place in such a work.

Like most great writers, Byron was, of course, torn in several directions. One side of him admired Pope and the Augustan poets of the eighteenth century. In spite of his own political outlook, he also revered the personality of Samuel Johnson, the typical English Tory. It is probably no chance that the idealised Englishman who occurs in *Don Juan* is called Johnson.

Professor Joseph, who is at times somewhat diffuse, and a shade hard to tie down as to dates, deals with these more general aspects in an effective manner. He points out that the epoch in which Byron lived and wrote has much in common with our own, and Byron's comments are at times singularly up to date in their relevance.

Byron was, for example, a great attacker of cant. He was at the same time perfectly aware that cant is nowhere to be found more flourishing than among those who regard themselves as particularly qualified to smell it out. His mixture of seriousness and burlesque is particularly good equipment in this polemical field.

The lack of sympathy between Keats and Byron is touched upon here; although a certain amount of rather formal commendation was exchanged between them, they remained profoundly unsympathetic to one another. Keats thought Byron lacked imagination; Byron thought Keats's poetry 'a Bedlam vision produced by raw pork and onions'.

Byron put Scott at the top of the poets of his day: then the now forgotten Rogers, followed by Moore and Campbell. It has to be admitted that, although Scott is perhaps today underrated, this critical taste has not held up well.

> Thou shalt believe in Milton, Dryden, Pope;
> Thou shalt not set up Wordsworth, Coleridge, Southey;

> Because the first is crazed beyond all hope,
> The second drunk, the third so quaint and mouthey;
> With Crabbe it may be difficult to cope.
> And Campbell's Hippocrene is somewhat douthy;
> Thou shalt not steal from Samuel Rogers, nor
> Commit – flirtation with the muse of Moore.

It surely must be admitted that this is the right sort of stuff.

Byron the Poet, 1964
M. K. Joseph, Gollancz *Daily Telegraph*

II

Profressor G. Wilson Knight begins his book with an enjoyable piece of information:

> In the Eton and Harrow match of 1805, Lord Byron went in directly after a boy named Shakespeare. Shakespeare was stumped for 8 and Byron caught for 7. In the second innings their runs were respectively 5 and 2. How far these figures should be regarded as symbolically relevant will perhaps be determined by my present study: I would not agree that they do Byron justice.

This is just the right tone for a subject so debatable as comparing one writer with another, especially Byron with Shakespeare; the differences are in so many respects enormous that the scale of the comparison must be kept reasonably fluid.

Unfortunately Byron is one of those figures people find hard to discuss without heat. There are moments when Professor Wilson Knight's book takes on a tone that is not far from heresy-hunting.

It must be agreed that Byron is not easy to write about. In one sense interest in him has greatly increased during the past thirty or forty years, which have produced several excellent studies of his life. On the other hand, even in the lowest ebb of his standing as a poet, Byron remained an unequivocally famous figure. There was never any real question of forgetting about him.

To this day he remains the prototype of all he stood for in his own period. His work has survived much hostile criticism. *Don Juan* is now generally accepted as a comic epic of genius. Nothing can dim the beauty of some of the short lyrics. His personal life retains an almost inexplicable interest.

In these circumstances too much insistence that Byron is not only the fullest human expression of what Shakespeare was aiming at, but hardly inferior as a writer, is adding a rather unnecessary burden to material already a trifle unmanageable owing to its variety and the difference of opinion it excites.

It is scarcely necessary to remark that in putting his theories forward Professor Knight, knowing the works of both writers very thoroughly, has much to say that is of interest, especially regarding the quotations he makes from them. All the same, the thread of the book's theme sometimes becomes a little tangled.

Byron himself was steeped in Shakespeare, a fact clear not only from his verse but from his letters. He certainly saw himself, not without reason, as a consciously Hamlet type. On the other hand, he put on record that he regarded Shakespeare as the 'most extraordinary of writers', yet 'the worst of models'. We are not always willing to be convinced by some of the Shakespearian resemblances on which Professor Knight insists.

On the personal side, he thinks homosexuality played a relatively large part in Byron's life, and that the break-up of his marriage was due more to a taste for abnormal relations with Lady Byron than to the accusation of 'incest' with his half-sister.

This question of homosexuality, if accepted, gives Byron an additional link, so the argument goes, with Shakespeare – the Shakespeare of the Sonnets, of course. Professor Knight speaks of 'a balance of homosexual idealism against engagements, which may be either heterosexual or homosexual, of a less ideal order'.

Others who have written admirably about Byron – Mrs Doris Langley Moore and Mr Malcolm Elwin, for example – have been inclined to underplay this particular aspect of Byron's life. They may be right. Byron himself wrote: 'all passions in excess are feminine'. Certainly this is true, one would think, of the inveterate Don Juan as he grows older, so the phrase really proves nothing about Byron's alleged sexual deviations.

On the whole, in fact, the question seems to be one on which everyone interested must make up his or her own mind. Generally speaking, I lean towards Professor Wilson Knight's side – partly because Byron's love of perversity for its own sake might easily have led him in that direction as much as appetite – but there seems no necessity to make the matter an issue on which an irrevocable decision must be taken.

In support of his own theories Professor Knight uses some rather doubtful ammunition:

> The Thyrza poems [written on the death of Edleston, the good-looking choirboy on whom Byron had undeniably had a 'crush' at Cambridge] belong to the great tradition of homosexual elegy to which so much of our poetry on such idealised relationships belongs: in ancient literature, in Milton's *Lycidas*, Arnold's *Thyrsis* and Tennyson's *In Memoriam*; and in the general tenor of Gray's *Elegy* and Housman's *A Shropshire Lad*.

This is surely going a little far. We would all admit the overtones of *A Shropshire Lad*. But, really, to call Matthew Arnold's poem on the death of his friend Clough 'homosexual' is either to demand another word for what is usually implied by the epithet, or to make aspersions on Arnold so ludicrously inappropriate that they can hardly be termed even unjust.

One would say the same was equally true of Milton and Tennyson while, even if Gray's deep melancholy could be traced to some extent to sexual maladjustment to describe the *Elegy* as 'homosexual' certainly does not convey the poem's salient feature.

In rather the same way, it seems no service to Byron to support him when he says silly things. For example, Professor Wilson Knight writes:

> Byron is cosmopolitan and international: is not, in any usual sense, English. He told Count D'Orsay on April 22, 1823 that he was only in part English; his mother was Scottish; 'my name and my family are both Norman' and he himself 'of no country'.

His mother – one of the most provincial women, one suspects, who ever lived – was certainly a Gordon. The Byrons may ultimately have been of 'Norman' origin, but for generations they had been allied to other Lancashire and Nottinghamshire families. A dash of Cornish blood adds that characteristic English variation, so that, apart from the maternal side, Byron was as 'English' as he could be.

If you wish to contrast Shakespeare with Byron, it might be thought that Shakespeare had an extraordinary grasp of what other people were like; Byron of what he himself was like. They are accordingly writers of precisely the opposite sort. However, the contrary view is vigorously put forward here for all those who want to argue the point.

Byron and Shakespeare, 1966
G. Wilson Knight, Routledge. *Daily Telegraph*

III

Thomas Medwin, the author of *Conversations of Lord Byron*, was a second cousin of Shelley.

He was the son of a prosperous Horsham solicitor and had served briefly in India as a subaltern in the 24th Light Dragoons, a regiment, incidentally, that disappeared in due course from the Army List, to be resurrected ('Light' omitted) as an armoured unit towards the end of the Second World War.

Medwin had the reputation of a bore, but there is evidence that Byron liked bores. The combination of cavalryman and man of letters was also one to appeal to him, for Medwin had written tolerable verse and made serious researches into the art and customs of India. The Shelley relationship did the rest. For five months during 1821–22, when Byron was living at Pisa in a villa on the Arno, they saw a certain amount of each other.

Ernest J. Lovell has already written a book, *Captain Medwin: Friend of Byron and Shelley*, though Medwin's captaincy was self-appointed. Here he contributes only a brief introduction, with very full – and conveniently arranged – notes to the memoir. Mr Lovell should, I think, just have mentioned that Medwin was born in 1788, so that he and Byron were the same age.

Medwin produced his book on Byron admittedly to make money. It was published in 1824, the year of Byron's death. During the next eighteen years the memoir appeared in fifteen editions and was translated into French, German and Italian. It caused a tremendous row.

No one can deny that it was full of inaccuracies. Byron is represented as saying all kind of things about himself that he could not possibly have said, simply because they would have been pointlessly untrue, e.g. that his mother-in-law's estates were in Lancashire, when they were in fact in Leicestershire. When howlers of that sort existed, there is nothing surprising in the outcry raised about Byron's alleged opinions.

All the same, the *Conversations of Lord Byron* do convey a keen sense of how Byron appeared to a man of Medwin's background. It must be remembered that almost everyone is affected to some extent by the person to whom he is talking. Byron was no exception.

If Medwin – after both of them had drunk a good deal of claret – misunderstood Byron in saying, 'I have been concerned in many duels as second, but only two as principal; one was with Hobhouse before I became intimate with him' – when in fact (according to Hobhouse) Byron had never been concerned in a duel in his life – that does not alter the picture provided of the kind of conversation that was to be heard at Byron's table.

Accordingly, if taken with a great many grains of salt, the memoir is extraordinarily readable and vivid. Goethe was upset because Byron was shown as travelling with 'seven servants, five carriages, nine horses, a monkey, a bull-dog, a mastiff, two cats, three pea-fowl and some hens'.

But, although Byron's mistress, Countess Guiccioli, denied the peacocks, Shelley agrees that at Ravenna he had met five peacocks, two guinea hens and an Egyptian crane on Byron's grand staircase. Shelley put the monkeys at two, the cats at five and the dogs at eight. In respect of pets, at least, the general panorama seems acceptable.

Byron himself (he said his name should be pronounced 'By-ron') is represented as saying that his own conversation was 'not brilliant', and one has the impression that it would not have been so judged at the time he lived. On the other hand, its range and liveliness break through. We learn, for instance, that he liked Americans, even thought of going to America and settling there. What a good subject for a story, that Byron emigrated to the United States and lived to eighty . . .

This is the kind of entry that arouses interest:

> No woman has so much bonne foi as Mme. De Staël; hers was a real kindness of heart. She took the greatest possible interest in my quarrel with Lady Byron, or rather Lady Byron's quarrel with me, and had some influence over my wife – as much as any person but her mother, which is not saying much.

Medwin also records the remark:

> Who would not wish to have been born two or three centuries later? Here is a savant of Bologna, who pretends to have discovered the manner of directing balloons by means of a rudder, and tells me that he is ready to explain the nature of his invention to our Government. I suppose we shall soon travel by air-vessels; make air instead of sea-voyages; and at length find our way to the moon, in spite of the want of atmosphere.

Medwin shows himself as sceptical, but Byron was right.

Byron talks about the period when he was on the Drury Lane Committee, when 'five hundred plays were offered to the Theatre during the year. You may conceive it was no small task to read all the trash, and satisfy the bards that it was so.'

He was on the whole critical of Shakespeare, and especially of the way that 'Garrick used to act Othello in a red coat and epaulettes'. Mr Lovell adds an amusing note to the effect that Garrick's witches in *Macbeth* wore wigs, rouge, red stomachers, point lace aprons and mittens. It sounds an enjoyable production.

Medwin himself lived on rather seedily, endlessly producing books, and filled with spleen against those who had attacked him for what he said about Byron. He was perhaps not a very admirable character, certainly not one to rely on, but the *Conversations* are well worth reading.

Medwin's Conversations of Lord Byron, edited by Ernest J. Lovell, OUP. — 1966, *Daily Telegraph*

IV

Byron's life, followed in his letters, makes absorbing reading. Here is something quite different from Byron's biography told in narrative form by someone else. Immediacy is conveyed in an extraordinary manner. This first collected edition of all the letters supersedes Prothero's work, published at the turn of the century. Unlike that edition, it is unbowdlerized and also contains many letters hitherto unpublished. Leslie A. Marchand, author of the definitive biography of Byron, has done an excellent job, providing a good index and notes that supply the information required without overweighting the page.

There arc at lcast a dozen ways in which the letters of Byron could be considered. For readers of *Apollo*, rather than emphasizing the psychology of the poet himself – his sexual ambivalence is particularly clearly illustrated here – or the general picture given of Regency society, one may say a word about Byron's approach to painting. It must be admitted at once that pictures did not provide a field in which he showed himself a particularly sophisticated critic, although he liked having his own portrait painted. On the other hand, his tastes throw interesting light on what was admired at the time by someone not primarily a connoisseur, but one moving in a world sometimes aristocratic or adventurous, sometimes intellectual or Bohemian, where an opinion on the subject would be required from a man of the world.

The tone is set in *Beppo*:

> They've pretty faces yet, those same Venetians,
> Black eyes, arch'd brows, and sweet expressions still;
> Such as of old were copied from the Grecians,
> In ancient arts by moderns mimick'd ill;
> And like so many Venuses of Titians
> (The best at Florence – see it, if ye will),
> They look when leaning over the balcony,
> Or stepp'd from out a picture by Giorgione . . .

Thus, writing to his friend John Piggot about a row with his mother, Byron (9 August, 1806) says: '. . . you with the rest of the family, merit my warmest thanks, for your kind Connivance at my Escape from "Mrs Byron furiosa". – Oh! for the pen of Ariosto to Rehearse in *Epic,* the *scolding* of that *momentous Eve,* or rather let me invoke the shade of *Dantè* to inspire me, for none but the author of the "*Inferno*" could properly preside over such an Attempt. – But perhaps where the pen might fail, the pencil would succeed; what a group would you form for the Colours of Poussin (who I think, but will not be positive, dealt in the *horrible*) Mrs B. the principle figure, you cramming your ears with *Cotton,* as the only antidote to total deafness. . . .'

Byron goes on in a similar strain about his mother's tiresomeness, which was considerable. The choice of Poussin, with the painter's calm and peculiar restraint, is an amusing one to make for the '*Horrible*', but perhaps Byron was thinking of something on the lines of Poussin's *The Schoolmaster of the Falerii* or *The Plague of Ashdod*, though he could hardly have seen them.

Some years later (18 March, 1809), in a letter to William Harness, one of his favourites at Harrow, Byron writes: 'I am going abroad if possible in the spring, and before I depart, I am collecting the pictures of my most intimate Schoolfellows, I have already a few, and shall want yours or my cabinet will be incomplete. – I have employed one of the first miniature painters of the day to take them, of course at my own expense as I never allow my acquaintance to incur the least expenditure to gratify a whim of mine – to mention this may seem indelicate, but when I tell you that at first a friend refused to sit, under the idea that he was to disburse on the occasion, you will see that it is necessary to state these preliminaries to prevent the recurrence of a similar mistake. I shall see you in town and will carry you to the *Limner*.'

The Limner was, in fact, George Sanders, who painted several portraits and miniatures of Byron himself, as well as these planned likenesses of fellow Harrovians. One of Sanders's life-size portraits of Byron is frontispiece to the first volume of the Letters (*Byron landing from a boat*, 1807) and an engraving of one of the miniatures, frontispiece of the second volume (showing the poet with an open shirt and fur-collared cloak, 1812).

Incidentally, other portraits of Byron listed in the DNB include a miniature by Kaye (at the age of seven); a half-length by Westall; two half-lengths by Thomas Phillips (one of them the well-known portrait in Albanian dress); a bust in marble by Thorvaldsen; a half-length by Harlowe; a miniature by Prepiani; a miniature in watercolours (in college robes) by Gilchrist; a pencil sketch from memory by G. Cattermole; a medallion by A. Stothard; a bust by Bartolini; a half-length by West; three sketches by Count d'Orsay; a silhouette cut in paper by Mrs Leigh Hunt. This is not a bad score.

In 1810, when he was travelling in Greece, Byron saw something of Giovanni Battista Lusieri, a Neapolitan painter, who had been employed by one of Lord Elgin's secretaries to make topographical studies of the Near East, when Elgin was Ambassador at Constantinople. Byron was, by the way, against the removal of the 'Marbles' from the Parthenon, whatever risk they may be thought to have run by remaining there. In the following year he employed a Bavarian artist, Jacob Linckh, to 'take some views of Athens &c &c' for himself, describing him (20 January, 1811) as a 'Bavarian Baron . . . who limns landscapes for the lucre of gain'.

Back in England later in the same year, Byron brought the painter John Vincent Barber to paint his wolf and his bear at Newstead. He writes to Francis Hodgson (13 October, 1811), a parson friend to whom he was inclined to send rather racy letters: 'The painter is not necessary, as the portraits he has already painted are (by anticipation) very like the new animals.'

A small point to be corrected is that Captain Massingberd, R.N., a husband of Mrs Elizabeth Massingberd, who let rooms to Byron, a distant relation, at No. 16 Piccadilly, was not dead, but on active service. The note states that it is not on record whether this family connexion was known, but, in the small world of county society, it would be unlikely not to be, especially as Byron himself was very preoccupied with kinship.

There is, of course, a lot more to the Letters than has been suggested here, touching mainly on Byron at painting, and they are much to be rccommended.

Byron's Letters and Journals: 1974
Vol I, *In My Hot Youth*; Vol II, *Famous in My Time,* *Apollo*
edited by Leslie A. Marchand,
John Murray.

THOMAS MOORE

Although *Lalla Rookh*, Thomas Moore's oriental epic – a wild success on publication in 1816 – is now all but totally forgotten, 'The Harp that Once through Tara's Halls', 'Oft in the Stilly Night', 'The Last Rose of Summer', 'The Canadian Boatsong', might all be allowed as stirring faint memories of early poetry reading. Perhaps even these last are unfamiliar to a younger generation.

Moore (b. 1779) had a remarkable career. His letters suggest that he was an unusually nice man, good-natured, an attractive companion, not in the least addicted to self-pity in face of some staggering blows, but, at the same time not, in the deeper use of the term, particularly intelligent.

Son of a Dublin grocer, he is an example of the manner in which the English *beau monde* has always been prepared to accept anyone, whatever his birth or background, if he happens to be amusing and to 'fit in'.

Moore's father managed to send him to Trinity College, Dublin, and afterwards to London with a view to reading for the Bar. Obviously this implies a certain sufficiency of means, that was all. Moore was not starving, but he was a typically impecunious young man and remained in money difficulties most of his life.

Almost immediately – through his patron, Lord Moira – he was presented, then aged twenty, to the Prince of Wales, and soon afterwards to Mrs Fitzherbert. From that moment to the end of his days, when he was not abroad or living quietly in a country cottage, Moore moved in a circle of grandees.

This caused a good deal of irritation among egalitarianly minded acquaintances. He was then, and still is, accused of snobbery. The *Letters* do not seem to bear this out, if an obsequious approach is implied. On the contrary, they are written with the same ease of manner, whomever Moore is addressing.

If his social success was not effortless, it was not offensively sought. Moore himself, after he had endured unusually shabby treatment from a journalist friend, says in a letter to Mary Shelley: 'Bad as my "aristocratic" acquaintances are . . . this is not the way to make me regret the sphere of society I have chosen for myself.' The fact was that Moore had no chip on his shoulder, and his singing of his own songs was certainly greatly enjoyed as a form of drawing-room entertainment at parties he attended.

Accordingly, he was fixed up by his patrons, in the manner of the period with the job of Registrar of Bermuda. He went out there found the place had little to offer a man of his sort, and the post in the hands of a deputy. A year or two later the deputy defalcated to the tune of £6,000.

Moore retired to the Continent. The government were eventually persuaded to reduce the demanded amount. The debt was at last paid off. Moore himself was getting advances from publishers of 2,000 and 3,000 guineas, huge amounts at that date.

He is now probably remembered chiefly for the unfortunate affair of the Byron memoirs. Byron and Moore had first come in contact over what Moore regarded as a disobliging reference to himself in *English Bards and Scotch Reviewers*. Later the two poets became friends. An extraordinary arrangement was made by which Byron should hand over what amounted to the copyright of his own *Memoirs* to Moore in order to help him out of his financial difficulties.

As is well known, this finally resulted in the *Memoirs* being burnt. Moore showed weakness rather than deliberate crime against posterity in his behaviour over this affair. He was in a hopelessly tangled position himself, financially and otherwise. Hobhouse and John Murray are the real villains of the piece.

The whole arrangement seems a very strange one. It is hard to know whether, in that day, it seemed less odd than now, or whether it must be thought of merely as a characteristically Byronic gesture, neither more nor less. Whichever it was, Moore at one moment might have preserved a copy of the manuscript. So at least appears from the *Letters*.

It has to be admitted that Moore's *Letters* on the whole are not breathlessly exciting. They confirm various matters; the usual personalities like Sydney Smith and Samuel Rogers stray through their pages. Moore lived at Sloperton in Wiltshire, an address Lady Holland – in what one imagines to be a characteristic example of her wit – renamed Hogwash Cottage.

Moore was a fan of Jane Austen. He enjoyed *Emma* and wrote to John Murray, 'I heard a little of the new novel (Persuasion &c) read at Bowood the other night, which has given me a great desire to read the rest.'

He always lived a very domestic life, when not going about in society, where his wife, in general, did not accompany him. He had several children, one of whom became an officer in the French Foreign Legion.

The editing by Wilfred S. Dowden might have been more painstaking. To refer to 'Earl Bertrand Russell' under the acknowledgements is a good joke in the circumstances, but one must regret 'Viscount Percy Strangford' in the text.

The Letters of Thomas Moore, 1793–1847, edited by Wilfred A. Dowden, Clarendon/OUP.

1965
Daily Telegraph

PERCY BYSSHE SHELLEY

Shelley was a favourite with the Victorians, being, for instance, the poet to whom Thomas Hardy most often turned. But the Romantics were in for a bad time, and Shelley, among them, was in the next few decades to be knocked about badly by T. S. Eliot and others.

There is probably some reaction so far as Shelley's poetry is concerned, but in a permissive age the mess he made of his own life now seems not so much romantic as depressingly banal. Besides, unlike Byron, Shelley never managed to do things in style.

Claire Tomalin tells the story, at times a fairly complex one, in an admirably compact manner, adding an excellent selection of illustrations. In Shelley's case this is a genuine addition to the account of his wanderings over England and Wales, later on the Continent.

Percy Bysshe Shelley (1792–1822), known to his family by the middle name, was an eldest son with five younger sisters, a circumstance dear to the psychiatrist. The Shelleys were a Sussex family of some standing and antiquity, but immediate forebears had only become rich (very rich) in the last two generations by resourceful eloping with heiresses. The poet's grandfather had been born in New Jersey of parents not at all well off who might perfectly well have settled in America.

Politics bulk large in Shelley's early life as he started off as a professional revolutionary. Mrs Tomalin writes from a rigorously Whig point of view ('Peterloo,' diminished by recent scholarship is swallowed whole), and I think she is a shade too willing to accept his father without sufficiently emphasising that the background of the Shelley home was in itself impeccably Whig.

Shelley *père's* political patron, the eleventh Duke of Norfolk, may have been disparaged by Shelley himself for not being Radical enough, but in 1798 the Duke had been deprived of all his offices for making a indiscreetly democratic speech, and in general the views that Shelley disseminated were largely those with which he had been brought up, even if he advocated them in a more violent manner. In short, Shelley was a classic example of Dostoievsky's theory that the Liberals of one generation begat the nihilists of the next.

Shelley was traditionally unhappy at Eton and (rather a Dotheboys Hall incident) stuck a fork into a schoolfellow, but Mrs Tomalin quotes a poem about picnicking with hot tea in bottles, hard-boiled eggs and radishes in overcoat pockets, which makes his school days sound not entirely intolerable. He was famous at Eton for 'cursing his father and the king'; the former of whom presumably paid for the printing of the two novels Shelley, somewhat unusually, produced while still at the school.

Shelley's most disastrous step was to marry Harriet Westbrook, daughter of a prosperous retired restaurant proprietor, when he was just nineteen; she was only sixteen. This inevitably led to trouble. Shelley's particular combination of egoism, high-mindedness, and certainty that he could put the world right, was attractive to women, and it is noteworthy that he tended to do much more real damage in other people's lives than Byron did by being cynical. The fact that the two poets got on well is to some extent unexpected, and a taped conversation of the two of them 'messing about in boats' together would be of superlative interest.

Shelley's second wife, Mary Wollstonecraft, daughter of that fairly frightful political philosopher William Godwin, outsoared her husband's fame by writing *Frankenstein* (not the most readable book in the world, it must be admitted), thereby creating a folk hero (albeit the Monster is usually confused with his creator) to be known to millions. There is an excellent picture of Mary Shelley's mother here, a proto-woman's libber, wearing a top hat to prove her point.

Returning to Shelley's poetry today one is surprised by its sheer extent – a fat volume even if printed on India paper – although he was drowned a month before his thirtieth birthday. There is a respectable amount that one would hesitate to condemn out of hand. For my own part, while never being much attached to Shelley as a poet, I should take my stand on *Adonais* and 'Ozymandias'. Mrs Tomalin's first choice is 'The Two Spirits: An Allegory' –

> O thou who plumed with strong desire
> Wouldst float above the earth, beware!
> A Shadow tracks the flight of fire –
> Night is coming!
> Bright are the regions of the air,
> And among the winds and beams,
> It were delight to wander there –
> Night is coming!

Some of Shelley's drawings are reproduced here. They are not without talent, and vividly suggest his neurotic state of mind. Mrs Tomalin very truly points out that, whatever Shelley's condition, he also possessed an extraordinary toughness and organising ability, which made it possible for him to take a party of women and children across France to Italy, a journey that must have set every sort of logistic problem at that period.

One of the most absurd incidents in his life was when, in his father's absence, he wanted to pay a clandestine visit to his mother, he disguised himself in military uniform. Shelley was, however, wholly lacking in the humour to appreciate such occasions.

Shelley and His World,
Claire Tomalin,
Thames & Hudson.

1980
Daily Telegraph

JOHN KEATS

There have been some good books about Keats – Aileen Ward's *John Keats: The Making of a Poet* (1963), for example – but a fair amount of misleading legend remains to be repudiated.

Robert Gittings's scholarly, understanding, above all eminently reasonable biography puts a lot of the material in new focus. It will give most readers a coherent picture of the poet that they have never had before.

Mr Gittings provides far the best picture available so far of Keats's origins. These have been bedevilled by both friends and enemies: the former, like Leigh Hunt, anxious to represent them as modest as possible for political and moral purposes; the latter keying them down simply because they wanted to make themselves disagreeable. I have to admit that I had always supposed Keats the son of an ostler who married the daughter of his boss, an innkeeper; and that at an early age he had unwillingly become an apothecary's assistant and sold pills over the counter.

All this is not precisely untrue, but has in general been propagated in a manner to obscure the facts. Keats's grandfather did indeed keep an inn in the City. It must have been a prosperous one, because he left £13,000, a very tidy sum in 1805. One son was an officer of Marines, and his daughter, Keats's mother, planned to send her boy to Harrow.

So far from being an unwilling apothecary's assistant, Keats went through the perfectly normal training to become a doctor, a profession he was keen to follow. At the end of his apprenticeship he would have emerged as a full-fledged GP, had the law not been altered, quite by chance, at that moment. It was during the additional eighteen months' training required from him that he decided to give up medicine in favour of poetry. Although he disliked pre-anaesthetic surgery, he was always drawn to being a physician. Even after abandoning it, he talked of getting a job as ship's doctor.

About Keats's father there is certainly a mystery. Perhaps he was indeed 'helper, ostler or waiter'. If so, he was no ordinary one. There was an obvious contemporary lack of desire to probe into the family background, and it would not be unreasonable to suspect illegitimacy.

Mr Gittings is far too good a scholar to do more than present the facts, but he shows how a family of Keate or Keats, deriving from a doctor born at the beginning of the eighteenth century at Wells in Somerset, show strong physical, temperamental and vocational characteristics resembling the poet's. Tiny, violent-tempered, red-haired, they tended towards medicine, though Dr Keate, headmaster of Eton, was also one of them. Keats himself was less than an inch over 5ft.

Keats was born in 1795 and died in 1821. It is astonishing how much work he packed into this brief period. As Mr Gittings points out, his special characteristic as a poet is an extraordinary sensitiveness to the impressions of the moment. Although it seemed to Keats himself that he never truly achieved recognition, one is surprised at what an early age he was accepted as a remarkable figure in literary circles. All literary journalists who hope not to go down to posterity as sunk in stupidity, vulgarity and complacency should occasionally re-read the attacks on him.

One of the strangest aspects of the nineteenth century's approach to Keats was the discomfort they felt about his love affair with Fanny Brawne. Mr Gittings goes into this in a good deal of detail. One cannot see what all the fuss was about. The Brawne family background was oddly similar to that of Keats in certain respects. Fanny was not as young as Keats thought at first. She was in fact nineteen when they became friends. This was quite mature by the standards of the time. She was attractive, lively, not unintelligent, apparently a perfectly reasonable girl to fall in love with.

That Keats went through a great deal of torture on her account is undoubtedly true, but this was to be attributed to a large extent to the tubercular disease from which he suffered. More than once one is reminded of Marcel and Albertine in Proust's novel, in the agonies of jealousy Keats suffered when, so far as can be seen, Fanny was in fact deeply attached to him.

If Keats's state of health is allowed for, it is hard to see what there was so greatly to disapprove. Keats, in the end, certainly thought Fanny should have given herself to him, and believed that his final collapse was brought on by her refusal. She can hardly be blamed in the circumstances, and it was not for this that she earned Victorian disapprobation.

Keats's circle of friends was not a particularly inspiring one, but one suspects he was one of those magnetic personalities who require a good deal of dullness round them. The friends, too, had a hard time of it often, though Keats himself, when not racked with disease, emerges as an attractive personality.

John Keats,
Robert Gittings,
Heinemann Educational Books.

1968
Daily Telegraph

CHARLES AUGUSTIN SAINTE-BEUVE

'It is as if an English author, possessing the curiosity of Isaac D'Israeli, the scholarship of Saintsbury and the skill of Edmund Gosse, were to leave us forty volumes containing essays on such diverse subjects as Beattie's *Minstrel*, the Blickling Homilies, Mrs Vesey, *Tottel's Miscellany*, the Army *Manual on Sanitation*, Jack of Newbury, Green's coneycatching, Wyclif and scholasticism, Adelaide Anne Procter, Drummond of Hawthornden, Lady Melbourne, Rifleman Harris, the Paston Letters, the Warwickshire coterie, Caroline Norton, Barclay's *Eclogues*, Jacob Tonson and the Two Angry Women of Abington.'

Thus does Sir Harold Nicolson describe the scope of Charles Augustin Sainte-Beuve (1804–1869), who, if not the greatest of French critics, he justly labels the greatest guide to French literature of the nineteenth century. If being a good critic consists in marking down the contemporary names that in due course impress posterity, Sainte-Beuve undoubtedly had his blind spots. He missed Balzac, Stendhal and Flaubert; Baudelaire and Verlaine. Modern French sentiment tends to be unsympathetic to him; Proust's *Contre Sainte-Beuve* charges him with imposing a blurred, artificial shape to the things of which he wrote.

Sir Harold more than once informs his reader that this book is little more than a study derived almost entirely from M. André Billy's monumental work on the same subject; and that it is his wish merely to present Sainte-Beuve to the English reader in intelligible terms, giving reasons for considering him to-day an underestimated figure. He has accomplished this task with clarity, humour and understanding. The book is that rare thing, a monologue over the dinner table of which one does not tire.

A large part of the biography is taken up by the great emotional event of Sainte-Beuve's life – his love affair with Madame Victor Hugo. This is a fascinating story from every point of view. Sainte-Beuve, as a young critic, was brought into contact with Hugo, then rising speedily to fame. By degrees he fell in love with Hugo's wife. He informed Hugo, who perhaps found the matter impossible to take seriously, or was not unwilling to have an excuse to embark on the career of record-breaking amatory adventure in which the rest of his own life was spent.

The piquancy of the story lies not only in the fact that Sainte-Beuve was a critic and Hugo a poet, or that Sainte-Beuve was unsuccessful, poor and hideous, while Hugo achieved fame in his early twenties, never had much trouble in raising money, and was unusually good-looking. On top of all that Sainte-Beuve possessed a physical disability which would have made a normal marriage impossible, while Hugo's powers were of a truly fabulous order. One is driven to the banal reflection that you simply cannot tell what a woman will like. My only criticism of Sir Harold's treatment of this incident is that he does not accept the extreme contrast as in itself a good reason for Madame Hugo's fall.

What the affair amounted to emotionally is, of course, another matter. When, towards the end of this life, Princesse Mathilde asked Sainte-Beuve whether he had ever truly loved a woman, 'he gazed in silence for a few minutes at the carpet. "That," he answered, "is a box which I never open."' There can be no doubt that an element of scoring off Hugo in this manner played a powerful part in the whole business.

It is impossible to say that Sainte-Beuve was an attractive character. He was treacherous, cowardly, envious, stingy, ungrateful, and no woman was safe from his advances. On the other hand, he was deeply devoted to literature, and, when he had made up his mind that he himself was never going to be a star of the first rank, he worked like a black (if that phrase is still permissible) to produce a guide to French literature that is unsurpassed. No one who possesses a good memory and a set of the *Causeries du lundi* need fear to be seriously caught out on that subject at the most intellectual party. Another fact should go on record. Sainte-Beuve once stood Matthew Arnold dinner at 'the only good restaurant in the quarter', Pinson's in the rue de l'Ancienne Comédie.

Sainte-Beuve, 1957
Harold Nicolson, Constable. *Punch*

EDGAR ALLAN POE
and
THOMAS HOOD

At first sight Edgar Allan Poe (1809–1849) and Thomas Hood (1799–1845) do not seem to have much in common except what comparative closeness of date inevitably gives, although Poe wrote a poem called 'The Haunted Palace' (not 'House', as John Clubbe quotes the title), and Hood 'The Haunted House'.

'The Haunted Palace' in 'The Fall of the House of Usher' (1839), was possibly read by Hood, though there is no evidence of it. Hood's poem was admired by Poe, who also expressed appreciation for:

> O saw ye not fair Ines?
> She's gone into the West,
> To dazzle when the sun is down
> And rob the world of rest . . .

One might think Poe immensely out of fashion at the moment, but in fact his complete works, in seventeen volumes, have quite recently been reissued in the United States (together with Woodberry's biography), so clearly interest in him exists. If reading his poetry in bulk is rather heavy going, that is true of all but very few poets, and the good bits are certainly remarkable for their peculiar individuality. Baudelaire and Yeats thought highly of Poe and it is hard to feel that they were mistaken.

Hood, on the other hand, has come into his own with contemporary emphasis on 'social criticism'. 'The Song of the Shirt' remains a powerful piece in its own genre, and 'The Bridge of Sighs' was also admired, indeed translated, by Baudelaire:

> Look at her garments
> Clinging like cerements;
> Whilst the wave constantly
> Drips from her clothing;
> Take her up instantly,
> Loving, not loathing.

It might be priggishly suggested that the suicide of an ill-favoured and middle-aged prostitute could, morally speaking, be just as tragic as that of a young and good-looking one, and there is no doubt that sentimentality of just that sort does flaw Hood's work in a manner that Poe, for all his dead child loves (his own wife was only thirteen when they married), manages to avoid.

Mr Clubbe mentions the difficulty of categorising Hood's verse, and the divisions of his selection into Romantic, Comic, Domestic, Narrative and Social Protest work well. Among these 'Miss Kilmansegg and Her Precious Leg', taking up eighty pages, has a section to itself. These verses tell how Miss Kilmansegg, a very rich young lady, lost her leg in a traffic accident, had it replaced by a leg of gold, married a foreign count who ill treated her, and was eventually done in by the count with this leg, the verdict being suicide as it was her own limb.

'Miss Kilmansegg' seems to me much too long and immensely boring, but it does show the odd surrealist side of Hood, of which his Joycean puns were also part. It illustrates too his sado-masochist strain, which made it possible for him to write a comic poem describing how a man, born blind, married, had his eyes opened 'like oysters, with a knife', murdered his wife because she turned out to be so ugly, and was hanged.

In Hood's sado-masochism and surrealism we seem to have a closer link with Poe than in the purely romantic element the two poets share – Hood's efforts to write like Keats were disastrous. Poe was, of course, hailed as one of their masters by early writers of a surrealist sort like Jarry and Apollinaire.

It is true that Breton said that 'in questions of revolt, none of us should need ancestors' and 'let us spit in passing on Edgar Poe', but that was later on. By then surrealist obeisance had already been made. The surrealists do not seem to have discovered Hood, who certainly has something to offer in their line.

Accordingly, it is interesting that this republication of Poe's poems has the Heath Robinson illustrations. It may not be generally known that Heath Robinson – later famous for his caricatures of incredibly complicated mechanical devices – started life drawing romantically in the Walter Crane/Beardsley manner. Although obviously derivative, Heath Robinson's work is never offensively so and has a certain charm of its own.

A not uncommon paradox is suggested by Heath Robinson's change from an extreme romanticism to a technique based on mechanism, that is to say the short step from the romantic to the grotesque. One cannot help playing with the idea of an edition of Poe's poems illustrated in Heath Robinson's later manner. For example:

> By a route obscure and lonely,
> Haunted by ill angels only,

Where an Eidolon named Night,
  On a black throne reigns upright
I have reached these lands but newly,
  From an ultimate dim Thule
From a wild weird clime that lieth, sublime
  Out of Space – out of Time.

Surely Heath Robinson would have done a splendid surrealist picture of that?

Mr Clubbe's Hood selection must be commended for giving the poet's own original illustrations. They are in the Leech/Thackeray manner, a shade scratchy, but add to the understanding of Hood's personality. He was typical of one kind of English literary figure, deeply imbued with middle-class respectability, hard-working, always pressed for money. His 'Pauper's Christmas Carol' is typical:

Ring the Day of Plenty in!
But the happy tide to hail
With a sigh or with a tear,
    Heigho!
  I hardly know –
Christmas comes but once a year!

Poe was a not uncommon American literary type (rather in the Scott Fitzgerald manner), just as hard up, but approaching life with a reckless, erratic violence which led to a bad end. He and Hood make an interesting couple.

The Poems of Edgar Allan Poe, illustrated by W. Heath Robinson, Bell. 1970 *Daily Telegraph*

Selected Poems of Thomas Hood, edited by John Clubbe, OUP for Harvard.

EDWARD FITZGERALD

About six months ago a longish poem called 'Letter to Omar', written in burlesqued metre of Omar Khayyám's *Rubáiyát*, appeared in a contemporary journal. It was by Dick Davis, the poet, presenting himself as having lived in Iran and now established in East Anglia. The gist of the verses was how good FitzGerald's version of the *Rubáiyát* is, whatever highbrows may say. 'Letter to Omar' seemed to me amusing, to the point and in its way rather moving.

What about Edward FitzGerald (1809–1883) whose '*Rubáiyát of Omar Khayyám, the Astronomer-Poet of Persia*' rendered into English verse, was printed at his own expense in 1859, and became one of the most popular poems in the language? Hundreds of editions have appeared in this country, even more in the United States, where, once known, the *Rubáiyát* was immediately pirated. T. S. Eliot, when young, found it 'overwhelming'.

Robert Bernard Martin gives an understanding, scholarly, and up-to-date account of FitzGerald, whose story is full of interest, both as an individual and for the friends of the book's title, who 'possessed' him. It should, at once, be added that possession was not in the physical sense. There is every indication that FitzGerald never had sexual relations with anyone throughout his life.

He came of an Anglo-Irish landed family called Purcell. His father, half a FitzGerald, married a FitzGerald first cousin, herself daughter of FitzGerald first cousins. FitzGerald himself disliked the change of name, but of four grandparents three belonged to that powerful Irish house. His mother was also a considerable heiress.

FitzGerald's parents at first got on well, then became estranged. They had several residences, living chiefly in East Anglia. His father, dim and eccentric, enjoyed country pursuits, and quite egregiously managed to bankrupt himself for an enormous sum trying to run a (uneconomic) coalmine. His mother, unlike some Victorian ladies, retained control over her fortune and lived – richly and rather vulgarly – mostly in a large house in Portland Place where she entertained a good deal but was not well looked on by Society.

FitzGerald went to Cambridge. He was up with Tennyson and Thackeray, both of whom were lifelong friends, as later was Carlyle. From his earliest days FitzGerald met such figures as an intellectual equal, though his extraordinary tactlessness and taste for working jokes to death – even by Victorian standards – sometimes caused trouble. In any case he disliked the poetry of Wordsworth, both Brownings (Mr Martin does not mention the row with Browning about FitzGerald's expression of relief when Mrs Browning died), Rossetti, Swinburne, Matthew Arnold, and later Tennyson.

An almost total inability to organise himself was FitzGerald's main characteristic. He remained throughout his life an untidy undergraduate who hated making arrangements, loathed social life in London, became bored in the country, but settled for the country (various places in East Anglia) in the end. One of the plagues of his existence was his dominating mother, who forced him to come to London to be her 'spare man', a humiliating chore which continued until his thirties.

Part of FitzGerald's immaturity came out in lack of understanding of his own homosexual temperament. We know that the Victorians were used to emotional talk about the affection male friends felt for each other, also that homosexuality was not understood or spoken of except in the sort of circle frequented by, say, Rossetti and Swinburne.

Even if he was quite open about his love for the two young men who meant most to him in his life, William Kenworthy Brown and Robert Cowell, it might be thought that FitzGerald would not have declared to everyone that he was seeking a friend among the longshoremen of Lowestoft. The fishermen themselves were by no means so unsophisticated. FitzGerald's ultimately unsatisfactory protégé, 'Posh' Fletcher (who looks remarkably shifty in a sou'wester photograph in his old age), seems to have been ragged on the subject by colleagues.

This failing on FitzGerald's part to know what other people were like (he was, in fact, not in the least interested in other people) led to his disastrous marriage to the daughter of a dead friend. It lasted less than a year. He was forty-seven, she was forty-nine. Quite apart from sex, he does not seem to have given a thought to what it might be like to exist with a woman in the house. By the time he was quite comfortably off, so all was settled amicably, but what seems so strange is the manner in which FitzGerald had in no way pondered and come to terms with his own nature.

He pottered about, lonely and melancholy most of the time, producing a book of aphorisms, translating Calderón, then when he was about forty-two became interested in Omar Khayyám through the second of his great loves, Robert Cowell, a young man of prodigious learning, who, oddly enough, married a much older woman whom FitzGerald himself had once thought of as a possible wife.

The story of how, after two years' publication, the *Rubáiyát* was put on a bookstall at a penny, found by a young Celtic scholar called Whitley

Stokes, then went through Monckton Milnes, Richard Burton, Rossetti, Swinburne, Ruskin, all the Pre-Raphaelites, like the proverbial salts, is well known. Mr Martin points out with truth that, in fact, two years was not an unreasonable time for a poem to become famous.

FitzGerald clearly felt a tremendous affinity for the *Rubáiyát* but his own life far from resembled that of its protagonist. True he liked living largely on tea and bread and butter, consumed at any time of day, which might represent the Loaf of Bread, but although he used to get tight occasionally, he was not very great on wine, tending to drink beer or brandy. All the same, the extraordinary thing about Persia, with its formal gardens that 'just divide the desert from the sown', is the way the country makes one think of Omar and his translator.

With Friends Possessed: 1985
A Life of Edward FitzGerald, *Daily Telegraph*
Robert Bernard Martin, Faber.

ALFRED, LORD TENNYSON

I

The amount of biographical and critical attention already devoted to Tennyson puts rather a strain on a new book about him, but Philip Henderson's study moves quickly and revealingly, making the essential points without too much cluttering of information, which the poet's long and full life can threaten.

It now seems strange that Alfred Tennyson (1809–1892) could ever have been regarded as anything but a very great poet at his best, even if he did have bad patches. He upset some by a taste for order, and a grasp that there were stormy times ahead. His father, a dispossessed eldest son, who had been forced against his will into the Church, produced a large family, not all of whom remained sane. Tennyson's early life was uncomfortable and chaotic, but not altogether unhappy. Tennyson *père* immediately recognised his son's poetic gift.

Mr Henderson rightly devotes a good deal of space to the Tennyson/Hallam situation, which has two aspects: first, the emotional impact on Tennyson personally; second, its place in the Tennyson myth. These are not quite the same. Arthur Hallam, a Cambridge contemporary, became engaged to Tennyson's sister, then died suddenly at the age of twenty-two. He and Tennyson had been the closest of friends at Cambridge, and for the rest of his life Tennyson regarded the loss of his friend as the greatest blow he was ever to suffer. The record of his grief is *In Memoriam.*

There is no reason why two young men should not feel mutually an enormous personal and intellectual sympathy without the smallest degree of homosexual implication; nor that the death of one of them might not come as a shattering blow to the survivor. This was especially true of the Romantic sentiments of the early nineteenth century, and Hallam's letter to Monckton Milnes refusing him friendship 'in the lofty sense', while agreeing they should write poems to each other, indicates very well the high-flown undergraduate exchanges of the period.

Nevertheless, Mr Henderson quotes passages from *In Memoriam* that do make laughing off Tennyson's references to physical closeness (anyway in his own mind) extremely difficult. Tennyson consciously paralleled

Shakespeare's Sonnets, but Shakespeare did not mince matters in expressing how inconvenient, physically speaking, he found falling in love with another man. Tennyson makes no such protestation.

So far as one can see there was not the smallest suggestion of any similar attachment to a man in Tennyson's later life. Soon after the death of Hallam he fell in love with a Lincolnshire neighbour, Rose Baring, was later happily married, and always enjoyed being flirtatious with pretty girls. We are somewhat reminded of Kipling's overwhelming affliction at the death of Wolcott Balestier, followed by marriage with Balestier's sister – a kind of variation on the Tennyson/Hallam family connection.

The second aspect of *In Memoriam* its myth, involved Queen Victoria, who identified the subject of the poem with the Prince Consort, and described it as her favourite reading after the Bible. Mr Henderson's book well brings out the real liking and understanding that Tennyson and the Queen felt for one another.

Mr Henderson draws attention to something now often forgotten, the extraordinary virulence and scurrility of Victoria journalism. Tennyson (very sensitive to unfriendly comment) was always under attack throughout his life. The equivocal side of *In Memoriam* did not escape reviewers, and *The Times*, in a caustic notice, referred to 'much shallow art spent on tenderness shown to an Amaryllis of the Chancery Bar'. A good deal of spite was also displayed when Tennyson (unwillingly) accepted a peerage – after turning down several offers of a baronetcy – though no man could have been less time-serving or place-seeking.

'Maud', 'Locksley Hall' and several other poems (the first two among Tennyson's most absorbing) celebrate his love for Rose Baring, and the situation that perpetually crops up in Tennyson's verse – the impoverished young man aspiring to a girl of higher position, whom he loves, while at the same time feeling uneasy. The two of them being caught embracing on the terrace is an often repeated, probably autobiographical, Tennysonian awkward moment.

Mr Henderson is good on the poet's financial position, always interesting. Tennyson was determined to do no other work than writing poetry, and it is hard to know what would have happened had not his father died in 1831, leaving him property worth about £200 a year. About ten years later, unbelievably, Tennyson sold this, investing all his capital in a crack-brained scheme for carving wood by machinery to bring 'artistic' furniture within range of the masses.

Naturally the money disappeared at once, but, by an inconceivably shrewd move connected with life insurance, his brother-in-law got most of it back for him. Soon after Tennyson was granted a Civil List pension of £200; he was only comparatively well off in later life.

The picture of Rose Baring illustrated here as 'from a portrait by Richard Buckner, a fashionable but not much documented painter of the mid-nineteenth century, the ideal artist for Lady Clara Vere de Vere.

Tennyson: Poet and Prophet, 1978
Philip Henderson, Routledge. *Daily Telegraph*

II

To get the hang of Victorian publishing it is well to bear in mind that between April 1852 and April 1853 *Uncle Tom's Cabin* sold one and a half million copies. That showed there was a book buying public to be tapped.

When Alfred Tennyson was confronted with the question of publishing his poems (which first appeared in book form in 1827) the usual gloom prevailed in the book market – complaints that all the great writers were dead; no one was buying any books; they couldn't afford them. A publishing climate with which we are all only too familiar.

To this was added Tennyson's own extremely complicated attitude towards the presentation of his poetry. On the one hand he was determined to make a living by being only a poet (which he managed to do in the early stages by a series of extremely lucky chances). On the other, although he would read his poems privately within a comparatively large circle of friends, he had a positive unwillingness to appear in print until he felt his work was absolutely satisfactory to himself.

He added a further paradox to these conflicting attitudes. He was a shrewd businessman in dealing with his publishers – though not, one would say, over-grasping, as has sometimes been suggested. In contrast to that, he possessed a pathological horror of publicity; not merely in the personal annoyance of being bothered by tourists who wanted to catch a glimpse of the famous poet, but in objecting to a publisher putting an advertisement in a paper to the effect that a certain poem was presented in a new edition with some lines added to it.

June Steffensen Hagen's detailed examination of all this makes extremely interesting reading, and produces all sorts of unexpected side effects. For example, I have a much better idea of Arthur Hallam than before, from the manner in which Tennyson's much beloved friend acted almost as his agent in help given where publishing matters were concerned.

Poems by Two Brothers – Alfred and Charles Tennyson – which appeared in 1827, was brought out by a bookseller in Louth, Lincolnshire. A London bookseller, Effingham Wilson, issued the first collection of solely Alfred Tennyson's poems (some of the best-known ones) in 1830. Of this undertaking Hallam wrote:

> I went again to Effingham Wilson's shop to-day, saw the old codger himself; he was bland and submissive, promising to send me the account as soon as he should have time to make it out. I am confident the £11 will be found a mistake – perhaps a bravado of that saucy cub his son. Come what may you need not pay it. Take no step yourself. Leave that to Moxon, Tennant, Heath and myself.

The Moxon mentioned by Hallam was Edward Moxon, who has claims to have been Tennyson's most congenial publisher. He had begun as a boy in a bookshop and seems to have had a real feeling for poetry and its marketing. He and Tennyson got on very well personally, but unfortunately Moxon died and the business passed to his brother.

This situation produced the classical literary disaster of one publisher possessing the instinct to handle a given writer, another totally failing to do so. Moxon had suggested an illustrated edition of Tennyson's poems, an idea that Tennyson himself had not greatly welcomed. This proved far less remunerative than Edward Moxon had supposed. The adjustment that had been made on this account by both Edward Moxon and Tennyson did credit to the common sense of both.

When Edward Moxon died, however, his brother claimed that Tennyson owed him nearly £900 for persuading Edward Moxon to produce this publishing failure. The correspondence shows that exactly the reverse had happened, Tennyson being wholly opposed to the venture.

Tennyson extracted an apology on this account, but had to find another publisher; though very honourably he paid an anonymous allowance to Edward Moxon's widow. He tried various firms, and his ups and downs with them eventually brought him to Charles Kegan Paul.

Kegan Paul was a former clergyman and schoolmaster who had turned publisher. He had been not, as Mrs Hagen states, headmaster of Eton – it would have been a remarkable metamorphosis for an Eton headmaster to resign and become a publisher – but 'Master in college', so to speak housemaster of the seventy King's Scholars at Eton.

Kegan Paul had resigned his orders because his religious beliefs were always changing. At first he and Tennyson hit it off pretty well, but Kegan Paul's business methods were sharp, to put it mildly, and, to be fair, Tennyson was in certain respects not easy to deal with, one of his foibles being to keep proofs of his poems for at least a year until he had made up his mind about corrections.

Finally Tennyson found himself with Macmillan's and there he seems to have been happy. Alexander Macmillan, the founder of the firm, took a great deal of trouble with him. There are all sorts of minor amusing points in Mrs Hagen's book, such as Bram Stoker, author of *Dracula* and

Sir Henry Irving's manager, travelling down to Faringford to discuss production of one of Tennyson's plays.

Tennyson and His Publishers,
June Steffensen Hagen, Macmillan.

1980
Daily Telegraph

III

These are the first two volumes of a projected three-volume edition of Tennyson's letters. The collection usefully includes letters from other people to the poet together with extracts from letters, and even from diaries, in which he is mentioned. It is extremely well edited and the notes shelter some quiet jokes.

Tennyson's background was like the plot of a rather improbable novel. His grandfather, an ambitious and successful solicitor who married well, was determined to establish his family with an estate in Lincolnshire, a county that thought a good deal of itself. His eldest son, the poet's father, was clearly not going to fit into this scheme of things, but the second son was all that might be desired. The eldest son was therefore forced against his will to become a clergyman, the second son treated as heir.

The curious thing was that this all worked according to plan. The second son added d'Eyncourt to the name, a medieval descent traced through various female lines, and built a neo-Gothic manor house where a d'Eyncourt castle had stood. This caused a great deal of laughter in Lincolnshire, but that branch of the Tennyson family undoubtedly attained its objective up to a point.

Meanwhile the poet's father, vicar of Somersby in the same county, a man of considerable talent himself, became drunk and mad, threatening his wife and numerous children with a loaded gun and carving knife. His sons (as well as Alfred) were Frederick, of whom Dr Keate, no less, said he was the best scholar he ever sent out to Eton but whom his father had removed from the house by the constable; Charles, involved with a governess and opium, but also a good poet; Arthur, an alcoholic; Edward, insane; Septimus, indolent and morbid. Of the daughters Emily is the most celebrated owing to her engagement to Arthur Hallam, hero of *In Memoriam.*

All this may be found in the vast Tennysonian literature, though much was watered down in such letters as have already been published. However, there is a vividness in letters, written often when feelings were high, which can never quite be reproduced in biography. I had not fully taken in the mutual detestation of the Somersby Tennysons and the Tennyson d'Eyncourts, though the poet's father's insistence that he had been 'disinherited' was not absolutely what happened.

In the same way we get a sense of the young Tennyson from his letters and what was said in letters about him at the time, which comes over with a strong impact: his good nature, striking conversation, shyness, hypochondria, occasional boorishness, deep melancholy, enjoyment of drinking with his friends. Unfortunately, no letters from him to Hallam seem to have survived, though Hallam's letters have a sharp character of their own.

Books and poetry are rarely discussed, and 'gossip is my total abhorrence', but letters to, say, Edward FitzGerald or Richard Monckton Milnes convey a feeling of friends who get on very well together. Within the family things could be rather different and his grandfather (26 January 1829 when the Poet was twenty) wrote:

> Charles and Alfred left me on Friday. They did not act disrespectably to me, but they are so untoward and disorderly and so unlike other people I don't know what will become of them, or what can be done with; or about them. I tried to impress them with the feeling that they and Frederick was spending or wasting half their Father's Income . . . Those three boys so far from having improved in manner or manners are worse since they went to Cambridge.

On the other hand Lincolnshire neighbours like the Massingberds were on good terms with the Somersby Tennyson's whatever their oddities.

One gets a good picture of Tennyson in his early thirties from a letter (February 1841) written when he was staying at seaside village of Mablethorpe:

> I being somewhat in a stew got up early next morning, hired (the only thing to be got) a fisherman's cart, drove over to Alford (three mortal hours going 8 miles) put three letters in the post, talk to the postman, agitated him a little being an old grayhaired man, then got yours, wrote three other letters to contract the first, and then thinking there was much ado about nothing, got all six letters out again though the old man said it was illegal . . . All being right, I invited the fisherman that drove me to a glass of gin, poor fellow got drunk, talkt wildly about God and the Devil, fell down like a corpse.

The first volume takes the story on to Emily Tennyson's marriage – which was violently disapproved by those friends and relations who thought she ought to have remained in a state of perpetual ritual widowhood from her engagement to Hallam – Tennyson's own marriage (interesting comments about his wife among those first meeting her); and to the laureateship, which had first been offered to Samuel Rogers but refused on account of his great age. Tennyson would have liked to refuse too, but as beneficiary of a Civil List pension felt that would be unbecoming.

When writing of Blenheim to FitzGerald (July 1842), Tennyson says: 'The great oaks are fresher in my recollection than the Raffaelle [*The*

Ansidei Madonna, now in the National Gallery] indeed I did not have much time to study the latter: I was just getting into it when the old Duke sent a special blue plush to me to turn me out.' A note says of blue plush, 'Usage not in O.E.D'; surely it just means footman (compare '*The Yellowplush Papers*').

The second volume gives a remarkably lively picture of an odd, awkward, gruff, kindly, simple-hearted poet, whose hatred of any form of publicity – combined with irritation when his own gifts were not adequately appreciated – was perfectly genuine.

At the close of this volume he was sixty, astonishingly famous compared with the manner in which writers and poets are regarded today, admired by Queen Victoria (whose ability as a writer herself is shown by her brief pen portrait of him), meeting everyone, doing a good deal of revelling in Europe, having a full family life with his wife (who seems to have been universally liked) and children, to whom he was devoted.

The editors, as in the previous volume, have included extracts from other people's letters and diaries to heighten the background. Among these the journal of the Irish poet William Allingham is one of the best. Allingham (whom Tennyson helped to a Civil List pension) notes (July 1865) that Tennyson told him:

> I was at an hotel in Covent Garden, and went out one morning for a walk in the piazza. A man met me, tolerably well dressed but battered-looking. I never saw him before that I know of. He pulled off his hat and said 'Beg pardon, Mr Tennyson, might I say a word to you?' I stopped. 'I've been drunk for three days and I want to make a solemn promise to you, Mr Tennyson, that I won't do so any more.' I said that was a good resolve, and I hoped he would keep it. He said 'I promise you I will, Mr Tennyson' and added 'Might I shake your hand?' I shook hands with him, and he thanked me and went on his way.

When (March 1851) Tennyson has to kiss the Queen's hand as laureate he tells the sculptor Thomas Woolner that Samuel Rogers (who had himself just declined the laureateship) lent him his court dress, which had already been worn by Wordsworth. Tennyson had feared that the 'inexpressibles' might be too tight, but happily that proved not the case.

There is a good deal here about 'The Charge of the Light Brigade' which Tennyson said he wrote in 'about two minutes' and, to another correspondent, that he did not pique himself on it. There was some doubt about the number of personnel in the charge (apparently 673), the poet hesitating as to whether he should alter the line to 'Rode the seven hundred'. The poem was an immediate furore, the troops in the Crimea apparently singing it (one wonders to what tune), a chaplain to the forces asking that 'printed slips' should be sent out for the purpose.

Edward Lear appears in the letters occasionally (though he and the Tennysons had a slightly awkward relationship), Tennyson thanking Lear in June 1855 for sending his Nonsense Book 'with which Hallam will be delighted'. In June 1858 Tennyson gives a vivid glimpse of himself, writing to his friend Charles Weld (librarian to the Royal Society): 'I had a dreadful journey home. Sneezing every moment all the way and both eyes streaming with tears: nothing excites my hay fever so much as the dust of a train. When I got out at Southampton, some one of the officials at the station said: "Sir, you look like a miller; brush the gentleman, Jacob." So Jacob brushed me.'

Tennyson, who had none of the inadaptability of modern poets when it came to writing to order on a given subject, produced an ode to be sung at the opening of the International Exhibition of 1862, but did not attend the occasion himself.

For most of the time during this period the Tennysons were living at Farringford in the Isle of Wight, where many celebrated persons came to visit the poet. He was also much plagued by sightseers, one of whom climbed up the wall, peering over, and was rebuked by him. Longfellow, then also at the height of a fame which these days has grown somewhat dim, came to luncheon in July 1868, accompanied by two sisters, a brother-in-law, a brother, three daughters and a daughter-in-law.

Eventually the lion-hunting tourists drove Tennyson to abandon the Isle of Wight for the Surrey-Hampshire border, where we leave him at the close of this volume.

From time to time Tennyson encountered Gladstone, with whom he seems to have got on well. The manner in which each spoke to the other with his own strong provincial accent was well worth hearing. There are a good many letters to publishers, with whom Tennyson was not always happy. He was, however, lucky enough to find an American publisher prepared to pay him something for his work, in an era when many other British writers were being shamelessly pirated without redress.

The letters are admirably edited and convey an extremely vivid impression of Victorian life, especially of being a Victorian celebrity and what that felt like, described by a man about whom there was absolutely no nonsense. It is impossible not to be struck by the directness of Tennyson's feelings, resulting, certainly, in opinions that may now seem rather absurd, but were never assumed to make a particular impression. In some respects one feels not that Tennyson was essentially Victorian, but that Victorianism itself, on the whole in its best aspects, owed a good deal to Tennyson.

The Letters of Alfred, Lord Tennyson: 1982, 1987
Vol I, 1821–1850; *Vol II, 1851–1870*, *Daily Telegraph*
edited by Cecil Y. Lang and Edgar F. Shannon Jr.,
Clarendon Press/OUP.

ELIZABETH BARRETT BROWNING

The story of Elizabeth Barrett Browning, as she is usually called, is well known. Something of an infant prodigy, herself a poet, she married Browning, six years her junior, when she was forty, a reprehensible act in the eyes of her dominating father.

E.B.B.'s father (whose elder sister Sarah was the 'Pinkie' of Lawrence's picture) was born Moulton, of a Durham family, taking his mother's name, Barrett, on inheriting considerable Jamaican estates from his grandfather. In 1809 he bought a property in Herefordshire called Hope End, and built an attractive neo-Gothic house there with Moorish windows and turrets. That is the background to E.B.B.'s diary.

She was the eldest of twelve children, two of whom were disinherited by their cantankerous parent, who even refused to open the letters his daughter sent him asking for forgiveness after decamping with Browning. These letters are known to have been still in existence in 1924. When, in 1961, a box containing family papers was opened in the presence of certain members of the Moulton-Barrett family and of Philip Kelley, one of the editors of this book, it was thought quite probable that they would turn up inside.

The letters were not there, but this diary appeared. The further history of the letters is not without interest – if they still exist. Their then owner was so infuriated by the play *The Barretts of Wimpole Street* (1924) that he said he had destroyed them. There is, however, reason to doubt that he actually took that step. If he did not destroy them, they remain in the secret drawer of a desk that was sold in October 1945, the furniture-dealer keeping no record of the buyer. Browning fans will like to note this.

The diary is of interest for several reasons, but, much as one likes to applaud scholarship, it is doubtful whether the devotional reverence applied to the reproduction of its form and style is quite what was required. It has been treated like one of the Dead Sea Scrolls, every addition and correction – even blots – scrupulously noted, the actual underlining (sometimes three, sometimes four lines) given, the whole in italics, not the easiest typeface for a full page. A simpler edition would have given E.B.B. more of a chance, and surely we all know now about most of the 'Psychoanalytical Observations' that are appended by Dr Robert Coles?

However, that may be hypercritical. There are two sides, as it were, of the record; life of local country society – Martins, Biddulphs, Coventrys, neighbours still unchanged after a century and a half – and E.B.B.'s intellectual interests:

> Miss Steers was there, & we had been talking of Keats & Shelley, & Colleridge's [sic] Ancient Mariner . . . On my return, I found a parcel from Mrs Martin containing Moore's Life, handsomely bound.

An amusing entry (and excellent piece of annotation) refers to the complaint of a friend that certain verses E.B.B. had published were 'horrible . . . some of those on Warren's Blacking are as good'.

It appears that the firm of Robert Warren advertised its boot-blacking poetically – for example:

> A NEW LIGHT
> To highly polished Boots and Shoes
> Warren's brilliant blacking use,
> From well-known Mart, at 30 STRAND,
> The most renown'd in ev'ry land.
> Fam'd ROBERT WARREN always adds a grace
> To *understanding* of the human race.

Now this was the notorious 'blacking factory' to which Dickens was apprenticed. Can we doubt that, had he stuck to the job, Dickens would soon have been promoted to the public relations side, and that Warren's, insufficiently in touch with their staff, lost a great ad-man?

A theme that runs through E.B.B.'s diary is her friendship – certainly an *amitié amoureuse* – with Hugh Stuart Boyd (1781–1848) the blind Greek scholar, then living at Malvern. At first she was not allowed to visit him but in due course they read classical authors together. Boyd seems to have exercised over her that curious mixture of demanding affection and bullying so characteristic of relationships of that sort.

Owing to unwise business ventures Hope End had to be sold, to the great grief of E.B.B. and the rest of the family. An important aspect of the diary is undoubtedly the picture it gives of the Barretts' relative happiness and fellow feeling, in spite of much that must have been hard to put up with.

No doubt there is a great deal we do not know, but, allowing for E.B.B.'s remarkable intellectual development, and existence in not always sympathetic surroundings, she seems to have been less at her wits' end than might be expected. The portrait (frontispiece) which is attributed to Eliza Cliffe is interesting in the light of better known ones, even though E.B.B. thought it 'not her'.

Diary of E.B.B.:
The Unpublished Diary of Elizabeth Barrett 1831–1832,
edited by Philip Kelley and Ronald Hudson,
Ohio University Press.

1969
Daily Telegraph

A. H. CLOUGH

Arthur Hugh Clough (b. 1819) came of a Welsh family shown in *Burke's Landed Gentry* of 1952 as still owning the estate in north Wales where they had lived for four hundred years.

It is notable that in the pedigree there given Clough's entry does not refer to him as 'the poet', nor mention any of his writings. The fact is that Clough is very generally forgotten. 'And not by eastern windows only', is about the best most of us could do; possibly followed, if pressed by:

> Do not adultery commit;
> Advantage rarely comes of it:

Katherine Chorley was written an interesting book about a curious, unsatisfactory, perhaps only moderately interesting man. That is the impression one has at the end of it. Clough was gifted in all kinds of ways. He also lacked some essential element.

To begin with, he was that dangerous thing, a prize pupil. He came up to Balliol from Arnold's Rugby with promise of a great career before him. He was hard up as an undergraduate, as his parents had not much money and his father's business affairs did not flourish. This fact, together with the moral and intellectual exhaustion brought on by having been one of Arnold's favourite boys, made him something of a recluse at Oxford.

Clough seems never wholly to have recovered from the Arnoldian method. He himself diagnosed the trouble, but he was unable to cure it: the appalling emphasis on moral worth, that quality being arbitrarily defined by Dr Arnold's own opinions. How fortunate, one sometimes feels, are schools – for example, Eton – which have never been plagued by a 'great' headmaster.

Lady Chorley handles the Clough story very well, skirting her way through the controversies in which he was involved, which are complicated without being eventful, far less dramatic. Her interest in him kindles the reader's.

Clough was a deeply religious man, who could neither accommodate himself to any religion, nor become a carefree agnostic. This state of mind did not even have the advantage of making him specially tolerant, either of those who belonged to specified creeds, or of those who were in much his own position. Jibbing at the 39 Articles himself did not make him any less argumentative about the views of others.

This state of mind would, in general, nowadays be merely a matter of interior discomfort. In Clough's day, for a man who hoped to earn a living in the field of education, it closed many doors, where getting any kind of teaching job was concerned.

Inability to commit himself arose to some extent from a kind of innate unworldliness, which Clough combined with regarding himself, in some respects, as knowing a good deal about the world.

This contradiction is illustrated by his serio-comic poems, something of a speciality with him. Lady Chorley, aptly – though damagingly to Clough – puts them beside a stanza of *Don Juan*. Not only is Byron's infinitely superior poetic facility immediately shown, but also Byron's grasp of the material he was writing about. Byron knew the world and was saying, even if frivolously, what he really thought. Clough, one feels, never really knew the world well enough to satirise it. He is too easily shocked. The pretence that he is finding it all very funny in a cynical way is not a genuine one.

Perhaps that is a little unfair to Clough, who certainly packs a lot of self-criticism into his poems. At the same time he never seems able to escape from his particular bugbears.

He married at the age of thirty-four. The marriage was happy, but there is evidence that it tended to dry up his gift for writing. He died at forty-two, apparently of a kind of stroke, never having found employment worthy of his early promise.

Crabb Robinson, famous for his breakfast parties, used to refer always to Clough as 'That amiable and accomplished man. You know whom I mean. The one who never says anything.'

Inevitably there must be much, in a case like Clough's, that we do not know. Lady Chorley suspects – and one would agree with her – that there may have been a sordid sexual incident in Venice that upset him in his youth. 'The Clergyman's Second Tale' in *Mari Magno* perhaps fits in with the implications of 'Dipsychus' in this respect. Even if true, it is strange that it worried him so much.

There can be no doubt that Clough felt sexual passion strongly and was able to commit his feelings to paper. 'Natura naturans', the poem his widow prevented from appearing in earlier collected editions of his works, describes with an extraordinary mixture of intensity and naivety the experience of sitting next to an unknown pretty girl in a railway carriage.

By temperament a somewhat indolent man. Clough also felt he should drive himself to drudgery. This probably explaines his curious interlude of doing odd jobs for Florence Nightingale, who was a cousin of his wife's. Lady Chorley terminates the biography with a convincing investigation of her subject in terms of Jung.

Arthur Hugh Clough, the Uncommitted Mind: A Study of His Life and Poetry, Katherine Chorley, Clarendon Press/OUP.

1962 *Daily Telegraph*

CHRISTINA ROSSETTI

Christina Rossetti has strong claims to be considered the greatest poet of her sex that this country has ever produced. No one who knows her work even superficially can fail to have been struck by the passionate tone of the occasional poems on the one hand, on the other by sexual symbolism and disturbing power of *Goblin Market.*

However, in spite of her fame, the background of Christina Rossetti's life has never been fully explained. Her brother William, after her death, seemed to go out of his way to emphasise the story of her emotional life, which amounted to two decidedly lukewarm proposals from a couple of men, neither of whom could be regarded, whatever their other good qualities, as calculated to stir specially violent feelings as a lover.

Lona Mosk Packer, in a long, sober, thorough, sympathetic study re-examines the situation. There seems little doubt that Miss Packer gets to the root of the whole matter. Her *Christina Rossetti* is a book of notable interest. It not only presents an intelligible account of the subject's life, but also adds material to the unending oddness of Victorian manners when closely investigated.

> O roses for the flush of youth,
> And laurels for the perfect prime:
> But pluck an ivy branch for me
> Grown old before my time.
>
> O violets for the grave of youth,
> And bay for those dead in their prime:
> Give me the withered leaves I chose,
> Before in the old time.

Christina Rossetti had reached her eighteenth birthday (in 1848) a couple of months before she wrote these lines, and, even allowing for the characteristic pessimism of the young, there is something genuine, quite unexhibitionistic about the verses. She seems to have known from the earliest moments of her poetic self-expression that she was in for a bad time.

The Rossetti family are interesting in a dozen different ways, their origins, what happened to them, what grew out of them. The daughters were brought up to be governesses, but Christina refused to take on this profession. Marriage apparently was the only alternative. That state, too, she never accepted. The fact appears to be that, deeply religious, she was all her life in love with a married man, regarding whom she suffered not only agonies of frustrated passion, but also tortures of guilt.

The man was William Bell Scott. It is all very well to say that Scott was 'unworthy' of Rossetti, but who is to say who is 'worthy' of whom? It was not so much a question of worthiness as blighting circumstances. Not much remains of Scott to explain his attractions, but that is no reason for supposing they did not exist.

He is described in the DNB as 'poet, painter and miscellaneous writer'. He came from Edinburgh, where his father was an engraver, and his family was closely associated with the arts, though he himself was not a very distinguished performer at any of them.

It is here that one feels the strangeness of the way of Victorians went on. Scott had a wife, but seems to have known the Rossettis for two and a half years before mentioning her: this can hardly be explained by the fact that owing to some indisposition of Mrs Scott the marriage was one only in name.

After having some sort of a flirtation with Christina Rossetti, Scott fell in with a Miss Boyd, who owned a small castle in Scotland. She lived with him for the rest of his life, presumably as his mistress, his wife's existence making the life *à trois* outwardly respectable.

Some of the time he spent in the Ayrshire castle, where Christina went to stay, some of the time in London. Scott appears, anyway in his early days, to have been something of a lady-killer. In later life he grew disgruntled and sour, rounding on his old friends.

One of the other two men in Christina Rossetti's life was James Collinson, a member of the original group of seven Pre-Raphaelite painters – not a very good one. Collinson was continually becoming converted to Roman Catholicism, then changing his mind. Christina, a convinced Anglican, took the opportunity of breaking off her engagement after one of Collinson's conversions, and he disappears from the scene.

Later she received a proposal from Charles Cayley, a philologist. William Rossetti said of Cayley:

> His manner was absent-minded in the extreme. If anything was said to him, he would often pause so long before replying that one was inclined to 'give it up,' but at last the answer came in a tone between hurry and confusion, with an articulation far from easy to follow. In truth one viewed his advent with some apprehension, only too conscious that some degree of embarrassment was sure to ensue.

Christina Rossetti seems to have been attached to Cayley throughout her life, but her brother William's efforts to suggest that Collinson or Cayley gave rise to the poems certainly cannot be accepted. It was a case of deliberately throwing dust in the eyes of those who might prove too inquisitive.

In later life Christina Rossetti grew into a somewhat formidable figure, anyway for the younger generation. She was consciously dowdy in her dress, almost totally without a lighter side. This innate seriousness was one aspect of the Rossetti character, and it was said that her sister Maria was unwilling to venture into the Mummy Room in the British Museum in case it happened to turn out to be the Day of Judgement and she found herself in a milling concourse of the dead come back to life.

Christina's powers as a poet remained to the end, showing no weakening as she grew older. Swinburne was a great admirer of her work, always sending her copies of his own books, which she did not reciprocate. Indeed, she pasted strips of white paper over the lines in them which seemed atheistic, such as the chorus in 'Atalanta in Calydon'.

Christina Rossetti died in 1892 in Torrington Square, Bloomsbury, where she lived in a comparatively large house, many of the disused rooms of which were kept shut and locked. Towards the end it was a somewhat gloomy existence, and she seems to have suffered at times from bouts of hysteria.

> I shall not see the shadows
> I shall not feel the rain;
> I shall not hear the nightingale
> Sing on as if in pain;
> And dreaming through the twilight
> That doth not rise nor set
> Haply I may remember,
> And haply may forget.

Christina Rossetti, 1964
Lona Mosk Packer, *Daily Telegraph*
CUP for California.

W. S. GILBERT

The operas of Gilbert & Sullivan are something about which people argue. To what extent does Clean Fun of one generation continue to amuse another? Are the tunes really as 'neat' as they are cracked up to be?

Whatever you think, it is undeniable that the epithet 'Gilbertian' remains valid, anyway where official procedure is concerned. The editor of this volume, James Ellis, states the case reasonably enough in saying that Gilbert's fame rests on the comic operas 'slenderly but securely'.

The *Bab Ballads* are another branch of Gilbert's writing, about which a word of explanation is required. Most of them were written (and illustrated) by him in the 1860s for a periodical called *Fun*, a rival of *Punch*. They were first collected in 1869. The nature of the contents of later editions was complicated by Gilbert raiding his earlier verse to provide material for the operas, and later on including 'Songs of a Savoyard', lyrics written specifically for opera librettos.

W. S. Gilbert (1836–1911) is an interesting figure. Mr Ellis in his introduction deals with biographical facts only relevant to Gilbert's poetry and journalism. No doubt the further field was too wide to be easily enclosed, but it might have been worth mentioning that as a child of two years old Gilbert had been kidnapped by brigands in Naples, then ransomed for £25. The lines in 'Gentle Alice Brown' ('whose father was the terror of a small Italian town') perhaps have bearing on this incident:

> I have helped mamma to steal a little kiddy from its dad,
> I've assisted dear papa in cutting up the little lad.

'Bab' was Gilbert's nickname as a child. It was a mere chance that he did not become a regular officer in the Gunners at the time of the Crimean War. He had employment in the civil service and as a barrister, contracts reflected in his work.

Speaking as a reader brought up on the *Bab Ballads*, I should say they do not wholly retain their former hold, except in a few cases. For example, both metre and subject matter of 'Lost Mr Blake' (who 'did not consider his soul imperilled because somebody over whom he had no influence whatever, chose to dress himself up like an ecclesiastical Guy Fawkes', and married a pious widow whom he made attend church twenty-two or twenty-three times a week) are still amusing.

Swinburne, a great fan of the *Bab Ballads* particularly liked 'Etiquette', which describes how two Englishmen, cast up on a desert island, keep rigorously to their own ends of it, as they have not been introduced. Somers is at the end where turtles flourish, which he will not eat; Gray being equally allergic to oysters, which teem on his shore – though 'turtle and his mother were the only things he loved'. This hint of an Oedipus complex perhaps gives the key.

Finding out (through Somers talking aloud to himself) that they have a Carthusian acquaintance in common in Robinson, they speak; then share the whole island together. Robinson turns up on a passing convict ship. By that time the pair prefer to remain on their island, but revert to their earlier ends of it at finding the other has such a disreputable friend.

Swinburne's influence is even perhaps faintly discernible in 'Little Oliver':

> The brilliant candle dazed the moth well;
> One day she sang to her Papa
> The air that Marie sings with Bothwell
> In Niedermayer's opera.

Gilbert's own verse, in turn, certainly left a strong mark on others, notably Kipling. Indeed it is in comparison with 'Departmental Ditties' that a certain lack of bite can be noticed in Gilbert. In the same way, his nonsense verses, not without talent, lack the surrealist abandon of Lear and Carroll:

> Under the beechful eye,
> When causeless brandlings bring,
> Let the froddering crooner cry,
> And the braddled sapster sing.
> For never and never again
> Will the tottering bauble bray,
> For bratticed wrackers are singing aloud,
> And the throngers croon in May!

Mr Ellis has brought the number of Bab poems up to 137, no earlier edition containing more than eighty-six. His notes – which are designed for Americans – are excellent but surely when the waiter threatened:

> *Je lui dirai de quoi on compose*
> *Vol au vent à la Financière!*

that was not because a Frenchman was going to give away a valuable secret recipe to an Englishmen, but rather that, hearing the true ingredients, Lorenzo de Lardy would never eat at the restaurant again?

The original 'insect-like' drawings are given, as opposed to the revised ones Gilbert made in the edition of 1898, which Mr Ellis calls 'sweet, amiable, inoffensive and wholly inappropriate'. While agreeing that the earlier drawings – which suggest the influence of Dicky Doyle and Linley Sambourne – are best for this definitive edition, the more Leech–Tenniel style of 1898 contain some quite good tough pictures, e.g. the King of Canoodledum with his rum bottle, or villainous Robinson, 'old chummy of the Charterhouse', rowing in his broad-arrowed convict clothes.

The Gilbert drawings embossed on the binding of *Fifty Bab Ballads* (1884) looked particularly effective, and would have been much nicer than the not very attractive cover of the present edition – but perhaps that would have been too expensive. Like everything quintessentially of its epoch, something compelling remains about the *Bab Ballads*, and one is grateful for them still, even if in a modified form.

The Bab Ballads,
W. S. Gilbert, edited by James Ellis,
OUP for Harvard.

1971
Daily Telegraph

ALGERNON SWINBURNE

I

In spite of vigorous critical efforts to curtail his reputation, Swinburne remains a towering figure. The arguments against him, so to speak, are well put in John Dixon Hunt's excellent general survey, *The Pre-Raphaelite Imagination 1848–1900*. Mr Hunt finds Swinburne a lesser poet, for example, than Rossetti. Yet, surely, of the two it is Swinburne's powers that strike one as the more truly unique, and it is certainly impossible to get away from him as an influence.

Jean Overton Fuller's extraordinarily interesting biography, *Swinburne*, although it deals, in the most usual sense, with the poet's life rather than with his work, has great bearing on this verse. Her book, largely through her own individual discoveries, and also because she has collated research that has been going on elsewhere for some years, presents the most intelligible version of the Swinburne story that has yet appeared.

Unlike Harold Nicolson and a lot of Swinburne's other commentators, Miss Fuller does not fight shy of the flagellation motif. In fact she tackles it in a big way. A legacy of Victorian primness, even after this aspect of Swinburne began to be ventilated, has still perhaps obscured the point that sexual psychologists regard the tendency as so common as to be scarcely categorised as abnormal. But in Swinburne's particular case it is of importance in becoming out of hand, not so much physically in that he occasionally went to brothels, but intellectually in that he allowed the obsession to distort his mind and disfigure some of his work.

The Swinburne myth – chiefly disseminated by that source of so much inexact information, Edmund Gosse – is roughly as follows: Swinburne, aged about twenty-five, fell in love with Jane Faulkner, niece and adopted daughter of a certain Dr Simon, whom Swinburne had known through Burne-Jones. He proposed to her, was greeted with laughter, went home and wrote 'The Triumph of Time' and never looked at a woman with love again.

Some years later, trying to keep his friend on the rails, Rossetti offered the circus-rider Ada Menken £10 to seduce Swinburne. This was a failure, but as a consequence of the rather absurd encounter, the poet wrote 'Dolores', 'Faustine' and all the poems of that tone to Ada Menken.

About fifteen years ago an American scholar, John S. Mayfield pointed out that Jane Faulkner would have been only ten years old when this incident is alleged to have taken place. In other words it was quite untrue, though Swinburne had indeed composed some stanzas 'To Boo', which was the little girl's nickname.

Miss Fuller, in a series of masterly references to known facts from letters and documents, together with inferences drawn from Swinburne's poems and strange, but, in certain respects, very talented novels, demonstrates that the heroine of 'The Triumph of Time' – and all the Dolores-type verse – was Swinburne's first cousin, Mary Gordon, who later married Colonel Disney Leith.

This attribution is not made for the first time, but owing to Mary Leith's strenuous efforts to scotch any such suggestion, and without the supporting evidence that is here collected, the lead has always seemed too slight to be followed up; especially in the light of other apparently more obvious solutions. Incidentally, 'Dolores' was written before Swinburne met Ada Menken.

Swinburne's mother, Lady Jane Swinburne, and Mary Leith's mother, Lady Mary Gordon (who inadvertently appear once or twice as 'Lady Swinburne' and 'Lady Gordon', to be corrected in subsequent editions) were sisters, Lady Mary having herself married a first cousin.

In this enormously inward-looking family circle, existing chiefly in the Isle of Wight, Swinburne developed a passion for his cousin, which had undoubtedly included some degree of 'necking' and the sharing of sadistic fantasies. The climax is not so likely to have been a proposal of marriage as some sort of attempt at a sexual act; the severance was Mary Gordon marrying a man twenty-one years older than herself.

Not the least fascinating aspect of the story is that Mary Leith wrote passable poetry herself, and also a long string of novels, a fact that suggests the literary talent came in through the Ashburnham, rather than Swinburne, family.

These poems and novels can sometimes be related to exactly the same themes as Swinburne's, first biographically speaking, secondly in their preoccupation with near-sadistic subject matter. Miss Fuller's detective work reached an apex when she discovered three letters from Mary Leith, written when both she and Swinburne were in their fifties, which unequivocally refer – though no doubt without modern psychological sophistication – to flagellation. Some sort of a relationship had been kept up, which sets the overheated poems, supposedly imaginary and artificial, in a different light.

Swinburne was a man of quite exceptional intelligence – he was more intelligent than Rossetti, even if Rossetti may have known more about everyday life. He was well aware of the anguishes of his own emotional condition. That is, in fact, what the poems are largely about – though, of course, to read them in terms of a conventional love affair usually makes nonsense of them.

Miss Fuller brings out the recklessly uncontrolled nature of Swinburne's emotions, for example, his obsessive affection for Watts-Dunton's child nephew. At the same time, I very much doubt that there were – as she suspects – homosexual relations with Simeon Solomon, though one must agree with her that Swinburne behaved badly, even abominably, to that unfortunate painter.

To return to a moment to Mr Hunt's *The Pre-Raphaelite Imagination*, he deals well with such questions as William Morris often producing just the kind of work he was supposedly attacking. He also recognises in Beardsley, what is so often missed, the great satirist – even comic draughtsman. Is there not something of this satirical aspect of Beardsley that is often disregarded in Swinburne, too?

Swinburne: A Critical Biography, Jean Overton Fuller, Chatto.
The Pre-Raphaelite Imagination 1848–1900, John Dixon Hunt, Routledge.

1969
Daily Telegraph

II

Everyone who met Swinburne (1837–1909), whether they liked him or not, thought him, mentally and physically, the most extraordinary personality they had ever come across. He made a monumental impact on the poetry of his own epoch, but later there was naturally a big swing against his verse.

It is interesting to note that this reaction came largely from the same sort of public as had been formerly so uncritically enthusiastic. Individual poets of a later date remained aware of Swinburne's colossal gifts – for example, Ezra Pound, whose championship of a totally different school of poetry might reasonably have made him antagonistic.

A good deal of biographical work has been done on Swinburne during recent years, but Philip Henderson performs a service in bringing together uncollated material in a readable form. Much of his book disposes of legends.

Mr Henderson takes his stand on 'The Triumph of Time' being a very great poem. Together with 'A Leave-Taking' and 'At the Month's End', this poem forms part of a group that records a turning point in Swinburne's life: the marriage of his cousin, Mary Gordon, to a man twenty years older than herself, after a close relationship – certainly mentally erotic, if not physically – with the poet.

Edmund Gosse's *Swinburne* is often to some extent deliberately misleading. Mr Henderson is becomingly polite about Harold Nicolson as a predecessor in Swinburnian biography, but Nicolson is condescending and often inept. Both Gosse and Nicolson attribute these particular three poems of a desolate and appalling despair to Swinburne's refusal in marriage by Jane Faulkner (adopted daughter of a Dr Simon).

Mr Henderson justly suggests that 'The Triumph of Time' and kindred poems celebrate not merely losing Mary Gordon as a potential (though utterly improbable) wife, but the acceptance by Swinburne that he was one who suffered all the agonies of love, but, morally and physically, was for ever excluded from love's fulfilment. He was perfectly aware of his own state.

The other myth of which Mr Henderson disposes is Watts-Dunton unexpectedly driving up to Swinburne's rooms in Guildford Street, and removing the drunken and dying poet by force to Putney. It is perfectly true that Swinburne would undoubtedly have died if left to his own devices, but his family had made all financial arrangements for the removal to take place.

It even appears that Swinburne and Watts-Dunton had enjoyed a seaside holiday together not long before, at a time when Swinburne's transit to Putney is likely to have been already in view. Swinburne always made a special point of the fact that he was not a boarder in Watts-Dunton's house, but was sharing Number 2 The Pines with his friend.

Like many men of genius, Swinburne is not easy to defend in several aspects. His own chosen alternatives, as professions for himself – cavalry officer or lighthouse keeper – well express his inconsistencies. His recent biographers, including to some extent Mr Henderson, tend to make rather heavy weather of the poet's patronage of the St John's Wood brothel, but there can be no doubt that, intellectually speaking, he did allow his obsession with flagellation to get harmfully out of hand. After years of lauding Sade, and every form of outspokenness, Swinburne will suddenly show himself anti-Zola for being 'filthy', he will encourage Simeon Solomon to do erotic drawings for him, then, when Solomon is arrested for soliciting, abuse him as disreputable. Swinburne's nature is totally divided.

One cannot help being struck by how extremely well Swinburne's parents behaved. His father, the admiral, gave his son a very reasonable allowance, paid for the publication of volumes of poems he did not himself like, and travelled sometimes to Scotland, when he was no longer young, to rescue Swinburne after his frequent collapses.

Swinburne was removed from Eton at sixteen, but it is not perhaps generally appreciated how remarkably high he was in the school for a boy of that age. At Oxford his industry was rather up and down, but the reason for not taking his finals was a bad fall from a horse when jumping a gate. Mr Henderson quotes a remarkable comment of Jowett, then Master of Balliol, in connection with the poet:

> I incline to believe that the greatest power older persons have over the young is sympathy with them. If we don't allow enough for the strange varieties of character, and often for their extreme, almost unintelligible unlikeness to ourselves, we lose influence over them, and they become alienated from fancying they are not understood.

What could be more up to date than that? Another contemporary touch is added by the delight Swinburne took (after retirement to Putney) in reading in the paper that a man named 'Robert Browning was taken up for running stark naked down Park Lane, through the Marble Arch, at noon' – an interesting early example of streaking, especially by so distinguished a poet.

Mr Henderson oddly speaks of the Light Brigade at Balaclava as a 'company of lancers', 'Lady Pauline Trevelyan' should read 'Lady Trevelyan' in future editions. Napoleon III's deathbed occurs on one page as at Chichester, instead of Chislehurst, and the classic scholar Lemprière gets misprinted more than once as 'Lamprière'.

Swinburne: The Portrait of a Poet, 1974
Philip Henderson, Routledge. *Daily Telegraph*

III

It takes all sorts to make a world – certainly a literary world. All the same, one sometimes gets surprises. For example, on the wrapper of these volumes of *The Swinburne Letters* a *Times Literary Supplement* reviewer is quoted as saying: '. . . if Swinburne is not a great poet . . . he is etc., etc.'

One is divided between wondering what desiccated, rightly anonymous henchman of Eng. Lit. wrote such – if one may say so – rubbish; and at the same time feeling surprise at the publisher choosing to quote such an opinion.

That many people should find Swinburne's poetry unsympathetic today is reasonable enough. Tastes in all art rightly change. To suggest that Swinburne is not a great poet, on other hand, seems to me merely silly; if for no other reason than because his influence can be seen on almost every subsequent poet writing in English, from Rudyard Kipling to E. E. Cummings and Dylan Thomas.

So much for people who think Swinburne not a great poet. Professor Bonamy Dobrée's new paperback selection gives them a chance of revising their opinion at a very reasonable price. I regret that the ballad of the Queens was not included in the Penguin *Swinburne,* not because it is in the top class but because it is so rarely printed.

Let us turn to the Letters. The first and second volumes opened when Swinburne was seventeen. They covered the stormy period of his early life in London. In them can be traced his development as poet and scholar, his less conventional friendships and perennial flagellation fantasies.

The two volumes under review continue these themes during the period 1875–1882 (age forty-two to forty-nine), thereby bridging the moment (1879) when the poet, reduced to a poor state of health by over-indulgence, was removed by Watts-Dunton in a cab from 25 Guildford Street, to be ultimately deposited under Watts-Dunton's own suzerainty at 2 The Pines.

It was once the fashion to excoriate Watts-Dunton for taking this step, some critics holding the view that it would have been more romantic to allow Swinburne to die of drink in Bloomsbury rather than live to a ripe old age in a humdrum manner in Putney.

More recent biographers have pointed out that Swinburne appears, in truth, to have tempered his more sober maturity with an occasional modicum of congenial dissipation, while the fact of writing his best verse when he was young applies to all lyric poets, irrespective of living in the suburbs with a friend generally regarded as a bore. (In any case, Watts-Dunton was perhaps not so prim as usually painted, since Swinburne refers here to his friend's 'too Paphian temperament'.)

The letters certainly bear out the view that the move left Swinburne in most ways unaltered. There seems to be remarkably little change of tone, except for more complaints about deafness, less about general ill-health.

Let it be admitted straight out that many of the letters are not very exciting. On the other hand, the fact that every available letter has been brought into the net does give an over-all picture of the poet's life; while certain specific letters are of the greatest interest and the collection in general very enjoyable.

Some of their attraction is the way in which they record social history. Swinburne asks his rather sinister friend, George Powell of Nant Eos (of whom a biography should certainly be written): 'By the by, how do you address a man of that sort, the head of a large business, who has no tail in the shape of a Co?, as Esq. or as Mr?'

A short time later, he writes: 'What a glorious thing is this triumph of Captain Webb, and O what a lyric Pindar would have written on him!' This was the famous Channel swimmer, later lyrically celebrated, if not by Pindar, at least by Betjeman.

The young Edmund Gosse was an acquaintance of this period. One of Swinburne's letters to him on the subject of Sappho makes one recall with amusement the coyness of Gide in fearing to shock Gosse. There is something oddly modern, too, when the poet writes about the name of a periodical to which he was to contribute: 'Chatto's Magazine or even the Piccadilly M. would be better, "Belgravia" *stinks.*'

Swinburne's views on literature and painting were go-ahead, including enthusiasms for Stendhal and Manet. They are well illustrated by his letter to John Nichol about the latter's *Tables of European Literature and History*. There is an amusing thumbnail sketch of Wilde.

> The only time I ever saw Mr Oscar Wilde, he writes to an American friend in 1882, was in a crush at our acquaintance Lord Houghton's. I thought he seemed a harmless young nobody, and had no notion he was the sort of man to play the mountebank as he seems to have been doing.
>
> A letter which he wrote to me later about Walt Whitman was quite a modest, gentlemanlike, reasonable affair, without any flourish or affectation of any kind in matter or expression. It is really very odd. I should think you in America must be as tired of his name as we in London of Mr Barnum's and his Jumbo's.

Swinburne particularly detested Zola and his works. He records that Wordsworth was the first person to tell him the story – now, I believe, frowned upon – about Wolfe reading Gray's *Elegy* on the way to capture Quebec.

Politically the poet was unpredictable. His Radical sympathies did not prevent detestation of the Boers – which would now put him on an easy wicket, but in those days made him as hard to assimilate on the Left as did his lack of feeling for Bulgarian atrocities.

> Have you – but of course you have – seen our grand old Kossuth's glorious essay? It supports me, under the charge from the lips of Radical friends of having *ratted* to the Tory party and his lordship of Beaconsfield, who at least must be allowed this merit – 1) that he is not Gladstone, and 2) that he keeps Gladstone out.

He enjoyed sending grotesque newspaper cuttings to his friends, e.g. one describing how 'Matthew Arnold, a printer' was fined for playing tip-cat in the street, commenting:

> The enclosed is the most scandalous example of genius degraded by eccentricity that I have seen since Robert Browning was taken up for running stark naked down Hyde Park, through the Marble Arch, at noon – his 'second offence', according to the *Times* reporter of some years ago.

There can be no doubt that the unidentified 'Mr Bowles' referred to in the letter to Watts-Dunton of April 16, 1876, is Thomas Gibson Bowles, MP, founder of *Vanity Fair*, grandfather of Miss Nancy Mitford, herself a fairly close relation of Swinburne's.

The Swinburne Letters,
Vol. 3, 1875–1877; Vol. 4, 1877–1882,
edited by Cecil Y. Lang,
OUP for Yale.

1961
Daily Telegraph

Swinburne: Poems,
Selected and Introduced by Bonamy Dobrée,
Penguin Poets.

IV

These two volumes conclude *The Swinburne Letters*. Having only recently emerged from one thousand letters by Oscar Wilde, one inevitably compares the two collections. It would be hard to imagine a greater contrast.

Swinburne was born in 1837, only seventeen years before Wilde, but the gap might be centuries. Wilde belongs to the modern age. If anything, he lived before his time. The TV studio awaits his return to earth.

Swinburne, on the other hand, is a Victorian of Victorians, never more so than in his own reaction from the period. These last instalments of his letters complete the picture, oddly absorbing in spite of its muted tones.

Not the least interesting part of these volumes is a long note by Edmund Gosse on Swinburne deposited in the British Museum and never before printed.

From Gosse's note it appears that Swinburne's drunkenness was particularly difficult to deal with on the part of his friends, as he himself was totally unaware of it. The effects the following day he always attributed to indigestion and general ill health. Indeed, one of the 'additional' letters in Volume 6 speaks of 'an attack of indigestion which . . . makes my hand still shake like a drunkard's'.

A comparatively small amount of drink overcame Swinburne, whereupon there was an almost instantaneous change from lively conversation to utter intoxication.

In this and certain other respects – the violently anti-Christian outbursts, the dancing, the scenes like Swinburne kicking top-hats about in the cloakroom of the Arts Club – one is reminded of the composer, Peter Warlock (Philip Heseltine), also a passionate student of the Elizabethan period. No doubt they belonged to a somewhat similar psychiatric type.

Gosse deals also, in the plainest terms, with Swinburne's practical solution of his flagellation fantasies, although feeling it necessary to add a few characteristically prim phrases about his commonplace of sexual deviation, which Gosse himself must often have heard about elsewhere in his day.

There are some amusing letters from the literary forger, Thomas Wise, trying to trap Swinburne into making admissions that would assist Wise's traffic in bogus editions. In this respect, Swinburne seems to have been on the whole unhelpful.

It is impossible not to be struck by the entirely different facets of character that Swinburne offers. Gosse says – and the letters bear this out – that Swinburne was never quite the same after the *crise* that led to his Putney retirement. 'Something luminous and vivid,' in Gosse's words, 'was quenched in his nature and that never reappeared after 1879.'

Even so, Swinburne alters entirely in relation to his different correspondents. This is far more than a matter of somewhat adapting his style to the person he addresses. For example, when he writes to his mother, who survived until the poet was nearly sixty, he throws himself into her approach to life. One would not expect him to impose his own atheistic views on her, certainly, but he seems to go much further than might be expected in apparently almost discarding these views.

There can be no doubt that Lady Jane Swinburne was a dominating influence on her son, a very worrying son to have. Ten years after the withdrawal to Putney, we find her writing an anxious inquiry to Watts-Dunton because Swinburne had left unanswered one of her letters, in which there were arrangements for paying her a visit. The possibility that Algernon might go off the rails again must always have been present.

Most of the letters are about fairly trivial matters, with a permanent undercurrent of Swinburne's interest in bringing little-known Elizabethan poets and dramatists, and others too, to the foreground. His efforts in this direction must have left a mark on contemporary appreciation of literature that is not always appreciated.

Together with these scholarly interests, an unwillingness to grow up led Swinburne always to read boys' books and *The Boy's Own Paper*, to the end of his days.

His political enthusiasms were of a kind to make him completely unassimilable to any party. When some Fenians were executed for shooting dead a policeman while attempting to rescue a political prisoner, Swinburne championed them; but he was equally violent in execrating the murders, cattle-maiming and other atrocities of Irish terrorists. Gladstone was his great aversion.

Cecil Y. Lang is painstaking, but at times a little self-satisfied in his notes. The Yale University Press cannot be congratulated on their style of production of the letters of a poet who appreciated good typography.

The Swinburne Letters,
Vol. 5, 1883–1890; Vol. 6, 1890–1909,
edited by Cecil Y. Lang,
OUP for Yale.

1962
Daily Telegraph

ADAM LINDSAY GORDON

Poets, generally speaking, are not pre-eminent in the field of sport and athletics. Byron could keep his end up; there are exceptions like Julian Grenfell, but they are on the whole rare. Adam Lindsay Gordon (1833–1870) was universally regarded as superb horseman. He was indeed a better rider than poet.

Gordon, rather exotically was born in the Azores. That was mere chance. His father was an army captain invalided from the service, who had married a Gordon cousin. Captain Gordon, an excellent linguist, taught Hindustani at Cheltenham College, the school his son attended for a time, but from which he appears to have been sacked. He was also sacked from the Royal Military Academy, Woolwich.

Adam Lindsay Gordon liked drink and girls, but his greatest troubles from earliest days were – and remained – those connected with horses. His family was remarkably forbearing with him, for the period. Even so there was evidently no hope of fixing their son up satisfactorily in England, and he seems to have felt no great objection to trying his luck in Australia.

Gordon went to Australia with introductions, the intention being that he should become an officer in the Australian Mounted Police. It is not clear whether he did not bother to carry through this plan, or whether a period in the ranks was in any case required, but he joined the constabulary as a trooper.

From his earliest days Gordon seems to have had an interest in poetry, and written it himself. He left the mounted police after two years for the profession of horse-coping, riding a great deal in steeplechases, though never for money and never betting. He composed much of his poetry while on horseback.

He married (happily) in Australia; inherited a small but useful legacy from his father; became briefly a member of parliament; dissipated his fortune, such as it was, embarking on a foolish lawsuit and ran into serious money difficulties. Then he committed suicide. By that time he had a certain name as a poet, though his verse was published at his own expense and sold miserably.

All this is described by Geoffrey Hutton in a not very polished style, but assembling the facts. In the last resort, Mr Hutton gives quite a good idea of Gordon's character – an odd mixture of inward-looking melancholy and need for constant action, preferably with horses, a temperament perhaps not uncommon in the horsey world. As a very young man he had hunted with the ill-fated L. E. Nolan, the cavalry lieutenant who, just before being killed, transmitted by word of mouth the order for the Charge of the Light Brigade.

Gordon was to become canonised as Australia's national poet. There has been some demur at this because he was only in Australia for seventeen years, most of the time behaving as if he fully intended to return in due course to England. He also wrote of Australia the disparaging lines:

> . . . where bright blossoms are scentless,
> And songless bright birds;
> Where, with fire and fierce drought on her tresses,
> Insatiable summer oppresses
> Sere woodlands and sad wilderness
> And faint flocks and herds.

As indicated by the above, Swinburne was a most unfortunate influence on Gordon. Even worse was Gordon's long narrative poem *Ashtaroth*, deriving from Byron, Goethe and Tennyson a version of the Faust legend. It contained the unhappy lines:

> Indeed, I have not the least idea:
> The man is certainly mad.
> He married my sister, Dorothea,
> And treated her cruelly bad.

Nevertheless Gordon's bust in Westminster Abbey, and his statue in Melbourne, are not altogether unjustified in their Australian connotation. Gordon went to Australia as a happy-go-lucky young man in the best tradition. When he arrived there, even if he became a policeman rather than a bushranger, his habitual behaviour was (even in Parliament) sufficiently slapdash to satisfy a national dread of anything that might be thought in the least pompous. He passes as an authentic Australian.

Adam Lindsay Gordon is represented by several poems in *The Oxford Book of Victorian Verse*, including what is probably his best work – from which perhaps Kipling derived something – 'The Sick Stockrider':

> Hold hard, Ned! Lift me down once more, and lay
> me in the shade.
> Old man, you've had your work cut out to guide
> Both horses, and to hold me in the saddle when I
> sway'd,
> All through the hot, slow, sleepy, silent ride . . .

Adam Lindsay Gordon: the Man and the Myth, 1978
Geoffrey Hutton, Faber. *Daily Telegraph*

VICTORIAN VERSE

It is rather like an election. 'How's it gone?' 'Well, Abou Ben Ahdem has lost his seat, and Heraclitus, but it's the women who've come off worse – "Rose Aylmer" is out, and "Dark Rosaleen", "The Lady of Shalott", "Mariana of the Moated Grange", even "Cynara".' 'Good Heavens, "The Scholar-Gypsy" is re-elected, I hope?' 'He's all right, though his majority's down a bit, the same with "The Blessed Damozel".' 'What about new members?' 'Quite a few. Danny Deever, for instance, and Omar Khayyám's quintupled his vote. More unexpected, *The Snark* is in, and "The Old Man on Some Rocks".'

Quiller-Couch imposed his taste in poetry (at which, on the whole, one would not grumble) for three generations in this country, which included two world wars, a great time for poetry reading. With characteristic luck he brought out *The Oxford Book of Victorian Verse*, a comparative side-show to the main volumes, in 1913, just in time for hostilities.

The epithet 'Victorian' is never easy to define, and, as Christopher Ricks points out in his own introduction to his revised collection, Quiller-Couch's started off ambiguously. He said: 'Though Wordsworth happened to be the first Laureate of Queen Victoria's reign, no one will argue that he belongs to it.' Professor Ricks remarks dryly that, in fact, Southey was Laureate for the first six years of Queen Victoria's reign, and Wordsworth did not 'happen' to be Laureate, he was appointed by the Queen. In addition to that, says Professor Ricks, 'not only his [Wordsworth's] earlier work but his continuing art was deeply consonant with so much that was esteemed in the Victorian England which could remember Regency England'. He adds of Wordsworth's poems: 'A stiff price is paid for denying that they are [Victorian], the price of a stultifying self-fulfilling notion, by which from a narrow range of Victorian poems a restrictive practice is first extracted and then erected.' When Professor Ricks goes on to speak of 'unseemly vying' among party politicians about 'Victorian values', I think what was said in the initial instance was 'Victorian virtues', something rather different which has become twisted.

The New Oxford Book of Victorian Verse has been purged of a good deal of poorish stuff, but not in a manner to exclude minor poets. On the contrary, there are plenty of them here, which is right, because a volume like this should give, so far as possible, an unprejudiced picture of the epoch. Professor Ricks is a great believer, if something is long, in printing the whole of it, for instance *The Rubáiyát*, *Goblin Market*, Clough's *Amours de Voyage*, *The Hunting of the Snark*. The only excerpts are where the poet himself allowed some autonomy, such as *In Memoriam*, Meredith's *Modern Love*, but not Arnold's 'Sohrab and Rustum', which never becomes disconnected from its main theme.

It is difficult to discuss a book of this sort without falling back on one's own tastes. *Amours de Voyage*, which particularly needs its entirety to make sense, is immensely polished, but I find myself never able wholly to forget that Clough was Dr Arnold's favourite pupil. Is it a shade smug? Perhaps I am wrong. Also, though devoted, on the whole, to Lewis Carroll, I have always felt that the *The Snark* was too long, though few seem to agree.

William Barnes has been upped from half a dozen in Quiller-Couch to twenty-three here. Again I rebel. I can stand only a limited amount of: 'Study in sheade o'bank or wallen,/In the warmth, if not in light;/Words alwone vrom her a-vallèn,/Would be jay vor all night.' I recognise that as no doubt a weakness, but stick to my guns in finding Mrs Browning's *Aurora Leigh* heavy going.

It was perfectly right to include the pictures with the Lear limericks, and a very good idea to give Aubrey Beardsley's two poems, something which would have delighted the artist himself, who liked to inscribe his profession as *homme de lettres*. The poems by Elizabeth Siddal (Mrs D. G. Rossetti) are fascinating too. Wilde is allowed two short ones together with *The Ballad of Reading Gaol*, all rightly included. How angry Lord Alfred Douglas would be at his own expulsion.

Gerard Manley Hopkins, unknown, of course, when the earlier volume appeared, is now well represented. I was not sure that I wanted sixteen by Robert Louis Stevenson, but his lines on reviewing Browning are funny. While on that sort of subject, Macaulay's 'Jacobite's Epitaph' survives here from the Quiller-Couch collection. Couldn't Professor Ricks have done better than that? What about 'Naseby', for instance (especially as the Professor seems a bit of a Roundhead), or *The Lays of Ancient Rome*, though with the latter I see there would have been difficulties in putting in the whole thing, as there are no specific authorial sub-sections.

I was sorry to see George Darley out, especially as his song, 'Sweet in her green dell the flower of beauty slumbers' seems to have influenced Meredith's 'Love in a Valley'. And what about Newbolt? Obvious objections, undoubtedly, but it is hard to deny that he was part of the Victorian scene. After all Roy Fuller said a kind word for: 'There's a far bell ringing/At the setting of the sun . . .'

Anyway, there's lots here to argue about and enjoy.

The New Oxford Book of Victorian Verse, edited by Christopher Ricks, OUP. — 1987 *Daily Telegraph*

NINETEENTH-CENTURY MINOR POETS

Anthologies are, it must be admitted, rather a vice, and, as with most vices, those who indulge in them find excuses for themselves. They would not (so they maintain) otherwise read the poems . . . only the best have been picked . . . here are opportunities for comparisons with similar work.

The point about anthologies – and W. H. Auden's *Nineteenth-Century Minor Poets* is a perfect example of this – is that everything depends on the person who does the selection. In a period as rich as the nineteenth century almost anything could be proved by judicious picking.

It should be said straight away that Mr Auden's volume is extremely enjoyable. The poems are often those that have not before found their way into collections. His own very distinctive personality gives just the right feeling that the book has been compiled as one person's individual taste.

The poets here represented were all British subjects born between 1770 and 1870; the poems all printed between 1800 and 1900. This imposes limitations that work out unfairly, Mr Auden noting that Crabbe was born too early to be included, although his best work appeared after 1800, while Housman is in, but not with his best work, because that was published in 1922.

Mr Auden's Introduction has some interesting things to say about 'minor poets' as such. The nineteenth-century major ones he defines 'justly or unjustly' as Blake, Wordsworth, Coleridge, Byron, Shelley, Keats, Tennyson, Browning, Arnold, Swinburne, Hopkins, Yeats, Kipling. These are excluded.

He makes the good point that 'one cannot say that a major poet writes better poems than a minor'. He emphasises the balance of taste and judgement in making an anthology, saying: 'It is just as dishonest for an anthologist to exclude a poem simply because his predecessors have used it as it is to include one for the same reason.'

The obvious comparison for Mr Auden's bunch of blooms is with Quiller-Couch's *Oxford Book of Victorian Verse*, though Mr Auden has admitted a lot of comic or light verse that was not in former times thought 'serious' enough to be poetry.

In the selection of the light verse, one has particularly the sense of an individual taste at work, and, with it, the feeling that, given the same poet, one would sometimes have chosen another poem. This adds stimulation to an anthology and makes you think.

For example, I can see that someone who liked Hood's 'Miss Kilmansegg and her Precious Leg' would also like 'The Lady of St Cuthbert' in 'The Ingoldsby Legends,' both of which have the same odd kind of discomfort about them that makes me prefer other verses by those particular poets. Mr Auden, as a personal taste he does not impose on others, regards Hood as a major poet.

In rather the same way, one feels that an opportunity was lost with W. S. Gilbert – good as the Major-General's song and Bunthorne's song are – by not reproducing the far less known 'Lost Mr Blake', with its amusing theme and metre. Perhaps it was thought too long, or too purely narrative in style.

It is, of course, impossible to do more than glance at some of the poets brought together here, but again one is struck by Praed's really extraordinary facility, and the fact that, had his field been even a shade wider, he would have been very good indeed.

Clare, also, brings the reader up with a start. 'Badger' is hair-raising in its horror, 'The Lout' and 'Gipsies' almost equally good, though the rural cruelty is not quite so painful. In any case, country life is wonderfully deeply felt.

The sensuousness of Heber is striking when read:

> Say, shall we yield Him, in costly devotion,
> Odours of Edom and offerings divine?
> Gems of the mountain and pearls of the Ocean,
> Myrrh from the forest or gold from the mine?

The same feeling of sensuousness, this time longed for, rather than achieved, is echoed in a different manner by Darley:

> In his green den the murmuring seal
> Close by his sleek companion lies;
> While singly we to bedward steal,
> And close in fruitless sleep our eyes

Also to be found here is the William Morris poem which contains those unusual lines:

> O sisters, cross the bridge with me,
> My eyes are full of sand.

Incidentally, it is notable what an influence Morris had on Kipling, indicated by the poem here 'Sigurd's Ride'. In this connection, it would have been useful if all the poems had been individually dated.

Lord de Tabley is not much heard of now, but his 'Medea', for example, is impressive:

Sweet are the ways of death to weary feet,
Calm are the shades of men.
The phantom fears no tyrant in his seat,
The slave is master then.
Love is abolished; well that that is so:
We know him best as Pain.
The gods are all cast out, and let them go;
Who ever found them gain?

One is a bit surprised that no Hardy is included (*Wessex Poems*, 1898?) Among others who do not make the grade are Lang, Symons and Dowson.

The notes, by George R. Creeger, which seem intended to equip this volume as a school textbook, are scrappy and, if required at all, inadequate. Many poets are biographically ignored, while surely it should be mentioned that Samuel Palmer was better known as a painter than a poet, and that Wilfrid Scawen Blunt had quite a lively career.

They also contain one ludicrous schoolboy howler. In Peacock's poem 'The War-Song of Dinas Vawr' with the well-known

The mountain sheep are sweeter,
But the valley sheep are fatter;
We therefore deemed it meeter
To carry off the latter . . .

Dinas Vawr was not a 'petty Welsh King supposedly contemporary with Arthur', but the earlier name – it means 'the Great Palace' – of Dynevor Castle in Carmarthenshire. Indeed, we read in *The Misfortunes of Elfin* where the poem occurs: 'Prince Rhun . . . was received at the castle of Dinas Vawr . . . then garrisoned by King Melvas.'

However, that makes us no less grateful for the poetic part of the book.

Nineteenth-Century Minor Poets, 1967
edited by W. H. Auden, Faber. *Daily Telegraph*

WILFRID SCAWEN BLUNT

In his book *The Cousins* (1977) Max Egremont gave an excellent account of chiefly the political activities of Wilfrid Scawen Blunt (1840–1922), including the career of Blunt's friend and cousin, George Wyndham: thereby elaborating a family background, some knowledge of which is essential for Blunt's character to be understood.

Lord Egremont deliberately – and wisely – omitted Blunt's copious involvements as an 'amorist', a separate, if major, part of his life. Elizabeth Longford's biography, rich in hitherto unpublished material from Blunt's diaries and papers, naturally has to re-examine aspects relatively familiar, but her picture of Blunt the lover gives her study a fresh and engrossing quality.

Blunt's approach to himself is best summarised by the fact that when (perhaps not altogether justly) he was given two months for joining in an Irish political rough-and-tumble, he later wrote a poem comparing his experience with Christ's Passion. His overwhelming narcissism arose out of his being undoubtedly very good-looking, articulate, courageous, and a startlingly successful womaniser.

Describing Blunt's love affairs is in every sense a Herculean task. Apart from anything else, he preferred his mistresses to be drawn from his own enormous cousinship, which means you have to keep your bearings in a maze of aristocratic family relationships. Lady Longford reduces these often not far from incestuous adulteries to comprehensible terms, though the publisher has not made reference to the pedigree charts on the endpapers any easier by using white type on a red background.

Blunt was brought up a Roman Catholic, married according to the Anglican rite, spent considerable stretches of his life as an atheist, and was at times a devout Mahommedan. He liked having affairs with Catholic ladies, preferably relations; as these kept him in touch with the Church, offering more chance of repentance. Today he could not only rejoice in the termination of the British Empire – for which he long battled – but also in what he looked forward to as of equal benefit, the resurgence of Islam.

Lady Longford gives the best vignette I have read of Skittles (Catherine Walters), already a successful *poule de luxe* when Blunt, as a very young diplomat, picked her up quite by chance in a fair at Bordeaux. Skittles used to hunt with the Cheshire (did she ever meet Marx's friend Engels, who also rode to hounds in that county?) and lived to a great age, keeping up with Blunt, not always without financial undertones. The Great used to call on Skittles – including Gladstone, who would measure the smallness of her waist with his hands. All rather on the lines of Rosa Lewis of the Cavendish Hotel.

Blunt married his wife more or less for her money, but was also attracted by her as granddaughter of Byron, whom Blunt liked to think he resembled. The comparison breaks down, not only because Blunt was a vastly inferior poet, but even more drastically on account of his total lack of humour.

Lady Anne Blunt, her husband's intrepid companion in Arabian journeys often hazardous to a degree, on the whole ignored his amatory goings-on, finally leaving him, when both were approaching seventy, because of his domination (apparently not physical) by a hospital nurse so bossy that she took charge of the tea-pot at Lady Anne's own table. Blunt had enormously desired a male heir for Crabbet Park, his ancestral Sussex estate, but only a daughter survived – though at least one illegitimate son grew up. At Crabbet, to some extent with Lady Anne's money, the Blunts set up a notable stud of Arab horses.

Blunt's conquests ranged from Janey Morris (recorded by him as preferring his embraces to Rossetti's) to Margot Tennant (whose virginity he allegedly took), later wife of H. H. Asquith, the prime minister. Occasionally a bedroom door was unexpectedly bolted. Once when he was bent on seducing a vegetarian peeress, she did not turn up, and he had to eat a solitary dinner of spinach, cauliflower and sago pudding, by himself in his Mount Street flat.

Among much else that is new, Lady Longford provides Blunt's own unpublished account of the 'Peacock dinner' in 1914, when a group of younger poets, including W. B. Yeats and Ezra Pound, organised a party for Blunt, then seventy-three. The photograph of him standing among them is familiar. It is interesting to find that Blunt himself, far from being a link between the generations, regarded the young poets as 'futurist' and unintelligible.

Blunt's sexual exploits cause him to fall somewhat short of the photograph taken of himself as a young man in the character of Sir Galahad, but so did the family rows that darkened the end of his days. At the parting with his wife these were mainly about the division of the stud. When (by that time Baroness Wentworth in her own right) Lady Anne died, she did not leave her share of the stud to Blunt as he expected, while certain horses he wanted to keep were claimed by his strong-willed daughter. The scenes that took place, Blunt being nearly eighty, were worthy of King Lear.

In the 1880s in Rome 'Mrs Waldo Storey, the wife of a sculptor', to whom Blunt (who had just had an audience with the Pope) talked 'not in a way profitable to my soul' was surely the wife of William Wetmore Storey, sculptor friend of Henry James (whom Blunt, incidentally, found 'dull-witted'). Lady Longford perhaps underestimates Mabel Batten (seduced by Blunt in India in 1879) in calling her 'a typically frustrated Victorian'. Mrs Batten, later not unknown in society, is rumoured to have enjoyed the unusual distinction of having her name coupled with both Edward VII and the lesbian novelist Radcliffe Hall.

A Pilgrimage of Passion:
The Life of Wilfrid Scawen Blunt,
Elizabeth Longford, Weidenfeld.

1979
Daily Telegraph

FELIX FENEON

Félix Fénéon (1861–1944) is the sort of literary man we do not run to in this country. His father, an unsuccessful travelling salesman, married a woman of Swiss origin who more or less supported the family by becoming a provincial postmistress. While Fénéon was doing his military service he saw an advertisement for clerkships in the War Office, obtained three days' leave, sat for the exam, passed top, and spent the next thirteen years in the section concerned with recruiting.

It might be noted here that French conscription then lasted for five years, but, by paying about £60 for his uniform, a recruit of reasonable education could reduce this term to one year. That was the method chosen by Fénéon, lifelong enemy of wealth and privilege.

From the War Office now began Fénéon's extraordinary career of critic, writing and editing 'little magazines' associated with the Symbolist, Impressionist and Neo-Impressionist movements in literature and art, of which he was one of the earliest to appreciate the importance. Contributors to these periodicals were not as a rule paid.

One of them, *La Vogue*, which only appeared for about six months in 1886, published poems and tales by Laforgue, also his translations of Walt Whitman; Charles Henry's translations of Dostoevsky's letters, Keats's *Hyperion*, various other studies; and Rimbaud's *Illuminations*. By that time Rimbaud himself had already departed to Africa, his poems being known only through Verlaine.

Fénéon's impact on the painting side took place earlier, when, in 1884, he had been delighted by Seurat's *Bathing at Asnières* (now in the National Gallery), and became promoter of the Neo-Impressionists on all occasions, Signac painting the portrait of Fénéon on the jacket of this book. Later there were differences with Seurat, but, when the painter died in his early thirties, Fénéon catalogued his works, about which he remained always enthusiastic. He was at first not equally keen on the Post-Impressionists, Gauguin and van Gogh, though he came round to them, too.

All this time Fénéon's political stance was that of an Anarchist. The tenets of Anarchism are stated here as (1) belief that a truly free individual is essentially good; (2) humankind is better without any form of government. Anarchists were deeply opposed to Marxists, who wanted a 'society in which each citizen will bear a serial number'. One branch of the Anarchist movement believed the best means of achieving their ideal society was by throwing bombs – this called 'Propaganda by Deed'.

Between 1892 and 1894 about a dozen Anarchist bombs were exploded. One of these resulted in the death of the office boy at the main offices of a mining company in l'Avenue de l'Opéra (also a few policemen), but a more effective testimony that man was naturally good and government unnecessary was provided by lobbing a bomb at the band in the Café Terminus, patronised by shopkeepers and clerks, where much more damage was done.

Joan Ungersma Halperin, whose book is not put together with great facility but collects a mass of information about Fénéon and has admirable illustrations, makes a good case for Fénéon himself planting a bomb. He appears to have fabricated a mixture of dinitrobenzene and ammonium nitrate, which he packed with bullets in a flowerpot, the fuse hidden by the stalk of a hyacinth. He seems to have set the pot on the dining-room window of the Hotel Foyot in the Latin Quarter, famous for its cuisine, and boarded a passing bus.

When the bomb went off, no one was hurt except a fellow Anarchist, having a night out with a girl, who lost an eye. By this time, however, the police were on Fénéon's track. He and other suspects, 'The Thirty', were arrested and tried for conspiratorial activities, which carries extremely heavy penalties. Fénéon was acquitted, but, perhaps not unreasonably, sacked from the War Office (where he had kept a set of detonators, which he somehow explained away).

All this time Fénéon was living in the greatest poverty, sharing a small flat with his father, mother, wife, sometimes other relations. He found no great difficulty in getting a new job, and in fact edited the famous *Revue blanche* (for which contributors were actually paid), a publication that contained all sorts of famous names, including Proust, Gide, Apollinaire, Claudel and many more of a younger generation.

By this time Fénéon had, of course, an unrivalled knowledge of the painters of the Modern school, and incidentally owned a collection soon to become of immense value. To the surprise of his friends he switched from journalism (by that time he was writing a column of 'news in three lines' for *Le Matin*) to selling pictures. He took a job with the well-known Bernheim Gallery, where he made at last a respectable income.

Fénéon left Bernheim's in 1923. There the reader is left high and dry. What happened to him during the next forty years? How did he maintain himself? Had he held stocks and shares, or had he bought an annuity? Did he sell his collection? What did he do during the German occupation? By then, having forsworn Anarchism, Fénéon was a Communist. One would like to know some of these things, in addition to the often very interesting material that precedes this later half of Fénéon's life.

Félix Fénéon: 1989
Aesthete and Anarchist in Fin-de-Siècle Paris, *Daily Telegraph*
Joan Ungersma Halperin,
Yale University Press.

MARCEL PROUST

In this excellent translation one is puzzled only by the title. If the book was named in the original French *Contre Sainte-Beuve*, why not call it *Against Sainte-Beuve* in English? This study is levelled against Sainte-Beuve. It is a most devastating attack on him. Why suggest, therefore, that Sainte-Beuve is merely the vehicle for expressing certain literary opinions?

Contre Sainte-Beuve was begun by Proust in 1908 as an article for *Le Figaro*, but like everything else he touched it soon became enormously elaborated, eventually growing into a volume. 'Vatelle won't take Sainte-Beuve, which no doubt will remain unpublished,' Proust wrote. 'It is too long, four or five hundred pages.' Miss Townsend Warner justly comments on the energy of a writer who cannot remember off-hand whether he has written four hundred or five hundred pages of a book.

The final result, to be read here with various short essays on George Eliot, Tolstoy, Dostoevsky, Goethe and others, including several painters, can be enjoyed for two different reasons.

First, the critical opinions are of the greatest interest. Sainte-Beuve, perhaps France's greatest academic critic of the nineteenth century, believed that criticism could be treated as 'a science'. He also believed that a critic's first duty was to spot contemporary talent. Unfortunately he wasted a great deal of time with nonentities – as Proust points out – and he was also not the foremost to recognise many of the names posterity now acclaims. He disapproved of Balzac's invention of the *roman fleuve*, he disliked Stendhal's novels, he was patronising to Baudelaire, he consigned Gérard de Nerval to obscurity . . .

On these and other subjects Proust gives Sainte-Beuve a tremendous knocking-about, incidentally expressing a great many of his own views about life and letters, notable not only for their subtlety but also for their humour and common sense. Academic critics are always with us, and it would do some of them a great deal of good to ponder some of these comments.

However, there is another aspect of this book that will fascinate all interested in how Proust's own great novel came into being, and in the literary vitality and iron discipline of this extraordinary man.

Before he wrote *Contre Sainte-Beuve* Proust had already written – and put away as unsatisfactory – *Jean Santeuil*, a matter of 340,000 words, or about four times the length of the average novel. This book tried out his method; and many incidents and characters, some considerably altered, some scarcely altered at all, appeared eventually in *A la Recherche du Temps Perdu.*

Now *Contre Sainte-Beuve* is by no means all 'straight' criticism. Large sections of the book are devoted to imaginary people the author knows, whose approach, for example, to Balzac is described as an extension of Proust's critical method. The Guermantes are introduced for the first time, and an early sketch for Monsieur de Charlus appears. The author's brother is sketched in as a child. In short, this is a second attempt at expressing the material he had within him; an attempt also doomed, in one sense, to failure.

Finally, in *A la Recherche*, like one who has a third try at the high jump, in which he puts every ounce of his energy, we see him clear the cross-bar magnificently. The absorbing point about the earlier books is to observe what material he later decided to abandon, and what modifications he made, the better to express the realities of his own ife.

For example, Proust has been taken to task for representing himself in *A la Recherche* as an only child. The few words about his brother in *Contre Sainte-Beuve* immediately convince one that he was right to abandon this additional complication of presenting the Marcel of his novel; and that it was no mere egotism that caused this final choice. There are innumerable small points to be noted of this kind, and also the building up and dramatisation of personages and situations which are at first only lightly suggested.

There are all kinds of minor points in *By Way of Sainte-Beuve* which are to be enjoyed: for example, a terrific side-kick at Romain Rolland for *Jean Christophe*. Everyone at all interested in French literature must read it. I suppose it was too much to hope for an index, as such things are unknown in France, but it would have been a great help and – as the song in *My Fair Lady* says – would have set a good example.

By Way of Sainte-Beuve, 1958
Marcel Proust, *Punch*
translated by Sylvia Townsend Warner,
Chatto & Windus.

PAUL VALERY

I

Born in 1871, the same year as Proust, Paul Valéry seems to belong to a distinctly later generation than the novelist. That is not entirely because Valéry lived on through the Second World War, dying in 1945. Although his roots were embedded in the past – the essence of the French tradition – there is something immensely 'modern' about him. Even today, though you may disagree with his ideas, they never have the air of being dated.

To explain these ideas is a formidable task, especially since Valéry himself was particularly averse from any paraphrase being made of his writings. However, Agnes Ethel Mackay settles down to a thorough investigation, forging through the material like a bulldozer. *The Universal Self* cannot be described as light reading, but one emerges at the other end knowing considerably more about Valérian theories than when one started.

Although so much the quintessence of the French spirit, Valéry came of a Corsican family and his mother was Italian. As a young man – naturally, a very promising one – he was a friend of Mallarmé, always a strong influence, and worked for a time in the editorial office of Cecil Rhodes's *Chartered*.

He met William Henley, an encounter certainly deserving a picture by Max Beerbohm. He also dined with George Meredith. However, the climate of London was inimical to Valéry's health. He returned to Paris, was employed for three years in the French War Office, then found a job as private secretary to the director of the Havas News Agency.

> Valéry [writes Miss Mackay] went there for four or five hours every afternoon. His chief duty was to read aloud news of the Bourse, events from the daily papers, or the sermons of Bossuet and of Bourladoue; of the latter, Valéry said, 'he was very pure and scarcely anything more than that' and confessed that he sometimes skipped the dullest pages . . .

This was in 1900, the year Valéry married (his wife was a niece of the painter Berthe Morisot) and he continued this work until 1922, when his employer died. He also lived in the same house near the Arc de Triomphe for forty years, from marriage to death. He had three children and was devoted to his family.

Valéry held strong views on the subject of a writer's ideas being what matters – not his life. It follows that he would regard these biographical details about himself as of little or no interest. Others, less intellectually puritanical, may find a certain fascination in speculating how much or how little Valéry's career could be guessed from his works.

Miss Mackay points out that even in a study of some length it is exceedingly difficult to explain Valéry's thought. Obviously this is even more impossible to summarise in a few sentences. However, the title of Miss Mackay's book – *The Universal Self* – refers to Valéry's conception of a Pure Self, which is not entirely unlike that of the religious mysticism of the Yogi, seeking revelation through a negation of all that is material. But there is this essential difference, that Valéry's aim was also to 'extend his own consciousness so as to acquire a greater power of *creation*'.

How he set about his is of the greatest interest. After his first burst of poetry, he remained silent for twenty-five years, concerning himself chiefly with mathematics and science, studies for which he had no particular aptitude. Purity of language and thought was his great preoccupation.

Some of this side of himself is illustrated by his 'La Soirée avec Monsieur Teste', and other writings describing the Teste family. Monsieur Teste is the man who is incomparable in the world of ideas, but out of his depth in dealing with everyday life.

Then in 1917, Valéry began to publish more poems, 'La Jeune Parque', followed in due course by 'Charmes', 'Fragments de Narcisse' and his famous soliloquy on the theme of death, 'Le Cimetière Marin':

Ce toit tranquille, où marchent les colombes,
Entre les pins palpite, entre les tombes.
Midi le juste y compose de feux
La mer, la mer toujours recommencée!
O récompense après une pensée
Qu'un long regard sur le calme des dieux!

Valéry also produced an enormous number of essays and introductions. This was partly due to the necessity of earning a living by his pen after the loss of the job reading aloud sermons and Stock Exchange quotations; partly, perhaps, to a somewhat changed view of life in his fifties.

By that time he had made a great name. He took to going out in the world, abandoning his former asceticism and frequenting the beau monde, where he thoroughly enjoyed himself.

Miss Mackay's study has all kinds of good points, including a brief gallop through the various forms of philosophy against which Valéry reacted. Perhaps she is a shade too reverential. It is possible to feel a little rebellious at all this Pure Reason.

Then one turns back to the frontispiece, with its portrait; bright-eyed; humorous; sensible; neat moustached; beautifully dressed; cigarette poised.

He obviously knew when Pure Reason had gone too far. What would one guess him to be? The nicest sort of English peer? A famous actor, not in his first youth, playing Bulldog Drummond? In spite of his desire to be known only by works, one would like to hear more of Valéry himself.

The Universal Self: A Study of Paul Valéry, Agnes Ethel Mackay, Routledge. 1961 *Daily Telegraph*

II

The French Spirit, unlike the American Idea, is essentially exportable. Indeed, an interesting study might be made of writers of un-French origin who particularly express it in France; and those, not Frenchmen in any sense, who like to feel they express it in other countries.

Paul Valéry, who died in 1945, is a good example of the former. His father was a Corsican, his mother Genoese, yet Valéry himself, as poet, critic, and essayist, seems to typify all we imagine to be most French. Perhaps when we look closer, as with another non-Frenchman, Apollinaire, there is a certain absence of tension, a kind of easy good-nature in approach that suggests an unFrench strain; but all the same, in Valéry one finds the clarity, logic, tolerance and hard thinking most to be admired in French writing at its best.

History and Politics is Vol X (though the fifth to appear) of Valéry's *Collected Works*, edited by Jackson Mathews, translated by the editor and Denise Folliot. It includes about sixty pieces, essays prefaces, interviews, radio and other public addresses, spanning a period from 1895 to 1945, with notes and an index.

The preface by François Valéry, the poet's son, is very well done. It gives an excellent idea of what Valéry himself must have been like. On the one hand, he accepted the life of 'the average Frenchman', positively chauvinistic in his political views (more than once in the essays Valéry returns to what might have happened if Bonaparte had not been defeated at Waterloo); on the other, he lived an inner life of complete scepticism as to the efficacy of any political forms whatever, describing himself as a 'government anarchist'.

These occasional writings well illustrate this mixture of anarchy and conformity. Anti-Dreyfusard and nationalist, Valéry, if he had been killed in the 1914 war, would probably have been thought of as a Rightist like Maurras or Sorel – men from whom he was in reality utterly different.

Later, when he was elected to the French Academy in 1926, he was considered by his old friends to have moved too far to the Left, into the orbit of Blum and Briand. By chance he was also designated to receive Pétain with the usual eulogy when the Marshal became an Academician in 1931.

As one turns the pages of these polished, perfectly turned pieces, full of ideas, admirably expressed, never boring or pedantic, yet at the same time never cheap or aimed at an easy popularity, one feels that all that Valéry stands for has taken a terrible beating.

It is hard to accuse someone so sceptical of being optimistic; yet Valéry was, in a sense, too optimistic. He attached enormous importance, for example, to Japan's campaign against China in 1895, and the United States' war with Spain in 1898; the former, as the first act of power by an Asiatic nation, remodelled on European lines; the latter, the first act of power against Europe by a nation developed from Europe.

Yet in writing of this Sino-Japanese war he depicts a Chinese scholar churning out – apparently with Valéry's approval – all the clichés about thousands of years of civilisation and philosophy, about inventing gunpowder merely to make fireworks, and so on – a lot of stuff of which Chinese communism has made nonsense.

It is true that Valéry was only twenty-four or twenty-five when he wrote this piece, but, with all his hatred of disorder and love of freedom of thought, it seems doubtful, again, whether he fully appreciated the crisis of the 1930s, until Germany had overrun France.

All the same, Valéry behaved honourably under the German Occupation and gave the funeral address for Bergson in 1941. Equally, he disapproved of some of the action taken after the Liberation, often an expression less of justice than party politics. As ever, to Valéry's mind, in the political sphere one myth was substituted for another.

> Freedom; this is one of those detestable words that have more force than sense; they sing rather than speak, ask rather than answer; it is one of those words that have been put to every sort of use, and leave the memory smeared with Theology, Metaphysics, Morals and Politics.

One of the most enjoyable of the writings here is a memoir (1924) of a brief meeting with Conrad. Their talk roused the nationalist in Valéry: 'Why and how has France never been able to hold supremacy at sea?' Conrad put forward the interesting theory that instructions from Versailles were to capture vessels rather than sink them, an interesting example of French economy. The English fired to sink. One would have liked more talks like this one, between Valéry and contemporary writers.

History and Politics, 1963
Paul Valéry, Routledge. *Daily Telegraph*

HILAIRE BELLOC

Although younger contemporaries of Hilaire Belloc (1870–1953) were associated with the Nineties, he remains essentially an Edwardian. His enthusiasms and hates were for a world as it was in Edwardian times, and he never changed or modified his views.

It is approaching thirty years since Robert Speaight's life of Belloc was published, a good piece of work. Since then Belloc's reputation as a writer has not greatly changed: admirable comic verse; a genuine minor poet, usually at his best with a satiric edge; a few political prophecies like 'The Servile State', which turned out not far off the mark; reams of Roman Catholic apologetics; history that was biased and often inaccurate. As a man, however, by no means all was said. A. N. Wilson gives a vigorous account of an extraordinary figure, adding appreciably to what has previously appeared. He does that in a most entertaining and understanding manner.

Belloc was one quarter French, his male line deriving from a Nantes wine-merchant called Moses Bloch or Belloc; a disconcerting name for the ancestor of one who, except in the case of certain individuals, can hardly be considered anything but obsessively anti-Semitic. Belloc's father, whose mother was expatriate Irish, died when his son was two.

At twenty-two Belloc went up to Oxford (Balliol), four years older than most freshmen. Oxford was the principal, formative period. He became an outstanding undergraduate personality, president of the Union, where his talent for speaking emerged and won a First in Modern History. But then came two blows from which Belloc literally never recovered. He was not granted an All Souls fellowship; nor any fellowship elsewhere either.

The young Belloc (whose photographs make him look a little like M. Mitterrand) married in spite of dim prospects, and settled down to hack work as a lecturer and what was to be a chronic struggle for money. He was incapable of putting up with a boss, keeping regular hours, or in any way trimming his sails, so that a living had to be earned by turning out books.

Belloc's mother, who brought him up, is a key figure. Daughter of a well-to-do Birmingham solicitor, she held radical and feminist views, which she combined with becoming a Roman Catholic convert after a rather chilly talk with Manning. She gave Belloc his head from childhood, lived to ninety-three, and bestowed on her son an entry into the world of intellectual London, which was to be extremely useful. I had imagined that Belloc had trodden his very successful social path wholly through his own efforts. That was not at all so.

From the beginning he was articulate, uncontrollable, hard to place in life. He fell in love at nineteen with the American girl he subsequently married (who until the last moment almost became a nun), tramped without any money from New York to California to see her, then served a year in the French Artillery as a volunteer, since he was still a French citizen liable for conscription. Later he passionately romanticised those army days, using them as pretext in the two wars for writing immensely inept articles on strategy and tactics.

It has been suggested – notably by Malcolm Muggeridge – that Belloc's opinions and temperament would have found far easier accommodation in France; for example, in the sphere of Charles Maurras, editor of *L'Action Française*, though Maurras merely considered the Roman Catholic Church the best bastion against the evils of capitalism and socialism.

For a time Belloc was a Liberal MP, the extreme radical end of the party, although he did not like Asquith, Lloyd George even less, and retained all sorts of tenets not at all suited to Liberalism. He was in short – in no reckless use of the term – a fascist. He believed in government by a 'king', that is to say one man, organisation of labour in guilds, small agricultural holdings; and it comes as no surprise to find that even to the end he admired Mussolini.

Fashions change in religion, as Mr Wilson truly remarks, and generally speaking nowadays it might be regarded as a not very convincing recommendation of the Roman Church to write, as Belloc did: 'Threaten we cannot because we are nobody . . . But we can spread the mood that we are the bosses and the chic and that a man who does not accept the Faith writes himself down as suburban.'

Because Belloc has become so largely forgotten this piece has been taken up with sketching a very unusual life, but there is much of a personal nature touched on here by Mr Wilson that illuminates a story at times not much short of tragic. The death of his wife in her early forties was an appalling blow, and for all Belloc's drinking, shouting, singing, smart friends, large family, militant religion, he was, especially latterly, often lonely and wretched.

One is interested to learn that in 'Do you remember an Inn, Miranda?' the person apostrophised was probably not a girl but a Spanish diplomat, who was Duke of Miranda. But surely, in Belloc's haunting song 'The Winged Horse' the phrase should read 'Roland of the Marches' (i.e., borderlands of France and Spain) rather than 'marshes'.

Hilaire Belloc, 1984
A. N. Wilson, Hamish Hamilton. *Daily Telegraph*

JOHN MASEFIELD

I

In his day John Masefield (1878–1967) achieved wide recognition. He was Poet Laureate for nearly forty years, received the OM, surviving to a great and honoured age.

At his centenary in 1978 there was a competent biography by Constance Babington-Smith; Heinemann issued a convenient Masefield selection with an introduction by the present Laureate, yet the picture seemed to have become already a little faded.

These *Letters* would have made a good opportunity for an essay briefly defining Masefield's life and verse. Unfortunately the chance has been missed. Corliss and Lansing Lamont, son and grandson of Florence Lamont, the American lady to whom Masefield wrote the letters, produce in their Introduction the familiar smokescreen of misty romanticism that seems always to hang between Masefield and anything like serious critical judgement.

Even *The Oxford Companion to English Literature* (1967) states that Masefield 'ran away to sea in early life', just as the Introduction here says 'a wander-lusting mariner with no riches save the gift of verse and a loving family . . . He came to America first in 1895 looking for adventure'.

That is all absolute rubbish. Masefield was an orphan and – most unsuitably, one would think – was sent into the Merchant Service by a callous aunt (so far from a loving family, at that stage). He had a nervous breakdown after his first voyage and was brought back to England as an invalid seaman. His horrible aunt forced him to go to sea again, and he jumped ship at New York. He found a job in a carpet factory, had various struggles, returned to England, worked as a journalist, married a woman somewhat older than himself with some money, and lived happily ever after.

One feels that Masefield was a very nice man, simple to the point of naivety in his behaviour and views on life, and that much is lost by trying to build him up into a figure like, say, Byron's friend Trelawny, whom Masefield did not in the very least resemble.

During the First World War when Masefield was thirty-eight, he was employed by the government on the Western Front as an historian and observer. He had quite a dangerous time, and was then sent to the United States to undertake propaganda through lectures and such means, to bring America into the war on the Allied side.

While he was in America on these duties Masefield met Mrs Florence Lamont wife of a rich Wall Street banker. The Lamonts had Allied sympathies, and gave Masefield all the help they could. Masefield and Mrs Lamont appear to have felt at once a strong mutual attraction. Indeed it seems not going too far to say that he fell in love with her. She was about six years older than he, evidently a woman of ability and charm. They continued to write regularly to each other from 1916 until Mrs Lamont's death at the age of eighty in 1952.

Contemporary biographical material is usually so full of awful revelations about revered figures that there is a certain novelty in reading of a relationship that seems, at least on Masefield's side, to have been quite intense, and remained for both at the same time wholly innocent. After rather more than twenty years, when Mrs Lamont was in her middle sixties – and not without some apology – Masefield allowed himself to risk repeating a doubtful joke about Hollywood to the effect that 'you either lay on the earth and looked at the stars, or lay on the stars and looked at the earth'.

Masefield although he belonged to the generation which brought revolution to the arts, was consciously an 'anti-modernist'. He says, for example, of Dostoevsky:

> There can be no doubt that he was a very great writer of the modern school [Dostoevsky was born in 1821] . . . he had a great, profound, simple mind, which sees & feels rather than thinks. He had a great profound and beautiful spirit . . . He remained great but instead of being what nature meant him to be, great in creative delight like Chaucer, Cervantes & Shakespeare, he was a great nerve specialist, with a wide knowledge of the damned. I hold no brief for the modern school. They have all got a fever or an axe to grind, and I can't read much of them, but I think D had a power and a sympathy beyond the rest of them . . .

One might suggest that there are passages in Shakespeare (for that matter probably Chaucer and Cervantes) quite equal in grasp of horrors of the nerves to anything in Dostoevsky, and Masefield's fundamental weakness was that he could not accept that. Masefield can get angry about all sorts of wrongs that he thinks should be put right, but such knocking about the world as he had done never shook him out of a kind of nineteenth-century vicarage cosiness in his point of view.

Accordingly, these *Letters* are at times rather humdrum, intellectually speaking, but they do give a good picture of the sort of life Masefield himself led, his absolute lack of pretension in the face of success, deep love of the sort of poetry and books which appealed to him. One gets rather tired of his constant ejaculation 'Golly' and to refer to Osbert and Sachie Sitwell as 'Ozzy and Satchie' opens up an abyss of social bewilderment. David Rice (29 February 1924), for whom there is no note, was undoubtedly David Talbot Rice, the archaeologist, then an undergraduate at Christ Church.

Letters of John Masefield to Florence Lamont, edited by Corliss Lamont and Lamsing Lamont, Macmillan.

1980
Daily Telegraph

II

In the course of the late war many in the services (among those who reflect on such things) must have been struck by the changelessness of the foundations of strategy and tactics. Even in the RAF the element of single combat marked a return to a form of fighting that seemed to be going out of fashion; while the preparations for invasion – defensive and offensive – recalled in different ways aspects of military science familiar in classical times and, indeed, in the earliest recorded epochs. *Badon Parchments* takes this changelessness for its theme; and Mr Masefield shows that the problems which faced King Arthur were, in their essentials, comparable with the problems that face the world today.

Bardon Hill was the battle where by tradition Arthur defeated the Heathen, and the novel is a chronicle of the events leading up to this victory, presented through the eyes of John of Cos, an envoy sent to Britain by the Emperor Justinian and the Empress Theodora. The author places Badon (variously located mostly in the south of England) at some period towards the middle of the sixth century, later, in fact, than 518, recorded as its date in the *Annales Cambriae*. 'Arthur' is Aurelian, king of the West of England, up to the borders of Hereford, Berkshire and Hampshire, or there abouts. In him survive the remnants of Christian and Roman tradition, pressed hard by the Red Heathen of Norfolk and the Black Heathen of Kent. Aurelian inaugurates a system by which his army is thoroughly reorganised, notably in units of fifty strong, specially dedicated to their leader and to one another. One of these detachments is called 'The Round Table'.

Although the book takes up only 150 pages, Mr Masefield covers with skill the many forms of internal and external antagonism that leadership must face. When the war broke out.

> Horses at the relay-posts were maimed, stolen or stampeded. Signal posts were cut down. Stacks of forage were burned. These things made our men much more alert, and some of the criminals were caught. They were all young Britons who had been persuaded that the Heathen stood

> for the worker, against the lord. Why this should ever have been believed, when the least knowledge of Heathen practice would have shown its falsity, we could not learn. The Britons expelled these young men from their communities, painted them red, and sent them to the Red Heathen further down the coast, who burned them for permitting themselves to be caught . . .

This lively experiment in suggesting what history might have been brings out points that seem too convincing to have been invented. It would have been interesting to know some of the authorities used by the Poet Laureate, though we must recognise that not all might have prejudiced the novel's present smooth and occasionally ironic tone.

Badon Parchments, 1947
John Masefield, Heinemann. *Times Literary Supplement*

EDWARD THOMAS

Edward Thomas (1878–1917) is an odd, interesting figure, both as a man and a poet. Full of contradictions, never quite fitting in wherever he was, he throws light on that equally odd period between the 1890s and the First World War when so much was coming to birth.

His father, a staff clerk for light railways and tramways at the Board of Trade, had raised himself from a poor background in Wales, and managed to send his talented son to St Paul's and Lincoln College, Oxford. The idea was, of course, that he should have a great career in the Civil Service. It is striking that he was already getting odds and ends published in papers by the time he was just seventeen. This was to some extent through the influence of his future father-in-law, J. S. Noble, a literary critic of the *Spectator* and other periodicals.

Noble's daughter, Helen, fell in love with Thomas; they lived together when opportunity arose; she became pregnant; they married without a word to either lot of parents. He was still an undergraduate, twenty-one and a few months. This was all the consequence of a deadly serious disregard of convention, the very reverse of anything like a dissolute attitude towards life. Helen Thomas was obviously a remarkable woman. Throughout trying financial difficulties, the marriage worked.

When he came down from Oxford, Thomas plunged into what was to be his life until he joined the army at the age of thirty-seven. He became a literary hack. He would review twelve or fifteen books at a time, himself producing perhaps as many as five books in a year, the subjects carrying from the Duke of Marlborough to Maurice Maeterlinck.

Not surprisingly, such activities drove him to the verge of insanity and suicide. At the same time, it cannot be pretended that such a life was not to some extent his own choice. He had an extraordinary facility for writing that highly decorated Edwardian prose which seems appalling now, but was well looked on by the literary pundits of the time.

The word 'decadence' is always chucked about with great gusto, usually in connection with aberrant sex, but in fact this sort of writing, the final dregs of Lamb and de Quincey, is far more 'decadent' – i.e. writing in decay – than much of, say, Wilde, in some respects an innovator followed to this day. Edward Thomas was himself half aware of what was wrong with his own prose, and he speaks more than once of his desire when young to impress by fine writing, rather than to express what he saw.

It is this curious state of being somehow poised between dying forms, and others coming to birth, that makes his position peculiar. These was a brief brush with Ezra Pound; Edward Thomas was at first enthusiastic, then changed his mind. Mr Pound thought Thomas 'mild, without enough vinegar'.

That was not a very subtle judgement, but Thomas – whose two slim volumes of verse appeared only in the last two years of his life – never really impressed himself on the Old Gang either. Eddie Marsh had a blind spot for him, and Thomas's name never appeared in *Georgian Verse*. In 1913 the American poet Robert Frost, at that time still not much regarded in his own country, came to England. Frost and Thomas became friends, with a noticeable effect on Thomas's poetry.

War broke out. Thomas joined the Artists Rifles in July 1915. He was gazetted 2nd Lieutenant in the Royal Garrison Artillery in November 1916, volunteered for France, and was killed at the age of thirty-nine on Easter Monday, 1917.

There is an element in every biography – the absence, so to speak, of the man himself – which always leaves something to be guessed. William Cooke gives an excellent account of Thomas in the first half of his book. Quiet, withdrawn, strong-willed, cantankerous, with a good deal of charm, but without much humour. That is the picture. Probably a formidable egoist.

In his critical section, also written with vigour and understanding, Dr Cooke is at pains to point out that rather a hash has been made by some writers on the subject of Thomas's army career. The tendency has been to present him as a harassed man who suddenly found his true life in the army, and wrote poetry about nature there.

That is no doubt an over-simplification of what has been suggested, but it is true that Thomas is, on the one hand, inadequately recognised as a 'war poet', on the other, he naturally found the army tedious enough in many respects.

The misunderstanding is because his particular form of disillusioned patriotism has nothing whatever in common with the highly coloured dramatics of a Brooke or a Sassoon. Thomas knew what he was in for, and expected nothing better, but, as Dr Cooke points out, although his poems were written before he went overseas, they are none the less 'war' rather than 'nature' poems. Where the war poets are in question Thomas has an important place.

It is unexpected to find that, as a young man, Thomas numbered among his friends unregenerate figures like Norman Douglas and that eccentric and bibulous lawyer E. S. P. Haynes. Had he caught from them some of their cheerful bohemianism, would there not have been a touch of Apollinaire in the way Thomas looked at things? They were much of an age, and verse like the following is not unlike the French poet (also a gunner) in one of his observant pastoral moods:

> By the ford at the town's edge
> Horse and carter rest:
> The carter smokes on the bridge
> Watching the water press in swathes about his horse's chest.

– but Apollinaire would then have added a verse about his mistress.

Edward Thomas: A Critical Biography, 1970
William Cooke, Faber. *Daily Telegraph*

GUILLAUME APOLLINAIRE

Guillaume Apollinaire is one of the names that will always be associated with 'Cubism' and the New Movement in the arts that took place at the beginning of the twentieth century, and which, so far as its originators were concerned, was really at its height by 1914. Although his eccentricities were legendary even in his own lifetime, and he was suspected of having stolen *Mona Lisa* from the Louvre – for a week he was imprisoned on that entirely baseless charge – his feet were firmly placed on the ground where his own work was in question, and it is probably true to say that his reputation as a poet never stood higher than it stands today. In this country he is not so well known as on the Continent, and a word or two about his life is therefore necessary to explain the three publications under a review.

Apollinaire's name was de Kostrowitzky. He was born in 1880, his mother being the daughter of a Polish colonel in the Papal service and his father an officer in the army of the King of Naples, of a family coming originally from the Grisons. This fact seems now firmly established after the stories current during his lifetime of high ecclesiastical parentage. He came to Paris as a young man and the various brief accounts by those who knew him in those days, reproduced in the present number of *La Table Ronde*, are of great interest. His mother was at that time living with a Jewish businessman named Julius Weil and M. Charles André-Royer, who let a flat to this couple in 1904, provides a somewhat startling vignette of their life together. Apollinaire was devoted to his mother and rather afraid of her. He was employed in a bank through Weil's influence and a really excellent account of his life at that period is given in the memoir of M. René Nicosia, a Sicilian who worked in the same firm. Mlle. Nathalie de Gontcharova's brief story of meeting the poet with Michel Larionov (two of whose drawings are included showing Apollinaire with Diaghilev) also deserves to be mentioned.

When war broke out in 1914 Apollinaire at once volunteered for the French army, although not at that time a naturalised Frenchman. Going on leave in January 1915, he met Madeleine Pagès in the train between Nice and Marseilles, and they talked of modern poetry. He told her his name. She had never heard of him, and he promised to send her a book of his verse. They corresponded, and in due course became engaged to be married. *Tendre comme le Souvenir* is the collection of some two hundred letters which he sent to his young fiancée, whose family lived at Oran in North Africa. They are of considerable interest, not only for their moving quality (which cannot be dismissed by the necessary admission that Apollinaire was at the same time writing to other women in somewhat similar terms) but also for the tragic change of tone that takes place after he was wounded – and for the various literary judgments he makes in the course of the correspondence.

Apollinaire is a great contrast to many if not most of the poets of this country whose names are associated with the First World War, in whose work a strong admixture of self-pity and even a kind of defeatism is as often as not the predominant note. For this reason he is usually spoken of as a man who 'enjoyed' the war. This is the kind of over-simplification, dear to the hearts of critics, which, to be just, could find some support in poems like 'Les Saisons' or 'Merveilles de la Guerre'. The letters in *Tendre comme le Souvenir* are, however, an excellent corrective to any cheap acceptance of Apollinaire's action. He joined the artillery as a gunner and was soon given the rank of bombardier. In November, 1915, he was promoted second lieutenant and transferred to the infantry. Some months later he sustained the wound in his head which is generally agreed to have weakened him in such a way as to make him an easy victim to Spanish influenza from which he died in 1918. The letters show the discomforts to which, like other soldiers, he was subject; the horrors by which he was surrounded, and the manner in which he adjusted his mind to the discipline to which he voluntarily submitted himself. They show him, in short, as being thoroughly uncomfortable and putting up with it all with great good humour and not a little gallantry.

Some of the remarks about books and writers to be found scattered through the text are worth quoting:

> Vous m'avez parlé de Claudel dernièrement. Cet écrivain de talent est l'aboutis sant du symbolisme. Il représente de façon absconse et réactionnaire la même monnaie d'Arthur Rimbaud. Celui-ci est un louis d'or dont celui-là est le billon. Claudel est un homme de talent qui n'a fait que de choses faciles dans le sublime. A une époque où il n'y a plus de règles littéraires, il est facile d'en imposer, il n'a pas eu le courage de se dépasser et surtout de dépasser la littérature d'images qui est aujourd'hui facile. (July 12, 1915)

> Romain Rolland fait de désagréables et très déplacées manifestations presqu'en faveur de l'Allemagne. (July 18, 1915)

He was interested in Conrad because he was a Pole, and admired his work. He had read little of Dostoevsky.

> Je le connais cependant mais il m'attriste et m'abaisse. C'est pourquoi il me répugne un peu, bien que je reconnaisse son grand talent et puis il a le détail psychologique plus important que le détail réaliste. J'aime une balance entre ces deux éléments littéraires. L'autre russe que je préfère et que je mets près de Shakespeare, Flaubert, Cervantès, La Fontaine, Molière, c'est Gogol . . . Je n'aime pas qu'on regarde les travers, les vices ou les laideurs de l'homme sans sourire ce qui est une façon de comprendre et une façon de remédier en quelque sorte à notre misère en la voilant de grâce intelligente, dût-on en sangloter après. Mais j'ai horreur qu'on reste sérieux ou qu'on fasse le tragique à propos de choses basses. Comme chez Zola ou Dostoievsky. (September 14, 1915)

These are interesting views and provide a solid defence of a whole school of writing. On October 7, 1915, he wrote:

> J'ai appris la mort de Remy de Gourmont qui était mon ami et m'avait amené au *Mercure*. C'est un grand esprit qui disparaît. Ses jugements allaient parfois de travers quand l'interêt [le] lui dictait, mais au reste c'était un puits de connaissances littéraires et qui sait même biologiques.

Writing exactly a week later, he had just heard of the death of Fabre,

> l'entomologiste dont j'aimais infiniment les livres car ses études sur les insectes m'ont appris à connaître les hommes et si j'en avais les loisirs je voudrais que dans mon oeuvre romanesque ils fussent étudiés aussi minutieusement, aussi précisément et autant en dehors de morales. Il y avait en outre dans les livres du savant Fabre une bonhomie et une bonne humeur qui me plaisaient beaucoup. Mais je me suis amusé à changer parfois dans des pages de Fabre les noms des insectes en noms d'hommes et de femmes, ce qui donne à ces passagcs un épouvantable aspect d'humanité trop réelle à la Marquis de Sade . . . ou encore à la Suétone . . .

He knew 'Willy', who, with the help of a Dutch passport had managed to travel to Düsseldorf to see a play there, and the difficulties that such a well-known writer experienced in making enough money to live on worried Apollinaire in connexion with his own future.

> J'ai reçu aujourd'hui une letter de Willy (Henri Gauthier-Villars). C'est un écrivian léger, mais de grand talent. Il vaut même mieux que ce qu'il à écrit, d'ailleurs tout n'est pas de lui. L'ancien mari de Colette et le père de Claudine a beaucoup d'esprit. (October 17, 1915)

> Je comprends que d'Annunzio te déplaise puisqu'il me déplaît aussi et d'une façon inouïe. (October 22, 1915)

> Tu juges bien Anatole France, tu le juges très bien même, ses romans sont mal composés et leur différentes parties ne se suivent pas, (January 26, 1916)

> Je lis par petits bouts avant de dormir et il détruit l'admiration (moyenne au demeurant) que j'avais pour Villiers de l'Isle Adam qui sort entire de là. Mais Vigny quel merveilleux confeur qui pense et sait dire que la scène historique du pape et de Napoléon n'est que là . . . L'histoire des P . . . m'a amusé, mais je n'aime pas autant Maupassant qu'on fait d'habitude. Je ne sais pourquoi par exemple. Mais c'est comme ça. C'est un conteur vigoreux mais son ton est à mon avis de ce ton bourgeois de nouvelles journalistiques du XIXe siècle qui ne me plaisent point quoi que j'en reconnaisse le mérites. (February 23, 1916)

Such quotations give an extraordinarily clear picture of Apollinaire's approach to literature.

Le Guetteur Mélancolique, with a preface by M. André Salmon and a frontispiece by M. Picasso showing Apollinaire as a coffee-pot of which the spout forms his pipe, is rather too clearly a collection of odds and ends that the poet had decided on the whole not to publish. There are, however, one or two pieces of some charm towards the end of the volume. Its chief interest is in showing how certain poems were changed and polished up. For example, the beautiful pair of verses usually entitled 'Signe' appear here as 'L'Automne et l'Echo', and have nine stanzas. The accustomed version is:

> Je suis soumis au Chef du Signe de l'Automne
> Partant j'aime les fruits je déteste les fleurs
> Je regrette chacun des baisers que je donne
> Tel un noyer gaulé dit au vent ses douleurs
> Mon Automne éternelle ô ma saison mentale
> Le mains des amantes d'antan jonchent ton sol
> Une épouse me suit c'est mon ombre fatale
> Les colombes ce soir prennent leur dernier vol.

In *Le Guetteur Mélancolique* we find in place of the last line of the first stanza:

> Et je vis anxieux dans un concert d'odeurs

while the second stanza ends:

> Les fleurs ne laissent plus tomber aucun pétale
> Les colombes le soir tentent un dernier vol.

We see there a complete change of sense which retains only the part of the poem with which Apollinaire was satisfied. These things are of interest to those technically concerned with the writing of poetry, but there is not much in the book for others who know Apollinaire at his best and do not wish specially to study his method.

Tendre comme le Souvenir,
Guillaume Apollinaire,
Gallimard.

Le Guetteur Mélancolique,
préface d'André Salmon,
Gallimard.

La Table Ronde,
Guillaume Apollinaire, 1880–1918,
Librairie Plon.

1952
Times Literary Supplement

II

If Guillaume Apollinaire were alive today he would be rising eighty-one, and no doubt a member of the French Academy, much of his early days forgotten. As it is, he remains like a mammoth caught and frozen whole in a glacier, the embodiment of the bright young men of his period, and what this study appropriately calls 'the Cubist Life'.

Cecily Mackworth has written a very interesting book about Apollinaire. She is to be congratulated. Nothing would have been easier than to have strung together innumerable Apollinaire legends and given the impression that his life was one long riot of highbrow jokes and glamorous love affairs.

Nothing, also, would have been further from the truth. Miss Mackworth tackles with ability and common sense the often complicated ideas for which Apollinaire stood: at the same time, she gives a convincing and moving account of the man himself. The bare bones of Apollinaire's story are in themselves unusual enough. He was a quarter Polish, three-quarters Italian, his mother's father being an officer exiled after the Polish revolt against Russia in '61 who married an Italian lady in Rome.

Apollinaire's father, Francesco Flugi d'Aspermont, came of an Italo-Swiss family, military and ecclesiastical in tradition. He was in his forties when he ran away with Angelica Alexandrine Kostrovitsky, then aged seventeen. They never married. In due course he faded away, and Angelica Alexandrine became, in the official language of the French police, a 'kept woman'.

Apollinaire has that quality peculiar to people of strong personality that the 'boring' things that happened to him are as enjoyable to read about as the 'interesting' things; that is to say we are as absorbed – perhaps even more absorbed – when, as a young man, he goes to Germany as a tutor and falls in love with the English governess, as when, later, he is living in

Paris in the centre of the intellectual life of the period, and falls in love with the now famous painter, Marie Laurencin.

In a surprisingly short space of time, Apollinaire met figures like Moréas and Jarry, and himself became a well-known figure in the lively Parisian world. He was soon friends with Picasso, about his own age, and the host of painters of that generation who were to become famous. He became their impresario. It was for this he was first known. His own much more important fame as a poet took longer to develop.

The point that Miss Mackworth brings out very well is that there was very hearty opposition in some quarters to this new movement in the arts, Parisian, but by no means necessarily French. French nationalism, and French xenophobia, had in any case been much inflamed not long since by the Dreyfus case. There was certainly a good case for complaining that this new generation of artists was flying directly in the face of French classicism and the French tradition in general, of all traditions the least open to outside influence.

Apollinaire, devoted to France, always felt himself a foreigner there. He was subjected to vicious attacks – for example, by that decidedly stodgy novelist, Georges Duhamel – calling him 'part Levantine Jew, part South American, part Polish gentleman and part *facchino*'.

Such onslaughts would have been all part of the game – in many ways what Apollinaire was asking for – if there had not been the scandal of the stolen statuettes. This somewhat complicated affair extended from 1907 to 1911, and is perhaps too abbreviated in Miss Mackworth's version. Picasso does not exactly shine in the story, with which Apollinaire had little or nothing to do, though it resulted for him in the most absurd misapprehension. That was the accusation that Apollinaire himself had stolen *Mona Lisa* from the Louvre; a crazy Italian workman having somehow made away with it.

Apollinaire was imprisoned for a short time. The whole business dreadfully upset him, because he feared that be might be expelled from France. The experience was in itself unpleasant enough. He celebrated it in verse.

> Avant d'entrer dans ma cellule
> Il a fallu me mettre nu
> Et quelle voix sinistre ulule
> Guillaume qu'es-tu devenu . . .

In 1914 came the war. Apollinaire, not without difficulty, joined the French army, serving in the artillery as a driver and gunner; later as second-lieutenant of infantry. He was wounded in the head, probably the indirect cause of his death in 1919 from Spanish influenza.

Again, Miss Mackworth treats Apollinaire's war service with the grasp of reality. That he behaved with notable gallantry in volunteering is generally recognised; but she points out that, although many of the writers and artists who were his friends showed themselves no less willing to risk their lives, there was, among others, also a strong opposition to such a line of action. In other words, 'intellectual' courage was required of Apollinaire, as well as physical. This fact is sometimes overlooked.

Minor criticisms that might be made are that Gertrude Stein would probably not have liked to be described as 'studying the technique' of Joyce; and the Douanier Rousseau had already surely made some name as a public figure when Apollinaire discovered him.

Finally, I was struck by how often I was reminded of Wyndham Lewis's novel *Tarr*, which deals with artists in pre-1914 Paris. In spite of some careless proof-reading *Guillaume Apollinaire and the Cubist Life* is perhaps the best biography yet to appear about one of the greatest of French lyrical poets, and a man whose life offers all kinds of fascinating surfaces, cubist and otherwise.

Guillaume Apollinaire and the Cubist Life, 1961
Cecily Mackworth, *Daily Telegraph*
John Murray.

JULIAN GRENFELL

In attempting to define Julian Grenfell in a word or two, clichés spring to the mind – 'a Greek Hero', 'a latterday Elizabethan' – and, however hackneyed such labels may be, they are, including their less attractive implications, undoubtedly applicable to him. Nicholas Mosley has produced a remarkable book, well informed, unusual, enthralling not only as a biography but also as a picture of the times.

Mr Mosley, almost certainly wisely, devotes at least three-quarters of the book to Julian Grenfell's mother, Lady Desborough; so that in a sense the study is as much of her as of her son – or sons, because 'The Grenfells' were a composite legend, which survived to my own schooldays; though quite why people talked about them was not at that period clear to me.

Lady Desborough, née Ethel ('Ettie') Fane, came from one aristocratic family, and married into another one. She had been orphaned as quite a small child, and circumstances combined to make her an exceedingly attractive young woman (though not a great beauty), who became in due course a famous hostess and formidable personality. Although in one sense always happily married (her husband utterly engrossed in politics, athletics and bimetallism), she had a succession of lovers, who increasingly tended to be a great deal younger than herself. To what extent these immensely emotional affairs were also physical remains very uncertain in all but about two cases.

Lady Desborough kept an exquisitely embarrassing record of Julian Grenfell's childish sayings. It is perhaps largely a true record because he seems to have been an exceptional small boy in many ways – though after his death his mother was capable of adding a sentence or two to his letters or altering the description of a friend as a 'cockney genius' to 'he has a cockney accent'. She was in the highest degree competitive, so that her sons were expected to be first in everything, work and games – and they usually were that, or not far from it.

People who are very good at both work and games are by no means unknown; nor are people who have an overwhelmingly emotional relationship with their mothers. What makes Julian Grenfell exceptional is that he added an oddly dissatisfied, self-examining dimension to an ability to knock out an ex-stoker professional at boxing, or to jump a record fence (6ft 5in in South Africa) on a horse. He was interested in the arts in a more than amateur way, and an undoubted poet. Vis-à-vis his mother, he fought back, did not allow her to dominate him, and had love affairs which she often attempted to thwart.

Lady Desborough did more of her entertaining at their horse, Taplow, described by Sir Alan Lascelles as 'an ugly, overgrown villa furnished like a hotel', filled with 'the cream of the political and literary intelligentsia, with a constant leaven of brilliant young men whose mother she might have been'. She had that curiously restricted Edwardian literary taste (Gilbert Murray's Greek translations, Chesterton, Belloc) which was a more effective way of shutting out new writers and painters than a total philistinism.

It had been decided from the beginning that Julian Grenfell should enter the army. He made no objection to that profession (going first to Balliol), preferring a Dragoon regiment because 'steady and old-fashioned' rather than something 'more swagger', but admitting to leaving choice of regiment chiefly to his mother. He served in India and South Africa, enjoying the former, but getting very bored with the latter, where he was quartered in a hutted camp of great dreariness.

Grenfell's less appealing side is illustrated by the gusto with which he describes the forcible dosing with a lot of filthy medicines of a fellow subaltern, who had got drunk at a Sergeants' Ball. Combined with high spirits and terrific physical exertions were bouts of awful gloom and ill health; the last sometimes brought on by sheer over-training and starvation. He also suffered from brain-storms.

When the war came in August 1914, Grenfell was in France with his regiment the following month. Now he found himself in his element. He won a DSO with an act of great bravery that was obviously a very useful piece of work, too, from the point of view of checking snipers. To this period also belongs his best known poem, 'Into Battle'. He was hit in the head by a splinter of shell in May 1915, and died about ten days later. His brother, Billy Grenfell, was killed leading a charge the following July.

My only demur at Mr Mosley's treatment of all this is that I think he exaggerates the mood of almost frivolous romanticism which he attributes to this country's – indeed to all Europe's – going to war in 1914, nationalist and revolutionary interests, in Eastern Europe particularly, that welcomed war for reasons of *realpolitik*. The impact on England – which I can remember as a child – was certainly very different from what Mr Mosley seems to suggest at, say, a regular army station, where the appallingness of what was going to happen was not at all underrated, even if a good face was put on the situation.

At one moment Julian Grenfell seriously considered leaving the army, and becoming an artist in Paris. How would he have developed had he met people like the French poet Apollinaire, who was later also stimulated by being in the army and by war?

Julian Grenfell:
His Life and the Times of his Death,
1888–1915,
Nicholas Mosley, Weidenfeld.

1976
Daily Telegraph

ISAAC ROSENBERG

Although usually thought of as a 'war poet' – because killed in the war – Isaac Rosenberg (1890–1918) had many other sides to him. Had he lived, it is likely that this label would not have been attached to him permanently, as it was to Sassoon, or even up to a point is to Graves. His life is an odd and interesting one.

Rosenberg was the eldest son (the survivor of twins) of Jewish immigrants to England from Lithuania. His parents, strictly Orthodox, seem to have been fairly prosperous in Russia as builders and decorators, though the truth is hard to get at because his father was something of a fantasist. In England they were desperately poor, but possessed a certain degree of 'cultural' life.

The family gravitated to the East End of London. From his earliest childhood Rosenberg showed a talent for drawing. One of the most remarkable aspects of the story is that, by the time he was nineteen or twenty, he was moving in a group (mostly a year or two younger than himself) of young Jewish East-Enders who were to make a name for themselves. Of these Mark Gertler, the painter, and John Rodker, writer, translator, publisher, were the only two I can speak of from personal acquaintance, but obviously the intellectual standard obtaining was remarkably high.

Rosenberg never seems to have had much in common with his own family (there were five children), who more or less recognised from the start that he was a person apart, and loyally did their best to keep him going. He managed to get some sort of instruction in drawing, and, when he was fourteen, was apprenticed to learn platemaking and engraving. This was in the firm of Karl Hentschel, who was, incidentally, the original of Harris in *Three Men in a Boat.*

While copying an Old Master in the National Gallery, Rosenberg attracted the notice of a lady called Mrs Herbert Cohen, who made it possible for him to go to the Slade School of Art, then under Tonks, with a brilliant array of pupils. Although Mrs Cohen was not always an ideal patroness, in that she wished to influence Rosenberg's style, she did provide the opportunity which brought Rosenberg into contact with most of the livelier elements of London intellectual life, from Ezra Pound to Eddie Marsh.

For a time, though in dire poverty, Rosenberg kept going, as a painter. Then he went for a year to South Africa where he managed to exist. On the outbreak of war in August 1914, he returned to England. Just why he did this is obscure, because he had inherited from his parents, who were Tolstoyans, certain conscientious objections to fighting, and only intermittently (in some poems) seems to have been at all moved by patriotism.

My own feeling is that Rosenberg had a strong sense of being required to suffer. He joined the army – in which he remained a private, and had a fairly awful time – and saw active service until he was killed in April 1918, a few months before the Armistice.

Of these two accounts of Rosenberg's life, which inevitably cover much of the same ground, Jean Moorcroft Wilson's *Isaac Rosenberg: Poet and Painter* is decidedly the better. It contains the fuller selection of pictures as well. Dr Wilson tells the story in a straightforward way, and makes a successful effort to set out fairly Rosenberg's by no means easy character.

Jean Liddiard in *Isaac Rosenberg: The Half-Used Life*, weighs down her biography with sometimes rather naive disquisitions about the intellectual, social and political life of the period. She says: 'It is obvious that Rosenberg's difficulty was not the usual late nineteenth-century inability of poets to admit the reality of sexual impulses and their tangible concern with the flesh.' But surely, many late nineteenth-century poets talked of little else. What about all those bought red mouths?

Admittedly Rosenberg had a roughish time, but Miss Liddiard is absolutely determined that it should be a hard-luck story all the way; for instance, when Rosenberg picked up a rare Thackeray item on a Farringdon Road bookstall, she omits the information (given by Dr Wilson) that he sold it for £40.

It was perhaps a misfortune for Rosenberg that he was born capable of practising both the arts of painting and poetry. He was obviously a gifted painter, but not, one would say, a very interesting one. His poetry, on the other hand, although much influenced by the Romantics and Blake, is of great originality. It is separated from both the Georgians and the Imagists.

> A July ghost, aghast at the strange winter,
> Wonders, at burning noon (all summer seeming), . . .
> A frozen pool whereon mirth dances;
> Where the shining boys would fish.

This must, surely, have influenced Dylan Thomas, though I do not remember reading about Rosenberg as one of Thomas's foundations.

In physique Rosenberg was small (in the army he had to join a Bantam battalion), and his demeanour seems to have been a mixture of shyness and assertiveness. He had a kind of humour (not a characteristic of either Gertler or Rodker), but Dr Wilson points out that he lacked protective irony. Eddie Marsh was a sympathetic patron, but did not really understand the path poetry was by then taking, therefore rather a mixed blessing. Marsh was in any case shattered by the death of Rupert Brooke, whose poems Rosenberg thought 'like a perpetual Flag Day'.

Rosenberg designed the 40th Division's Christmas card for 1917, with a verse, a fascinating memorial to his army career.

Isaac Rosenberg: Poet and Painter, 1975
Jean Moorcroft Wilson, Cecil Woolf. *Daily Telegraph*
Isaac Rosenberg: The Half-Used Life,
Jean Liddiard, Gollancz.

JEAN-PAUL SARTRE

The existentialism of which Jean-Paul Sartre might reasonably be described as the high priest teaches, roughly speaking, that man finds himself in a frightful mess, a state he can pass through in almost total unawareness.

When man does realise the awfulness of his situation he is filled with a sense of absurdity and despair. Religion, philosophy, ordered morality are all merely methods of avoiding the issue; but some individuals, by a terrific act of will, manage to free themselves. They become 'committed'. This can only be effected by adherence to an extreme left-wing near-communism.

The Communists themselves have more than once disowned M. Sartre. That is not surprising, because it is certainly hard to see how his approach to life – of course ludicrously over-simplified above – does not often land him in a host of practical contradictions. One of these is, surely, that, looking back to the past, as he does in *Words*, the first volume of an autobiography, is in itself a form of decadence. However, that is M. Sartre's own affair. One must be grateful that he has done so, because this book about his childhood is unusual, immensely well observed, full of wit and acute self-examination.

The author's father was a naval officer who died young. His mother belonged to the Alsatian family of Schweitzer (Albert Schweitzer is a cousin), who had moved to France after the Franco-Prussian war. After her husband's death M. Sartre's mother went back to live with her parents. She was at once demoted to the status of an unmarried girl who had to be in by ten o'clock every night.

We suffer from many social ills in this country, which our publicists are never tired of holding up to censure. It is therefore a pleasure to draw attention to an infliction of which England is almost entirely free. We do not possess a high-minded, well-intentioned, scrupulously educated, totally self-satisfied *haute bourgeoisie*. That is something to be thankful for.

The English have often been blamed for being obsessed with their schooldays. Is childhood – and especially its element of grandparents – any less obsessive to the French? Again and again in French literature one gets back to childhood, even more to the horror of respectable bourgeois life.

Little Sartre knew nothing of his father, although he inherited from him a book called *Vers le positivisme par l'idéalisme absolu*, a work which, in the hands of a retired naval officer, probably boded no good for the future. He was brought up by his Schweitzer grandfather, who, as his grandson says, 'thought himself Victor Hugo'; Jean-Paul was the apple of his eye.

His family decided at an early age that Jean-Paul was a genius. In justice to them, a lot of people have said so since; but no doubt it was not the best way to bring him up, especially as this conviction was combined with a good deal of dodging the problem of education, as the boy was assumed to be so clever he scarcely needed any.

M. Sartre is exceedingly funny about all this, not letting anyone, including himself, off anything. There were dreadful educational revelations when he did go to school for the first time. Where has one read something like this before? Like, yet at the same time differently? Then all at once it comes – *Enemies of Promise* by Cyril Connolly. Since *Words* has been published, Mr Connolly himself has commented on this parallel, and, allowing for different circumstances, it is really remarkable. What, one wonders, would have happened if Sartre had gone to Eton, Connolly played in the Luxembourg Gardens?

At times the simplicity of characterisation attributed to the Schweitzer and Sartre relations seems a little too good to be true. Situations and relationships are rarely quite so clear cut as the way they are here represented. All the same, that does not take away from the vividness of the picture, which, in the Alsatian background, is a little reminiscent of the family meeting in André Malraux's *Les Noyers d'Altenbourg*, though approached of course in a very different mood.

M. Sartre's effective manner of reconstructing the atmosphere of his childhood by an incident is well illustrated by the occasion when he wrote a fan letter to Courteline, the comic writer and dramatist, especially known for his satires on civil servants:

> I doted on Courteline . . . My infatuation was thought amusing; care and attention enhanced it and made it into an avowed passion. One fine day my grandfather said to me casually: 'Courteline must be a good fellow. If you like him so much, why don't you write to him?' I wrote; Charles Schweitzer guided my hand and decided to leave a few spelling mistakes in my letter. Some newspapers reproduced it, a few years ago, and I read it with a certain annoyance.
>
> I ended with the words 'your friend-to-be', which seemed quite natural to me: Voltaire and Corneille were my familiars; how could a living writer refuse my friendship? Courteline refused it and did right: by replying to the grandchild, he would have got involved with the grandfather. At the same time, we judged his silence severely. 'I grant,' said Charles, 'he was a lot of work; but even so, you do answer a child.'

The tone of this and other anecdotes is admirably muted. However, when M. Sartre says, 'The bourgeois of the last century never forgot their first evening in the theatre . . . I challenge my contemporaries to tell me the date of their first experience of the cinema', I must take up the glove. Born the same vintage year as M. Sartre, the flickering screen of the Blue Hall, Edgware Road, *c.* 1911, is a very decided early memory.

Words is a good introduction to M. Sartre's study *Baudelaire*, because, having seen how he treats himself, the reader is in the right frame of mind to listen to his views on other people.

Here, a specifically existentialist approach is on the whole more obviously in evidence than in the autobiography. The line taken is that Baudelaire's troubles were almost entirely his own fault. He could perfectly well have avoided the Family Council, bankruptcy, syphilis, madness, early death. The fact was he really courted all these things.

Baudelaire, such is M. Sartre's thesis, positively required his stepfather. General Aupick; the rows with his publisher whom he threatened with physical assault never carried out; fear of damnation. He needed all the things that made up his unhappy life, in order to keep him going. He was not like Rimbaud, for example, who cashed out. Rimbaud did indeed set about making himself a life of quite a different sort.

All this is very closely argued and well worth reading. Yet the fact remains that, however unsatisfactory, existentially speaking, Baudelaire may have been, he could write the poems – and, paradoxically enough, it is probably General Aupick himself who would most heartily agree with what M. Sartre here has to say.

Words, Jean-Paul Sartre,
translated by Irene Clephane,
Hamish Hamilton.

Baudelaire, by Jean-Paul Sartre,
translated by Martin Turnell,
Hamish Hamilton.

1964
Daily Telegraph

DELMORE SCHWARTZ

The poets of the United States associated with the 1930s were on the whole younger than the similar group in this country, accordingly started later, but Delmore Schwartz (1913–1966) got off the mark early with praise from Eliot, Pound, Allen Tate, Wallace Stevens, lots more. By the time he was twenty he was making a name for himself.

Schwartz's beginnings provided a powerful myth which as material lasted him all his life, and from which he never deviated to any considerable extent: that is to say, the clash between the children of Jewish immigrants, who had been brought up as Americans, and their parents, born in Europe, or at any rate still affected by a European manner of looking at life.

Both Schwartz's parents were of Jewish-Romanian peasant stock. His father, arriving in New York at the age of thirteen, made a considerable fortune in real estate, lost most of it in the slump, then died in 1929. His son, expecting to inherit $100,000, found himself dependent on a hard-up and not very understanding mother.

That was an awkward situation in itself, and it came on top of a troubled childhood. The energy that made Schwartz's father a good businessman also expressed itself in keeping a string of mistresses. His wife greatly objected to this habit, but refused to divorce him.

On one occasion, when he was a child, Schwartz's parents woke him up in the night and told him he must choose between them; on another, when he was out driving with his mother and grandmother, his mother noticed her husband's car outside a road-house. Surmising that he was entertaining a lady there, and taking the seven-year-old Delmore with her, she dragged him from the dining-room. These were occasions to excuse Schwartz's tendency to bring up his childhood as reason for later erratic behaviour.

By the time Schwartz was seventeen he had done an astonishing amount of reading and, at an academic level, he remained almost to the end a fairly competent lecturer on philosophy. This does not mean that he always found earning a living easy. One of the interesting aspects of James Atlas's exceedingly readable biography, *Delmore Schwartz*, is conjecturing how Schwartz would have fared had he been a poet of the same sort of temperament working in this country. On the whole worse, I think.

Mr Atlas describes Schwartz's life with understanding, scholarship, humour. He says:

> For Delmore the religion of art differed from the more orthodox variants espoused by Baudelaire, Rimbaud and the new-Thomists who had such a considerable influence over him in one crucial respect: where for them art promised escape from the world, for Delmore it promised salvation in this world. His aspiration was to transmute the ordinary into something luminous and enduring, and only when he could no longer write did he begin the long descent into madness that culminated in his death.

Drink and sleeping-pills took their toll. 'It was Delmore's unhappy fate to be at once iconoclastic, irascible, egalitarian, and to find himself yearning for acceptance from the very society he so vociferously criticised.' Schwartz, who was by no means without humour, usually of a fairly macabre kind, noted of himself in his journal: 'Soon he succeeded in putting everyone in the wrong, the one art he had learned from his mother.'

Schwartz was married twice, both times unsuccessfully, but neither case altogether lovelessly. He wrote:

> All poets' wives have rotten lives,
> Their husbands look at them like knives
> (Poor Gertrude! Poor Eileen! No longer seventeen!),
> Exactitude their livelihood
> And rhyme their only gratitude,
> Knife-throwers all, in vaudeville,
> They use their wives to prove their will –

Unfortunately he was bedevilled with the desire to distinguish himself by an immense immortal work rather than such satirical flashes, and wrote a huge poem called *Genesis*, which, with a few exceptions, received a discouraging reception. Mr Atlas – whose opinion one would be inclined to accept – thinks *Genesis* does express quite vividly Schwartz's great theme, the drama of the Jewish immigration, but is best when not too ponderous, instead showing 'the fantastic wit and irony of his conversation'.

Schwartz's stories in the collection here (with a helpful foreword by Irving Howe) make an appropriate background for Mr Atlas's biography, because, even when writing in the Kafka manner, Schwartz was always autobiographical. The title story of *In Dreams Begin Responsibilities* (which appeared in the first number of *Partisan Review*) is the best. The Narrator is in a cinema watching a film that seems to be taking place in 1909. He sees his father and mother. They go out together. His father proposes marriage. His mother accepts. The Narrator jumps up in his seat and tells them not to do it. Evil will come. He is thrown out into the street, waking to find himself on the morning of his 21st birthday.

Schwartz can convey the atmosphere of young New York Jewish intellectuals endlessly talking, or the *Partisan Review* crowd giving a New Year's party, but his imaginative gifts were those of a poet, not a short-story writer or novelist. In most of his stories he notes in the margin of the manuscript who are the actual models, but only he himself comes to life. That does not mean the stories lack interest; while Mr Atlas's biography should certainly be read.

Delmore Schwartz: 1979
the Life of an American Poet, *Daily Telegraph*
James Atlas,
Faber with Farrar, Straus and Giroux.
In Dreams Begin Responsibilities and Other Stories,
Delmore Schwartz,
edited with an Introduction by James Atlas, Secker.

CONRAD AIKEN

I

Conrad Aiken is an American poet and critic too little known in this country. John Davenport gives a good account of him on the jacket of this book. It is perhaps a pity that these two or three biographical paragraphs have not also been incorporated in the text of the collected pieces.

Mr Aiken, friend and near contemporary of T. S. Eliot and, like him, a New Englander by upbringing, is a famous man in his own country; an early admirer of the French Imagists and one of the first poets to make use of the discoveries of psychoanalysis.

In *A Reviewer's ABC* we have over forty years of his critical writing. It is exceedingly lively and to the point. One may at times disagree, but nothing seems to date, and I strongly recommend it. Here is an opportunity of toning up one's own ideas about all kinds of writers by reading criticism of them offered from a different angle from that available in England. At the same time, the reader is given a vast plum-pudding of what a very intelligent American thinks about books.

There are over a hundred critical articles brought together, so that it is impossible to do more than draw attention to a few of the points made by Mr Aiken.

He is an admirer of George Moore; so much so that he can write:

> *The Brook Kerith* is fresher in my mind [than some other named Moore books] and I can say with unhesitating insanity that I believe it to be the finest novel in the English language, so far finer than any other I know that there is indeed no comparison.

I choose this as an opening, since it is an opinion with which few will be in sympathy, yet one does not in the least hold it against Mr Aiken. On the contrary, one feels it to be just that kind of individual peculiarity of taste which gives a firm basis to the best criticism.

There are several excellent articles on D. H. Lawrence, written between 1924 and 1929. In one of these Mr Aiken makes some very damaging quotations from Lawrence's book on American literature (which, even when it contains interesting stuff, is often phrased in an insufferable manner), commenting:

> In his passion for the direct, for the naked and unashamed, he insists on drawing our attention to the very odd clothes he wears (stylistically speaking) and, not satisfied with this, flings them off in a kind of dance of the seven veils.
>
> At bottom, this is nothing but intellectual vanity. Mr Lawrence is convinced that anything he says, no matter how he says it (and he tries perversely to make his saying of it as aggressively and consciously and peculiarly naked as possible), will be important.

In a different way, Mr Aiken offers much the same, equally relevant objection to Wyndham Lewis, to whose good points he is, of course, at the same time not in the least blind:

> One gradually becomes aware, as one reads these delightful and highly idiosyncratic stories, that Mr Lewis is adopting a role: he is, in fact, being forced into a special part. His awareness, whether vague or definite, of an audience there in the background – an audience waiting to see whether Mr Lewis is clever or not (and, if so, *how* clever) – is an unresting one and an uneasy one.
>
> It gives him a nervous manner, a high degree of self-consciousness; it takes away from him precisely that pure freedom of mind with which he appeared to be starting out.

Mr Aiken draws attention to Gertrude Stein's early interest, when still at the university, in automatic writing. He insists that there, contrary to her own assertion, are to be found the foundations of her 'experimental' work. Again, he is perfectly conscious of her undoubted abilities, at the same time pointing out that when it came to writing an autobiography she chose a perfectly normal manner of expressing herself.

Writing in 1927, he find Virginia Woolf oddly old-fashioned, a judgement of considerable acuteness. Katherine Mansfield delights him, however – a reputation that has perhaps not quite lived up to all he says.

Many other names are dealt with here, American and English, from Thomas Hardy to Dylan Thomas. *A Reviewer's ABC* makes a very good reading.

A Reviewer's ABC: Collected Criticism of Conrad Aiken from 1916 to the Present, W. H. Allen.

1961
Daily Telegraph

II

A notable poet, lively and perceptive critic, author of several novels, Conrad Aiken, now in his eighties, is one of America's most distinguished men of letters. At Harvard he was a contemporary of T. S. Eliot, and he belongs to that American infusion of the early 1900s which did so much in England to ginger up the arts.

Mr Aiken's family, came from the South, but after his parents died when he was a child, he was brought up on the Eastern Seaboard. There, when in his own country, he has usually lived, except for a time at Washington, when he held the Chair of Poetry at the Library of Congress. Much of his life was spent, however, in England, at Rye, a town which, as 'Saltinge', plays considerable part in this book.

Ushant is an autobiography told in the third person, in which many, though not all, names of people and places are changed. It appeared originally in the United States in 1952, but is now published over here for the first time, a key being provided to the concealed identities, i.e. 'the Tsetse' T. S. Eliot, 'Rabbi Ben Ezra' for Ezra Pound.

A great deal of the book is written in a style that, roughly speaking, derives from such writers as Sterne, Melville, James and Joyce. For those who value clarity in prose, the achieved result is little short of torture in an autobiography. There were, indeed, moments in the earlier pages when I thought I should not be able to hold out, and would have to surrender *Ushant* to a stronger man, or at least a seasoned addict of *Moby Dick*; but I clung on, in the end finding much of interest and enjoyment.

One of the most striking passages of Mr Aiken's book is that describing how an American Unitarian-minister-and-clairvoyant, encountered in a Guildford Street boarding-house, told his fortune when he was a young man.

This is a mere summary of what goes on for about a page and a half. It is a measure of Mr Aiken's acuteness that he reproduces what is, even if in a more literate form than offered in the first instance, so searching a description of his experiences and himself, not forgetting a certain failure of communication and some taste for the hackneyed. To be able to recognise this in oneself is no small achievement.

> Yes, you will write, but not too successfully. You have, I think, a streak of genius, maybe a little more than that, maybe a little less. . . . It is, I fear, in the communication that you will fail . . . a certain glibness and triteness will tend to spoil your excellent ideas . . . at least two or three times you will have the most wonderful of experiences . . . you will be bedevilled by sex . . . a dreadful, if delicious, pattern here awaits you . . . a quite extraordinary life, one that most of us should profoundly envy.

Mr Aiken is wonderfully good describing, without frills, how, beginning a five-hour railway journey, he wondered if he could endure sitting opposite a man with an appallingly mutilated face, and how the man himself, at the first stop when Aiken had planned if possible to move, got out, returning almost immediately and without a word handing Aiken a cup of tea.

The sex, of which there is a good deal, is perhaps less satisfactory, quite simply because sex is so exceedingly difficult to write about. Mr Aiken's first experience was with a tart outside the old Gourmet Restaurant on the corner of Wardour Street and Lisle Street. It made a great impression on him. One does not in the least want to underestimate that, but he does not manage wholly to escape sentimentality in relating it.

In rather the same way, several marriages and affairs get obscured in misty verbiage and all the chronic difficulties of dealing on paper with these happenings in a manner that tells the truth, yet avoids brutality. At the same time, the description, one of the quite straightforward ones in the book, of how the author decided to commit suicide while his wife was at the cinema, is excellently done. He turned on the gas, thinking there was plenty of time, to do the trick, but the programme was so awful at the local cinema that his wife came back an hour earlier than expected, so life was renewed.

The general picture of an impecunious, gifted young American in Edwardian London has many good moments, even if they have to be worked for. For example, the Eliot who appears in these pages is far from the bland great man of later years. Mr Aiken, recovering from an operation, his head full of ether, having written what the other poet considered an over-fulsome review of his latest work, received a page torn from the *Midwives Gazette* with certain words and phrases underlined, such as 'purulent offensive discharge'.

Eliot is also met coming out from the room where Harold Monro, of the Poetry Bookshop, was in the last stages of raving drunkenness and homosexual despair. Eliot remarked 'He doesn't seem quite himself'. There is also a telling record of the author sitting between Virginia Woolf and Katherine Mansfield, each breathing hatred of each other across him.

One's chief regret is that so much of what could probably be equally good in *Ushant* is obscure, but writers have to be what they are. Certainly no critic knows more about Mr Aiken than he does about himself, even when this knowledge is not communicated with complete success. He hints at something of the sort in one of his own poems:

> Walk with the world, upon my right hand walk,
>   Speak to the Babel, that I may strive to assemble
> Of all these syllables a single word
>   before the purpose of speech is gone.

Ushant: an Essay,
Conrad Aiken,
OUP.

1972
Daily Telegraph

BALLADS, ANCIENT AND MODERN

In his introduction to *The Faber Book of Ballads*, Matthew Hodgart defines a ballad as a 'song that comments on life by telling a story in a popular style'. This is a good rough and ready description, although of course, as Mr Hodgart points out, it covers many other forms of verse as well. At the same time, something pretty extensive is required to enclose even what is included in this volume.

Some of the Australian ballads and songs that occur in the two Penguin collections are to be found in the *Faber Book*, though sometimes with variant readings.

Mr Hodgart disallows what he calls the Great Tradition – 'serious' literature from Chaucer onwards – and he subdivides ballads into Town and Country; the latter, the traditional songs of the Borders, for example; the former, 'broadsides', very different in many ways from the country songs but also stemming from popular expression, rather than the production of an individual poet or writer.

Pondering these books, one does indeed begin to understand what a ballad is, although, with this grasp of its nature, a closer definition than Mr Hodgart's is no easier to come by. Meanwhile, various reflections are provoked.

One of these is the predominant part that self-pity plays in ballad production. True, Mr Hodgart gives us a few things such as Suckling's well-known poem in which are the lines:

> Her feet beneath her Petticoat
> Like little mice stole in and out.

But the cheerfully ironic tone of these verses, even though entitled 'A Ballade upon a Wedding', is in complete contrast to most of the material here.

On the whole, the ballad was at pains to point out how hard life is, and what bad luck the person or persons experienced who form its subject. The early, traditional ballads naturally treat of violence and bloodshed – with an occasional touch of the occult – and it is noticeable that they appear to be, most of them, the product of a given locality, the north of England and south of Scotland.

This strain of self-pity is particularly observable in the large number of ballads that stem from Ireland, dealing with the troubles of that country. At the same time, there are the broadsheets, no less full of self-pity, describing individual criminals of all sorts before execution.

Accordingly, a whole genus of ballad is found in Australia, the Irish convict there, as it were, combining two strong and separate streams of traditional self-pity. Russel Ward contributes an excellent introduction to *The Penguin Book of Australian Ballads*. He makes the important literary point – to be borne in mind in many other connections – that the 'typical' is not the same as the 'average': in this case that the typical Australian ballad does not deal with the average Australian.

In these Australian ballads and songs (to the latter, music is provided) one has to confess to getting a little tired of Ned Kelly the Bushranger. He is always enjoyable in the pictures of Mr Sidney Nolan, but in verse it is possible to have too much of him and his iron mask.

There is, indeed, a certain monotony about the squatters, swagmen and convicts, surprising in a country like Australia, with her really remarkable and lively achievements in all the arts. Why, for example, are there no ballads about Australian wine and Australian vineyards?

No doubt the answer must be sought in the special nature of the ballad itself. It is not a form of verse applicable to all subjects and all moods, but a specialised production, the result of certain relatively narrow, localised characteristics and circumstances.

Having raised objection to Suckling, it is possible then to have doubts about Bishop Corbet's 'Farewell, Rewards and Fairies'. However, the instructions given as to its rendering perhaps give this famous poem the necessary public nature required by a ballad: as the author added a note: 'To be sung or whistled to the tune of "Meadow Brow" by the learned to the tune of "Fortune".'

Two points are very evident: the enormous amount Kipling derived from the ballad; and, scarcely less, the amount that balladry might be said to owe to Kipling. His influence is noticeable in almost all ballads that postdate his work.

Among ballad-makers included in the Australian collection is the unfortunate Harry Morant ('the Breaker'), who was court-martialled and shot in the South African war for executing some Boer prisoners.

The story was not, I think, as noted here – that orders had been given for 'no prisoners to be taken'. The Boers in question were surely wearing captured British uniforms, and their liability turned on some technical question of what alterations, if any, had been made for this act to have been permissible. Kitchener was anxious that peace negotiations, then in progress, should not be prejudiced, and Morant, with another British subaltern, was convicted of murder. Morant obviously had some talent, and his own death, in itself, would have made a very suitable subject for a ballad.

J. S. Manifold, in his Introduction to *The Penguin Australian Song Book*, says that in the old days a strict etiquette prevailed specifying how local ballads should be learnt by a beginner. Having got them by heart, he was not immediately entitled to sing them.

Mr Hodgart points out that in the last few years folk-songs of every kind have become available through books, gramophone records and radio programmes. No tribes now are too fierce or too remote to fight off the folklorist and the tape-recorder.

The Faber Book of Ballads, edited by Matthew Hodgart, Faber.

1965
Daily Telegraph

The Penguin Book of Australian Ballads, edited by Russel Ward, Penguin.

The Penguin Australian Song Book, compiled by J. S. Manifold, Penguin.

DYLAN THOMAS

I

Every age has its myth-heroes, and Dylan Thomas is one of ours. It is therefore more than ordinarily difficult to place him in perspective.

When the memorial reading of his works took place at the Albert Hall after his death, people were streaming in there, some of whom would have been hard put to it to name half a dozen contemporary poets, certainly unable to give any account of their verse, or, indeed, Dylan Thomas's own.

This is particularly interesting because Thomas himself was, one might suppose, not at all marked out to capture contemporary popular imagination. His poetry was obscure, even in the eyes of a professional poetry critic like Richard Church, one of his early promoters. He was not in the smallest degree equipped for identification with popular politics, or fashionable social controversies.

The fact that he was Welsh started him off with no great advantage, especially as he lacked knowledge of the Welsh language, and did not indulge in any of that more superficial self-conscious 'Celticness' that always goes down well in England. It is true that, in fact, the roots of his own Welsh background lay very deep, but not until *Under Milk Wood* could they be said to have offered any lifeline to a public wanting to rationalise and simplify his personality.

Constantine FitzGibbon sets out here to do no more than narrate the circumstances of Dylan Thomas's life and death. He does not judge the poetry. His biography, extracts from which are appearing in the *Sunday Telegraph*, is an excellent job, piloting the reader through a jungle of painful and sordid incidents with good nature, energy, knowledge, and a grasp of what should be shown and explained.

Dylan Thomas was born in 1914, in Swansea, of Welsh-speaking farming stock. His father, a schoolmaster, to whom he was always devoted, had himself wanted to be a poet. He reacted strongly, however, against the Welsh language and Chapel standards. There had been a great-uncle, a bard, with notable talents. The setting is a classic one for producing what it did. Indeed, Thomas's story might be said to be classic in almost every respect.

Rather unusually bad at his books, except 'English' – and obviously very spoilt by his parents – he had a spell of working as a journalist locally, managing to get to London from time to time from the age of about eighteen onwards. The Sunday Referee poetry competitions, and other largely chance contacts, introduced him to literary circles almost immediately.

As Mr FitzGibbon's narrative progresses, it has to be admitted there was much to regret. To what extent some things could have been avoided is impossible, of course, to say, but it is hard not to feel that a certain degree of inner stiffening was lacking that would not in any way have reduced Thomas's force and powers as a poet.

As against that view, it is equally true that he endured a life of almost consistent poverty, discomfort and often disagreeable human relationships which would have made work impossible for a less forceful figure. To have behaved slightly better could have immensely reduced this martyrdom, attributable perhaps partly to an innate need for self destruction, partly to his taste for a somewhat journalistic 'image' of himself.

Certain notable points emerge from Mr FitzGibbon's book. One of these is Thomas's extraordinary early maturity as a poet. The essay on 'Modern Poetry' written when he was at Swansea Grammar School, only fifteen or possibly even fourteen, is a remarkable production for a boy of that age, however derivative. Many of his poems, too, were composed at this period, even though they may have been worked over later.

It is a commonplace that lyric poets tend to have written their best work by the time they are twenty-five, but few begin with such originality and assurance, even though an unexpected influence like Swinburne can be seen in Dylan Thomas's much later productions.

The other important point made by Mr FitzGibbon is that Dylan Thomas, so far from being bullied and cajoled into going to America to lecture – as has been suggested – was already making every effort to arrange something of the sort immediately after the war. He even thought of settling in America.

The fact is that at times the combination of ability to behave with practical competence when practical competence was required, combined with the total disregard for family, friends and even work, when in a less amiable mood, is a trifle disconcerting for those readers of this book who would prefer to avoid moral judgements.

When it came to working in a film unit during the war, or when he gave his lectures in America, Thomas is generally agreed to have done both exceedingly well. Having once allowed these bourgeois concessions, it is impossible not to feel that there were occasions when he could have pulled up his socks, practically speaking, without loss of dignity, personality or poetic status.

For example, his letters here quoted, on the whole, seem to me tiresome, pseudo-poetic, blarneying rigmaroles, that must have taken hours to write, time which could well have been devoted to a better – and often, one feels, less bogus – purpose. When he wanted to write a sensible letter he was perfectly capable of doing so, as may also be seen.

Dylan Thomas died in America in 1953. Myth has been particularly luxuriant round the story of his death, and it is true that its circumstances – the whole machinery of the lecture tour, the public side of a modern poet's life – has a macabre drama that gives some excuses for this. There is, perhaps, something of Poe's end about it, but could it have happened to Baudelaire or Rimbaud? Read Mr FitzGibbon and make up your mind.

The Life of Dylan Thomas, 1965
Constantine FitzGibbon, Dent. *Daily Telegraph*

II

The Americans, it must be admitted, have been at pains to build up the 'drunk' – especially the literary 'drunk' – as a figure of romance. You may get strongish whiffs of alcohol from time to time in Continental writers like Dostoevsky or Zola; but the real *mystique* of getting drunk for the sake of getting drunk belongs essentially to the literature of the United States. It is no doubt true that in the contemporary world dipsomania is the commonest expression of a personality at war with itself; and, as such, should receive proper attention in books. But it is also undeniable that in real life people who drink more than they can hold can become wearisome in the extreme.

However, anything suffered in the past from that ritualistic and insatiably violent devotion to the bottle that occasionally puts a particular strain on transatlantic friendships can now be considered a settled account. Dylan Thomas, as representative of our own tight little island, saw to that. If the Americans have ever boasted too freely their endemic literary alcoholics, they met in him an exotic example hard to surpass. The pages of Mr John Brinnin's absorbing book reveal every facet of the picture.

If I may be permitted a brief personal reminiscence, I ran across Dylan Thomas two or three times not very long after his first volume had been published. He came to dine. We talked again at the Surrealist exhibition of 1935, when I remember a pungent remark of his regarding a young lady who arrived there wearing a kind of fencing mask made of roses and carrying a false leg. In those days he seemed a modest, witty, gnome-like little creature, still fresh from 'the high hill of Wales', and said – with one lung – to have only a year or two to live. Obviously greatly gifted, he did not drink noticeably more than anyone else.

I never encountered him in that later period when he had achieved a public reputation of the rather unornamental kind which can only be a handicap to any writer's work. That stage had been in existence for some time when the present story opens.

Mr Brinnin had long been an admirer of Dylan Thomas's poetry, although they had never met until 1950, at Idlewild airport, after Mr Brinnin had arranged for Thomas a reading tour throughout the universities of America. This was followed by three subsequent tours; the last culminating in the poet's death.

It is the great merit of Mr Brinnin's book that he produces a human and sympathetic portrait without ever attempting in the smallest degree to modify the horror of the various American tours; or, indeed, the horror of the author's own visit to this country. Clearly Thomas's readings were often – perhaps even usually – admirably executed and greatly enjoyed. There was also the ever-present fear – only too frequently justified – that something would go badly wrong. Mr Brinnin gives his own convincing theories as to Thomas's torturing anxieties that caused him sometimes to behave so atrociously.

Could the situation at any stage have been improved? Mr Brinnin, I suspect, thinks there was never anything to be done. No doubt this is true. One has only to imagine Swinburne with a job in the BBC, or Beddoes lecturing in New England, to see that we have not yet solved the problem of how to deal with our poets. It was not a question of recognition; no one could reasonably have expected more public recognition than Dylan Thomas received. It was not a question of money; he was earning three times the stipend of Mr Brinnin himself, a don at an American university. Mr Brinnin, yielding nothing to his own personal friendship and admiration for the poetry, suggests that the interior machinery was lacking for transforming an early lyricism into a solid critical approach – the traditional progress of the poet. Thomas, he thinks, was not sufficiently interested in ideas. It was the knowledge of this weakness in his own intellectual equipment that he could never forget.

The rather facile wave of emotionalism at the time of Thomas's death among persons, many of them, not particularly notable for their everyday interest in art and letters, has cast an aura of journalism over the poet which somewhat obscures the field of serious criticism. That he was in a high class of his kind seems undeniable. The determinedly baroque language of much of his poetry becomes at times a trifle strained in spite of its brilliance – his simplicity is rare, but always delightful. We owe him at least a considerable debt for breaking free from the half-baked political pedantries of his immediate predecessors.

Mr Brinnin's book will no doubt be attacked for its plain speaking. It can hardly fail to present a painful side to many who were close to the poet. I like its realism. It certainly proves that, among Dylan Thomas's American hosts, the Biddles can take it.

Dylan Thomas in America, 1956
John Malcolm Brinnin, Dent. *Punch*

HISTORY IN VERSE

To present English history through the medium of a verse anthology is one of those simple ideas which, so far as I know, have never before been attempted. Kenneth Baker has produced an absorbing volume, providing brief notes from time to time. His selection is traditional and innovative, serious and funny, major and minor, sparing neither individual nor party, always giving both sides of the question.

It is essential that everyone in this country should be brought up knowing about Alfred burning the cakes, Lady Godiva, Robin Hood, et al; nor does it matter that Sir Richard Grenville probably fought fifteen Spanish ships rather than fifty-three, or that Magna Charta (I prefer Magna Carta or the Great Charter) was a somewhat class-orientated measure. To have heard of them is what matters.

We rightly begin with William Cowper's Boadicea, moving on via Tennyson's King Arthur to Caedmon's 'Hymn', *c.* 670, translated from Anglo-Saxon, the first poem in Old English. Here I make my one complaint of omission on the part of Mr Baker. If the first Old English poem, why not the first British poem, *c.* 600 (filling the gap between King Arthur and Caedmon)? *The Gododdin* (tr. Kenneth Jackson), describing a commando raid by three hundred Romano-Celts on Saxons at Catterick in Yorkshire, from which only three of the attackers returned, is a splendid piece of writing.

An extract from Keats's play about King Stephen was an excellent idea. In general Shakespeare, superb as he is on the Middle Ages, is not allowed wholly to dominate those centuries. For instance, Philip Larkin's 'An Arundel Tomb' finds a place, with several poets of the period who are new to me. Mr Baker (perhaps rightly) accepts Chaucer's Knight without mention of Terry Jones's theory (which slightly appeals) that Chaucer was satirical, all the engagements mentioned being fearful massacres.

The attack on Cardinal Wolsey by our first Laureate, John Skelton, is richly offensive. One is glad to find what is probably Wyatt's beautiful poem, 'The Death of Anne Boleyn', when she considers the various courtiers accused (improbably) of being her lovers. There is a characteristic verse by John Taylor (the seventeenth-century 'Water Poet'), explaining why Edward VI shillings were used for playing shove-halfpenny. Lady

Jane Grey is unexpectedly celebrated in a play by Webster. Queen Elizabeth herself is shown to be by no means a bad poet, her style slightly reminiscent of George Gascoigne.

In the seventeenth century Mr Baker really gets into his stride. He points out that, unattractive as James I may have been, we do owe to his reign the King James Bible and the First Folio of Shakespeare's plays. Samuel Butler deservedly crops up quite often (how good Butler's lines on Prynne, how up to date: 'This grand scripturient paperspiller/This endless, needless margin-filler'). Mr Baker has energetically dug out many interesting anonymous items, presumably from broadsheets.

'Ring-a-ring o' roses' celebrates the Great Plague, nosegays of herbs supposedly an antidote; sneezing, confirmation that the victim had been struck down. Milton, Marvell, Dryden, are represented by less obvious works as well as some famous ones. Also Rochester, whose own goings-on made him no less disapproving of vice.

The eighteenth century is better supplied with Jacobite verse than pro-Hanoverian; 'the wee, wee German lairdie' is a good comic example (anon) of the former. Swift's 'The Bubble' is an anti-Stock Exchange diatribe, assailing in verse an institution from which much verse of a ribald order has also emanated. We are apt to forget that the great actor-manager David Garrick wrote 'Heart of Oak' for a pantomime. 'The Lincolnshire Poacher' ('Oh! 'tis my delight on a shiny night') was a favourite song of George IV, who did not care for hunting and shooting.

The Victorian age opens with an unfriendly anonymous jingle about the Prince Consort ('My father lives at home/And deals in nice polonies'), soon followed by Wordsworth's Protest against the Ballot ('Forth rushed from Envy sprung and Self-conceit'). 'We don't want to fight, but, by Jingo, if we do' has managed to get a bad name, but was a perfectly healthy instinct, especially in insisting that the Russians shall not have Contantinople.

In the next century we find all the sort of people who grumbled at Jingo's complaining about the Munich agreement. John Davidson's 'Thirty Bob a Week' is included; Betjeman's 'Arrest of Oscar Wilde' – which, Mr Baker tells us, Lord Alfred Douglas found inaccurate – suitably closes the era.

In the twentieth century, history, as such, is less easy to pinpoint. Hardy marks the sinking of the *Titanic*; Kipling the Marconi scandal. The two wars have their respective poets. The Abdication is recorded in 'My Lord Archbishop, what a scold you are', the rebuke delivered to Lang, the Archbishop of Canterbury – 'how full of cant you are!' – and attributed to Anon, but surely written by Gerald Bullett. We close with Eliot's 'Little Gidding'.

All in all an admirable collection, giving rise to much thought; not least the reflection that poets dealing with contemporary events, if often the scourges of hypocrisy, equally often lack immunity from that failing themselves.

The Faber Book of English History in Verse, edited by Kenneth Baker, Faber.

1988
Daily Telegraph

PORTRAITS OF POETS

In a recent television series portraying Sir John Betjeman one sequence showed the unexpected arrival of eight or nine fellow poets come to congratulate the Laureate on his seventieth birthday.

Suppose the soundtrack had not been working and a chance viewer, knowing none of those concerned by sight, had switched on. Would poets and poetry have been the immediate thought? Might this not be a deputation of local officials come to break gently to a distinguished resident that a compulsory purchase order had been issued to enable the new bypass to be routed through his house; or the committee of the Dingley Dell Golf Club arrived to deliver a testimonial to their president after fifty years' membership?

There is indeed no earthly reason why poets should look poetic: some of them have; some have not. David Piper's book (based on his Clark Lectures) throws a great deal of light on this subject which turns out to be well worth examining and is made highly enjoyable by Sir David's scholarship and humour.

The first English poet of the top rank to be represented is Chaucer, in a fifteenth-century manuscript, where he appears more like himself, in his capacity as Controller of Customs, than poet. Even more so in another picture about a hundred years later, which shows him as decidedly plump, standing beside the Chaucer coat-of-arms.

The humdrum appearance of the author of *The Canterbury Tales* does not seem to have worried posterity much, but Shakespeare's image has caused fearful heart-burnings. Sir David uses the Shakespeare theme as a kind of leitmotif to his narrative, doing this to great effect.

There are only a couple of certainly authentic portraits of Shakespeare; the Droeshout engraving on the title page of the First Folio and the memorial bust in Stratford Church. Both these have been submerged in floods of abuse. Even Sir David, at heart a romantic (who agrees they evidently indicate the same man), feels a little badly about them.

Admittedly the Droeshout is a rotten engraving, and the bust is by a far from first-rate sculptor, but are they as hopeless as all that? The Droeshout depicts an unusual, intelligent, melancholy face, which is much more striking than innumerable later fanciful efforts to brighten it up. Sir William Empson, himself a poet, has called the Stratford bust 'Evelyn

Waughish', but might one not rather say Max Beerbohmish? Anyway not a negligible personality. There have been complaints that he looks like a successful businessman, but Shakespeare seems to have been by no means incapable on the business side of life, so why not?

We can only glance at a few of the poets considered here, many of whom deserve comment. They are apt to fall into those who took a good deal of trouble to be painted or sculpted as they would like, and those who did not much care. On the whole the most poetic-looking ones also took the most trouble, like Donne, obviously something of a film star in youth, who had himself carved in his shroud in later life, when he looks a trifle like Lord Olivier as Lear.

For being thoroughly humdrum, Browning's portrait by R. Lehmann in 1884 goes as far as any great poet's reasonably could, because the photograph of T. S. Eliot in a bowler hat suggests all sorts of under-currents in the poet's expression. Wyndham Lewis's drawing of Edith Sitwell in the National Portrait Gallery seems to me perhaps the best drawing Lewis ever did, and probably the best portrait of Edith Sitwell, though Guevara's, in which the chair seems to be sliding from the floor, has both charm and period feelings.

Thomas Hardy remarked of a drawing by Augustus John: 'I don't know whether it's like me – but it's what I feel like.' The latter is obviously an important point where poets are in question, and many painters have tried to achieve that, often with poets long dead. Tennyson was clearly a rewarding subject, and the Watts oil painting side by side with the Julia Margaret Cameron photograph should not be missed.

Pope, on the other hand, handicapped by small size and awkward body, was clearly interested in making the best of things in a series of portraits. There is a remarkable picture of Mathew Prior without a wig. His career in diplomacy obviously left a lasting mark on Prior, making him seem the conceited Foreign Office official of all time, though in fact, even if he was an efficient diplomat, the poem 'Jinny the Just', for instance, shows quite another side of him.

Byron was of course by far the most romantic of romantic poets, but although there are many portraits of him, none of them conveys as much as d'Orsay's light-hearted sketch, taken at an off-duty moment. Sir David rightly regrets that Byron never sat to Lawrence, who might have laid it on thick, but would undoubtedly have given us something memorable.

Apparently Rupert Brooke himself suggested the well-known photo-graph displaying the elegance of his throat. What a pity we do not have one of Brooke in uniform and one of Wilfred Owen intended to indicate how good-looking he was, rather than the other way about.

Of the imaginary pictures of poets *The Death of Chatterton* is probably the best known, painted by Henry Wallis with George Meredith as model. The painter subsequently ran away with the novelist's wife. Wallis also painted a hilarious picture of the Stratford bust of Shakespeare (which Blake thought not too bad) actually being carved.

There is an immense amount of interesting stuff in *The Image of the Poet*, but Sir David is kinder than I should be about Picasso's horrible scribble of an imaginary Shakespeare which adorns a paperback series of the Bard's plays.

The Image of the Poet:
British Poets and their Portraits,
David Piper, Clarendon Press/OUP.

1983
Daily Telegraph

PART TWO

The Artists

SELF-PORTRAITS OF PAINTERS

This study of self-portraiture in drawing is tackled in an amusing even eccentric manner and is no routine collection of old favourites like Leonardo da Vinci or Vincent van Gogh, though both of them appear. Not only are quite minor painters considered but some who, professionally speaking, were not painters at all.

In his Introduction to the book, David Piper, director of the Ashmolean, and former director of the National Portrait Gallery, writes illuminatingly of the peculiarities of self-portraiture and of the tendency of painters – something many people must have noticed among artists known to them – to make the sitter resemble the painter himself, if not too utterly different in feature.

Mr Piper also emphasises that the self-portraitist, forced to use a mirror – none of us knowing what we look like except in reverse – to some extent necessarily enters an Alice-through-the-Looking-Glass world.

Together with the portraits chosen, Joan Kinneir provides a page or more of text to give some idea of the individual artist's nature. This may vary from, say, a letter to a friend written by Gwen John (with a nice drawing), to a newspaper extract about the row in 1908 regarding the sculptures on the British Medical Association Building carved by Jacob Epstein (not at his best as a draughtsman).

The artists are arranged in order of the age at which each made his or her picture. Thus we begin with Albrecht Dürer, a silverpoint of extraordinary skill executed at the age of twelve or thirteen, and end with Hokusai at eighty-two or eighty-three, full of vitality, and expressing the hope that he might become a really accomplished draughtsman at the age of a hundred and ten.

In the early age group comes a moving self-portrait illustrated here, done in black printing ink on newspaper, by Michael Biggins in 1969, then aged fourteen. He came from Doncaster, and when efforts were made to get him into an art school his parents did not reply, and he has been lost sight of. For a boy with no formal training the head is certainly powerful. Perhaps he will turn up again one day.

Even more disturbing, though in a different manner, because manifestly belonging to the genre of art that emerges from such a source, is the self-portrait of Franz Pohl, drawn in coloured crayon in 1918, at the age of fifty-three or fifty-four in a psychiatric hospital. Pohl, who died a couple of years later, was a locksmith, also apparently with no art-school training.

Another – and more sinister – self-portrait, done in pencil this time in a psychiatric institution in 1974 at the age of twenty-four or twenty-five, is that of Alexander Kalugin. Kalugin was confined there by the Soviet authorities as an 'avant-gardist painter' – and for no other reason. The delicate drawing here – somewhat in the manner of Chagall – shows Kalugin in his cell. The text, an interview, describes his persecution by the KGB. The 'plain-clothes art critics', as they are caustically termed in Russia, accused him of imitating Salvador Dalí, a splendid comment on the knowledge possessed by official art critics in the Soviet Union.

In this area of avant-garde portraiture, bordering on caricature, is the dry point of Masuo Ikeda, born in Manchuria of Japanese parents. It is called *Myself, Staring at Me*, and was done in 1964 at the age of twenty-nine or thirty. Ikeda was repatriated to Japan after Hiroshima and tried to earn a living as an artist in Tokyo. The relevant text is an extract from what sounds an extremely lively autobiography.

Among compulsive self-portraitists was Aubrey Beardsley (1872–1898). Here we are given a no-nonsense head and shoulders, pen and ink on off-white paper, not one of those in strange fancy dress, for instance, that fastened by a tasselled cord to a statue of Priapus.

Cézanne did a striking pencil drawing – on off-white paper – of himself at the age of about forty, perfectly academic so far as it goes, though immensely skilful. Odilon Redon, on the other hand, even if he does not let himself go in his most impish manner, does suggest in a charcoal and black crayon self-portrait, towards the end of his forties, that half-humorous fantasy of which he was master.

There are four crayon drawings of Matisse, done at the age of sixty-nine, and the artist himself comments on them:

> These drawings seem to me to sum up observations that I have been making for many years on the characteristics of a drawing, characteristics that do not depend on the copying of natural forms, nor the patient assembling of exact details, but on the profound feeling of the artist before the objects which he has chosen, on which his attention is focussed, and the spirit of which he has penetrated.

Naturally one could comment on many more of the artists illustrated in this enjoyable volume. If there had been more room a slightly larger assembly of female painters might have been included, as these were always inclined to do pictures of themselves – but perhaps paintings rather than drawings.

The Artist by Himself: 1980
Self-Portrait, Drawings from Youth to Old Age, *Daily Telegraph*
edited by Joan Kinnier,
introduced by David Piper, Elek.

THE BAYEUX TAPESTRY

A sense of the past – like being musical or playing a good hand at cards – is one of those gifts granted to some and withheld from others; but one would have to be unusually tone-deaf to the appeal of history to visit, without some faint stirring of interest, that room at Bayeux in the former Bishop's Palace round which is displayed the Bayeux Tapestry. Here is the story of the Norman invasion of England in a strip cartoon 230 feet long by 20 inches wide, constructed within thirty years of the event. It is a work of propaganda, of course, but propaganda that has taken art into close alliance.

Views of the invasion vary according to fashions in history. One school has regarded the Normans as noble paladins, French – but not too French, owing to their Nordic blood – who introduced into this country, with many other good things, magnificent architecture and a taste for law and order. At the other end of the scale the Normans have been denounced as a miscellaneous gang of ruffians from all over Europe who combined under William the Bastard to descend upon a peaceful and more civilized country to plunder and dispossess.

The romantic anti-romanticism of contemporary taste tends to prefer the latter opinion. Simple Faith is now rated above Norman Blood. The former is certainly easier to claim, at least from the first phase of the immigration, since only fifteen names survive of those known for certain to have fought at Hastings; to which five may be added, established as personnel of the Duke's army, very likely to have been at the battle. They were probably seven thousand men in all: a small division, or perhaps two brigade groups. Harold's army seems to have been rather larger, but must have been still weary from its recently completed forced march of two hundred and fifty miles in twelve days.

The editors of this admirable volume (which reproduces the entire length of the Tapestry, including some excellent detail in colour) somewhat pander to a nationalistic view of the episode by calling the defending force 'the English'. Any other translation of 'Angli' was perhaps felt to be cumbersome, but this label rather weights sympathy against the Normans by implying a sense of modern nationality that could hardly have existed.

The fact was that William had quite a colourable claim to the throne of England; at one moment Edward the Confessor had fully intended him to succeed. The Tapestry is much concerned in the earlier sequences to prove this, showing Harold not only swearing on the relics that he would not stand in William's way but also fighting in Brittany as William's 'man'.

Why did Harold allow himself to fall into William's hands on this occasion? It seems most improbable that as the Tapestry indicates he went over to Normandy of his own free will. More likely he was shipwrecked as tradition has suggested.

The Saxons are shown with moustaches: the Normans, clean shaved. The whole representation is of extraordinary liveliness, not in the least unsophisticated. On the contrary, there is throughout the narrative design not only a rhythm and complete conviction of approach but also an underlying feeling of violence and sinister intrigue.

Two Norman knights, Wadard and Vital, are portrayed individually ('*Hic est Wadard*'), both to be found later with grants of land in Domesday Book. One incident remains wholly obscure: that captioned 'Where a certain clerk and Ælgyva'. The tonsured cleric seems to be pulling the lady's nose or adjusting her headdress. This happens during Harold's period in William's hands. Very few women appear in the Tapestry, but many horses. The bearded and trousered dwarf holding the horses in one of these early sequences should not be missed.

The borders of the Tapestry are of great charm. They are on the whole made up of mythological beasts, interspersed with occasional naturalistic incidents, including what Professor Wormald designates some 'mildly erotic' figures. The editors incline to think that these trimmings represent merely that light-hearted, disorganized approach to decoration so often to be seen in medieval ecclesiastical carving. One wonders. The Bayeux Tapestry is so packed with the history and psychology of the moment when the Dark Ages were ending that one is unwilling to discard any of it as a matter of chance.

The Bayeux Tapestry: A Comprehensive Survey, 1957
Sir Francis Stenton, Simone Bertrand, *Punch*
George Wingfield Digby,
Charles H. Gibbs-Smith, Sir John Mann,
John L. Nevinson
and Francis Wormald,
Phaidon.

THE HIGH RENAISSANCE

These two admirable books deal with the art period much out of favour among the *avant garde* in the earlier years of this century. For example, in 1914 Wyndham Lewis wrote: 'Michelangelo is probably the worst spook in Europe, and haunts English art without respite'; and, in the following year, 'Buonarroti is my *Bête-Noir.*'

I suppose it would be reasonable to describe Picasso as the 'worst spook' today. Perhaps even that state is passing. By 1935 Wyndham Lewis had relented sufficiently towards the High Renaissance to write of Michelangelo:

> . . . there again you have a poet of the first rank; not in output to be compared, certainly, with the immensely industrious painter and sculptor . . . There are people to be found, even – in spite of the marvellous abundance and facility of his creations in the plastic arts . . . – who prefer Michelangelo the poet. On the other hand, although the poems prove him to have been the intellectual peer of Dante, the poems alone would not have given him in literature the place occupied by Michelangelo Buonarroti in the art of painting.

Sir John Pope-Hennessy, in *Italian High Renaissance and Baroque Sculpture,* a revised edition of a work that first appeared in 1963, points out that Michelangelo was the first artist in history to be recognised by his contemporaries as a genius in the modern sense. Michelangelo and Bernini dominate Sir John's vigorous and readable study, though many lesser masters are also considered. Amongst a mass of absorbing illustrations, one might pick out the grotesque second-century head of Commodus, showing, for purposes of comparison, what the Romans could do when they wanted to be rococo, and, also in a light-hearted mood, Bernini's jolly, sexy *Truth Unveiled.*

This business of lesser masters is brought to the fore strongly in S. J. Freedberg's *Painting in Italy, 1500 to 1600.* Although the number and variety of High Renaissance Italian painters of the first rank is staggering, the phrase 'High Renaissance' brings a certain type of painter to the mind: Leonardo, Michelangelo, Raphael, Giorgione, Titian, Correggio, Tintoretto, Bronzino, and so on.

Professor Freedberg deals thoroughly with these masters, and a lot more, but his unusually well chosen illustrations of the lesser men prompt the thought that at the time – to the average amateur of painting – the High Renaissance may not have been quite what it is to us. At least, without a few of the top geniuses, things might have taken a very different turn.

To begin with, a great many bad pictures, which High Renaissance picture-lovers had to endure in their own day, must have happily perished. More important, if the great men had not settled what painting was to be, lesser painters could have accepted quite other influences. For example, Polidoro's *Noli Me Tangere* (*c.* 1525, S. Silvestro al Quirinale, Rome) is in the style of landscapes painted by Ancient Roman artists. The skill of these painters has only been appreciated comparatively recently. It might well have swept the board without the influence of, say, Leonardo.

Again, Bartolommeo Passarotti's *Butcher's Shop*, in the Galleria Nazionale, Rome, obviously Flemishly influenced, is an attempt to get away from 'Mannerism' – though Sir John Pope-Hennessy feels this label has by now lost its descriptive force – and paint something that almost foreshadows Hogarth. Passarotti had a special line in butcher's shops, and, if you think of Hogarth in one direction, you can easily think of the Royal Academy in another.

On the other hand, Girolamo Macchietti's *The Baths of Pozzuoli* (1570, Palazzo Vecchio, Florence) immediately recalls the Belgian Surrealist painter Paul Delvaux; though it is true that the bathers at Pozzuoli are all men – of a fairly epicene kind – and M. Delvaux tends always to paint women. It would be interesting to know if the Macchietti/Delvaux influence is already established.

Also among somewhat lesser-known painters, Il Rosso's *Dead Christ Supported by Angels* (Museum of Fine Arts, Boston) might be mentioned; Baccafumi's oddly Blake-like *Marriage of the Virgin* (Oratorio di S. Bernardino, Siena); and Bertoia's *Sala del Bacoi* (1566, Palazzo del Giardiro, Parma), which might have been painted during the French Directoire.

Where better-known names are concerned, Professor Freedberg has very sensibly not excluded old favourites like Veronese's *Alexander and the Family of Darius* in the National Gallery, but he has successfully avoided banality in his examples. Raphael's *Three Graces* (1517, Villa Farnesina, Rome), for instance, comes freshly to the eye, as do Giorgione's *Judith* (1504, Hermitage, Leningrad), Titian's *The Adultress Brought before Christ* (1509, Art Gallery, Glasgow), and Bellini's *Feast of the Gods* (1514, National Gallery, Washington), together with his very enjoyable *Drunkenness of Noah* at Besançon, where there is also an unexpected *Pietà* by Bronzino.

This concentration on the plates does less than justice to Professor Freedberg's scholarly letter-press. Armed with his book and Sir John Pope-Hennessy's, one need not fear being caught out about High

Renaissance painting or sculpture and may learn about those subjects in the pleasantest way.

Painting in Italy, 1500 to 1600, 1971
S. J. Freedman, Penguin. *Daily Telegraph*

Italian High Renaissance and Baroque Sculpture,
Sir John Pope-Hennessy, Phaidon.

II

Sir Roy Strong's *Art and Power* carries further his earlier work *Splendour at Court* (1974), which dealt with the complex and fascinating aspects of the spectacular entertainments put on by the princes of the Renaissance, a subject on which Sir Roy is a recognised authority.

Their prodigal public performances derived in many respects from Roman Triumphs, and were themselves forerunners of, say, the Lord Mayor's Show and Trooping the Colour. If the last might be held to be too specifically military for inclusion, in spite of the mesmeric and theatrical formality of the parade's music and movement, it must be remembered that the Renaissance festivals also drew on a medieval military tradition of tournaments and State entries. On the purely showbiz side these pageants and masques gave us ballet, opera, even the proscenium arch and the moveable scenery of the theatre today.

The practical purpose of all this lavish expenditure was to glorify the ruler, and establish his (in the case of Queen Elizabeth I, her) 'image' in the public mind. Sir Roy's theme is that these spectacles are perhaps the most consummate example of the arts, by the use of emblems, being called in to emphasise and define governmental power and aims. The horrible little facetious drawings with which officialdom nowadays sometimes embellishes its explanatory pamphlets might be likened to an enormously decadent example of the use of the emblem for the ignorant, with the aim of explaining and instructing in a tasteless age.

To make things easy for those who were none too bright was far from the method of the Renaissance, even if the display was intended to teach a simple lesson in who was ruler and what that implied. The festivals of the Emperor Charles V, Catherine de Medici in France, the Grand Duke Ferdinand in Tuscany and the court masques of Charles I in this country, were often obscure to a degree in the allegories they used. Some of the greatest artists, from Leonardo da Vinci to Inigo Jones, and Brunelleschi to Rubens, contributed to what Sir Roy calls these 'humanist dreamlands'.

The Roman architect and author Vitruvius (*c.* 40 BC), who had an immense influence on the Renaissance approach, wrote a propos staging:

> There are three kinds of scenes, one called tragic; second, the comic; third, the satyric. Their decorations are different and unlike each other in scheme. Tragic scenes are delineated with columns, pediments, statues, and other objects suitable to kings; comic scenes exhibit private dwellings with balconies and views representing rows of windows after the manner of ordinary dwellings; satyric scenes are decorated with trees, caverns, mountains, and other rustic objects delineated in landscape style.

One has from this an impression of tragic scenes done against backgrounds like those of the Surrealist painters Chirico or Delvaux; comic scenes against the old Harlequinade row of shops, or Aldwych farce front hall; satire (by which Vitruvius no doubt meant plays about nymphs and satyrs rather than, say, those of Alan Bennett) against a Salvator Rosa canvas. The interesting thing is that, anyway for the first two, this view is not all that out of date – for instance, Shakespeare productions on television.

The Renaissance changed the outward face of imagery and style by bringing in classical allusions – a king would be Jupiter, a queen, Diana – but much of the thought remained medieval. Richard II had watched knights led in by silver chains held by ladies mounted on palfreys; and a visiting German nearly two hundred years later described scenes at a tournament in which the combatants' servants were 'disguised like savages, or like Irishmen, with hair hanging down to the girdle like women . . . who addressed the Queen with a ludicrous speech, making her and her ladies laugh'.

Ballet, says Sir Roy, is the most elusive of all festival forms to recapture. There was then no form of choreographic notation, while its scenery and costumes, with music and poetry, survive today as vividly as in their own time. The ballet numbers of the court masques were particularly associated with Ben Jonson and Inigo Jones, one of many brilliant features of the period of Charles I ended by the Civil Wars. It is hard to exaggerate Charles's part in bringing superb pictures to the country; and the other arts were no less well represented in his reign.

Sir Roy has some interesting comments to make on the famous quarrel between Ben Jonson and Inigo Jones. He thinks that the row cannot be defined purely as the visual against the verbal elements of the masque. On the contrary, both men had very much the same ideas as to the court seeing itself in the mirror of art. They could not however agree on the presentation of what Jonson called 'removed mysteries'.

The Renaissance aspirations to universal harmony and order through the arts have much to teach, and the technicalities of the festivals, their staging and décor, are well indicated here by the illustrations.

Art and Power: Renaissance Festivals 1450–1650, 1984
Roy Strong, Boydell Press. *Daily Telegraph*

III

In 1917 T. S. Eliot could write: 'In the room the women come and go/Talking of Michelangelo.' Even a decade later, that would have been unlikely, or, if they were talking of Michelangelo, the women would probably be denigrating him for having been responsible for the disagreeable sculptural romanticism of Rodin. In the 1920s and 1930s Michelangelo, whatever his greatness, represented all that the fashion of the period most deplore.

This year is the 500th anniversary of Michelangelo's birth. He lived to eighty-nine, dying the year that Shakespeare was born. Howard Hibbard gives an excellent account of his life; clear, well illustrated, conveying a convincing impression of his personality, without unduly dwelling on his sexual proclivities (he was admittedly homosexual, but deeply religious, possibly exercising great self-control). He shows, too, what a literally epoch-making figure he was.

Michelangelo came from a comparatively impoverished family, but one fairly high up in the social scale – unusual for an artist in Italy of the period. His genius was incredibly precocious, but even when his name was famous he had difficulty in making ends meet. Finally he became a rich man, and, like Shakespeare, greatly appreciated the advantages attained. His own circumstances of birth, allied to material success, made him a crucial figure in raising the position of artists everywhere.

He was intensely melancholy by temperament, and in his letters reminded me more than once of Delacroix's diary, which I happened to be re-reading. Then, by coincidence, at the place I had reached in the diary a friend of Delacroix quoted an opinion of Michelangelo, already noted by me in Mr Hibbard's book: 'In my opinion painting is to be considered the better the more it approaches relief, and relief is to be considered the worse the more it approaches painting.'

This passion of Michelangelo's for human anatomy – his use of it being one of the ways in which he broke the bonds of traditional form – can be seen particularly well in the sculptural style of the figures in the frescoes of the Sistine Chapel. (Strange as it may seem, these were an unwelcome commission to the painter himself.) Those muscular, intensely individual studies of the human body are the beginning of Mannerism, a later stage of the High Renaissance, and one of its developments investigated in Michael Levey's new paperback study *High Renaissance.*

Mr Levey's admirable book, dates Mannerism at about 1520, when Michelangelo was in his middle forties. Mannerism has been called 'the stylish style'. In it can be seen some of the feelings that were later to burst out as Baroque. The transition from 'High Renaissance' to 'Mannerism' is, of course, a delicate one, and no hard and fast line can be drawn.

Mr Levey is particularly good in relating the other arts of the period to painting and sculpture. In this connection he remarks: 'What finally separates the High Renaissance from the periods of art which had preceded it is that, at last perhaps, an artistic style and a civilisation are in full accord. The arts – writing, fighting and gardening, as well as the visual arts and music – were not merely received in society but became part of its fabric.'

In the North, Dürer (who exchanged work with Raphael) was the first artist of the period to produce self-portraits in both painting and writing. In short, the anonymous craftsman of the Middle Ages had finally come to an end. And there was another development. When a tomb was put up in Naples to the poet Sannazaro, the inscription was a classical one – the two guardians, Apollo and Minerva; the central relief, Pan, Marsyas, Euterpe and Neptune.

One of the most interesting aspects of Mr Levey's book is the attention he devotes to Sir Philip Sidney's views on painting. One is apt to think of Sidney as a poet, an idealised public figure of the time, rather than a man of keen intelligence. The taste of the time for painting (except perhaps for painters themselves) was concentrated merely on identification and likeness in the crudest sense. Sidney's comments in his *Apologie for Poetrie* show how wide of the mark that was for a patron like himself.

He wrote: 'As betwixt the meaner sort of Painters (who counterfeit only such faces as are sette before them) and the more excellent, who, having no law and wit, bestow that in cullers upon you which is fittest for the eye to see . . .'. When Sidney was in Venice he had himself to choose between Tintoretto and Veronese for his own portrait. He plumped for Veronese (rightly, I think), but the picture is now lost.

Mr Levey lingers a moment over Shakespeare's taste in painting. The prime version of Titian's *Venus and Adonis* (now in the Prado) was, as it happens, forwarded to England by Philip II, when he married Bloody Mary. That was, of course, before Shakespeare's birth, but the picture appears to be the first treatment, either in painting or literature, in which Adonis is shown as being reluctant – the attitude Shakespeare gives him in his own *Venus and Adonis*. It is certainly tempting to think some connection of ideas may have existed.

Michelangelo, 1975
Howard Hibbard, Allen Lane. *Daily Telegraph*
High Renaissance,
Michael Levey, Pelican.

ANTHONY VAN DYCK

There has not been a comprehensive study in English of van Dyck's life and work since 1900 – Lionel Cust's – which as Christopher Brown points out was not altogether sympathetic to the painter. Mr Brown's own well-handled and informative book is almost a shock in its relegation to the right proportion of the van Dyck the name inevitably conjures up. The vision of melancholy Cavaliers and ladies, all seeming to accept the doom that hangs over them, was a comparatively late development (van Dyck was only forty-two when he died), and the majority of his earlier pictures express the preoccupations of an almost excessively devout man, rather than a romantically minded courtier. The two different emotional approaches could obviously find fairly easy accommodation in the same personality.

Anthony van Dyck (1599–1641), younger son of a prosperous Antwerp silk merchant, had remote connexions through his mother with several other painters, the Brueghels for instance, and was apprenticed to Rubens (some twenty years older than himself) not long after coming of age. In short, there was never any doubt about van Dyck's talent. He settled in London in 1632, drawn there by that superlative patron of the arts King Charles I; married one of the Ruthven family; transformed English painting, indeed the whole aesthetic point of view.

It is generally supposed that van Dyck was vain, though if painting seductive self-portraits is to be the basis of the accusation not many painters would wholly avoid that imputation. Off the cuff I can think only of Edward Lear and some (not all) by Wyndham Lewis that avoid some degree of self-flattery, though no doubt others can be suggested. What is perfectly clear is that van Dyck loved Court life, and presented a vision of the Caroline Age that has imposed itself on history.

Titian was van Dyck's admired example, one always before him (also King Charles's favourite painter), and since El Greco is thought to have been Titian's pupil, that may be the explanation of the curiously Greco-like air of van Dyck's *Moses and the Brazen Serpent.* On the other hand, had van Dyck seen paintings by Greco? Possibly he had. Alternatively, since this picture is at the Prado, have we here merely a question of Spanish taste in buying what might be called a Spanish-type picture? This is an interesting subject which van Dyck's works more than once illustrate: e.g. is there not something a shade American about *Henrietta Maria with her Dwarf, Sir Jeffrey Hudson* (the attractive portrait of the Queen wearing a broad-brimmed hat on the side of her head), which is in the Washington National Gallery? Or Russian about *Sir Thomas Wharton* in the Hermitage at Leningrad? *The Continence of Scipio* (Christ Church, Oxford), the influence of Veronese predominating, was painted during van Dyck's first brief stay in England. It shows the Roman general restoring the captured Spanish beauty (who looks only moderately pleased at the transaction) to her fiancé. Could van Dyck have used himself as model for the fiancé? There seems a look of the self-portraits.

An interesting pair of van Dyck portraits at Petworth House are Sir Robert and Lady Shirley. Shirley, an Englishman in the service of the Shah of Persia – an early example of British employments of that kind – had married a Circassian noblewoman. On a diplomatic visit to Rome they were painted in Oriental dress by van Dyck during his own first stay in the city. Sir Robert wears a turban, his wife a gown that would have not looked at all odd in the first half of the nineteenth century. One is struck by the manner in which van Dyck has treated the Shirleys as if they might be some exotic ramification of the East India Company in 1840. Sir Kenelm Digby 'in the dress of a philosopher' has this same Victorian look. The enchanting child Clelia Cattaneo could be nineteenth-century, too, and one is not at all surprised to see that she has found a home at the Washington National Gallery.

Van Dyck did not paint many mythological pictures, but brought very much his own style to such allegories as *Time Clipping the Wings of Love* (Musée Jacquemart-André, Paris), or *Venus at the Forge of Vulcan*. The *putti* in the background of the last, ragging with a visored helmet and unsheathing a sword, are surely meant to contrast Venus's oncoming attitude to Vulcan with her subsequent unfaithfulness to him, when her husband, with Mars? In a similar vein Tasso's *Rinaldo and Armida* (bought by Charles I, after the dispersal of the royal collection owned by the Dukes of Newcastle) is a splendid rich composition.

Rubens, who was in a position to speak on the subject, described Charles as 'the greatest amateur of painting among the princes of the world', the words spoken at an epoch when royal and archducal patrons set a high standard. Queen Henrietta Maria was particularly fond of the myth of Cupid and Psyche – a subject on which that obscure poet Shackerley Marmion, who rouses one's curiosity, wrote a long poem – and her cabinet at Greenwich was to have been decorated with canvases by Rubens and Jordaens telling the story, alas never accomplished.

Van Dyck's *Cupid and Psyche* is at Kensington Palace. The luscious Psyche is said to be modelled on the painter's mistress Margaret Lemon, of whom van Dyck painted a straightforward portrait, now at Hampton Court. According to that excellent topographical artist Wenceslaus Hollar, she was a 'dangerous woman' and 'a demon of jealousy'. Van Dyck had a daughter by his wife just before he died, and another daughter by some earlier liaison in Antwerp for whom he provided in his will.

Van Dyck's marvellous profusion of what may be categorised as Court paintings prompt all sorts of reflections. The well-known triple portrait *Charles I in Three Positions* (Windsor Castle), of which several copies exist, was made in the first instance to be sent to Bernini in Rome for the sculptor to use as model for a bust. It seems to me notable for the manner in which the right-hand profile of the King (left figure to the onlooker) resembles Charles II; on the whole uncommon in the case of this father and son.

Another pair of portraits at Windsor Castle on one canvas that catches the eye is that of Thomas Killigrew and a man who is probably his brother-in-law Lord Crofts. Killigrew, who was a favourite companion of Charles II and Master of the Revels, with a monopoly of running all the newly permitted playhouses (all closed by Cromwell), built a theatre on what is now the site of Drury Lane. Does not Killigrew there somewhat resemble photographs of Mr John Osborne? It would in any case surely be true to say he represents a characteristic type of the Theatre.

A word should be said of van Dyck's extraordinary skill with children, which stops short (if only just) of Victorian sentimentality. Also with animals. He has produced a gallery of dogs that might well be collected in a volume of their own. The dogs perhaps – and Mary Villiers's lamb – are less safe from the charge of sentimentality. But then it would be true to say that dogs are very sentimental.

For those critics who see the arts as an annex of economics and sociology there is much in van Dyck to which objection may be taken. Many of his contemporaries, puritans of a different complexion but no less opposed to certain forms of aesthetic expression, objected to him at the time. Indeed, they took the first opportunity of getting rid of van Dyck's or any other great works of art brought together by his royal patron. Others, of less limited viewpoint, will find much to ponder and admire in Mr Brown's book.

Van Dyck, 1983
Christopher Brown, Phaidon. *Apollo*

WENCESLAUS HOLLAR

When years ago I was working on the Aubrey papers for *John Aubrey and His Friends* (1948) I came across a short note from Wenceslaus Hollar (1607–77) telling Aubrey, who was evidently going to visit the artist at his lodgings, to ask for 'the French limner'; Hollar's Bohemian origins evidently defeating the neighbours.

It would be interesting to know whether Hollar was a Bohemiam of Teutonic or Slav extraction, something that Graham Parry's absorbing study does not mention. Aubrey thought Hollar's family were rather like baronets in England, but in fact, so Mr Parry tells us, Hollar's father was Registrar to the Bohemiam Law Court at Prague, and the patent of nobility Hollar acquired was chiefly through his mother's family, which was of *petite noblesse.* The point was that when he came to England Hollar operated as a 'gentleman', which had advantages in the seventeenth century for an artist.

Hollar had wanted to be a miniature painter. There seem to have been the usual family objections to a son taking up the arts, but he overcame these, and, like many famous painters, began professional life as an engraver and etcher. His natural turn for topography steered him towards this comparatively practical area of the graphic arts. It was in that capacity that he first impressed the great Earl of Arundel, then travelling in the Rhineland, to which Hollar himself had gravitated. Hollar managed to attach himself to Lord Arundel's retinue, through which he was brought to England.

This was a great coup because the brilliant Arundel was an unsurpassed patron while Charles I – something still not sufficiently appreciated – was the first of our kings to take a truly important part in promoting the arts, especially painting, in this country. All seemed set fair, but clouds had in fact been gathering for some time, and Hollar found himself involved in the Civil War. There is a tradition that he actually took part in the famous siege of Basing House in October 1645, when, in Mr Parry's words, 'the House was defended by what was virtually a contingent of the Artists' Rifles, including Inigo Jones, Thomas Fuller, William Faithorne, the engraver', the last of whom executed the most familiar portrait of Aubrey.

As the Royalists had the worst of the war Hollar was forced to retire to the Low Countries, where he subsisted to some extent on hack work of one kind and another, engraving pictures and illustrating books. He also produced a great many English 'prospects', which perhaps had some sale among the exiles, and in any case the Civil War had probably excited interest in the country. He also did still-life studies of shells and fur muffs. Mr Parry observes: 'It has very often been remarked that Rembrandt's etching of a shell (*c.* 1655) is very likely a tribute to and emulation of Hollar's artistry in these designs.'

Hollar appears to have returned to England about 1650/51, probably through the good offices of William Dugdale, the celebrated antiquary, who had several books in preparation, and no doubt regarded Hollar as the best man to illustrate them. There seems to have been some trouble on his return, possibly due to Commonwealth religious intolerance. For a brief period Hollar was arrested. His religion has in fact never been established with absolute certainty, but whatever took place was in due course smoothed over.

Aubrey records that Hollar noted that before the Civil War 'the people, both poore and rich, did looke cheerfully, but on his returne he found the Countenances of the people all changed, melancholy, spightfull, as if betwitched'. Nevertheless Hollar got a lot of work done, nearly two hundred engravings of Dugdale's *The Antiquities of Warwickshire* (1656) alone. There was much else, too.

During his first visit to England Hollar had been appointed drawing-master to the Prince of Wales, later Charles II, and at the Restoration he might reasonably have expected something in the way of a pension or at least royal favour. Neither came his way, probably because he no longer possessed a powerful patron. Within a few years he was badly hit by the Great Plague of 1665, his only son dying. Of the Great Fire that followed Hollar has left some considerable record in striking pictures of gutted London.

After the Fire plans had to be considered for rebuilding London. Hollar was employed as a cartographer, for which he had a peculiar gift, and was accorded by the King the title of Scenographer Royal; but without any financial benefit. Hollar executed many panoramas of London, including a terrible impression of the city burning, taken from the South Bank. His gift for drawing 'long views' that approximate almost to an air photograph is a truly extraordinary one.

Practically all that has been transmitted of Hollar's personality is through Aubrey, who described him as a 'very friendly good-natured man as could be, but Shiftlesse to the World, and dyed not rich'. Aubrey also recorded the death of Hollar's son, who apparently also drew well, and the fact that Hollar's daughter was 'one of the greatest Beauties I have ever seen', but we do not know what happened to her. Hollar himself married again in later life and died on 25 March 1677. John Bowle's just published *John Evelyn and His World* (Routledge & Kegan Paul) says that Hollar's dying request was that his creditors should not remove his bed first, such penury was he in. He was buried in St Margaret's, Westminster, the register describing him as 'the Famous'.

Mr Parry's book, scholarly and well produced, is full of good things. Hollar produced many costume studies, which are authoritative for dress of the period. He also did four particularly charming designs illustrating the Seasons, one of the most piquant of these female figures having for its verse:

> As Autumes fruit doth mourne and wast
> And if not pluckt it dropps at last
> So of herselfe (she feares) she shall
> If not timely gather'd, fall.

Hollar, as well as his many studies of London in different aspects, drew many English country houses, castles and churches, one of the most attractive of the first category being his picture of Lord Arundel's house Albury in Surrey. Even more interesting, if less enchanting as a setting, is Arundel House in London, an extraordinary conglomeration of nondescript constructions dating from late-medieval and Tudor times, where Hollar lodged in one of the outbuildings when under Arundel patronage on his first visit to England. Hollar's picture gives a vivid impression of how, in the seventeenth century, a great nobleman lived in London surrounded by his dependants; something very different from the Whig palaces of the next century.

One is continually struck by the appalling damage that was done to English arts and architecture by the Roundheads, even apart from breaking of statuary and stabling of horses in churches. For example, one of Hollar's views of the Thames shows among other residences York House, which belonged to the second Duke of Buckingham, whose father had bought Rubens's collection of paintings and antiques, which included nineteen Titians, thirteen Veroneses, seventeen Tintorettos, three Raphaels, three Leonardos, thirteen canvases by Rubens himself. These masterpieces were quickly dispersed under Cromwell, and York House given to General Fairfax.

John Aubrey himself had some turn for drawing, and it is interesting to note, in some of Aubrey's sketches of his old home, Easton Pierse in Wiltshire, that the convention used for threes and foliage seems to owe something to Hollar's method.

Hollar's England, profusely illustrated, is a book to be strongly recommended, not only to all historically concerned with seventeenth-century England, but also more generally for Hollar's astonishingly accomplished arts, topographical and otherwise.

Hollar's England: A Mid-seventeenth-century View, Graham Parry, Michael Russell. — 1981 *Apollo*

WILLIAM HOGARTH

I

Hogarth is one of the great figures this country has produced. So far as his paintings are concerned, it seems extraordinary that this should not always have been immediately clear. A work like *The Shrimp Girl* could hang advantageously beside any Impressionist masterpiece, not merely for its technical handling, but for the timeless manner the canvas rises above changes of taste.

Joseph Burke, in the Introduction to this volume, rightly castigates Roger Fry and Clive Bell as art critics for their insensitiveness – one might almost say their crassness – in making little or no distinction, where 'literary' painting was concerned, between some ludicrous nineteenth-century 'subject-picture' RA and Brueghel or Poussin. Obviously drastic arguments were required fifty years ago to make people aware that a new modern school of painting had come to birth on the Continent. That was no reason to carry doctrine to lengths that almost disallowed Hogarth.

The fact is as Mr Burke points out, that there exists always a puritanical prejudice against comedy and wit. Their presence arouses disquiet. Any artist who traffics in them is at best likely to encounter efforts to relegate his work to the second rank.

Of course if Hogarth had drawn and painted in a mediocre way, and at the same time been the first to conceive sequences like *The Harlot's Progress* or *Marriage à la Mode*, he would have been no more than a byway of illustration, more or less interesting according to his skill. As it happens, he was not merely a painter of genius, but one immensely interested in the technical abstractions of his art.

Hogarth's work was, and to some extent still is, known chiefly by the engravings of the pictures. This volume comprises every engraving made of a Hogarth picture or drawing, and includes a commentary on each subject, not simply a *catalogue raisonné*, but one that can be read consecutively, which is very acceptable.

Hogarth was born in 1697. He was therefore a generation older (a slip here says 'younger') than Reynolds and Gainsborough, with whom he is apt to be classed. He was the son of a schoolmaster with literary ambitions, and married the daughter of another artist, Thornhill, best known for the painted dining hall he executed at Greenwich.

Hogarth was first apprenticed to a goldsmith, where he designed such things as letters, emblems and coats-of-arms, his first known piece of work being the advertisement card he made when he set up on his own as an engraver.

This goldsmith association is worth noting, because Aubrey Beardsley came of a family that designed gold ornaments and jewellery, and one cannot look through these Hogarth engravings without noting what an enormous effect they had on Beardsley's style. For example, compare Hogarth's picture of Fielding with Beardsley's Volpone, or the use in Hogarth's *Sigismunda* of masses of flat dark and light with a whole lot of Beardsley designs.

No painter qualifies more than Hogarth as a painter of 'social criticism', but none, at the same time, was more level-handed in his use of that criterion. If the rich were called to order, the poor were certainly not sentimentalised.

Hogarth's own strong feelings about the need to safeguard children, and his hatred for cruelty to animals, were given practical expression and he had close charitable connections, as well as the pictures he painted there, with the Foundling Hospital. Incidentally, he is also an important figure in the history of copyright – today still threatened by countries not subscribing to international agreements – as he was an early victim of pirated engravings.

The first picture in perhaps Hogarth's most famous sequence, *The Harlot's Progress*, began simply with a single canvas of a tart rising in the morning, to which someone suggested adding a second scene to make a pair, a popular commission in France at this date. The Rev. Dr Trusler's *Hogarth Moralised* (1831) remarks that there are 'many little objects in this plate, met with in the chamber of a prostitute, that sufficiently explain themselves to the more knowing part of mankind, which decency will not permit me to make such of my readers acquainted with as these pages are calculated to improve'. The accumulation of symbolical material in all Hogarth's pictures is remarkable. An even fuller investigation than it has been possible to give in the present volume would be of psychological value.

One hesitates to disagree with the present editors (and also with Dr Trusler) as to the detail of plate III in *Marriage à la Mode*, the *Visit to the Quack*, but has the young nobleman, in truth, brought the two women there to find out 'which infected him'? He looks, in the first place, much too cheerful for this. Surely the little girl is pregnant, and he is complaining that the pills have not brought on a miscarriage; while the other woman is not threatening him with a knife, but preparing to procure an abortion. However, there may be documentary evidence for the other view.

Hogarth is a fascinating figure. Although quite a lot is known about him, there is also much that we do not know. The important point that is brought out here – and can be followed in the plates – is that he was not an illustrator of naive moral maxims, but a classicist who knew what life was like.

Hogarth: The Complete Engravings,
Joseph Burke and Colin Caldwell,
Thames and Hudson.

1968
Daily Telegraph

II

If the first half-dozen great English painters were in question, the name of William Hogarth would certainly be canvassed for inclusion. To define his position in painting might be less easy.

The marvellous facility of *The Shrimp Girl* (sometimes called *The Market Wench*) in the National Gallery could be the work of a master of almost any period – perhaps an Impressionist's. On the other hand, one of the painter's own favourites, *Sigismunda Mourning over the Heart of Guiscardo,* is a subject not really in Hogarth's line – though it seems rather hard that the Tate (so we are told here) has banished *Sigismunda* to its storeroom at Acton, where she can only be seen one day a week by special request.

Derek Jarrett makes a most interesting and thorough attempt to plumb Hogarth's attitudes. If at the end one is left wondering what Hogarth really did feel about his art, that is due to the painter's own complexity, not Mr Jarrett's often sparkling examination of Hogarth's various changes of standpoint. These were, of course, closely connected with the position of a painter at that particular period, but also owed a good deal to a fairly cantankerous temperament.

Hogarth, son of an unsuccessful schoolmaster who had been imprisoned in the Fleet for debt, had begun life engraving coats-of-arms in silver – a fairly normal apprenticeship for a painter in those days – not really establishing himself on his own until he was about thirty. His early aim was to be an 'historical painter in the grand style', in the manner of James Thornhill (the first painter of English birth to be knighted), who was to become Hogarth's father-in-law.

In order to earn a day-to-day living Hogarth produced popular engravings. Some of these – notably *Gin Lane* – have become classics, but he did not himself regard them as more than a kind of pictorial journalism, to give time to paint the pictures he preferred. Mr Jarrett is instructive on the subject of 'emblems' used in Hogarth's work, then thought of (in a manner that derived from the Renaissance) as a kind of poetry, and more important than the actual marks the painter made on the canvas.

The third Earl of Shaftesbury, whom Voltaire judged England's boldest philosopher, had written on this subject, holding that allegory should be contained within the limits of probability. For example, the figure of Time with a scythe walking along a London street was not convincing, but an old woman pushing a wheelbarrow full of old books labelled 'waste paper' would be symbolically acceptable.

Hogarth's mind was much devoted to this problem. His line about himself was that of being a rough, straightforward Englishman, beef-eating, beer-drinking, freedom-loving – direct antithesis of the starved, enslaved, affected French. His picture, usually known as *Calais Gate* (though entitled *O the Roast Beef of Old England*) expresses this view, given added force by the fact that Hogarth was arrested as a spy when painting it.

While projecting this image of himself, which was in certain respects not at all untrue – the account of a five-day drunken rampage on which the artist embarked with several friends might well be called Hogarthian – Hogarth attacked the fashionable world on the grounds that its masquerades and operas were vulgar and plebeian. These productions were just a lot of Swiss and Italian rubbish; the theatres should have been playing Shakespeare and Ben Jonson.

Mr Jarrett points out that some of the autobiographical material left by Hogarth needs to be accepted with caution, and shows the political complications the artist was unavoidably involved in when seeking patrons.

Hogarth, Protestant and Hanoverian, had been brought up in a world where opposing parties had seemed an evil; an attitude that was changing to government and opposition being held jointly to represent a guarantee of liberty. Hogarth started often with a comparative political neutrality, but found himself in a maze of complexities that often makes the meaning of his prints hard to determine.

Frederick, Prince of Wales, was one of Hogarth's patrons, and, in the 1730s, the Prince's Master of Horse, Lord Cholmondeley, took delivery of a painting of himself and the Prince with four companions out hunting, which gives an idea of the sort of remuneration a painter received. The whole picture cost £246 15s, of which £157 10s went to John Wootton (the accomplished painter of sporting subjects) for the figures and the background, £57 15s to the framer, £31 10s to 'Mr Hogarth for painting six faces in the picture at five guineas a face'. The cost of the frame represents more than a fifth of the expenditure.

Hogarth's last years were not happy, and there seems no doubt that he was a difficult man to get on with. His theories were a strange mixture of the original and the doctrinaire. 'Action is a sort of language,' he observed, 'which perhaps one time or other may come to be taught by a kind of grammar rules.' He also said: 'Drawing and painting are a much more complicated form of writing.' Hogarth possessed an extraordinary versatility. His engraving *Royalty, Episcopacy and the Law* (1724) could have been hung in a Paris exhibition of the Surrealists in the 1920s without the least incongruity.

The Ingenious Mr Hogarth, 1976
Derek Jarret, Michael Joseph. *Daily Telegraph*

JOSIAH WEDGWOOD

In the catalogue to the exhibition of Wedgwood portrait medallions now taking place at the National Portrait Gallery, Robin Reilly, co-author with George Savage of this finely illustrated and informative study of the medallions, draws attention to the 'passion of the British for portraiture [that] amounted almost to frenzy' in the last quarter of the eighteenth century. 'Likenesses of the great, of family and friends, were demanded and provided in a variety of media as wide as it was extraordinary,' says Mr Reilly. 'Portraits in oils, miniatures in watercolour on ivory; life-size figures and busts in marble or bronze; small busts in relief, carved, modelled, or cast in ivory, wax, glass, paste, jasper and basalts; profiles cut out or painted in silhouette; bronze medallions; even needle-work portraits worked in the sitter's own hair: all illustrate a fashion never equalled in any other country.'

This is particularly remarkable because the great realistic portraits of Holbein had never been developed by British artists, and – although miniaturists like the Elizabethan Hilliard, with Faithorne and others in the next generation, were native painters – the seventeenth century was dominated in this country by portrait-painters from the Netherlands. It was Hogarth who laid the foundations for Gainsborough, Reynolds and the great English School.

This interest in individuals, as such, might not unreasonably be linked with the eighteenth-century growth of the novel, leading to its nineteenth-century flowering in England. Whether this fascination with recording what people were like struck painters and writers at much the same moment, or whether the proliferation of portraits in all forms exercised direct influence on the imagination of nineteenth-century novelists, is a question worth considering.

In this field of portraiture, Josiah Wedgwood (1730–1795) plays a unique and fascinating role. The Wedgwoods (a formerly landed family of some antiquity) were potters, remaining so to this day, Josiah himself being the fourth in line.

His achievement (he started with little money) was to commission appropriate artists to design these portrait medallions – Flaxman, for example – which vary in size from many at 2 inches, or less, to Peter the Great at 17 by 14 inches. In all there must be not far short of two thousand of these medallions in existence.

Wedgwood would not allow its artists to sign their works, so that a great deal of research has gone into listing the medallions, their subjects and designers. The subjects vary greatly. There are, for example, seventy-eight Roman emperors and empresses, 256 popes, together with kings of England and France, the two last sold in sets only. Religious subjects were the Virgin Mary, Mary Magdalene, the Four Evangelists.

The 'Heads of Illustrious Moderns' provide the full range of greatest interest, from, say, Voltaire (in black for the clergy, white for the laity) to unremembered persons – some unidentified, some included because they helped Wedgwood in the production of required material for his workshops. Lively – at times rather controversial – biographical notes are given under each medallion reproduced in this book.

The different aspects of these medallions that might be discussed are innumerable. One is worth mentioning because not always remembered in connection with the Romantic movement, that movement certainly playing an essential part in creating Wedgwood's public.

On the one hand, the Romantics pointed the way to Gothicism, Byronism, 'horrid' scenes; on the other, they emphasised refinement of feeling, exaggerated delicacy, a tendency to puritanism.

Messrs Reilly and Savage give instances of this prudishness, describing how Wedgwood quarrelled with the modeller Jean Voyez because he found Voyez modelling the naked daughter of his coachman. Wedgwood was also afraid that some of the Roman designs in his pottery (Pompeian excavations were a recent attraction as an art influence) might be difficult to sell on account of their nudity, so that it would be necessary to accept the additional cost of clothing them.

The authors quote Wedgwood's admonition of the painter Wright of Derby (noted for his candlelight pictures), in 1784:

> I could not speak to you when I was with the ladies at your home about the particular sort of drapery of the Corinthian Maid which I liked the least, but finding afterwards that some of the ladies had seen that part of the drapery in the same light as myself . . . I begged Dr Darwin to mention it to you. The objections were to the division of the posteriors appearing too plainly through the drapery, and its sticking too close . . . giving that part a heavy hanging-like appearance . . . It is unfortunate in my opinion that the maid shows so much of her back.

It would be arguable that prejudices of that sort had persisted from Roundhead times and earlier into the eighteenth century, sometimes too much characterised by its robuster writers.

Mr Reilly is the author of many books on the decorative arts, and Mr Savage has specialist knowledge of relief portraiture from working in the Wedgwood firm. The medallions always seem to have had the quality to make them admired after the fashion for them had died down.

Wedgwood: The Portrait Medallions is one of the oddest and most interesting contributions to European and American historical portraiture.

Wedgwood: The Portrait Medallions,
Robin Reilly and George Savage,
Barrie & Jenkins.

1973
Daily Telegraph

JAMES BARRY

If any picture by James Barry (1741–1806) is familiar today it is likely to be his unfinished oil sketch of Samuel Johnson in the National Portrait Gallery, which gives an excellent idea of the Doctor.

It was roughed out for the artist's *The Distribution of Premiums in the Society of Arts*, a large affair (11ft 10in by 15ft 2in) executed for the RSA and containing the likeness of many eminent persons.

Barry himself regarded portraits as a demeaning activity for a painter. Although the rule of 'significant form' and 'pure paint' has been to some extent shaken during the last sixty years, it is still hard to take in how much the idea of the 'history painter' dominated the eighteenth century. Even so vigorous a figure as Hogarth felt throughout his life a gnawing guilt that his pictures were not sufficiently 'sublime'.

Barry, son of a Cork publican, managed to get some training as a painter and saw a patron in Edmund Burke. He was a radical in politics and rather unusually cantankerous, possessing an infallible instinct for quarrelling with anyone likely to be of practical use to himself. He had, for example, a bitter row with Reynolds (though once unexpectedly supporting him at a Royal Academy meeting), and he is the only Royal Academician ever to have been expelled for causing trouble there.

It is desirable that biographers should feel enthusiasm for their subjects, and William L. Pressly's book opens up many fascinating aspects of late-eighteenth-century art. At the same time I cannot go all the way with him as to Barry's capabilities. Barry does not seem to me to draw very well and he has a certain banality of mind.

As against that, his *Elysium and Tartarus or the State and Final Retribution*, painted in 1783, subsequently added to, is the first mural to bring into a single picture the intellectual history of all humanity, a genre that was to be popular in Victorian times. He undoubtedly influenced both Blake and Fuseli (possibly also Ingres), though temperamentally without the profound mysticism of the former, or the surrealist inventiveness of the latter.

I would, however, grant the haunting quality to which Mr Pressly refers, for instance in Barry's *The Temptation of Adam* or *Jupiter and Juno on Mount Ida*.

When Benjamin West painted *The Death of General Wolfe* in 1770 the daring innovation of putting the figures in the military uniforms of the period rather than in togas was considered no less revolutionary than Picasso's *Les Demoiselles d'Avignon* (1907). Some years later, in 1776, Barry produced his own *Death of Wolfe*, also in contemporary dress, attempting to be at once more realistic than West and also more heroic.

Mr Pressly thinks that this return to the subject may have been connected with the outbreak of the American War of Independence, in which Barry as a radical would have taken a keen political interest. But he adds that George Romney had used this popular hero in a picture (now missing) much earlier, as had Edward Penny – whose enjoyable canvas *The Marquess of Granby Assisting a Sick Soldier* is in the National Army Museum.

Barry's contempt for landscapes and still lifes is well illustrated by a letter he wrote after seeing the royal collection of Netherlands masters at Turin: 'God help you, Barry, said I, where is the use of your hairs-breadth niceties, your antiques, and your &c. Behold the hand-writing upon the wall against you; in the country to which you are going, pictures of lemon peel, oysters, and tricks of colour and other baubles, are in as much request as they are here.'

Barry became increasingly unmanageable and hard up. A collection was made for him which would have kept him going, but he died just at the moment of receiving it. Sir Robert Peel arranged for him to be buried in the crypt of St Paul's and for a tablet to be put up. There is something about Barry of Benjamin Robert Haydon, some years his junior.

Mr Pressly, in a book devoted to his subject's life and art, quite rightly relegates to only a short note an odd postscript to Barry's life. Nothing whatever is recorded here about Barry's relations with the opposite sex, probably because no information is available, but no one could doubt from his pictures that he felt a deep appreciation for female attractions. When he died another James Barry turned up to see if there were any pickings, and, although described as a nephew, seems perhaps to have been an illegitimate child.

That in itself might be commonplace enough, but the particular James Barry the Younger, as described in June Rose's *The Perfect Gentleman* (1977), appears to have started life as a girl, undergone a sex change, become Inspector-General of the Army Medical Department and in that capacity to have given Florence Nightingale a tremendous ticking-off.

The Life and Art of James Barry,
William L. Pressly,
Yale UP
for the Paul Mellon Center.

1981
Daily Telegraph

SIR GEORGE BEAUMONT

The lasting memorial of Sir George Beaumont (1753–1827) is that he was not only largely responsible for the establishment of the National Gallery but also presented sixteen of its pictures, which included three Claudes, a Poussin, a Rembrandt, a Rubens and a Canaletto. Unlike many of the persons I find myself writing about in these columns, George Beaumont was happily married, lived a life entirely without scandal, but, to the great grief of himself and his wife, had no children. By that the public subsequently benefited through this munificent gift.

The position of an aristocratic patron of the Arts is never an easy one. Beaumont's case was perhaps made even harder than usual by the fact that he was himself a talented painter. There is no question that he could have earned a living by his brush; lack of any great originality, or devotion to a given school, was unlikely to have been a handicap where selling was concerned. I don't think I have ever seen a picture by him. The many reproduced in *Collector of Genius* show a most competent performer.

The Beaumonts are a family of immense antiquity and considerable distinction (for instance Beaumont and Fletcher). Various branches flourished for a time, then produced no male heir, a pattern to be repeated by Sir George Beaumont, 6th Baronet, who came into his inheritance at the age of six. He made no particular mark at Eton or Oxford except that at New College a lively drawing-school existed, run by a musician and art-master from Cologne, John Baptist Malchair.

The account here of Beaumont's education in painting is perhaps the most interesting section of a book that covers in a fascinating manner the changeover from eighteenth- to nineteenth-century painting and connoisseurship. Felicity Owen (a descendent of Sir George Beaumont) and David Blayney Brown handle adroitly a lot of different complicated material, including Beaumont's preoccupation with the stage and passion for the Lake Poets.

When he was twenty, Beaumont met Joseph Farington, landscape-painter and topographer, with whom he visited various East Anglian country-house collections. Farington was a pupil of Richard Wilson, and at North Aston, the house of Oldfield Bowles near Oxford, Beaumont met, as well as the great Wilson himself, another of his pupils, the Radnorshire squire Thomas Jones, the importance of whose paintings, especially the later ones, has recently been examined in a long essay by Lawrence Gowing. Oldfield Bowles himself was a fairly gifted amateur, if not in the class of Jones, a professional in spite of his background. North Aston must have provided a remarkable centre for professionals and amateurs to meet.

All this seems worth emphasising, because it shows Beaumont as having got off very much on the right foot so far as painting was concerned, a hopeful start that was not entirely consummated by his final years. As the authors comment, he always remained with eighteenth-century values, strongly influenced by the Romantic Movement, never fully understanding the exploding creative forces of the new century.

Beaumont was, for example, intensely anti-Turner, and, although on good terms with Constable, never bought any paintings by him while Constable was alive. That was also true of Wilson and Gainsborough, though Beaumont was later accustomed to speak with regret of this omission, so far as the last two artists were concerned. Inevitably there was grumbling among those he did not patronise.

Reynolds always remained Beaumont's great hero, and it was Reynolds who was probably responsible for Beaumont treating his own painting, and his connoisseurship, with a seriousness that was something more than just pottering about as a 'virtuoso'. When Beaumont went to Italy in 1782, he could still think Domenichino's *Last Communion of St Jerome* the 'finest landscape background in the world'.

The authors suggest that during the years between the death of Wilson and Gainsborough, and the emergence of Turner and Constable – a period dominated by topographers – Beaumont, had he been a true professional, might have occupied an important position in British painting. There was indeed a moment when he was suggested, perhaps rather frivolously, as a possible president of the Royal Academy.

One notes that Beaumont fell for the so-called 'Venetian Secret', a nostrum hawked by a certain Thomas Provis, which purported to reveal how the great Venetian painters obtained their effects. That was in 1794. In the same way Beaumont could latterly see some qualities in a perfectly awful picture (by an American painter, Washington Allston) called *The Angel releasing St Peter from prison*. Although David Wilkie, even Benjamin Robert Haydon, might be better than that (the former was much admired by Beaumont), they were no alternative to Turner.

There is much else about Sir George Beaumont that is worth reading, but the promising beginning in painting, combined with the comparatively disappointing end, is particularly striking. He was for some years an MP, enjoying political work, if that did not become too unpleasant. Unfortunately the French Revolution and the Napoleonic Wars made it so.

There was a great deal of entertaining in Grosvenor Square, though the Beaumonts lived much of the time at Coleorton Hall in Leicestershire, now owned by the Coal Board, who jealously guard the reproduction there of Michelangelo's tondo, the original of which went to the Royal Academy.

Collector of Genius:
a Life of Sir George Beaumont,
Felicity Owen and David Blayney Brown,
Yale UP.

1988
Daily Telegraph

THOMAS ROWLANDSON

The name of Rowlandson immediately conjures up cartoons of Bonaparte and the Prince Regent, which, however accomplished, are in the coarsest and most knockabout vein of the period; together with a John Bull Englishness of the most aggressive sort.

This superb collection of some 350 drawings (a volume not expensive for these days) shows how one-sided any such view of Rowlandson can be. Not much is said of Thomas Rowlandson (1756–1827) himself in the Introduction, indeed in one sense not much is known about him, in spite of a formidable list of studies of his works.

He was the son of a fairly well-to-do merchant in Soho, and lifelong friend of Henry Angelo (son of the famous fencing-master), who went on to Eton, where the younger Angelo later also taught fencing – a drawing here shows him fencing with a woman. Rowlandson's gift seems to have been accepted early on by his family, for he was attending the Royal Academy school when about eighteen.

Quite soon Rowlandson got himself over to France, where he had a French aunt. So far from being the intensely insular figure that some of the cartoons might suggest, he spent a good deal of time in France, speaking French well; he seems also to have travelled in Germany, perhaps elsewhere in Europe.

The French aunt eventually left Rowlandson £7,000, a respectable sum then, but her nephew was a gambler, and, one imagines, not indifferent to other ways of getting through money quickly. He was accordingly almost always in a condition of having to produce a great deal of work to order.

Although Rowlandson's drawings are by no means of equal merit (and forgeries abound), his facility as a draughtsman is staggering. He has a particular ability in handling fields of recession in a picture – seen here in landscapes of the rolling country of Devon, Cornwall, or the Isle of Wight – and was equally at home with complicated architectural compositions. These powers of dealing with receding planes are again noticeable in his handling of groups or boats in a harbour of scenes at racecourses, where no doubt a good deal of the artist's money disappeared.

In fact Rowlandson is on the whole not at his very best in the Hogarthian scenes for which he is most known. His more brutalised subjects (for example, *A Sporting Cove*) have less feeling than Hogarth's. Rowlandson shone in subtler comment, and, where representation of the human figure was concerned, in his extraordinary grasp of foreshortening (*New Shoes*, an undergraduate stooping down to see a pretty girl's feet).

Perhaps the strangest impression that these drawings from the Paul Mellon Collection give is the resemblance between some of Rowlandson's work and that of later French masters in somewhat the same genre. It must of course be remembered that the predominance of France in painting was a later, nineteenth-century development. At the beginning of the century the French to some extent looked to English painters like Bonington, and possibly Rowlandson had more influence on subsequent French drawing than might be expected.

Anyway, there is a powerful tang of Daumier in Rowlandson's *Three Clerical Scholars*, while *The Love Letter*, *Two Girls Tippling*, and *The Duchess of Devonshire and the Countess of Bessborough*, with several more, all strongly recall Constantin Guys.

One of the most impressive sides of Rowlandson – especially in an artist who enjoyed having a fairly uproarious time – is his capacity for doing painstaking academic studies of such objects as marble thrones (of which there are examples here) or a series of *Loyal Volunteers of London*, with all the positions for the musketry exercise.

Many of the drawings undoubtedly attached to incidents that have now been forgotten. An interesting example is the comic drawing entitled *The Historian Animating the Mind of the Young Painter*. Rowlandson has written on the drawing: 'Thompson the Poet Reading his Seasons to Wilson the Painter.' – the artist at his easel listens to an elderly man, while in the corner a woman plays with a child. The editors comment: 'The subject was etched by Rowlandson in 1784 with the above title, two years after the death of Richard Wilson. Thus, the inscription on the drawing must be an obscure joke alluding to Rowlandson's old teacher at the RA, as there is no sure evidence that Wilson was ever married or had offspring.'

The joke surely has some connection with the fact that Richard Wilson was never at ease with the 'Romantick' tastes of his period, preferring to paint pure landscape in which he would insert a few classical figures, but Wilson did in fact take at least two of his subjects from James Thomson's (rather than Thompson) *Seasons*. It is also true that Wilson is not known to have been married, but in the 1790s the Royal Academy made a small grant to a petitioner who claimed to be Wilson's son, which would all fit in with Rowlandson's drawing.

Thomson the poet was, in truth, only about a dozen years older than Wilson the painter. Rowlandson's drawing of Wilson is not altogether unlike the Mengs portrait.

The Drawings of Thomas Rowlandson, 1978
in the Paul Mellon Collection, *Daily Telegraph*
John Baskett and Dudley Snelgrove, Barrie & Jenkins.

PORTRAIT PAINTERS IN INDIA

The slightly austere title of this book – which might suggest no more than a sequel to Mildred Archer's admirable two volumes on *British Drawings in the India Office Library* (1969) – does not altogether do justice to both sides of its scholarship and readability.

The lively account of the individual artists who went to India at this period to earn a living might have been expected; less so the absolutely convincing impression of India itself at a period when the subcontinent was gradually being taken over by the British. There are plenty of books of social history to describe this, but the approach through painting – the attitude of the Honourable East India Company's merchants, officials, soldiers, that of the Indian princes, the relations between the two elements – shows by implication how both Indians and Europeans really lived. Especially so in the mixing of races by what was, in effect, intermarriage – something that did not survive the increasing missionary zeal of the nineteenth century.

In 1810, according to the *East India Vade Mecum*, there were about four thousand European 'male inhabitants of respectability' and about two hundred and fifty women to be similarly described, so that, except for 'those platonic few whose passions are unnaturally obedient', the answer was an Indian mistress, or *bibi*, since the Company made marriage of its servants to an Indian virtually impossible. These unions were treated with the same respect as marriage by both Europeans and Indians, and, so far were they from the clandestine love affairs between the races often touched on by Kipling (notably in the story 'Without Benefit of Clergy'), that the civilians and military officers of the eighteenth century would be painted in a 'conversation group' with their *bibi* (sometimes two *bibis*) and offspring.

Owing to damp and insects the large rooms lived in by the British in India, designed for coolness, could not be decorated with wallpaper or tapestry, so that oil paintings provided a suitable relief from a too stark severity. In the case of portraiture and the recording of martial or political events, pictures were popular in an expanding world of commence and government.

Painters had to receive permission from the Company to ply their trade in India, but in practice no painter of any standing was refused. The artists themselves would sometimes arrange to ship as supposed 'midshipman' on an East Indiaman, having made a private arrangement with the captain to 'desert' at Bombay, Madras or Calcutta.

Mrs Archer is particularly good in characterising the painters who went to India, none perhaps in the top rank, but, at worst, good, competent performers. Almost all had strong personalities, something required if the very real difficulties and dangers of the enterprise were to be faced.

Tilly Kettle, son of a London coach-painter, has claim to be looked on as the first British painter of some distinction in India. He painted the Nawabs of Arcot and of Audh, and was in general attracted by 'Indian' subjects as such. Kettle travelled as far as Tibet, and did a picture (1775) of the British emissary being received by the Panchen Lama. Probably John Zoffany, over and above his work in India, is the best known of the artists dealt with by Mrs Archer. Zoffany, who was born in Frankfurt, did not reach India until he was fifty. He was already established in England as a successful painter of the Royal Family and had been made a baron by Maria Theresa, which accounts for his sometimes being called 'Sir John'.

Zoffany had been patronised by Garrick for theatrical conversation pieces, and there is always a touch of the theatre about his groups. That trait is something to be grateful for in Zoffany's representation of the British in India, apt to be depicted with the gravity of Roman senators or generals. One of his most enjoyable scenes shows the artist himself with his friends, Colonel Antoine Polier (a Swiss officer in the employ of the Nawab of Oudh), the French adventurer Claude Martin (to end as a British major-general) and John Wombwell (the Company's paymaster at Lucknow), the last a richly comic John Bull figure in blue tailcoat rather too tight for him.

Warren Hasting's enthusiastic patronage of painting in India should not be forgotten. Zoffany painted Hastings and his wife (a beauty removed by Hastings from her former husband, a German baron) several times. Zoffany's impish humour is well illustrated by his picture of 'The Last Supper' for St John's Church in Calcutta. In this altarpiece

> The worthy Greek priest, Father Parthenio, was acceptable as Christ, but the somewhat effeminate police magistrate, W. C. Blacquière, who at times adopted female disguises, was a startling model for the effeminate apostle John, and the auctioneer, William Tulloh, was far from pleased to find himself Judas.

Catherine Read (1723–1778), 'the Rosalba of Britain', should be mentioned as the first female painter to go to India, which she did, as a spinster, a the age of fifty-four. She had already impressed everybody, including Fanny Burney, as a thoroughly eccentric figure. Unfortunately none of her Indian canvases seems to have survived. Later there were lady miniaturists.

There is so much in Mrs Archer's book that names can be picked out only here and there, omitting many that deserve a mention. Among painters of special note were Arthur William Devis (who started his journey to India by being shipwrecked off Borneo, where he painted the inhabitants), Thomas Hickey (no relation to the contemporary diarist in India, William Hickey) and George Chinnery, whose drawings are of particular interest. Mrs Archer makes interesting comments on that very popular subject for Indian history pictures, Lord Cornwallis receiving the sons of Tipu Sultan as hostages.

India and British Portraiture 1770–1825, 1979
Mildred Archer, Sotheby Parke Bernet. *Daily Telegraph*

JOHN CONSTABLE

It will be remembered that about two years ago many of the paintings attributed to John Constable (1776–1837) were conclusively shown by the authors of this extremely scholarly study to have been painted by Constable's son Lionel. Their book deals not with Constable's life but with the vicissitudes of his name and works after his death, a story of extraordinary complication.

Constable himself had a simple biography. His family came originally from Yorkshire, but his grandfather had settled in East Anglia, where the artist's father was a well-to-do miller. Constable himself was a miller for a year, and I have heard it said that he prided himself on having a 'miller's thumb'.

He fell in love with a girl whose family regarded themselves as a cut above a miller's son who was only a comparatively successful painter. They held off the marriage until their daughter was twenty-nine and Constable forty. The couple married, however, at last, lived happily (though she died relatively young) and produced a large family.

Constable's pre-eminence as a landscape painter would hardly be questioned nowadays, but he was regarded as not particularly exciting in his own period. He was attacked by Ruskin, and his pictures were, naturally enough, unsympathetic to the Pre-Raphaelites. On the other hand, by the 1850s he was claimed as 'the father' of modern French landscape by Delacroix, who had repainted his own *Massacre of Scio* after seeing Constable's *The Hay Wain*. (The emphasis on the *painting* rather than the *subject* is to be noted on the part of the Frenchman).

A change for the better, so far as Constable was concerned, took place in this country towards the end of the century. By the 1920s he had begun to be hailed as the forerunner of the Impressionists – which he can be called only rather obliquely.

Apart from occasional money difficulties, Constable was reasonably well off, always led an ordered life, in which he was totally immersed in his art, and was comparatively little sought after by rich collectors. He therefore kept a great many of his paintings, even from time to time 'buying them in'.

Accordingly, on his death the family found itself in possession of some seven hundred of his works, many of them in a totally unclassified state.

Constable's eldest son (who died before he was thirty) was only twenty at his father's death, and most of the continuing administration of what was left fell to the next son, Charles, an officer in the East India Company's Naval Service, therefore not always available.

There was a good deal of bitterness within the family as to distribution of the pictures and drawings, aunts playing what the children regarded as malign part. Although appreciating their father's work, no one seems to have been very much at ease in the practical handling of the problems that arose.

The youngest son, Lionel, was the most talented in a family where all seem to have been able to draw a bit. His drawings were sometimes preserved with his father's in portfolios, as father and son would go out painting together.

From illustrations reproduced in this book, Lionel Constable's style appears to have been rather 'fussier' than his father's, but he chose much the same subjects, naturally enough, and was clearly far from an incompetent performer, indeed might at times have been mistaken for his father.

There was certainly no deliberate intention on the part of Constable's children to mislead, but they were young at their father's death, and became increasingly out of touch with what he left behind. At the same time one cannot fail to be struck by the rapid appearance of forgers of Constable's works. As early as the 1850s the family was worried about this. By 1869 several notorious forgeries were shown up.

The picture-forger is a peculiarly noxious form of criminal, and one regrets the publicity, even a kind of half-baked popular regard, evoked by such vermin, whose productions, it is true, are sold on the whole to the uninstructed and credulous, but at the same time muddy the waters of the genuine art market.

By the time of Constable's grandchildren there seems rather less certainty as to whether anyone knew that drawings by Lionel – or even the other brother, Alfred – were sometimes included in the saleroom descriptions as those of Constable. Ian Fleming-Williams and Leslie Parris write: 'A reasonable case could be made out for Constable's grandchildren simply being unable to tell what was what amidst the huge residue of [their aunt] Isabel's estate.'

To add to the difficulties of sorting out Constable's pictures and drawings is the existence of at least a dozen competent near contemporary painters who follow his style – including, maddeningly enough, George Constable of Arundel, who was no relation – of whom George Frost and the Rev. John Fisher deserve a mention.

The authors have undertaken a monumental task in sorting out so thoroughly Constable's work and its history since his death. They show up some past attributions, both acceptances and dismissals, as incorrect, sometimes made by eminent art-historians. There is an excellent, and very necessary, chart pedigree of the Constable relations. In short, they have done an admirable job.

The Discovery of Constable,
Ian Fleming-Williams and
Leslie Parris, Hamish Hamilton.

1984
Daily Telegraph

SAMUEL PALMER

On the whole the troubles of artists – anyway as they are popularly thought of – stem from loose living, drink, women, recklessness about money, rather than from quarrels with their relations over religious doctrine, or too much dependence on the opinions of fathers-in-law.

Van Gogh and Rouault had, of course, strong religious preoccupations. No doubt many others could be found, but Samuel Palmer (1805–1881) is in his way a unique figure, and, for English painting, an outstanding one.

Palmer's father was a shiftless bookseller, younger son of a fairly well-to-do mercantile family. Both Palmer's parents were Nonconformists, and he had a lonely, unconventional childhood, in which one of the few illustrated works to which he had access was Joseph Glanvill's *Philosophical Considerations touching Witches and Witchcraft* (1666). This, incidentally, was 'Glanvill's book', where Matthew Arnold, in the poem, pondered on the story of the Scholar-Gypsy. Raymond Lister does not mention the Scholar-Gypsy in his full and absorbing story of Palmer's life, but one feels there is a link.

Palmer showed his talent at an early age, selling his first picture for seven guineas when he was only fourteen. Although his father was a Particular Baptist, his mother a Wesleyan (with Roman Catholic relations), Palmer himself turned to the Church of England with great enthusiasm. This does not seem to have upset his father, but eventually led to difficulties with his father-in-law, John Linnell, whose Nonconformity took the shape of a religion revealed by God only to himself.

Linnell, who was thirty when Palmer first met him at the age of seventeen, is the ever-looming figure in the Palmer story. Linnell, too, was a painter, not a particularly gifted one, but with an immense amount of energy and push, so that he ended up a relatively rich man. He was also a skilled teacher of drawing. Even his energies must have been extended to the full in instructing some of his pupils, such as Beckford (of Fonthill), Wainewright, the art critic and poisoner, and possibly Mary Godwin.

In 1826 Palmer went to live at Shoreham in Kent, about twenty miles from London. At Shoreham his most notable 'visionary' work was done. He was associated with the group of painters known as the Ancients. Blake, then in his late sixties, came to visit Palmer there, and for some time Palmer was treated by art critics as a mere appendage of Blake.

A certain similarity of style clings to all this mystical group, but, so far from being a hanger-on of Blake, Palmer was the more considerable painter.

I happen to have lived at Shoreham myself for a short period, and – if personal comment may be allowed – a cloud of smoke at times hangs over London, sometimes to be seen against a perfectly clear sky above the country further south. This must have been no less, possibly even more, a marked feature in Palmer's day, and it produces dramatic effects sometimes at sunset, which must have delighted a band of painters in the manner of the Ancients.

Palmer, with many weak, even silly, characteristics, was an immensely professional worker. He took up etching late in life and wrote of the work involved: 'You are spared the dreadful death-grapple with colour which makes every earnest artist's liver a pathological curiosity . . . the tickling [of the etching plate] sometimes amounts to torture, but, on the whole, it raises and keeps alive a speculative curiosity – it has something of the excitement of gambling without its guilt and its ruin.'

Palmer married Linnell's daughter when she was nineteen, he thirty-two. The religious opinions of all concerned were so much at odds that the ceremony had to be a civil one. In the beginning the couple were much attached to each other. They set out for Italy (with very little money) and stayed there for about two years.

Marriage, Italy, a new sort of life, had a strong effect on Palmer; the mystical influences were swept away. In his own day critics like Ruskin took this to be a change for the better – Palmer's later pictures were somewhat in the manner of, say, Edward Lear – but modern critical taste greatly prefers the Shoreham period. The emotion of those earlier days was undoubtedly deeper, though the later work is by no means to be dismissed.

What matters about an artist is his painting, but those who enjoy a personal story will find an extraordinary one in Palmer's life, too – chiefly in his relations with Linnell. The older man was a monster in the top class of Victorian horror. Strong-willed, eccentric, he built his own houses without an architect, devised extraordinary ways of saving money – his long-suffering wife drew the line finally at travelling in an empty furniture van – and tyrannised over his relations.

Palmer at first welcomed this domination, indeed never entirely freed himself from finding a certain fascination in it, but finally Linnell drove a wedge between his daughter and her husband. Not for the first time in reading of Victorian family strife is one reminded of the novels of I. Compton-Burnett, from one of which Linnell might have emerged bodily.

All this is told in a well-documented, straightforward manner by Mr Lister, who has made a close study of Palmer, his art and his associates. In the end Palmer, far from well off, was forced to live, in a conventional style totally unsympathetic to himself, on Linnell's doorstep. There is much quiet horror, and a great deal of interest, in the story of one of England's really notable painters.

Samuel Palmer: A Biography, 1975
Raymond Lister, Faber. *Daily Telegraph*

SALON PAINTING

Between the conflict of the Classical and Romantic schools of painting at the beginning of the nineteenth century, and the eventual triumph of Impressionism, Post-Impressionism, Surrealism and Abstract art in the twentieth century, stretches an enormous area of pictures that once filled the public galleries. To these Aleksa Celebonovic (whose book is translated from the French) has given the not unreasonable name of Bourgeois Realism.

On the whole these canvases from the Royal Academy, the Salon and their equivalents on the Continent and in America, have been relegated to the cellars as *art pompier*. This does not mean 'fire-brigade, i.e. philistine' – as the blurb to this volume incorrectly explains – but refers to the helmets (resembling firemen's helmets) worn by figures in Classical paintings (David, for example). The jibe was originally launched by the Classicists' enemies, the Romantics.

Mr Celebonovic (of whom we might be told a little more by the publisher than just that he is 'the Yugoslav critic and art historian') makes out a good case for these forgotten pictures. At the very least they are of great social interest. Some of them, even if out of fashion in subject matter, are extremely skilfully painted – after all the final criterion. And it should not be forgotten that, to the end of his days, Sickert – an undeniably fine painter himself – used to tease Bloomsbury by reiterating his view that 'Every Picture tells a Story'.

Mr Celebonovic is faced with the difficulty of having to lay down some overall standards for what he should include. He is ingenious in doing this, having sections devoted to such subtitles as Devotional Pictures, Torture and Mortification, Gesture and Eroticism. Reconstruction of the Life of Antiquity, Mediaeval Legend, Warlike Patriotism, Orientalism, Social and Family Life, and so on. Even so, it's almost impossible to assimilate all the types (excellently illustrated) under one critical umbrella.

For example, very different, extremely talented painters like John Frederick Lewis (1805–1876), and James Tissot (1836–1902), can perfectly well be judged by their taste in design and technical skill. Ruskin may have objected that Tissot's pictures look like photographs, but nowadays photographs are fetching high prices in the art market.

In contrast with these, William Adolphe Bouguereau (1825–1905), admired in his day – and most execrated of all the Salon painters by those who wanted a reformed style of painting – remains, one would say, perfectly frightful in almost every way a painter can be frightful; while Jean Béraud (1850–1936), born in St Petersburg, and P. Andrez (probably Spanish, second half of nineteenth century) both move into an area of painting that is not far short of being Surrealist.

Andrez, in *Portrait of a Woman*, 1890, shows a lady bursting right out of the canvas, and gripping the actual frame with her hands. Béraud, in a large oval canvas entitled *St Mary Magdalene before Christ*, conceives the New Testament story as taking place at an all-male dinner party in nineteenth century Paris, the guests including portraits of Renan and Alexandre Dumas the younger, the repentant Magdalene represented by the well-known courtesan Liane de Pougy.

A remarkable link between what are usually regarded as two very different types of painter is shown by Jean Ernest Meissonier (1815–1891), famous in his lifetime for his genre painting, chiefly of military scenes. Meissonier drew well and could handle paint. It is pointed out by Mr Celebonovic that, when Meissonier's *Napoleon III at the Battle of Solferino* was hung in the Luxembourg, Degas copied several of the horses there shown into his book, and used them later in his own work.

Looking at this volume it is impossible not to reflect on the attitude of Communist and Fascist governments to painting. Both discourage – sometimes actually persecute – everything that could possibly come under the heading of Modern Art, instead of which 'Socialist Realism' (or its Fascist equivalent) is advocated. The paradox of such a policy is that regimes which pride themselves on being 'anti-bourgeois' are recommending a style which, of all schools of painting, is most rooted in 'bourgeois' society.

An interesting example of 'social criticism' is found in the picture reproduced here by the Russian painter I. E. Repin (1844–1930) called *They Had Given Up Waiting for Him*. This shows a haggard man returning to his home from imprisonment in Siberia, a subject perfectly acceptable, one would think, as 'Socialist Realism', and as topical now as when it was painted. It is, at the same time, unlikely to be produced in a contemporary version by any Soviet artist.

Mr Celebonovic's generalisations are sometimes a trifle precarious; for instance, I doubt whether, anyway in this country, a very strong division of taste could be drawn in the nineteenth century between 'aristocratic' art patrons and 'bourgeois' ones, and sometimes he seems to falter on the actual subject of a picture.

For example, Solomon J. Solomon (1860–1927) in his *Conversation Piece* clearly shows a couple looking at a *carte de visite* photograph, just taken from its album, not a 'valuable *objet d'art*'; while Sir Luke Fildes's *An Alfresco Toilet* is surely not 'a young servant and her mistress', but a group of sisters, who look like the concierge's family, in an Italian palazzo probably turned into flats. Nevertheless, there is much to be enjoyed here.

The Heyday of Salon Painting:
Masterpieces of Bourgeois Realism,
Aleksa Celebonovic, Thames and Hudson.

1974
Daily Telegraph

DICKENS'S ILLUSTRATORS

Several books before this one have appeared on the subject of the illustrators of Dickens's works. Jane R. Cohen's study is not very attractively produced (the plates incline to be indistinct), but information about the original illustrators (there were many subsequent ones) is conveniently brought together and makes an extremely interesting story.

The life of Charles Dickens (1812–1870) spans tremendous changes, both personal ones in his own rise to fame, and general ones of a social and intellectual kind that took place between the world of the Regency and that of the middle Victorian years. The literary difference between *Sketches by Boz* and *The Mystery of Edwin Drood* is very great, and that difference could not possibly be better expressed than by comparing, say, George Cruikshank's illustration of *Public Dinners* in the former with Luke Fildes's *Jasper's Sacrifices* in the latter.

Dickens took a keen interest in his illustrations, and was not an easy man to work with. He raises the interesting question of to what extent the author knows best in giving instructions for how his stories are to be depicted. On the face of it there seems no argument as to which should have his way, but one finishes Miss Cohen's book with certain doubts. Does the material of a novel stretch out beyond the knowledge of the writer? Could it be that sometimes the artist knows best? These reflections are generated by the fact that so often Dickens had rows with his best illustrators, and liked those whose work seems to a later generation indifferent.

George Cruikshank was twenty years older than Dickens, a famous figure when the writer was still unknown, and a man of considerable eccentricity. This last was sufficiently shown by choosing to depict Fagin in his own likeness, something admitted at the time, and shown here in a self-caricature. Dickens disliked Cruikshank's illustrations for *Oliver Twist*, which must seem to most people inseparable from the novel. Baudelaire was a great admirer of Cruikshank, speaking of him in the same tones as of Brueghel and Goya. Cruikshank illustrated something approaching nine hundred books in all, and contributed only to five of Dickens's twenty-four illustrated works.

Cruikshank grew fanatical in later life on the subject of abstention from drink, which he preached in pictures displaying the frightful consequences of having a drop too much, but he was unable to practise teetotalism with complete success himself. He parted with Dickens on bad terms, and nursed a grievance on the subject to the end of his life.

Dickens moved on to Robert Seymour for *Pickwick*, an artist comparatively well known in his own day for comic sporting sketches. He is now forgotten, though not altogether deservedly. The style Seymour used for Dickens was very similar to Cruikshank's, and I should guess that, of the many people who must remember Seymour's haunting picture of the dying clown in *The Pickwick Papers*, the large majority suppose it to be by Cruikshank. Seymour was in a permanent state of being hard up, and financial troubles, coupled with rows with Dickens about how the author's characters should be illustrated, caused him to commit suicide. His widow subsequently waged something of a vendetta against the novelist.

Dickens found his most appropriate illustrator – anyway in the eyes of posterity – in Hablot Knight Browne, better known as Phiz. Browne was a withdrawn, diffident man, uneasy in society, and prepared to fit in with Dickens's wishes. One feels that there must have been all sorts of complicated interior emotions for Browne to produce the figures he did; Squeers, for instance, or Quilp, and his crowd pictures are usually good. In *Martin Chuzzlewit* Browne was required to draw scenes taking place in the United States, a country he had never visited, not an easy assignment.

Browne's picture of a pawnshop in *Martin Chuzzlewit* is set side by side in Miss Cohen's book with one by Cruikshank of the same subject in *Sketches by Boz*, and although Browne's may have owed something to the earlier conception, both have very much their own individuality and vigour. Dickens got on pretty well with Browne, even contriving to involve him with the amateur acting that was almost a *sine qua non* of being on good terms with Dickens at all. That did not prevent a certain amount of Dickens grumbling, especially in relation to Browne's work for *David Copperfield*, which had a special place, naturally enough, in Dickens's affections. Dickens complained, too, that Paul Dombey was represented as sitting in the wrong sort of chair and Mrs Pipchin looked too young, though she can't be said to seem particularly juvenile.

Browne's illustrations for *A Tale of Two Cities*, a fruitful subject one might think, must be admitted to be not very exciting. Miss Cohen suggests reasonably enough that Browne was by that time worn out with illustrating Dickens, and doing his best to fit in with the author's whims. Dickens quite ruthlessly dropped him from the new Dickens venture from *Master Humphrey's Clock*, which in practice meant illustrating *The Old Curiosity Shop*. It should be mentioned that several illustrators would often have a hand in the same book, which makes generalising about different Dickens novels difficult so far as success of their pictures is concerned. Browne was upset about being jettisoned. He suffered money difficulties, and as usual a philistine government refused a Civil List pension, which Browne well deserved as one of the most distinguished illustrators of his day.

Times were changing and so was Dickens as a writer. Public taste was moving away from the touch of caricature which once had been popular in illustration. An artist who makes one doubt whether a novelist, anyway Dickens, always made the best choice in this field is Robert Cattermole, for whom Dickens felt great enthusiasm. Cattermole, unlike his predecessors in the Dickens books, was a professional artist who exhibited at the Royal Academy. He was a personable young man to whom Dickens took a great fancy on social grounds. Cattermole can indeed produce attractive drawings, but these are usually work not immediately concerned with illustration. For Dickens he is apt to be over elaborate, whimsical, and, where human figures are concerned, bloodless.

A whole host of illustrators now follow who did a few drawings for Dickens books but are on the whole not chiefly remembered in the Dickens field. Samuel Williams, for example, must be credited with one very lush rendering of Little Nell asleep in bed, but a good deal of pressure was required from Dickens himself before the picture was judged just right. When *Master Humphrey's Clock* ran into difficulties Williams was unshipped. John Leech, a great artist in his own sphere, is rather another matter. Leech had applied early on and unsuccessfully for the job of doing *Pickwick*. It might therefore well have been Leech to have imposed Dickens's characters on history. As it is, one remembers Leech's Scrooge sitting in his nightcap when visited by Marley's ghost, and the exuberant figure of the Spirit of Christmas Present greeting Scrooge, still in his nightshirt.

This last Leech picture (with many other Dickens types) was later used by John Tenniel as a *Punch* political cartoon, showing Gladstone as Scrooge confronted by a very different Christmas Present bearing a torch labelled Anarchy. Tenniel himself did a few pictures for *The Haunted Man*, but he had no great desire to become a Dickens illustrator.

The Royal Academy world in Dickens illustrations is now growing increasingly, in evidence with Daniel Maclise, who executed what is probably the best-known portrait of Dickens himself as a young man. The objections to Maclise as an illustrator are much the same as those which make Cattermole unsuitable. *The Christian Remembrancer* took umbrage at Maclise's frontispiece for *The Chimes* as 'a monstrous melange of kicking, sprawling nudities', and it must be admitted that some of the amorous couples romping together in the design would now be deemed to have a distinctly lesbian connotation.

An artist to do a few of the drawings for *The Chimes* was another *Punch* figure, Richard Doyle, but his well-deserved reputation was made in other spheres. Edwin Landseer became a close friend of Dickens, but did only one illustration for him, a dog (savage rather than sentimental) in *The*

Cricket on the Hearth. Clarkson Stanfield, not a very interesting illustrator, now quite forgotten, also contributed to *The Haunted Man* and *The Chimes*, but he was mainly concerned with landscape and decoration rather than people. He too was roped into Dickens's theatrical activities, among other things designing sets for the plays.

In Samuel Palmer an unusually distinguished painter became connected with Dickens, but this was to illustrate *Pictures from Italy*, a Dickens work far from well received, the artist unjustly taking some share of its unpopularity.

By this time we have moved into the period of *Our Mutual Friend* and the unfinished Dickens novel, *The Mystery of Edwin Drood.* It has to be admitted that neither of these would have been very suitable for illustration by Cruikshank or Browne, and, apart from the gradual change in the style of Dickens himself, methods of reproduction had by then been radically altered. Francis Topham, a rather humdrum performer, had illustrated Dickens's *A Child's History of England*, and Frank Stone, another personal friend, had also worked on *The Haunted Man.* Neither of these would have been adapted to this final Dickens period, but Marcus Stone, the second artist's son, was chosen for *Our Mutual Friend.*

Marcus Stone, not without all gifts as an illustrator, is the essence of mid-Victorian sentimentality and archness presented in a naturalistic manner. His implied comments on the story are certainly less acceptable than the same sort of thing done by Cruikshank or Browne, both of whom always manage to get a certain bite into their drawings. With Charles Collins the complications of Dickens's family life enters into the role of illustrators, because Collins married (as her first husband) Dickens's daughter Kate. Miss Cohen says that they became attached while posing for Millais's *The Black Brunswicker.* It has been suggested elsewhere that the male figure in this picture was a professional model, but perhaps one such stood in when Collins was busy elsewhere, because the hussar certainly appears to have the features of Collins.

Finally there was Luke Fildes (painter of *The Doctor*) for *Edwin Drood.* Like Marcus Stone this Royal Academician overflows with sentimentality and phoney drama, but his illustrations have acquired a certain period charm. The drawing is a trifle messy and Du Maurier did the same sort of thing more effectively. Dickens himself liked them, and Fildes had greater influence than most in deciding what was to be illustrated in the novels.

Dickens, as we know, died before *Edwin Drood* was finished. The Dickens family felt that Fildes deserved well of them as the work was necessarily at an end, so that Fildes continued on the outskirts of the Dickens industry, notably with a watercolour called *The Empty Chair*, showing Dickens's study. This work was greatly admired by Van Gogh, who, fantastic as that may seem, himself painted a picture called *Gauguin's Chair* which indicates a decided Fildes influence.

Miss Cohen has produced a useful and scholarly work, and, because her book is not casual journalism (where all such solecisms are common enough) one must put in a plea for more careful use of the English language: 'fortuitous' means 'by chance', not 'fortunate'; 'oblivious' (endlessly misused) means 'forgetful', not 'unaware', and is followed by the genitive 'of'; 'anticipate' means to 'use in advance', not to 'expect'; 'befriend' does not simply mean 'to be friends with', it conveys a sense of 'help, favour', e.g. Landseer did not 'befriend' Dickens, since they met as equals, if anything Dickens the better known. I don't think any of these are 'American usage', which naturally one respects, but merely loose employment of English found on both sides of the Atlantic, and preferably to be avoided.

Charles Dickens and His Original Illustrators, 1981
Jane R. Cohen, Ohio State UP. *Apollo*

JOHN LEECH

Many small children seem geniuses at drawing, but even so John Leech's watercolour of the Bath Mail done at the age of six has quite unusual vigour and charm. It would have been surprising had nothing emerged from such early talent. In fact, Leech never attended an art school. All his drawing was executed by the light of nature.

Leech (1817–1864) had an unusual background for an artist. His great-uncle worked as a waiter in London Coffee House on Ludgate Hill; was taken into partnership, became sole proprietor, then left the restaurant to his nephew, Leech's father. This Micawberish figure, apparently of some cultivation, went bankrupt, though not before sending his son to Charterhouse, when that school was still in London.

Leech left Charterhouse, where he was not happy, at the age of fourteen. He later became a medical student, but the family's money troubles forced him to make immediate use of his turn for drawing. In a surprisingly short time he found a place on the newly founded magazine *Punch* (though at first the paper was not disposed to admit artists on equal terms) and from then on Leech was established throughout his comparatively short life.

Although one might not go all the way with the claims Simon Houfe makes for Leech, he was a brilliant artist within his limits, who more or less invented the comic drawing with two- or three-line caption (so long to hold sway until displaced by *New Yorker* style jokes), and defined many strata of Victorian life from the heavy swell to the cockney errand boy. He was also a delightful colourist, to be particularly noted in the illustrations to the Surtees novels, though Mr Houfe also provides examples of some of Leech's rare oil paintings.

Mr Houfe invokes comparison with Constantin Guys in two of Leech's pictures. In the first, a pair of pretty but bedraggled little tarts stand in the Haymarket, with rain coming down, one remarking: 'Ah! Fanny! How long have you been *gay*?' (that is to say, a prostitute). In the second picture two ragged soldiers chat in the snows of the Crimea: 'Well, Jack! Here's good news from home. We're to have a medal.' 'That's very kind. Maybe one of these days we'll have a coat to stick it on?'

These cut deep enough to demonstrate the shallow self-righteousness of contemporary journalists who attacked Leech for lack of humanity in a preoccupation with the rich, in his art; but neither as draughtsman nor as observer of life does Leech ever quite equal Guys in profundity of feeling, an artist whose influence may be seen in, among others, Picasso. Leech, one would say, is superior to Gavarni, and his drawing-room scenes are comparable with those of Eugène Lami, certainly as deft.

Leech had a very considerable contemporary reputation, and for one of his profession did well, but he was always in financial difficulties owing to generous treatment of his many relations, not least his father. While not extravagant he liked to live a comfortable family life, and stay away in country houses where he enjoyed hunting, shooting and fishing. His drawings express these country tastes and his own simple nature. He seems to have suffered from melancholia though he liked a full social programme.

Mr Houfe quotes occasional comments made about art, which suggest an odd mixture of sound natural instincts inhibited by a conscious refusal to look at pictures in at all an intellectual manner. He had after all to earn a living as a comic artist, and perhaps felt that danger lay that way. All the same, it is impossible not to feel curious as to how Leech might have developed had that particular necessity not been his.

How would he have reacted for example, had he gone to Paris to study art in the manner of the characters in *Trilby*, who would have been about his contemporaries? As things were, he never used a model as such, though he was for ever taking notes and making small sketches.

A fascinating point brought up by Mr Houfe is that, probably about 1862, Leech met Manet, who presented him with a little ink drawing inscribed 'à John Leech E. Manet'. One can see that the two artists had something in common, and, in the arid desert of relationships between the main stream of British mid-nineteenth-century painting and the Impressionists, this contact is of great interest.

Thackeray – who had known Leech as a junior at Charterhouse – said with more truth than tact that *Punch* might have remained unwritten had it not been for Leech. On another occasion he contrasted Leech's 'wholesomeness' with the French cartoonists who satirised adultery and other vices. No doubt Leech was a man with a personal preference for domesticity, and, in the paths open to an artist of his kind in Victorian London, had to toe the moral line.

John Leech and the Victorian Scene, 1984
Simon Houfe, Antique Collectors Club. *Daily Telegraph*

G. F. WATTS

In 1930, Evelyn Waugh dined with the Duchess of Malborough at Carlton House Terrace, and afterwards recorded: 'Sat next to Edith Sitwell. The dining-room was full of ghastly frescoes by G. F. Watts. Edith said she thought they were by Lady Lavery.'

Thirty years later Waugh visited the Watts Gallery at Compton in Surrey (of which Wilfrid Blunt, author of this book is curator) and was 'fascinated' by Watts's *Jonah*, which (wrote Watts himself) shows the 'full-length, gaunt-like figure of Jonah, standing facing, with outstretched arms; behind him, on a mural tablet, are depicted scenes representing the sins of the people, drunkenness, gambling, racing, etc.'.

Mr Blunt mentions these two facts, without underlining that Waugh's reactions to Watts (1817–1903) indicate much of what has happened to the painter's reputation since his death. Mr Blunt's account of Watts is perhaps rather over-chatty in tone – as if he were taking visitors round the Watts Gallery after a good lunch – but he has an interesting story to tell both about the painter's professional and personal life.

Watts, son of a Hereford piano-tuner, had considerable gifts as a painter from the start. At the age of twenty, he showed at the Royal Academy a picture called *The Wounded Heron*, which might reasonably be compared with the animal studies of Oudry. He also possessed good looks and a charm which almost immediately involved him with aristocratic patrons. He was soon taken on by Lord and Lady Holland as a member of their household in Florence, where Lord Holland (son of the famous hostess of Holland House) was British Minister.

Mr Blunt deals tactfully but firmly with his subject's sex-life, without being able to arrive at any final conclusions. Some such enquiry is not mere idle curiosity, being demanded by the pictures themselves, to which contemporary objection was quite often taken on the grounds of too great a sensuality.

At the same time, speculation must remain indecisive. Watts was deeply shocked when an Italian married woman, young, beautiful, well-born, made at pass at him, which suggests prudence, if not a certain indifference to the opposite sex. We are then confronted with the forty-seven-year-old Watts proposing to the lovely Ellen Terry, just turned seventeen. No man who did that could conceivably be blamed for being too cautious, nor for sheering off women.

The Ellen Terry marriage was, of course, a disaster. There is argument as to whether it was consummated. One is inclined to think that, if nothing had taken place, the marriage would simply have been annulled. In fact, Ellen Terry herself was not at all pleased when Watts insisted on a legal separation. In the end, though years later, there was a divorce.

Watt's second marriage – this time a success – was equally risky. Then he was sixty-nine, the bride thirty-six. The second Mrs Watts was one of those Victorian wives – of whom there appears to have been an inexhaustible supply for writers and painters – who took complete charge of her husband, his art output, money, friends. It was characteristic of this sort of widow to insist that at the Watts Gallery, where all other postcards were a penny, those of her husband should be tuppence.

Mrs Watts did not have it all her own way at the start, because there was another dominating lady who regarded Watts as her private property – though a physical relationship is altogether unlikely. This was a pattern in his life – a similar female dragon having done much to make his first marriage go as badly as possible. Even Lady Holland fits to some extent into this dynasty of controlling women.

The adulation showered on Watts at the height of his fame has to be read about to be believed. It was certainly true that he retained an extraordinary energy in producing work – including sculpture, which he took to late in life – until the very end of his days. *Physical Energy* (the naked figure on horseback in Kensington Gardens) was finished when he was about seventy. It is now the cap-badge of the Lusaka Boys' School, Zambia.

Watts suffered a great deal from depression. He was in many ways a modest and simple man, at times rather a twister about money, a habit that seems more neurotic than grasping. There was certainly a strain of silliness in him, and he was totally without humour. To prove that the latter was not the case – and that he could enjoy a joke with the best – he painted a huge picture called *B. C., or Tasting the First Oyster*, in which 'the primitive woman watches with anxious curiosity the effect of the first courageous gulp of the primitive man'.

As a painter Watts could claim a good deal of versatility. He did not like painting portraits, and took them on only to gain an income, but many of his famous sitters are admirably represented in terms of the period. His *The Cedar Tree* (1868) has something of Samuel Palmer about it, and *Freshwater in Spring* (1874), before it was quite finished, must have looked like some of the landscapes produced by comparatively go-ahead English painters in the 1920s.

Watts's shortcomings were not so much in painting as in the sources of his 'literary' side; to be seen by comparing him with, say, Delacroix. Some of the small drawings are very talented.

England's Michelangelo: 1975
A Biography of George Frederick Watts, O.M., R.A., *Daily Telegraph*
Wilfrid Blunt, Hamish Hamilton.

JOHN RUSKIN

I

Dr Joan Evans has written an excellent biography of Ruskin, well-balanced, informative, sympathetic, though not without both humour and severity. Among the great Victorian figures, John Ruskin (1819–1900) has claims to being considered at once one of the most typical and the most extraordinary. His private life is inseparable from his public career, the latter taking its shape from the former, almost as if designed to illustrate a textbook of abnormal psychology.

There was suicide and madness in the family of Scots tradesmen from which he was sprung. His father made a fortune in the sherry business – apparently about £150,000 – and married a cousin, who, even in the world of dominating mothers, sounds unusually horrifying. He remained under the sway of his parents as long as they lived, he himself luxuriantly developing all that time: a plant of monstrous exoticism enclosed in that domestic hot-house.

In the end his egocentric nature brought him to insanity, but the annulment of his marriage to Effie Gray (later Lady Millais), and the extraordinary love affair with Rose La Touche (beginning when she was only thirteen), had to be played out. In these personal relationships nothing but his weaknesses is displayed. Parallel with them are his contemporary triumphs as an 'art historian' – to use a designation which to modern ears has perhaps acquired a somewhat satirical ring. It might almost be said that Ruskin was the first of his particular kind.

As the story of his career unfolds it is impossible to remain unimpressed by the ineradicable mark Ruskin left on the aesthetic views not only of his own generation but even down to the present. Indeed, the popular view of painting today, certainly among older people, might be said to derive almost entirely from him, scarcely affected by *fin-de-siècle* reaction from his views, or the twentieth-century movement of 'modern art'.

In later life he became interested in socialism, which inevitably appealed to his intense, earnest, authoritarian temperament. He saw at once that its system could be truly imposed only by despotic measures, striking at the root of individual freedom. He was consistent in his attitude towards a 'planned society', for example, writing, during the American Civil War, in which he supported the Southern States, on the legitimacy of slavery.

As Dr Evans indicates, it would be almost impossible to build up a coherent appreciation of art from what Ruskin says. It was the intensity of his feelings that moved people, not the fact that he was strikingly original, or even well-informed. He was forty before he visited the art galleries of Dresden and Munich. He disliked the architecture of St Paul's, wanted to stop the National Gallery from buying Rubens, loathed among many other painters of high distinction, Canaletto, Claude, Poussin, Cuyp, and thought Wallis's *Chatterton* (death of) 'faultless and wonderful'.

The fact is, judged by any conceivable standards, he often talked arrant rubbish. Not content merely to advance his views, they had to be advanced, even from his earliest days, in the most aggressive and tyrannical manner. It is arguable that he and the Pre-Raphaelites between them did irreparable damage to English painting. Incidentally, he knew nothing whatever of the growth of Impressionism on the other side of the Channel.

Dr Evans has something to say in favour of Ruskin's highly coloured literary style. His influence on Proust is, of course, well known, the French writer even finding a certain affinity in the rich, middle-class background they possessed in common and also in their childhood's coddlings. Perhaps Ruskin's true importance, good and bad, always lay as it were at a second remove, rather than in his immediate teaching. He himself even complained that such was the case, that 'scarcely a public house near the Crystal Palace but sells its gin and bitters under pseudo-Venetian capitals copied from the Church of the Madonna of Health or of Miracles'.

For myself, I find agreement with the reviewer of *Blackwood's*, writing in 1848, who found Ruskin's prose 'verbose, tedious, obscure and extravagant'. I think it would be a great pity if his many inadequacies were forgotten in the general revival of Victorian sentiment that has brought him once more to the foreground as a critic. He is the essence of all that is 'unclassical' in his approach to art. Fortunately, with such an effective biography as this available, his failings may be easily understood and there can be no doubt of his interest as a man and a portent. In appearance he was described by Ford Madox Brown as 'half-way between a fiend and a tallow chandler'.

John Ruskin, 1954
Joan Evans, Cape. *Punch*

II

Tim Hilton's biography promises additional material about Ruskin's later life, when he was a 'finer writer and, if I dare say so, a better man'. This will be something to look forward to in a further volume, as the present one takes us only just up to the appearance of Rose La Touche, Ruskin's little girl love. Here, what is by now a fairly well known story of the earlier years is solidly and intelligently retold.

Mr Hilton says that when he himself was an undergraduate, in the 1960s, an interest in Ruskin was regarded as 'as foolish as an enthusiasm for modern art'. He survived that, and now speaks for the defence, not least for Ruskin's extraordinary output (two hundred and fifty titles, apart from lectures, periodicals, diary, published correspondence). In any case Ruskin is a figure who needs to be reassessed from time to time.

His private life is inseparable from his public (which began at a very early age). In a sense he himself would have wished that to do so. He wrote: 'I wholly deny that the impressions of beauty are in any way sensual: they are neither sensual nor intellectual, but moral.' Accordingly, a man's life, his moral status, so to speak, is his work.

His parents kept Ruskin entirely within their own household. This he totally accepted. When he went up to Oxford, his mother took rooms within the university, and he spent every weekend with her. One notes, however, that far from encountering the snobbish prejudices always so emphasised nowadays as a nineteenth-century characteristic, Ruskin, who in addition to being *nouveau riche* must have been an exceedingly odd fish, had plenty of friends at Christ Church, including several young noblemen.

He himself noted that he was on terms with gamblers, 'men who had their drawers filled with pictures of naked bawds', and 'walked openly with their harlots in the sweet country lanes'. This seems worth noting, as it disposes of any question of Ruskin, at his marriage, being absolutely innocent about the sexual side of life. So far as we know, however, sex was no bother to him, except purely emotionally when falling in love.

He fell passionately in love with the daughter of his father's Hispano-French partner when he was seventeen, a prelude to the disastrous marriage with Effie Gray. That marriage, as we know, was never consummated, though lasting six years. Ruskin shows up at his worst in all this marital mishap. First he said that he did not want children and made other excuses. Finally he blamed things on some alleged physical defect of his wife's. One is reminded of an equally self-worshipping man, D. H. Lawrence, similarly excusing his own physical failure with 'Brett'.

Ruskin's marriage was annulled. Mr Hilton gives an excellent account of the events leading to the break-up. Effie married the painter Millais, and gave birth to eight children. One imagines that Millais's portrait of her in *The Order of Release*, represents just what she looked like.

It might almost be said that Ruskin was the first 'art historian'. He was an extremely capable painter and draughtsman himself, though, as Mr Hilton aptly remarks, his drawings 'imitate not so much Turner as steel engravings after Turner'.

Turner was, of course, Ruskin's greatest admiration as a painter. His passion for Turner always seems to me utterly unexpected in the light of his other tastes in pictures. For example, Ruskin thought Claude Lorraine's paintings so awful that he would have included them in an imaginary exhibition in which he would show everything that was to be avoided in art. How he managed to deny to himself the obvious Claude element in Turner's pictures is inexplicable.

It fell to Ruskin to do the clearing up after Turner had died leaving a cantankerous will (from which art lovers are still feeling the effects). *The Fighting Téméraire* was found covered with dust in Turner's shuttered studio in Queen Anne Street. Ruskin thought it the last large picture Turner ever painted. Ruskin also, to his horror, found work which he described as 'grossly obscene'. This he burnt. One can't help wondering what it was like!

Mr Hilton is naturally, and rightly, concerned with presenting Ruskin at his best (though not at all concealing his faults), but it is hard not to feel that Ruskin did a good deal of harm from the side of him which would have liked to pull down St Paul's. We owe much neo-gothic hideousness to Ruskin as well as what was admirable in its encouragement of interest in painting, and preservation of ancient buildings (he was particularly upset by the way the French were wrecking their medieval churches).

Ruskin's drawing *Stone Pine at Sestri*, is remarkable in its apparent Japanese influence. Could he have seen a Japanese print as early as 1845?

John Ruskin: the Early Years, 1819–1859, 1985
Tim Hilton, Yale UP. *Daily Telegraph*

CHARLES BAUDELAIRE

This selection from Baudelaire's critical works makes an extraordinarily attractive book. It is rather like spending the day with someone who talks very well, but always on the same subject, and finding that on this particular occasion the talker has a new theme – and is as good as ever.

Charles Baudelaire (1821–67) is chiefly known in this country for *Les Fleurs du mal*, which, as *The Oxford Companion to English Literature* primly states, are 'poems in which the melancholy romantic spirit is carried to a morbid excess'. This is the side of Baudelaire with which we are most familiar: opium, the mulatto mistress, the '*affreuse juive*'. As an art critic he is known to a few in this country as author of the essay on Constantin Guys called '*Le Peintre de la vie moderne*', but his general writings on the subject of painting are on the whole sadly neglected.

These pieces are admirably translated and edited by Mr Jonathan Mayne. Here are Baudelaire's articles on the Salons of 1845, 1846 and 1859: his analysis of laughter: notes on caricaturists, French and foreign: the Exposition Universelle of 1855: and his essay on Delacroix. Space has not allowed the account of Guys to be included. It has been translated into English twice before; and I rather suspect that Mr Mayne is a shade impatient with Baudelaire for so much admiring what he calls 'this delightfully gifted but essentially minor artist'.

However, the great point of this volume is the fact that it is profusely illustrated. Great trouble has been taken to find some of the pictures Baudelaire singles out for praise or blame. The illustrations, not to be found even in French editions of Baudelaire's prose works, are an excellent thing. With the best will in the world it is hard to read the essays, and understand them, if there is no clue to the appearance of the pictures considered by the critic. Collated here are merely writings regarding drawing and painting (including caricature which involves laughter) and one is not, so to speak, bothered by Baudelaire's *coeur mis à nu*, his views on literature, or his dislike of the Belgians. This is a great advantage from the point of view of sorting out what he has to say about the graphic arts.

Baudelaire's critical language is remarkably clear: 'A picture is a machine all of whose systems of construction are intelligible to the practised eye: in which everything justifies its existence, if the picture is a good one; where one tone is planned to make the most of another; and where an occasional fault in drawing is sometimes necessary, so as to avoid sacrificing something more important.'

He could be devastating when he disliked a painter, for example, Vernet, painter of soldiers and battle scenes (and incidentally, it will be remembered, ancestor of Sherlock Holmes): 'Furthermore, in order to fulfil his official mission, M. Horace Vernet is gifted with two outstanding qualities – the one of deficiency, the other of excess; for he lacks all passion, and has a memory like an almanack.'

Baudelaire was a passionate adherent of Delacroix, but Delacroix's almost invariable tendency to depict scenes from the past prevented him from achieving Baudelaire's ideal of 'true romanticism'. He thought that 'to call oneself a romantic and to look systematically at the past is to contradict oneself. . . . For me, Romanticism is the most recent, the latest expression of the beautiful'.

He could be – some will think justly – critical even of such great painters as Ingres and Courbet, and Mr Mayne sounds a trifle shocked at his dislike of Millet's work. Baudelaire has been blamed for praising a host of forgotten nonentities among the painters of his period, and failing to 'discover' Manet, whose enchanting portrait-drawing of him decorates the wrapper. But, as Mr Mayne points out, Baudelaire is not really of the class to be judged by a kind of 'hit' and 'miss' accumulation of marks.

It was an excellent idea to include among the illustrations Tassaert's lithograph *Ne fais donc pas la cruelle!* in which the lady wears the pantaloons and the top hat.

The Mirror of Art: Critical Studies, 1955
Charles Baudelaire, *Punch*
translated and edited by Jonathan Mayne,
Phaidon.

THE PRE-RAPHAELITES

The first of these two books is the official catalogue of the exhibition recently opened at the Tate Gallery of the Pre-Raphaelites (never previously shown so comprehensively); the second, a collection of fourteen essays by different hands (including Holman Hunt's granddaughter), all worth reading, which discuss different aspects of the Pre-Raphaelite movement.

Quentin Bell opens the batting vigorously with a lively and instructive piece in which he draws a parallel between the horror in which Rubens was held by the Pre-Raphaelites and the horror in which the Pre-Raphaelites were held by Bloomsbury in the 1920s, by which time Rubens was somewhere near the top of the critical tree. The Pre-Raphaelites are now in favour again – anyway so far as prices are concerned – and Jeremy Maas closes with an amusing piece about how he quite simply grew up as boy in the 1940s with a love for the Pre-Raphaelites, eventually finding himself in a position to promote their sales through a gallery of his own.

Having said that, just what the Pre-Raphaelites were is extremely difficult, indeed impossible, to define. There were various periods, dating from the very young art students of 1848 – notably Millais, Holman Hunt, Rossetti – who wanted to get back to a simple pre-Raphael approach in painting. They painted what were intended to be deeply moving human incidents, usually historical or legendary, in what Quentin Bell calls 'hard edge'.

In due course the movement, in a sense via Rossetti, was to become transformed into what is nowadays much more popularly associated with Pre-Raphaelitism, the pictures of Burne-Jones and the theories of William Morris – not least through the actual physical image of Morris's wife Janey.

From this later stage of Pre-Raphaelitism stems Beardsley (who owed something especially to Burne-Jones's innate sense of design), and subsequent Beardsley influences on the Continent, extensive and at times bizarre, which might be thought not much less than the precise opposite of what the original Pre-Raphaelites had set out to achieve.

The more one looks at the Pre-Raphaelites the less one feels able to contain them in a single assessment. It might be helpful to suggest that, setting aside purely religions implications, Millais's *Christ in the Carpenter's Shop* (which so violently upset Dickens) has more in common with *Family of Saltimbanques* (1905) by Picasso (another great upsetter) than Holman Hunt's *The Awakening Conscience*, although nearer in time, has with a picture also representing a man with his mistress, Degas's *Au café, ou L'absinthe.*

As a matter of fact it does appear that Picasso, as a young painter in Barcelona, came across the Impressionists before he came across the Pre-Raphaelites. More material is the way in which the Pre-Raphaelites, when attempting to deal with down-to-earth contemporary subjects, are miles away from the pictorially less verbose though no less equally felt pictures of sexual tension by, say, Manet.

Whatever one thinks of Pre-Raphaelitism it was a purely English phenomenon, and it is worth glancing at it to see whether its characteristics were ever repeated in other forms. For example, is there a touch of Vorticism to be traced in the earlier group? That would hardly be expected, but two of the lesser known Pre-Raphaelites give a hint of it: F. G. Stephens in *Mother and Child*, in which the mother's face might almost have been painted by Wyndham Lewis; and *The Glacier Rosenlaui*, by John Brett, where both colouring and shapes come near being given a Vorticist touch.

Of the earlier Pre-Raphaelite subject pictures it is easy to feel that some were not so different from those of a Victorian painter like Augustus Egg, who was not a Pre-Raphaelite; while the sculptors (treated by Benedict Read) are apt to take on this more general Victorian tone. *Pegwell Bay*, by William Dyce, retains its charm as a seascape. It is a pity that pictures are not listed under painters in the index, but the survey is all the same an admirable one.

Ruskin's influence on the Pre-Raphaelites remains obscure. He attempted to force his views in a manner that seems out of all proportion in the relation of a critic to an artist, an attitude far from acceptable to a temperament like Rossetti's. Swinburne also gave encouragement to the group (over and above employing Simeon Solomon to do pornographic drawings). In Rosalie Mander's brisk account of the Pre-Raphaelite murals in the Oxford Union, Swinburne appears in the rare role of offering good advice: 'The idea of marrying her [Janey Morris] is insane. To kiss her feet is the utmost one should dream of doing.' Swinburne seems, in fact, only to have pinched Janey's ankles under the table.

Several of the less-well-known Pre-Raphaelites repay attention. Mary Lutyens gives an account of W. H. Deverell, for instance. Mary Bennett has interesting things to say of prices, patrons and Madox Brown's picture

Work. There is a good biographical section of the beginning of the catalogue with information about nearly thirty of those involved in Pre-Raphaelitism.

The Pre-Raphaelites, 1984
Tate Gallery/Allen Lane/Penguin. *Daily Telegraph*
Pre-Raphaelite Papers,
edited by Leslie Parris,
Tate Gallery/Allen Lane.

DANTE GABRIEL ROSSETTI

Dante Gabriel Rossetti is a particularly difficult figure to treat in biography because his impact on those brought in touch with him was due to 'personality', something hard to express that is possessed by certain people, over and above their executive gifts, and almost impossible to convey later on paper. To attempt to describe it is like trying to define the genius of a talented actor.

Neither as a painter nor as a poet can Rossetti be assigned a very high place, although he obviously grades as a respectable starter in both races. He was not much of a draughtsman, but there is something about his pictures that bears the mark of originality of mind; while his poems, too, have an indefinable atmosphere that recognisably filters down as an influence through the slim volumes of a horde of later and far worse versifiers.

In fact, a case could be made against Rossetti as a bad influence in the arts, anyway a bad influence on painting, turning away, as he and the other pre-Raphaelites did, from the classical truths of good drawing and skilfully applied paint to follow 'socially significant' and basically sentimental themes.

However, all this does not prevent Rossetti from being a figure of very considerable interest in the history of the arts in England as well as through the flamboyance of his own life. New material has come to light about him during recent years, notably the letters between himself and Jane Morris, wife of William Morris. These letters were deposited at the British Museum and made available for publication a year ago.

Rosalie Glynn Gryll's book contains a great deal of useful information about Rossetti and some perceptive comments. She does not, however, quite manage to weld the material, some of it pretty intractable, into an entirely satisfactory, biography. *Portrait of Rossetti* has good paints, but the one thing the book never manages to achieve is a convincing portrait of Rossetti.

That is, I think, because Miss Glynn Grylls does not herself seem to possess a keen enough sense of character. This emerges especially in her treatment of minor personalities like Howells, Watts-Denton and Knewstub, who scarcely ever get adequately defined when they appear in the narrative, while even Morris and Swinburne move through the pages with less conviction than is required.

The main new point here is, of course, Rossetti's relationship with Jane Morris. Was she his mistress? If so, did Morris know? If Morris knew, did he care? 'Whether their companionship extended to consummation of the sexual act would not be so all-important for him [Rossetti] as it seems to a post-Freudian generation,' writes Miss Glynn Grylls.

This seems a surprising judgement. It is hard to see what Freud has to do with it. Freud did not invent sexual intercourse, he merely propounded certain theories about the subconscious mind. For a man as well disposed as Rossetti towards the opposite sex, one would certainly suppose – unless strong evidence were produced to the contrary – that Rossetti regarded the question as of the first importance.

The affair took place after they had known each other for a long time, when he was already in his forties. The tragedy of Rossetti's marriage is well known. His wife, the beautiful, neurotic, melancholic Elizabeth Siddal had died from an overdose of laudanum, in circumstances that have never been wholly cleared up. Rossetti buried the manuscript of a projected volume of unpublished poems with her; but later obtained Home Office permission to disinter them.

Miss Glynn Grylls comments with great truth:

> What is surprising is not Rossetti's lack of sentimentality over the affair, nor his apprehension as to what friends would think about it, but his obsessive need for the book. Considering how good his own memory was and how many other people had received copies of the poems (including Swinburne, who never forgot a line) there can have been very little that could not have been reconstructed.

At the time of Lizzy's death, and to the end of his life, Fanny Cornforth (whose real name was Cox), jolly, romping, sinister, maintained a hold Rossetti could never throw off. There were undoubtedly many other ladies, too, picked up at Cremorne and elsewhere, though the probability is that his models were required primarily as models and not expected to be more intimate.

Such a background is always hard to document. Miss Glynn Grylls is inclined to take the line that Rossetti was promiscuous because things never worked out happily for him where his wife and others were concerned. Perhaps she is right. We cannot be certain. The letters to Jane Morris do seem to reveal a very genuine and deep affection. The impression they give, so it seems to me, is that Rossetti and Mrs Morris went the whole way.

Among other famous stories that have to be abandoned is the one that Rossetti found a copy of FitzGerald's *Omar Khayyám* in a penny-box outside a bookshop in Leicester Square. On the contrary, the *Rubáiyát's* translation was sent him by Whitley Stokes, the Celtic scholar; but there seems no reason to disbelieve Swinburne's account of Rossetti going down to the stall later and making a great fuss when he found the stall-keeper had put up the price to twopence.

In the latter part of his life, when he lived in Cheyne Walk, with a collection of odd animals like wombats in the garden, Rossetti was a famous Chelsea character, treated with great respect by those who came to see him. This is the side which is so difficult to transmit to posterity, the dominating personality which has to be taken so much on trust.

Although in theory 'anti-Establishment' in his point of view, Rossetti cannot claim a good record in grasping the way the arts were moving. He could just tolerate Courbet, but Manet provoked no response at all in him.

He took little or no interest in his own Italian origins, which may, indeed have encouraged him in his sometimes rather aggressive cockney Englishness and intolerance of anything that came from abroad. He was also well endowed with that characteristics which we think of as specially Victorian (though still in good supply) of saying one thing and doing another. Miss Glynn Grylls justly speaks of his 'English governess' side. The fact that his own life was pretty irregular never in the least inhibited him from taking a high moral line.

Rossetti was, indeed, very upset by the notorious article by an obscure, forgotten journalist on 'The Fleshly School'. He showed himself at great pain to prove that his work was not 'fleshly'. He remains a highly enjoyable person to read about.

Portrait of Rossetti, 1965
Roslie Glyn Grylls, Macdonald. *Daily Telegraph*

II

These letters were held up for publication until 1964. They are the survivors of a large correspondence, most of which was deliberately destroyed, or has been lost. They are well edited by John Bryson, who has been able to trace most of the references, in association with Janet Camp Troxell, an American authority on Rossetti.

There have been quite a lot of books about Dante Gabriel Rossetti (1828–1882), none of them, owing to his complex life and character, ever quite conveying the reason for the fascination he exercised over his contemporaries. That is perhaps impossible to do now, especially as there remains so much that we do not know; particularly regarding his relationship with Janey Morris.

Evelyn Waugh's *Rossetti: His Life and Works* (1928), where emphasis is chiefly on the paintings, scarcely does more than hint that Rossetti was romantically attached to his friend William Morris's wife. Waugh had, of course, no opportunity to read these Letters. On the other hand in *Portrait of Rossetti* (1964), by Rosalie Glynn Grylls, the biographer had access to the Letters, and Janey Morris, accordingly, occupies a far more prominent part in the story. Nevertheless, the role of Mrs Morris remains there, too, an enigmatic one.

In this collection, therefore, the reader has a limited amount of the evidence provided from which to make his own judgment, and it is well worth attention for that reason. There is also the interest of the daily life and problems of a man like Rossetti, by now (the 1870s) a relatively successful painter and established poet in middle-age.

Jane Burden, a striking beauty in the Pre-Raphaelite manner, was daughter of a groom employed at Oxford. Rossetti speaks of 'your costermongering relations'. She was brought into the Pre-Raphaelite circle as a model, then married William Morris (called 'Topsy'), painter and poet. Morris's name, perhaps more than any other, summons up the essentials of the Pre-Raphaelite Movement. He and Rossetti were of course, associated for a short time in what was (in the widest sense) a decorating business that revolutionised contemporary taste.

Janey Morris, intelligent, a strong personality, not much short of a professional invalid (though she lived to the age of seventy-five) seems to have been far from happy with her husband. Morris, with an undoubted streak of brilliance, was famous for his rages, combining passionate enthusiasms for philanthropic causes with personal stinginess about money. His Socialism, and the people brought round them by its theories, bored his wife. Among friends who figure in her letters are the fanatically teetotal Earl and Countess of Carlisle. The Countess, incidentally, poured away all the vintage wine in their cellar.

Rossetti – though in an odd way he had his puritanical side too – was a very different sort of artist from Morris. The partnership had not lasted, though a remnant of it – something not quite explained here – was their income from Rossetti's capital in the business paid by Rossetti to Janey Morris after leaving it. Of one thing there can be no doubt; Rossetti was very deeply attached to her. At first it is possible to wonder whether his letters are not deliberately written to suggest stronger feelings than actually existed, but soon that seems put out of court.

Yet it is hard to feel otherwise than that, at some moment, there had been a physical affair. Evidence exists, perhaps not very reliable, that Rossetti once spoke of that. In the Letters he appears to refer from time to time to some crisis in their connected lives, raising speculation as to whether there had been a time when Rossetti had wanted Janey Morris to run away with him. A possibility might be that she had refused to do so – Morris, whatever his failings, a safer harbour than any offered by Rossetti – the affair then breaking down.

Rossetti constantly refers to the importance to himself of keeping up this link by writing, even when he has little or nothing to say. He had no particular turn for composing chatty letters (neither had she) but there is almost always something sympathetic about him, even when airing his prejudices (December 24, 1879): 'I wish I had more news – for instance such tidings as that Ruskin was hanged or something equally welcome.'

Rossetti was enthusiastic about the poetry of Donne – often represented as a discovery of the early 1900s – and he felt detestation for Manet and the rising Impressionist School. He disliked G. H. Lewes (who had left his wife to live with George Eliot), and said that there was a suggestion that the first move had in fact been made by Mrs Lewes, who had found an uglier man than her husband.

The illustrations are an excellent feature of this book. There are some twenty portraits of Janey Morris, most of them paintings or drawings of her by Rossetti. The self-consciousness of her beauty – shown in all sorts of exotic settings of Pre-Raphaelite romanticism – is to be set against the figure who appears in the Letters, cool to the point of chilliness, usually complaining of her health. Rossetti would be dreadfully upset, for example, if she wrote in pencil because she felt unable to hold a pen. The relationship, as shown by what fragments remain here, has plenty of interest.

Dante Gabriel Rossetti and Jane Morris: Their Correspondence,
edited with an Introduction by
John Bryson and Janet Camp Troxell,
Clarendon Press/OUP.

1976
Daily Telegraph

EDGAR DEGAS

The implications of the title of *My Friend Degas* are something considerably less than the book itself. It is a volume to be strongly recommended to those who like reading about the social life of the personalities involved in that extraordinary flowering of art and letters in late nineteenth- and early twentieth-century Paris – the world of Proust and the Dreyfus case.

Daniel Halévy, author of this book, essayist, critic and historian, is probably less well known in this country than his brother Elie, because Elie Halévy made the political, economic and religious evolution of England his special study. They came from a formidably intelligent and lively family, Jewish in origin, Catholic and Protestant in connections.

The general form is indicated by Daniel Halévy deciding (on the advice of Renan) to take his university degree in Arabic, and, while still an undergraduate, translating Nietzsche's attack on Wagner and subsequently writing a biography of the German philosopher.

Daniel Halévy died in 1962, aged ninety. Mina Curtiss, in her introduction, gives a delightful account of visiting him in old age, and of the select society which met at his house in homage to the sixth Earl of Derby as true author of the works attributed to Shakespeare.

The painter Degas (1834–1917) was a close friend of the Halévy family. He was, as is well known, a tremendous personality. Daniel Halévy, at the age of sixteen, conceived the idea of keeping a journal which was to have special reference to the doings and sayings of his hero, Degas. This project he followed up from 1888 to Degas's death. The result is very enjoyable. The book is illustrated with splendid photographs of the period, one of them showing Degas posed with the Halévy family and friends in a parody of Ingres's *Apotheosis of Homer*.

Degas was a man oppressed with melancholy, though by no means unable to make a joke. With an enormous sense of family honour (the name was originally 'de Gas', pronounced 'de Gass', with no accent, as sometimes given) he had chosen a life of relative poverty in order to pay off the debts of a bankrupt brother – something in no way required of him in law.

If Degas felt such a social obligation to weigh heavy on him, his feelings about his own work were no less overwhelmingly severe. Painting was treated with a religious gravity. Those interested in such things will find here absorbing material about his 'anti-art' approach, which might, in certain respects, be said to link up with similar revolt in the Modern movement, especially among the Surrealists.

> Whereupon [1896] a great explosion from Degas: 'Let us hope that we shall soon have finished with art, with aesthetics. They make me sick. Yesterday I dined at the Rouarts'. There were his sons and some young people – all talking art. I blew up. What interests me is work, business, the army!'

Those critics who praised – who even mentioned him in a general article about contemporary painting – incurred Degas's deep displeasure. They were lucky if they were not cut by him in future.

> Taste! It doesn't exist. An artist makes beautiful things without being aware of it. Aesthetes beat their brows and say to themselves, 'How can I find pretty shape for a chamber pot?' . . . No more art! No more art! No more art!

It is not surprising that Degas's eccentricities led to some odd results. Halévy says he 'never tired of a friendship or a hatred, nor of an admiration, a joke or a grievance'. Unfortunately, as things fell out, he became a furious anti-Dreyfusard, which inevitably shook the Halévy relationship.

Late in life, Degas began writing sonnets, making Berthe Morisot, perhaps the greatest of female painters, remark when told about this switch to poetry: 'And those women in their tubs? What will he do with them?'

> Degas was passionately opposed to the restoration of Old Masters. 'What do I want? I want them not to restore the paintings [in the Louvre]. If you were to scratch a painting you would be arrested. If M. Kaempfen were to restore the Gioconda they'd decorate him . . . Time has to take its course with paintings as with everything else, that's the beauty of it. A man who touches a picture ought to be deported.

Degas never married. He said he could never risk a wife saying: 'What a pretty picture you painted this morning.' His friends ragged his maid to find out if she were his mistress, but received a violently negative answer.

The whole picture of a lost world is revealed by this book, in a manner hard to convey by merely reviewing it. Perhaps the most striking impression is that the life it describes was enjoyable as well as being intelligent and immensely talented.

My Friend Degas,
Daniel Halévy,
translated by Mina Curtiss,
Hart-Davies.

1966
Daily Telegraph

AUGUSTUS HARE

The twenty-second edition of Augustus Hare's *Walks in Rome* (1871) appeared, somewhat revised, in 1926 and no doubt many of his guidebooks, at least for the more out-of-the-way parts of Europe, are still worth a glance.

He was born in 1834 and died in 1903, thereby neatly enclosing the Victorian epoch, in which he was a peculiarly characteristic figure.

The Hares were a predominantly ecclesiastical family, with aristocratic connections, who had become possessed of Herstmonceux Castle, in Sussex, about the middle of the eighteenth century and remained round about the place until 1832. Augustus Hare's father belonged to a younger branch. His wife was the daughter of a banker-baronet, Sir John Dean Paul, whose bank eventually went bust, causing much dismay all round.

Augustus Hare's parents, although extravagant, had just enough money to wander aimlessly about Europe, but were continually inconvenienced by Mrs Hare producing a child regularly every year. Augustus was the fifth, and, when his aunt Maria (née Leycester) lost her newly married Hare husband, they were delighted that she should informally, but completely, adopt Augustus, then an infant.

Maria Hare was steeped in Evangelicalism and her main object in getting a child into her clutches was that it should be brought up in the way she thought best, which was to break its will and see that it had no outlets whatever for enjoyment. Augustus was allowed to meet no other children, kept short of food, and fitfully beaten with a riding whip by his uncle Julius Hare (subsequently Archdeacon of Lewes), who lived conveniently nearby, on call to perform this office when required.

These unalluring relations were, however, nothing to the woman the Rev. Julius Hare married, who was called Esther Maurice and was regarded by the Hares as being of lowish origins. She was also a sadist. She deliberately hanged Augustus's pet cat from a tree, and took him to see it. This was simply and solely because he loved the cat. The name of Esther Maurice, later Esther Hare, should be remembered, and execrated, as that of one of the vilest hags of history.

After being sent to a series of schools (including very briefly Harrow), most of which might reasonably have played athletic fixtures with Dotheboys Hall and taught him little or nothing, Augustus was sent up to

University College, Oxford. There he was kept very short of money, but managed to get breathing space to read a few books.

His adoptive mother by now, and throughout the rest of her life, completely obsessed him. Gradually a pattern emerged of his going abroad, often in her company, and the career of becoming mainly a writer of guidebooks began to take shape.

It turned out that Augustus Hare had another gift. He was the 'spare man' of all time. No enemy to smart society, he soon found himself in demand at every great house in the country. The Season at an end, he would wander from Chatsworth to Panshanger, Hatfield to Glamis, Holland House to the Roman palaces, while his books gradually accumulated for him quite a nice little fortune, notwithstanding the shortcomings, not to speak more harshly, of nineteenth-century publishers.

Malcolm Barnes, who edited and abridged some of Augustus Hare's very abundant autobiographical writings in the 1950s, recounts Hare's life story. He seems surprised that Hare managed to get about in Society as much as he did. There is no particular mystery about this. He had a great many relations.

His temperament, licked into shape by having lived entirely with persons much older than himself, was by nature adapted to making himself agreeable to dowagers and the like. A certain number of guests of that sort were needed to oil the wheels of a country-house community. Somebody was required, too, when most of the men went out shooting, to keep the ladies amused. Hare perfectly fitted the bill.

Even Hare became rather tired of this sort of life as he grew older, but one is impressed by the shattering discomfort of the journeys he was prepared to make on the Continent, even when getting on in years, in order to write about them. He had a strong strain of real toughness. When eventually he had accumulated a certain amount of money he used to have small house-parties of his own in Sussex.

Somerset Maugham, as a young man, would stay with Hare, later writing about him. Maugham said Hare had discussed sex with him, admitting he had no experience until the age of thirty-five. Hare in later life was certainly involved with somewhat dubious young men, who took money off him, but everything seems to point to the relationships being merely sentimental. As Maugham himself was on the whole setting up as being heterosexual in those early days, it would be interesting to know how down-to-earth their talks were. Nancy Mitford, who had remote family connections with Hare, also wrote about him.

Mr Barnes is no great stylist, and occasionally indulges in fairly banal reflections on the changes wrought by Time. He also seems to miss occasional opportunities of unifying the picture over and above Hare's own writings. For instance, when Hare had difficulty in finding a companion for the wild country of the Abruzzi, 'eventually an artist named Doyle agreed to go there'. Surely Richard Doyle is worth a word?

One of the striking aspects of Hare's story is the fury of reviewers when he made known what an awful time he had experienced as a child. It was somehow felt not to be playing the game to say so.

Augustus Hare, 1986
Malcolm Barnes, Allen & Unwin. *Daily Telegraph*

VICTORIAN PAINTERS

This book sets out to be no more than a catalogue of 'Victorian' painters, giving their dates, a résumé of their work, current prices at auction, and illustrating a very fair proportion of them with characteristic examples.

About the same amount is said of every artist, the most famous getting a few extra lines, and they are in alphabetical order. The reader is, therefore, not bothered with anyone else's views, except insomuch as is necessary to give an accurate idea of any given painter. The result is a fascinating panorama of painting in Great Britain during this period.

There is, of course, some little difficulty in defining who can reasonably be called 'Victorian'. Some painters who worked for several years during the period 1837–1901 obviously belong to an earlier tradition, others to a later. Christopher Wood has judged shrewdly in his inclusions and exclusions, so that we get, say, Henry Alken's coaching scenes at one end of the scale, suggesting the Regency: Wilson Steer or Sickert at the other, undeniably Victorian, though penetrating into a much later area of painting.

It is impossible to browse through Mr Wood's volume without reflecting, not for the first time, what an extraordinary age was the Victorian epoch in England; how much we are the heirs to its confused and romantic thinking. It has been said that England has the best 'bad painters' in the world. Here that is certainly suggested, though in an untendentious manner; an extraordinary amount of talent, for a variety of reasons at the time, never came to much.

The Pre-Raphaelites, in spite of the tempered affection one cannot help feeling for them, in many ways did a disservice. How strange they could be, often entirely unexpected. Rossetti's *Dante drawing an Angel on the Anniversary of Beatrice's Death*, reproduced here, is a picture with almost Vorticist implications – at least I thought at once of Mr William Roberts's work. So much pure painting became sidetracked by them into not always the best sort of historical romanticism.

Sickert – in the face of utter disapproval from Bloomsbury – used always to insist that 'Every picture tells a story'. The 'stories' in Sickert's own pictures were invariably stark and witty (he is represented here by *Noctes Ambrosiane, The Mogul Tavern*), but with many painters the stories approached the fatuous.

One would not for a moment be without *The Last Day in the Old Home* (Robert Martineau), *The Death of Chatterton* (Henry Wallis), *Le Mariage de Convenance* (William Orchardson); but, say, *Herod's Birthday Feast* (Edward Armitage), *The Babylonian Marriage Mark* (Edwin Long), *Unconscious Rivals* (Laurence Alma Tadema), never get to grips with their subject.

James Tissot, a Frenchman, though one who painted in England, has great charm in his own genre. One wishes that he could have done an illustrated Conrad, so convincing are his officers of the Mercantile Marine and their ethereal ladies – just like Conrad heroines. There is a touch of Tissot's inspired naturalism in Edward Gregory's *Boulter's Lock: Sunday Afternoon*, a remarkable composition in its way.

Henry O'Neil's *Eastward Ho! August, 1857*, also somewhat in the Tissot manner, recalls the composition of Tenniel's *Dropping the Pilot.* John Frederick Lewis, an artist of great originality, might also be considered in this group. His *Lilium Auratum*, illustrated, is not one of his best.

British artists are great illustrators left to themselves and it is interesting that an American, Whistler, put something of a bomb under them in the middle of the century, just as the new way of looking at things in Edwardian days owed so much to the American origins of Wyndham Lewis, T. S. Eliot and Ezra Pound. Surrealist debts to Victorian painting are very obvious as one turns the pages of Mr Wood's book. That mysterious picture *My Macbeth* by Charles Hunt (dated 1863) might almost be School of Magritte.

I was quite unaware until studying this book that Simeon Solomon, a familiar figure in the Pre-Raphaelite Circle, who knew Swinburne, and fell on evil days after a homosexual scandal, had a brother and sister, who were both painters. Abraham Solomon, who died in his thirties, achieved great success in his day with the railway subjects *1st Class – The Meeting* and *3rd class – The Parting*; while Rebecca Solomon painted such canvasses as *Peg Woffington* and *Fugitive Royalists.* She too as the DNB says 'developed an errant nature and came to disaster'.

A portrait painter who might well be given a show one of these days is Richard Buckner, illustrated here by his *Adeline, Countess of Cardigan.* This is the lady of the *Memoirs*, wife of the Charge-of-the-Light-Brigade Cardigan. Her portrait may have led (or vice versa) to Buckner painting *Drummer Barber: the Balaclava Drummer*, which sold for £1,680 in 1964. Buckner, whose paint is inclined to go rather black, never became RA. He seems to have irritated his contemporaries by his success. Mr Wood could have noted that in *Trilby* George du Maurier writes:

> Hideous old frumps patronised him [Little Billee] and gave him good advice, and told him to emulate Mr Buckner both in his genius and his manners – since Mr Buckner was the only 'gentleman' who ever painted for hire; and they promised him, in time, an equal success!

One could go on for ever about such painters as Charles Jones, known as 'Sheep Jones', because of his skilful painting of sheep; or surmising just what had happened in Emily Mary Osborn's *Nameless and Friendless* or August E. Mulready's horrible little girl in *Her First Earnings.*

The Dictionary of Victorian Painters, 1971
Christopher Wood, *Daily Telegraph*
Antique Collectors' Club.

VICTORIAN SCULPTORS

Purely on grounds of topicality the Victorian sculptor who deserves first word is George Rennie (his *The Archer* belongs to the Athenaeum Club), who was also an extremely successful governor of the Falkland Islands. Rennie (says the DNB) resisted, without rupture, the 'extravagant claims' of the United States; Argentina is not even mentioned.

Benedict Read gives a very comprehensive picture of a subject that is not at all easy to handle. Sculpture – anyway Victorian sculpture – makes frequent inroads into fields only occasionally shared by painting and likely to be much less easy to define, such as contemporary politics and local patriotism. It is almost impossible to write of sculpture without reference to these extraneous elements.

Mr Read steers clear of any temptation to make fun of nineteenth-century sentiments, often seen at their most exaggerated in sculpture. The Victorians felt differently from people today about all sorts of things, but not necessarily more absurdly. Their sculpture must be judged, at least to some extent, by their own standards. In fact Victorian critics (says Francis Turner Palgrave) were by no means lenient in assessing sculptured art of the time, on which they delivered violent attacks.

A certain pattern stands out. Neoclassicism, long dead in painting, continued as a sculptural approach until the 1860s or 1870s. Then the New Sculpture (Leighton, Watts, Hamo, Thorneycroft, Gilbert) produced a fresh attitude, especially towards materials, though without hint of what was to become 'modern'.

It is sometimes forgotten that Thomas Woolner, one of the best Victorian sculptors, was of the founding seven of the Pre-Raphaelite Brotherhood. To appreciate sculpture from photographs is always difficult, but Woolner's *The Housemaid* (The Salters' Company) looks an attractive work.

The much-abused Albert Memorial can hardly be side-stepped at the Mid-Victorian period, when, as Mr Read says, sculpture 'could be said to have ranked virtually as an industry'. The groups of Continents at the four corners might be worse. My own order of preference is: *Africa* (William Theed), *Asia* (J. H. Foley, who also did Prince Albert under the canopy); *America* (John Bell); *Europe* (Patrick MacDowell).

Bell also exhibited a bronze Andromeda, a nude with an oddly modern look about its chunky configuration (so far as can be seen from the photograph) which was bought by Queen Victoria. This shows the Queen as quite impervious to contemporary objection to nudity.

None the less the bishops made a fuss about nakedness in sculpture. Henry Weekes (sculptor of *Manufactures* on the Albert Memorial) wrote: 'Absence of colour from a statue removes it so entirely from common Nature that the most vulgarly constituted mind may contemplate it without causing any feeling of a sensuous kind.' In lecturing to sculptors he added, perhaps rather recklessly, '. . . the Beauty of your work must be in the representing all the organs of the living being you are endeavouring to portray in the state most suited to the use they are intended for'.

The *Virtues* and *Sciences* of the Albert Memorial were to some extent echoed on Holborn Viaduct by Henry Bursill: former City magnates like Gresham and Myddelton, amongst whom one must regret the loss (by enemy action?) of the Lord Mayor, Sir William Walworth, who struck a blow for law and order by killing Wat Tyler.

Alfred Stevens has been put forward as the best of the Victorian sculptors. He executed the Wellington Memorial at Hyde Park Corner. One would say that the romantically realistic soldiers at the base (I speak from memory) – Grenadier; 23rd (Royal Welch) Fusilier; 42nd (Black Watch) Highlander; 6th (Inniskilling) Dragoon – are just what is required.

Local patriotism has been mentioned above, and Mr Read ascribes that as in part responsible for more than twenty statues of Sir Robert Peel in the North of England. Scotland has interesting statuary – Glasgow even more than Edinburgh – and it is to be noted that Sir Walter Scott's memorial in Princes Street, the first major memorial in Scotland of its kind, was to a literary figure.

One notes that Thorneycroft's *Boadicea* at Westminster Bridge was actually begun in 1856, though not erected until 1902. A favourite sculptor of the Prince Consort was Baron Maroquetti – regarded as a bit flashy by his colleagues – who among other works did *Richard Coeur de Lion* outside the Houses of Parliament. *Oliver Cromwell* by Hamo Thorneycroft (son of Thomas) is kept outside Parliament, too, though it is hard to see why Cromwell should be associated at all with an institution he closed down.

Alfred Gilbert's so appropriate *Eros* in Piccadilly seems to have come there almost by chance. D. G. Rossetti turns up unexpectedly in Llandaff Cathedral with *The Pelican Feeding her Young*, and again at the Oxford Union with *King Arthur and the Knights of the Round Table.*

In the Lincoln Cathedral precinct G. F. Watts appears to have put in Tennyson's dog largely as physical support for the poet himself in his voluminous Inverness cape; while the same sculptor's *Hugh Lupus*, founder of the Grosvenor family (ordered by the Marquess of Westminster for Eaton Hall), is only a very slightly varied design from Watts's *Physical*

Energy in Kensington Gardens. Mr Read's book is one to be rambled through, where much else of interest is to be found. There is an excellent index.

Victorian Sculpture, 1982
Benedict Read, Yale UP. *Daily Telegraph*

AUGUSTE RODIN

One might demur at Denys Sutton's choice of *Triumphant Satyr* as a title for his book about Rodin on the grounds that, however well the sculptor qualifies in other respects for the label, no satyr ever worked as hard as he did. He lived to seventy-seven. Even so, his output shows great industry.

It would be hard to think of any artist more out of fashion than Rodin thirty or forty years ago, the moment when Modern art might be said to have gained popular recognition. He was everything to be disapproved of by the 'Significant Form' pundits: emotional, 'literary', unpredictable in style. He also started in those days with the scales badly weighted against him by his passionate admiration for Michelangelo.

Mr Sutton, in an entertaining and well-illustrated study, puts the picture in perspective. Moving quickly but thoroughly through the life and work, he shows what an extraordinary, interesting figure Rodin is, irrespective of whether or not you like his sculpture.

Rodin was born in 1840. His father had been a lay brother in early life, and Rodin himself always possessed a strain of religious mysticism, though this did not take an orthodox form. Rodin *père* was employed at the Paris Préfecture of Police, a similar background, as it happens, to that of Huysmans, the novelist, and other French nineteenth-century figures of the intellectual world.

Although he was not able to free himself entirely from hack work until he was nearly forty, Rodin got off the mark with great speed as a young man. The bronze head of his father, executed when he was twenty, shows tremendous ability, and he was only twenty-two or twenty-three when he produced *The Man with the Broken Nose*, an absolutely mature piece of work.

This precocious talent brought him immediately into contact with the great French artists – and some of the writers – of the period. That fact contributes one of the most striking aspects of Rodin's career. In his early life he met Delacroix and Ingres, Alexandre Dumas and Théophile Gautier; in his later days figures appear like Augustus John or Diaghilev and members of the Russian Ballet, who seem to belong so essentially to an era immensely separated in point of time and other implications from the days of the early Classicists and Romanticists.

It is, indeed, hard to think of any artist of comparable stature who spans the nineteenth and early twentieth century in quite the same way. There are reasons for emphasising this in Rodin's work, apart from the mere chance of the period through which he lived.

Mr Sutton points out that, although Rodin was in due course regarded as a revolutionary force in art, this view can easily be exaggerated. When he set out on his career, although in due course he became the most outstanding sculptor of his time, he owed a good deal to his contemporaries, some of whom were themselves very able performers.

In fact, aesthetically speaking, Rodin was a conservative, who wanted to 'interpret the contemporary situation (as he saw it) in terms both monumental and modern and yet retain a link with the past'. This last determination was closely connected with Rodin's deep feelings for Michelangelo's Medici tombs, which he regarded as weakly modelled compared with the antique, but at the same time full of life and energy, and with important bearing on his own aspirations.

In this Michelangelo connection, Mr Sutton touches lightly on the suggestion – made at the time of Rodin's bronze of Nijinsky – that the sculptor's marked preoccupation with the muscularity of the male body, and his particular relationship with the famous dancer himself, hinted at homosexual leanings, even if repressed ones.

Rodin, a compulsive womaniser, was very reasonably angry at this implication; but – as Mr Sutton notes – the overvaluation at times noticeable in his male figures does suggest the psychological interpretation of Rodin's 'Don Juanism' as an escape from homosexuality.

Rodin was always very well received in England, a country, on the other hand, so slow to recognise Impressionism. W. E. Henley did all he could to make Rodin's work known, introducing him to, among others, R. L. Stevenson, who became a great admirer. Rodin was sometimes classed with Zola, a writer then under heavy attack in this country. Stevenson defended Rodin from this supposedly damaging comparison, not wholly inappropriate in certain respects.

Wilde, too, was a great admirer of Rodin, particularly the statue of Balzac in the Salon of 1898. In order to deal adequately with his *Monument to Balzac*, Rodin found out what tailor had made Balzac's clothes and ordered a pair of trousers and waistcoat to be made to the novelist's measurements.

He was one of the competitors in the entry for the Byron statue that was to stand just off Hyde Park Corner. Whatever the subsequent period charm of Byron and his dog, Bosun, there can be no doubt that London missed a lot by the committee failing to grasp their opportunity in 1880.

Although his personal behaviour left a good deal to be desired, Rodin is an impressive figure, one of those geniuses a little larger than life. His many affairs included one with Gwen John, the talented, if softly keyed painter, sister of Augustus John. She was thirty at the time and the sculptor sixty-six.

Rilke, the Austrian poet, was for a time Rodin's secretary. They must have been a well-matched couple, not only in the range of their gifts, but also in their respective egotisms and determination to come out on top. Rodin was enormously well read and his powers of assimilating forms of art foreign to his own – that of the Far East, for example – were remarkable. More than once he produced work that shows affinities to that of the Surrealists in the juxtaposition of dissociated objects. One feels that he has also a decided influence on such a 'modern' sculptor as Giacometti.

Speaking of sculpture in his own day, Rodin said:

> It is not the *type* which is and must be antique, it is the modelling. For want of understanding that, the neo-Greek school has produced nothing but cardboard.

He was against the young student beginning with the Antique; to do so he thought would make him 'die an old scholar, but not a man'.

The whole of Rodin's story, as told by Mr Sutton, is well worth reading, both as a study of sculpture and the social history of the epoch.

Triumphant Satyr: The World of Auguste Rodin, Denys Sutton, Country Life. 1966 *Daily Telegraph*

ARTISTS' MODELS

Probably the best known incident in fiction involving an artist's model is the scene in George du Maurier's *Trilby* where Little Billee flies distracted from a French painter's studio on finding that Trilby, the woman he loves, is posing before a concourse of art students in the 'altogether'.

In spite of its many absurdities *Trilby* retains an awful vitality. Du Maurier knew the world he was writing about (and illustrating), which is more than can be said of some of his successors who wrote of models. His novel certainly bears out Frances Borzello's complaint that when an artist's model is mentioned people always think of a female model, one like Trilby posing naked, also like Trilby suggesting erotic undertones; whereas in the history of models – not much shorter than that of art itself – many models were male, many were clothed, and, so far as we know, many lived lives of the utmost respectability.

Du Maurier (himself impeccably heterosexual) goes on to say that no genuine artist undergoes the smallest temptation when at work and that in any case Little Billee's friend and fellow painter, the huge ex-cavalry officer, Taffy, was far more beautiful in his tub than any woman could hope to be. This is a typical piece of undercutting of his own premises on the part of du Maurier, and not all who have experience of artists as friends will be in total agreement with him.

Miss Borzello's book has the air of being a series of lectures brought together for publication. She has collected interesting information about her subject, but is it a pity that she has not digested this very well, especially where chronology is concerned. There are constant repetitions, and additional remarks about subjects or painters already dealt with. For instance, Vasari's anecdotes of Renaissance artists and their models come somewhere near the middle; Greek and Roman painters and sculptors, instead of at the beginning, almost three-quarters way through.

The author is right to insist that to suppose models were always women, always naked, always promiscuous, is patently incorrect. Male models were just as much in demand for painters of History, Mythology, Genre, in which both sexes might require to be clothed in some particular manner.

At the same time it is undeniable that many painters did use their mistress as model – van Dyck, for instance, has a fine wash drawing of

Margaret Lemon in the current show at the National Portrait Gallery – and the fact that they also painted their wives does not entirely clear up the question of whether mistress or model (or for that matter wife) came first.

Miss Borzello has not avoided getting caught up in a lot of dubious contemporary sociological fads, which do not always make sense in this context, indeed are sometimes self contradictory. Her manifestly condescending attitude towards the Victorians implies approval of 'permissiveness', but at the same time she censures any tendency to find female models sexually attractive, or suggest they were easygoing in that respect, as a displeasing form of male aggressiveness. It is hard to know how either artist or model should conduct themselves.

There is also a tendency to urge (perhaps on the analogy that hospital porters are more significant than hospital patients) that artists are mistaken in persistently regarding themselves as superior to models. But surely the artist at work is superior to the sitter, whether model or patron?

Certainly, few persons who have ever sat for a portrait can have felt anything but inferior while the process is going on, and they are ordered to do this and that. There seems no reason why professional models should be the exception.

The statement that bohemian life in England came into being only with the 1890s is a precarious one. D. G. Rossetti (often mentioned here and clearly a key figure in the artist/model syndrome) undoubtedly qualifies as making a centre of bohemian life that stretched from, say, Monckton Milnes to Simeon Solomon (whose models would certainly have been male). In another direction were Thackeray (as a cartoonist) and his cronies.

The subject of the artist's model in fiction is a tempting one. Miss Borzello would have been justified in letting herself go about the incident of the publisher's packer's wife who sat for an artist in Galsworthy's *The White Monkey*. It will be remembered that the packer subsequently recognised her in the artist's show, which he had strayed into. It is all wonderfully silly and improbable.

On the subject of male models something might have been said of some of the notable ones like Samuel Strowger (possibly an ex-Life Guards Corporal of Horse), who sat a good deal for Etty, the last apt to be stereotyped as predominantly a painter of nymphs. Charlotte M. Yonge, in *The Pillars of the House*, has her hero call on a painter. The studio is in great disorder, breakfast uncleared away, a bottle of brandy on the table, and a half-naked brawny sailor posing as Samson or Hercules.

The famous Paris model Kiki, who wrote her memoirs and married the photographer Man Ray, deserved a mention. Also Mary Renault's novel *The Last of the Wine*, where, during the Atheno-Spartan war, the hero is forced to become a sculptor's model during the siege of Athens and finally is reduced to seduction by one of the sculptors; a complete reversal of the stereotype to which Miss Borzello draws attention in her book which has imperfections, but is not without interest, and contains some appropriate illustrations.

The Artist's Model, 1983
Frances Borzello, Junction. *Daily Telegraph*

LONDON STATUES

To have a statue set up to you depends, like most other things in life, a good deal on luck. If you are a monarch you start with a great advantage but even statues of monarchs are pulled down, or decay and are vandalised; the former like that of Charles II, removed to make way for the Mansion House; the latter like George I, in Grosvenor Square, a splendid gold equestrian affair which simply disappeared about 1838 after a good deal of damage.

Charles II was eventually commemorated in Soho Square, an eminently appropriate neighbourhood for him; an interesting study of the genial king unfortunately recently cemented over, obliterating its former subtleties of expression. He is also to be found among his Chelsea Pensioners in the Royal Hospital. George I, on the other hand, has been relegated to the stepped pyramid steeple of Hawksmoor's St George's, Bloomsbury. Not a few others, royal or otherwise, have simply vanished.

John Blackwood has produced a really admirable illustrated compendium of London's free-standing statues; scholarly, thorough, often funny, dealing in an even-handed manner with the subjects' careers (a matter not always without problems), while at the same time not too bland. He also bends his own rules occasionally to include things like Kensington Gardens favourites such as G. F. Watt's *Physical Energy* (Cecil Rhodes) and Frampton's *Peter Pan* (J. M. Barrie).

As a writer you stand little or no chance of a personal statue; if a novelist, absolutely none. It might be thought that Dickens, simply on grounds of his celebration of London in a manner no other author ever achieved, might be gratefully remembered, but no. Even Shakespeare muses only among the squalors of Leicester Square. He once shared a drinking fountain with Chaucer and Milton, at the bottom of Park Lane, which I remember. After being slightly damaged by enemy action, the authorities felt £2,000 too much for repairs, when the more attractive prospect of demolition was offered.

The Leicester Square Shakespeare had an amusing history. He was erected in 1874 by an extremely dubious figure called 'Baron' Albert Grant, born in Dublin as Gottheimer (one imagines a dishonest version of Bloom of Ulysses), who was to be congratulated in this case but otherwise only just missed his bankruptcy being criminal. The statue is a copy of Scheemakers' memorial in Westminster Abbey.

So far as I know, Bo'sun, Byron's dog, is the only dog commemorated individually; the cat sleeping under the chair in the *bas relief* (showing Richard forgiving the archer who killed him) on the side of Richard Coeur de Lion's statue being anonymous. I rebel (coming from an ancient Nottinghamshire family) at Byron being described here as a Scot, even if his mother was a Gordon, but Burns and Carlyle are undeniable. They are among the rare poets and writers London shows itself aware of.

In spite of the efforts of the Irish Members, Cromwell managed to get a statue outside Parliament, an odd situation for an institution he closed down. Mr Blackwood remarks that it is 'strangely placed well below the level of the road'. Surely also the Irish Members managed that, after failing in total exclusion! Constant Lambert (who bequeathed the comment to Osbert Sitwell) said Cromwell already had his most suitable memorial in the Cromwell Road.

Sir Wilfred Lawson, on the Embankment, cannot be remembered by many people nowadays. He was a bearded Victorian Liberal MP, passionately anti-alcohol, managing to inflict 'Local Veto' on certain districts. By one of those enjoyable tricks of fate, the statue was unveiled in 1909 by the then Prime Minister, H. H. Asquith, among the country's more notable non-total-abstainers.

On the whole I am in favour of having the nonentities left where they were put, as monuments also to what was thought at the time. The French are infinitely more keen on commemoration of artists and literary men (I once saw a barge on the Seine named *Verlaine*), and one may love the emotional sub-Rodin manner of French war memorials, but England's – especially London's – nonchalance, and eccentricity of choice, has this charm too.

There is not much doubt that Charles I (Le Sueur) in Whitehall is, aesthetically speaking, the winner. Mr Blackwood rightly prints the whole of Lionel Johnson's wonderful poem on it. The statue had a picturesque history: ordered to be destroyed by the Roundheads, concealed by a brazier, who sold souvenirs allegedly made from its melting down, during the Commonwealth, then produced the statue triumphantly at the Restoration.

There are a great many Victorian soldiers, also a selection of Americans. When George Washington was put in front of the National Gallery at one end, somebody suggested putting Kruger at the other. The United States also presented Abraham Lincoln.

There were two Lincoln statues, and a row broke out in America (there are almost always rows about statues) as to which should be erected. One, of course, is that which rises in Parliament Square, a copy of the Saint-Gaudens (by no means a bad sculptor) in Chicago. It was then thought that Barnard's waif-like Lincoln, in old clothes and huge boots, which is in Cincinnati, would do more justice to that side of Lincoln, and be more sincere. However, Lincoln's son, 'known as something of a snob', found it 'grotesque and defamatory', so a home was found for it in Manchester.

There is immense wealth in Mr Blackwood's volume, and purchasers are given a voting form on the jacket on which to say who they would like to see commemorated. My choice is Rudyard Kipling.

London's Immortals: 1989
The Complete Outdoor Commemorative Statues, *Daily Telegraph*
John Blackwood, Savoy Press.

ALFRED GILBERT

By far the best known work of Sir Alfred Gilbert (1854–1934) is the (miscalled) *Eros* at Piccadilly Circus, unveiled in 1893, set up to commemorate the reformer and philanthropist, the seventh Earl of Shaftesbury. The figure, generally taken to be Cupid, is really Anteros, the spirit of Charity.

Alfred Gilbert is an interesting man. He had a long, eventful life, which is admirably recorded here by Richard Dorment, formerly assistant curator of paintings at the Philadelphia Museum of Art. Mr Dorment is scholarly, informative, and tells a very good story, but he must promise never again to commit the horrible solecism of using 'cohort', a Roman military unit, as if it meant an individual who was a co-partner.

Gilbert's background was modest. His father was a struggling musician from Salisbury. His mother, Charlotte Cole, daughter of a shoemaker and church organist of Tarrant in Herefordshire, was also musical. She – of whom more later – was a woman of powerful ambition and the strongest single influence on his life.

Pugnacious, wilful, bad at his books, Gilbert managed to get his father to send him to Heatherley's art school, which many well-known people attended. He was determined to become a sculptor, married a Gilbert cousin when they were both very young, and lived in Paris and Rome, where the young couple suffered considerable privation. He succeeded in making a name by the time he was thirty.

In Paris it was possible for a sculptor to send a piece called, say, *Gorilla Carrying Off a Woman*, to the Salon in 1859, a subject that would not have been welcome at the Royal Academy of the same period. None the less, nineteenth-century British sculpture had its merits and has gone through a long stage of unjust neglect. The masters Gilbert admired were Donatello, Verrocchio, Cellini. He himself represents a kind of Victorian baroque, never what could be called Pre-Raphaelite but latterly showing signs of Art Nouveau, even aspects of Beardsley. Mr Dorment aptly compares Gilbert with Fabergé where work in gold is concerned.

Gilbert's sculpture may not have much appeal for those who think of the art solely in terms of Brancuse, Giacometti, Hepworth, Moore, Reg Butler – still less for enthusiasts for stacks of bricks and used motor-tyres. This does not prevent Gilbert from being an extremely talented and original performer whose mastery of elaborate scroll-work and variation of design in metals is often breathtaking.

Alfred Gilbert was always fortunate in his friends. As a young man he was often helped by Leighton and Boehm, a sculptor now not much remembered but very successful in his day and one of those who introduced Gilbert into a glamorous social world when success arrived. Gilbert was taken up by the Royal Family and inundated with commissions in a manner that might have gone to the head of a man of steadier personality. He was, unfortunately, less than reliable.

His enormous capacity for work made him also incapable of refusing anything offered. In consequence he was always behindhand in finishing what he had set out to do. Although large sums of money poured in he was very extravagant, and perpetually living on what were advances for uncompleted work. There were later rumours of drink, even drugs, but these seem quite baseless. He simply possessed an understandable taste for sitting up late at the Garrick Club and going to a lot of parties.

These tastes, however, considering Gilbert's temperament, were quite sufficient to get him into a terrible mess. The Duke of Clarence, elder brother of King George V and then heir presumptive to the throne, had died suddenly in 1892. Gilbert was commissioned to design the Duke's monument in St George's Chapel. This was to take the form of a sarcophagus flanked by statuary.

What Gilbert produced was of notable originality (although it dwarfed the other memorials in the chapel), but he could not be induced to finish it. Not only that, he sold one of the statues elsewhere – in any case a most dubious proceeding – with the consequence that he outraged King Edward VII, hitherto his most distinguished patron. One way and another Gilbert's life fell into complete disorder. He went bankrupt, resigned from the Royal Academy, and retired to Bruges.

Mr Dorment tells all this story well, and the illustrations are excellent. One gets a good idea of the enormous physical labour in which Gilbert was involved, not to mention the technical skills required in the kind of work he did, the demands on his inventiveness, and the strains of a highly social life among all the nobs of the period. It was not surprising that his wife and family felt themselves neglected. Alice Gilbert suffered a complete breakdown from the pressures to which she was subjected.

How Gilbert subsequently contrived to re-establish himself, even finish the Clarence Memorial twenty years later, is really a most extraordinary story. Although his last years were spent – like many figures of his kind – in being fought over by elderly ladies who had a passion for him, he managed to complete the memorial to Queen Alexandra in front of Marlborough House, another work of undeniable originality.

I think I can add a footnote to Mr Dorment's rather doubtful acceptance of the emphasis Gilbert's mother (née Cole) laid on the family's close association with the Foleys of Stoke Edith, the local big house at Tarrington.

My friend the late E. J. Cole, FSA, a remarkable man, told me that the Coles were in the parish register at Tarrant from the 1530s and he himself was descended from the postilion at Stoke Edith about 1720. This meant a connection with the Foley family over a period of at least a hundred and fifty years which for retainers would have been highly regarded in Victorian times.

Alfred Gilbert,
Richard Dorment,
Yale UP for the Paul Mellon Center
for Studies in British Art.

1985
Daily Telegraph

ARTISTS AS REPORTERS

This is a comparatively unexplored subject and, as it turns out, an extremely difficult one to define. First of all what do you mean by an 'artist'; secondly, what is implied by the term 'reporter'? How far should a study of this kind go back in history; what standard of pictures should be included?

To take a case which obviously qualifies, there is Constantin Guys (1808–1892), not only a superb artist, much admired by Baudelaire in his own day, but one whose influence has been seen on, say, Picasso. Guys is completely entitled to be called artist (some of his work might well have been illustrated in this book) and he was also sent, simply as a journalist, by the *Illustrated London News* to make drawings of the Crimean War. His pictures there of landscapes, troops, brothel scenes, make him the representative reporter or special correspondent of the book's title.

Paul Hogarth, himself an RA, gets a shade entangled in what might be called the purely literary and political (he has decidedly left-wing sympathies) side of this complicated investigation. He is far and away at his best in chronicling the nineteenth-century draughtsmen who were sent simply to provide pictures for periodicals that would today employ a photographer.

Mr Hogarth begins with China in the Middle Ages, and does a brief gallop through Callot, Hollar, Goya and such things as sixteenth-century drawings of American Indians, or eighteenth-century ones of Captain Cook's voyages. But where is one to draw the line? Why not Uccello's *Rout of San Romano* (with its early examples of perspective), or Velázquez's *Surrender of Breda*? The latter are nearer 'reporting' than William Hogarth's *Gin Lane*, which is simply a Temperance tract of genius.

Then there is Mr Hogarth's inclusion of comic periodicals in the chapter recording the rise of the illustrated paper. No doubt the histories of *Punch*, *L'Assiette au beurre*, *Simplicissimus*, *Jugend*, a thousand more, are of considerable interest, but they can hardly be called 'reporting'. They are personal views for the most part, which, so far as possible, reporting should, at least in theory, aim at avoiding.

The nineteenth-century artist correspondents Mr Hogarth singles out for special praise are William Simpson (1823–1899), who had a long connection, like Guys, with the *Illustrated London News* covering the Crimea, the Far East, the Abyssinian Campaign, Franco-Prussian War, and so on; Alfred Waud (1828–1891), the greatest of the American Civil War Special Artists; Melton Prior (1845–1910), another *Illustrated London News* man covering many African campaigns. Charles Fripp (1854–1906) worked for the *Graphic* in the Spanish-American and the South African wars; Frederick Villiers (1852–1922) did the Egyptian campaigns (like Dick Heldar, hero of Kipling's *The Light that Failed*, prototype of such artist-correspondents) and Balkan wars. By that time the camera was taking over, movies already beginning.

The French were always extremely adroit at illustrative reporting, for instance on the Dreyfus case. So were the Americans, particularly of their own Civil War. Mr Hogarth might have mentioned those really excellent four volumes *Battles and Leaders of the Civil War*, which have been reprinted since their first appearance, and are packed with really excellent drawings, more often than not executed on the spot.

Sydney Prior Hall did a lot of lively work for the *Graphic*. He should be particularly remembered for two hundred brilliant off-the-cuff sketches of the Parnell Commission (1889), when drawing was still allowed in the courts. I have a weakness for Caton Woodville (1856–1927) and Fortunio Matania (1881–1963), neither of whom Mr Hogarth likes, because they are too blatantly patriotic, although Matania is, I fear, more at ease with Roman orgies.

The next jump to what must be regarded as authentic artist-as-reporter material (as opposed to what is specifically satire or propaganda) was when well-known painters were sent officially to record the First and Second World Wars. This government patronage of the arts reaped a splendid harvest, as can now be seen.

The employment of artists in the true sense (not what were merely craftsmen, however competent and dedicated) also produced interesting individual idiosyncrasy, which did not at the same time wholly depart from reporting. In that last sphere one might, for example, cite Wyndham Lewis (whose *A Battery Shelled* I would have preferred for reproduction to the C. W. Nevinson), or Paul Nash's *The Menin Road*.

In a similar manner in the Second World War Edward Bawden has his own particular angle, or Ronald Searle from his Japanese PoW camp. Linda Kitson in the more recent Falklands campaign also certainly deserved to be mentioned. Her *Rapier Missile on Sapper Hill* gives a better idea of the terrain than any photograph I have seen.

Mr Hogarth has dug out interesting stuff, together with a certain amount of perhaps inevitable old hat. His history is sometimes a trifle bland: 'the Russians had asked General Anders and General Sikorski of the Polish-army-in-exile to help form a Polish army on Russian soil'. Surely Mr Hogarth hasn't forgotten that in 1939 Communist Russia was allied with Nazi Germany and the Soviet Union had invaded Poland at the same time as Hitler? When Stalin made this benevolent gesture after the treachery of his former ally, General Anders was in Russian prison cell, where Stalin himself had put him.

The Artist as Reporter, 1986
Paul Hogarth, Gordon Fraser. *Daily Telegraph*

HENRI DE TOULOUSE-LAUTREC

Famous men might be said to fall into two classes where biography is concerned: those whose lives were so picturesque that legend obscures any balanced picture of them; and those whose days were passed in apparently so humdrum a fashion that even their washing bills must be closely studied in order to preserve a convincing image for posterity. Toulouse-Lautrec falls very decidedly into the former category. Journalism and the cinema have already helped themselves generously to his story. The aim of this magnificently illustrated volume is both to provide a full record of Lautrec's work by copiously reproducing his paintings and to correct some of the too highly coloured myths that have grown up round the great painter, who was born a hundred years ago last year.

Madame M. G. Dortu, through inheriting Lautrec's pictures and correspondence from the artist's friend and dealer, Maurice Joyant, has had access to a certain amount of unpublished material. This has been presented by Philippe Huisman. It must be admitted that the translation is not a masterpiece of flexibility in the rendering of French into English.

The book has the avowed intention of keying down Lautrec's career to sober terms. The extraordinary thing is that, even when a severe discipline is observed, the facts remain as incontrovertibly striking as the colours and forms of his own canvases.

The authors write:

> Lautrec was no more a French nobleman of the highest rank than he was a monster. The direct descent of the Comtes de Toulousse-Lautrec from the former reigning Comtes de Toulousse is a matter for surmise. The de Toulousse dynasty may have became extinct in the 13th century, and Lautrec was, in any case, descended from one of its younger branches.

Still, even if Lautrec's family did not necessarily link on to the semi-royal house of Toulousse going back to Charlemagne, the thirteenth century is very respectable antiquity for any family. The Lautrecs may not have been in quite the Guermantes class, but they inhabited an impressive château, and theirs was one of the two great families of that part of France. It is often possible to reduce aristocratic pretensions, especially on the

Continent, to mere technical affiliation with an impoverished noblesse. This was not in the least the case with Lautrec.

In the same way it is impossible to reduce beyond a certain point the chronicle of his father's eccentricities. (Count Alphonse de Toulousse-Lautrec was a Lancer officer, by the way, not a Dragoon, as the caption states under his photograph reproduced in the book.) Lautrec's immediate relations were not only eccentric, however; they were also gifted. His uncle's drawing (an example is reproduced in the book) obviously put him in a class far beyond that of the usual talented amateur; and, from the time when he could first hold a pencil, Lautrec himself was entirely devoted to drawing.

As is well known, a bone disease stunted Lautrec's growth as a child, although his passion for drawing was not at all the consequence of his disability; nor did it arise from a lack of attraction to an outdoor life. On the contrary, Lautrec all his days was devoted to such activities as swimming and sailing; although no doubt his disablement – he seems always to have walked with discomfort – threw him more and more, both imaginatively and physically, into the secret recesses of his art. One is reminded – although there were many differences, of course – of the background and temperament of the poet Swinburne.

Lautrec seems to have possessed an almost incredible facility for drawing from an early age. Some of the drawings executed by him as a boy, illustrated in this volume, show a skill and sophistication which are staggering. We have only to think of the drawings Aubrey Beardsley was doing as a schoolboy to grasp how unusual this blossoming is, even among artists of ability. Beardsley's juvenilia are the sort to be found in any school magazine that has a boy who draws fairly well amongst its contributors, even though it was work done only a year or two before he produced the illustrations for which he is now famous. The drawings done by Lautrec at the same age, on the other hand, are in quite a different class and are far superior to Beardsley's.

It is not surprising, therefore, that Lautrec, as soon as he was launched as an art student, settled down to produce work that in some respects he never bettered. The influence of his friendship with van Gogh is perceptible in the early stages – indeed, throughout his career – but at the same time there is always something individualistic about everything Lautrec created. Financially he was not very successful (he never sold a canvas for more than about £10), but those with an eye for true originality and faultless technique recognised his genius from the start.

Then came the drinking and the brothels. The latter, in these days, can be passed off as a form of 'social significance', a line of approach to which the authors of this book seem from time to time to be attracted. No doubt Lautrec did, indeed, appreciate that the women of the Grands Numéros were human beings like everyone else, with simple pleasures and sadnesses that had nothing to do with their profession. At the same time, a preoccupation with all the strange *mystique* of prostitution was something deeply embedded in his creative imagination. In the same way lesbianism held for him (as for Proust) a peculiar fascination. These are not characteristics to be explained as some kind of social virtue, as the authors explain them here: that is surely as inappropriate as to think of Lautrec as a 'monster'.

Sometimes, too, the authors make generalisations that are palpably inaccurate. For example, they say of Lautrec's emergence as a painter: 'In Paris itself art, literature, and politics were becalmed by the conversation which is a feature of all periods of prosperity.'

Yet the 'period of prosperity' of Lautrec's youth, which might reasonably be said to reach to 1914, contained one of the greatest revolutions in the arts which has ever been known. Conversely, a period of non-prosperity, such as that of the French Revolution, produced only, aesthetically speaking, a totally traditionalist painter like David.

However, although the authors do not make much of a case for their claim to present an entirely new picture of Lautrec, they do insist on two points about his character which are both well worth emphasising. The first is that he was absolutely without self-pity where his infirmity was concerned; the second, that, having jettisoned self-pity, he did not indulge in a savage cynicism that set out to hate the world and all that was in it.

In short, Lautrec comes out of it all as an attractive and charming personality, as well as a great painter. That he must have suffered dreadful inner miseries is not to be doubted. Apart from anything else, he was often in pain; and his relationships with women had always to be carried on against the background of his own unusual appearance. That these relationships were often successful and pleasurable to him does not preclude a basis of horror and isolation; and this for a man of strong passions.

The reproductions of the paintings and the photographs of Lautrec, his friends and relations, have been arranged in this book with effectiveness and taste, though the purist will regret that one or two of the pictures appear to have been cut down to accommodate them as illustrations. The method of showing photographs of a sitter on one page, with Lautrec's portrait on the opposite page, is of assistance in demonstrating Lautrec's manner of working and the characteristics that impressed him in the people he painted.

Lautrec was a great Anglophil. He talked English well and liked to begin and end his letters with an English phrase. 'Old Chump' was an expression that particularly took his fancy. It is, however, sad to learn that the Moulin Rouge does not stand on the site of a real red windmill, but was merely a name that appealed to the first proprietor of that establishment.

Lautrec always kept in close touch with his parents, although his father would have preferred him to have applied his talents to the painting of large battle-pieces in the manner of Vernet or Detaille rather than to the paintings he did produce. More than once in letters to his mother Lautrec reminds the reader of Proust, though the resemblance is probably no more than the characteristic tone of the period found in the correspondence of any intelligent, well-to-do French family.

'Lautrec by Lautrec' is a splendidly produced volume – a record of his painting, drawings, lithographs and posters worthy of this great painter's centenary year.

Lautrec by Lautrec,
P. Huisman & M. G. Dortu,
translated by Corinne Bellow,
Macmillan.

1965
Apollo

MODERNISM IN FRANCE

Rather a silly title has been given this book – *The Banquet Years*. The opening chapter, describing late-Victorian and Edwardian France – *La Belle Epoque* – threatens a rather silly book. If you are going to write history in epigram you must make more sparkling efforts than 'the only barrier to rampant adultery was the whalebone corset'.

However, those who persevere with, or indeed omit, this introductory glance at 'The Good Old Days', written in the most excruciating manner of Hollywood, will find information about the birth of the Modern movement in Art, not only of the greatest interest, but here presented in an easily intelligible form for comparing the respective development of painting, writing and music.

Roger Shattuck examines four men whose personalities colour different aspects of the growth of 'Modern Art': the painter Henri Rousseau (1844–1910), called 'Le Douanier'; the musician Erik Satie (1866–1925); the writer and dramatist Alfred Jarry (1873–1918). This is an excellent way of tackling the subject.

Many people to this day wonder what the whole thing is about. Is 'Modern Art' all absolute rot? If not, what does it mean? Some write it off as the former; others blindly accept what they are told – so that one finds action paintings owned by persons who probably possess only the vaguest idea of the merits of a drawing by Bonington or Keene.

Mr Shattuck's book helps to clarify the situation. His world of the past from which the Modernists reacted may be a cardboard one, but he has real feeling for the Modernists themselves. He does not get lost in verbiage in describing their aims.

Briefly, the nineteenth century saw the final exuberance of an approach to art that had begun with the Renaissance. A writer, for example, like Victor Hugo, enormously gifted and imaginative, probably France's greatest, poet, was also pompous, unreal, sentimental, utterly lacking in certain forms of human understanding. At least that was how he – and a host of other distinguished persons in the world of literature and art – appeared to intelligent younger people growing up. (If anyone doubts the reasonableness of these sentiments, let him have a go at *Les Misérables*.)

Accordingly, the younger artists looked around for hitherto unexploited fields – popular forms of art as seen at the circus or music hall: the sculpture of Africa or the Pacific; the apparently meaningless association of objects and ideas that individuals secrete within them, expressed later by Surrealism. The interesting thing is how early this movement began and how difficult its origins are to trace. Before you know where you are, you are back in the eighteenth century, heading for a yet more distant past.

Henri Rousseau, for example, was born in 1844. He was not really a Customs officer who went through travellers' luggage, but a rate collector. His position is hard to summarise because, so far from being in reaction from the academic painters of his day, he greatly admired them. His own naive skill in painting was written about before he was taken up by the Modernists. Indeed, it is interesting to note that he was not attacked in the press until the Modernists expressed admiration for his work.

Satie is quite a different figure. He was of seafaring stock, and his mother came from this country. Eccentric and witty, he loved to give his compositions disconcerting titles. The story is well known of how he rushed through the foyer of the concert-hall where some of his pieces were being played during the interval, shouting: 'Talk! Talk! Whatever you do, don't listen!' This was on the grounds that the orchestra was playing 'furniture music', intended only as a background to what was going on. Mr Shattuck points out with great truth that this was an extraordinary prophecy of the never-switched-off wireless, music-while-you-work, and all the other non-stop musical tortures of a later day.

Jarry is in some ways the most 'modern', most extraordinary, and most French, of the quartette. The brilliant son of the manager of a wool factory, he was only five feet high. He compensated for this by extreme eccentricity and aggressiveness, although also by no means without kindness and charm. In the *lycée* where Jarry was educated he encountered a well-meaning but utterly incompetent teacher of physics, already a legend in the school. Jarry transformed this unhappy pedagogue into the title figure of *Ubu Roi*, his famous play which appeared in 1896 and caused a great to-do in Paris.

How Jarry subsequently identified himself with Ubu, how he rode about Paris on a bicycle with two pistols at his belt, and how he died paralysed but never giving an inch where his fantasy life was concerned, makes fascinating reading.

Apollinaire presents yet another type. His mother was the daughter of a Polish colonel, exiled to Rome and married to an Italian. She became the mistress of a Swiss officer of good family in the army of the King of Naples. Apollinaire was his son – not, as he liked to imply, the offspring of a cardinal. Later, she had other protectors, and Apollinaire was brought up in France, where for a time he worked in shady banking.

Apollinaire is one of the finest French lyric poets. Also closely associated with the painters of his period, he was to a great degree the impresario of

Cubism. Known as a leader in escapades of all kinds, he was suspected of having stolen the *Mona Lisa* from the Louvre when Leonardo's famous picture disappeared. He was held in prison for a week during interrogation.

Apollinaire fought with enthusiasm in the artillery and infantry during the First World War, the wound he received in the head probably lowering his resistance to Spanish influenza, from which he died. His writing is to a large degree traditional, but with Satie he was the most conscious of 'Modernists'.

The Banquet Years makes one wonder whether it is not high time for another turn-over in the arts: and wonder also what form that turn-over would take.

The Banquet Years: 1959
The Arts in France, 1885–1918, *Daily Telegraph*
Roger Shattuck, Faber.

GEORGE GROSZ

This splendid book of eighty-four black-and-white and sixteen colour plates was first published in 1923. As Henry Miller points out in his Introduction, it has lost none of its freshness during the passing of nearly half a century. Human beings remain just as distasteful – if you like to see them with George Grosz's eyes – though perhaps, today, slightly different social labels might be hung round their necks. How admirable, for example, would Grosz be with the Beats and Flower People.

He is one of the great satirical artists of the modern age. Mr Miller gives a few biographical details, and one would have welcomed more, because Grosz was a complex figure, far from the draughtsman of genius who happens to take a simple revolutionary view of the social order. On the contrary – Mr Miller is perhaps even a little disingenuous in omitting this piece of information – Grosz very violently reversed his political opinions during the course of his life.

He served in the First World War and was invalided out of the German army with brain fever and dysentery. However, he was later recalled to the colours, found guilty of desertion, sentenced to death, then sent to a lunatic asylum, from which he was in due course discharged. Grosz was, naturally, always in trouble with the authorities for insulting, by his pictures, governmental institutions – the police, the army and so on – or being too outrageous in his sexual commentary. He only just managed to get out of Germany in time before the advent of Hitler in 1933.

Mr Miller points out that as late as 1962 there was opposition to showing Grosz's work in Germany on a large scale. I think he should have added something on the more personal side: the artist's romantic passion for things American, his love of boxing and his early association with Dada, which arrived in 1918 in Berlin from Zürich.

Although more on account of its attitude of being anti-everything than from any deep regard for the actual doctrines of Marx, Dada was pro-Communist. Accordingly, Grosz, with his strongly felt sentiments of revolt, at first held Communist sympathies. As late as 1924 he could write: 'The answer to the question, whether my work can be called art or not, depends on whether one believes that the future belongs to the working class.'

However, Grosz visited Russia a year or so later, as a result of which he became fanatically anti-Communist. So greatly did his political views alter in this respect that, when an unsuspecting fellow guest rattled on in praise of the USSR at a dinner party, Grosz listened for a time and finally socked him on the jaw.

Hans Richter's history of Dada (1965) suggests that Grosz had quite a hand in the invention of photo-montage as an art-form. He was also in the forefront of those who felt that good manners were a danger to good art, expressing themselves – as with the unfortunate Communist fellow traveller – in rows and violence.

One of the most enjoyable stories Richter tells is that Schwitters, another well-known German artist in the Dada movement, decided to call on Grosz, whom he had never met, and introduce himself. Grosz was notoriously surly. He opened the door of his studio himself.

'Good morning, Herr Grosz. My name is Schwitters.'

'I'm not Grosz' was the answer.

The door slammed. Schwitters retired. Halfway down the stairs, he changed his mind and returned. He rang again. Grosz, this time in a towering rage, opened the door again.

'I'm not Schwitters, either,' said the other artist, before Grosz could speak.

Grosz died in 1959. By that time he would allow no mention of Dada, modern art or Communism. He had lived long in America, but, appropriately, his end was in his own Berlin.

For anyone who knew pre-Hitler Berlin, the pictures in this book provide an incredible resurgence of the past, a real burst of period feeling, the very smells of the Kurfürstendamm. I dare say the nightclubs of West Berlin are not so very different now and the East Berlin streets at least equally sordid. To go back only so far as the fifteenth or sixteenth century, the Old Masters show how little people change in appearance, how similar the people who lived in Italy or the Low Countries are to those who live there today.

All the same, Grosz catches in a quite peculiar way the particular note of vulgarity, lust, cruelty, poverty and wealth that haunted Berlin in those days, all for some reason a little different from anything on view in any other great city.

Among so much here to choose from it is hard to know what specially to pick out for commendation. The brothel scenes, it strikes one, are occasionally reminiscent of the work of the Bulgarian, Pascin, in other respects a rather different, far less angry, observer. Grosz's colours are particularly his own – *Beauty, Thee I Praise*, for example, or *Soirée*. The drawing is always extraordinarily skilled. Above all, one feels, what a lot of energy nowadays is put into saying so much that has already been said – and said so much better and more succinctly by a great cartoonist like Grosz.

Ecce Homo, 1967
George Grosz, *Apollo*
Introduction by Henry Miller, Methuen.

ART NOUVEAU

When, in Proust's novel, Saint-Loup gives Marcel luncheon at a restaurant to meet his disreputable but very highbrow mistress, Rachel, it will be remembered that she talked of Art Nouveau and Tolstoyism. By that time Art Nouveau probably meant something later than the Eiffel Tower (1889), which was one of the first focuses of the phrase.

One would guess that Rachel brought up the subject with some reference to the latest number of the *Revue des arts décoratifs*, which had some splendidly characteristic examples on its covers.

In Britain today the question 'What is Art Nouveau?' might receive such varied replies as 'Aubrey Beardsley's drawings; the Peter Pan statue in Kensington Gardens; the interior of Ritz hotels' – or even mention of some of the old-fashioned pubs of gin-palace type which remain in London: alas, all too few of them.

The interesting thing is that Art Nouveau in Great Britain derived from diametrically opposite enthusiasms from those of France, ending up as much the same type of art. Of course, looking into the origins of any art movement takes you further and further back – it becoming increasingly hard to pin down – but roughly speaking, English Art Nouveau derived from Ruskin and William Morris, who dreamed of the Middle Ages, when there had been no hard-and-fast division between arts and crafts.

In addition to that, Morris was dedicated to a socialism of the extreme Left, wedded to sentimental belief in the virtues of the peasant craftsman. It is true that medievalism necessitated a certain amount of going along with such contemporary aspects as chivalry, and this movement of the Right – a bridge between the Royalists and less left-wing of the Republicans – recognised a common enemy in socialism. However, the image of the Republic on the familiar coinage of 1895, showing a beefy barefooted wench, wearing a Phrygian cap and sowing corn, did revive memories of the Revolution in an Art Nouveau form.

The Franco-Russian Alliance of 1897 also played a part. The Russians took to Art Nouveau with avidity, contributing their own idiom to what they produced. The Astoria Hotel in Leningrad is, or was, a prize example of decadent Art Nouveau, with perhaps a touch of Empire. Probably it still is. In fact Peoples' Republic art and architecture in general owes a good deal to Art Nouveau.

Less expected is to find Art Nouveau's alliance with medicine and psychology. An interest in neuropathology was stirring in other places than Vienna in the latter half of the nineteenth century. Among French pathologists, Dr Jean-Martin Charcot is notable for turning his attention to the arts, in particular Art Nouveau, though he was at first greatly interested in Leonardo da Vinci. This was in connection with treatment for hysteria, into which inquiries were now being made.

Leonardo took him to the world of fantasy and the imagination. Charcot had personal affiliations with Rodin – as characteristic of Art Nouveau as any artist to be named – who liked to frequent the Ecole de Médecine, where he would study medical anatomy.

That taste explains much in Rodin's sculpture. In fact, as Debora Silverman says, 'The discovery that the interior of the human organism was a sensitive nervous mechanism, prone to suggestion, visual thinking and imagistic projection in dreams . . . would alter the meaning of interior decoration in the *fin de siècle*.'

Zola, in a novel of 1888, made his hero think: 'down with Greek temples . . . Down with Gothic cathedrals . . . Down with the Renaissance . . . the solid elegance of metal girders'. But later Zola himself changed his mind: 'We are sick and tired of progress, industry, science.' Certainly the last thing the Modern movement was to like was Art Nouveau.

What I take to be these lectures of Dr Silverman are packed with fascinating matter, leading in all sorts of directions – including heraldry, which had rather an aristocratic ring – but these again could be accepted within a romantic convention, notwithstanding an equally strong belief in progress.

Art Nouveau in France was quite otherwise. Dr Silverman's fine study is researched with exceptional skill and thoroughness. As might be guessed, the French were keen on the abstract implications of a movement which might be said to start with the Goncourt brothers, who, so far from being on the Left, were on the extreme Right.

Edmund and Jules de Huot de Goncourt, half aristocratic, half bourgeois (they could claim a grandfather who had been guillotined), possessed modest private means, which allowed them to devote their time to painting and writing. They combined these with the passionate conviction that (even in the first half of the nineteenth century) modern life was perfectly awful. The brothers regarded the French Revolution as the first enemy, democratic individualism as the second. They wanted a return to the taste, politeness and cultivation of the Old Régime.

This was a tall order. However, by living a reclusive life in an attractive little house in Auteuil, on the outskirts of Paris, the Goncourts did have a most remarkable influence on the development of the arts. Dr Silverman's account of all this is absorbing. A single example will show how the Goncourts went to work.

French eighteenth-century rococo had incorporated certain Oriental motifs and objects including Japanese. Japonism was now spoken of as 'hardly foreign at all', part of the French tradition. This was quite a different, nationalistic, approach to Japanese art from that of, say, Beardsley or Whistler, both influenced by Japanese artists such as Hokusai, in their broad expanses of light and shade. This indicates the extraordinarily complex nature of Art Nouveau.

Dr Silverman gives a comprehensive outline of French political matters in the latter half of the nineteenth century, showing how the third Republic managed to a surprising degree to use Art Nouveau.

Art Nouveau in Fin-de-Siècle France: Politics, Psychology And Style,
Deborah L. Silverman,
University of California Press.

1990
Daily Telegraph

THE SYMBOLISTS

The word 'decadent' is a favourite term of abuse. Its imprecision makes denial difficult. If, as often, the epithet is directed against persons of ambivalent or irregular sex life, such essentially robust historical figures as Alexander the Great, Julius Caesar, Michelangelo, Nelson, a host of others, all risk inclusion.

Employed critically, the word is often no clearer. For example, 'Western Art' is condemned as morally 'decadent' in the USSR, yet Soviet painting and architecture represent an undoubted technical 'decadence', or at least falling off, of nineteenth-century styles. The French 'Decadent movement' of the late nineteenth century makes things easier by consciously adopting that description of itself.

Philippe Jullian, illustrator of Proust and biographer of Robert de Montesquiou, has produced an immensely enjoyable and well documented account of the painters, European and American, of this period, who equally reacted against the academic art of the time and that of the Impressionists. Robert Baldick's translation is lively and fluid, M. Jullian knows his subject thoroughly, not omitting fabled items like the Russian artist Elisarion's 'sanctuary of art' at Locarno, or the German Alastair, rightly called 'disquieting', whose pictures persisted into the 1920s. It would have been an advantage for all pictures reproduced to have been dated.

Dreamers of Decadence was called *Esthètes et magiciens*, when it first appeared in France, and is appropriately dedicated to Mario Praz, whose great work *The Romantic Agony* provides the earlier background, most of it literary, to the painters here investigated.

It should be emphasised that, interesting as is M. Jullian's book to those with a taste for exotic painting, there is quite another angle which makes it worthy of attention. This is the striking resemblance between the appearance and way of life of the professional Decadents of eighty years ago, and that of our contemporary Hippies.

There is the same alleged reaction against a materialistic society, the same drug-taking, the same long hair, the same style of dress, the same abhorrence of excessive washing, the same yearning for Oriental wisdom. No doubt such movements go back to the earliest times. All that is happening now is that a much wider sweep is being taken in a more affluent and egalitarian world. Are we having a pop 'Nineties? In a similar connection Gautier is quoted here, writing more than a century ago:

> Est-ce un jeune homme? Est-ce une femme?
> Une déesse ou bien un dieu?
> L'amour ayant peur d'être infâme
> Hésite et suspend son aveu.

M. Jullian makes clear that 'modern art' springs far more from the roots of these Symbolist painters than from the puritanical dedication of the Impressionists, thought so revolutionary in their day. This is very obvious in the case of the Surrealists, especially Delvaux and Magritte, in what they owe to their fellow Belgian Symbolist, Khnopff.

Through all the luxuriant jungle into which M. Jullian lures us, two guides must never be abandoned: can he draw? can he paint? In certain cases the answer is decidedly in the negative, though we are often grateful for being given an opportunity to consider the matter.

In this Symbolist world it is odd to find what a large part English art played, when one remembers Bloomsbury fanaticism about all pictures having to be (a) subjectless (b) French – even Brueghel being dismissed as an 'illustrator'. The Pre-Raphaelites were, in fact, an influence on Picasso, whose Blue Period also resembles some of the followers of the Symbolist Puvis de Chavannes.

Beardsley was a colossal influence on the Continent, and, as M. Jullian points out, this was not only on account of the excellence of his drawing at its best, but for his biting comic wit. It is the wit that redeems Beardsley from mere affectation. A third-rate figure like Rops, who tried to outdo Beardsley in shocking the bourgeois, not only drew far less well, but was also a pompous self-satisfied moralist with no wit at all. M. Jullian has a word for that excellent artist Arthur Rackham, pre-eminent in his own line.

Among the remarkable performers in the Symbolist group should be named Gustave Moreau and Odilion Redon, very different in manner, but both in a high class. I believe Matisse got some of his training in Moreau's studio, though M. Jullian does not mention this. Some of the Moreau pictures reproduced here suggest that might well be so.

We take a glance at Klimt and the Viennese *Sezession* school, perhaps a little disappointing when exhibited in London recently. There are also the beefy Art Nouveau nymphs of Mucha. Freud, by analysing dreams, gave a twist to the Symbolist aesthetic, based on aspiration towards the world of dreams.

The Symbolist or Decadent painters lead directly to the Surrealists and then logically to the art of the cinema; the film being the most successful expression of such ideas. Again we find a movement that was in the first instance addressed to an elite, carrying an aesthetic revolution into a popular field.

M. Jullian's book shows the necessity of distinguishing between the word 'decadent', as an adverse comment, and 'Decadent' as school of art. At the same time, it is hard not to feel that, when so much that was subtle and witty in the same vein went before, much contemporary pop art is 'decadent' in the former sense or at best very derivative, with far less wit.

Dreamers of Decadence:
Symbolist Painters of the 1890s,
Philippe Jullian, translated by Robert Baldrick,
Pall Mall.

1970
Daily Telegraph

BERNARD BERENSON

I

Bernard Berenson died last year at the age of ninety-four. The family had come to America from the Pale of Settlement in which Jews were segregated in Russia, his parents living in Lithuania, the northern most part of this region. Increased persecution and domestic misfortunes caused them to emigrate. They arrived in Boston when Berenson was ten.

Berenson's father made some sort of a living in his new home by selling pots and pans. Far from prosperous, he somehow manages to send his son to Harvard. It became clear that the boy's interests were entirely directed to the study of art. There were early struggles.

Before long Berenson emerged as the foremost expert on Italian painting of the age: his house, I Tatti, at Florence, became a legend as a centre of intellectual life, a place to which famous people of every sort crowded to meet the owner. In short, Berenson's is a success story the equal of which would be difficult to find in our own or any other time; particularly taking into consideration the gifts, tastes and character of the man himself.

Sylvia Sprigge has handled with much skill the difficult task of writing Berenson's biography. Berenson was devoted to women, and one feels it right that a woman should give this first full-length account of him. Mrs Sprigge's manner is in the best meaning of the term feminine. She conveys all the brilliance of Berenson and his world: she conveys also his own sense of failure in spite of this dazzling career.

In addition she entirely avoids in *Berenson: A Biography* what must have been an overwhelming temptation when writing of such a circle, any tendency to be spiteful about individuals or the Berenson way of life, certainly open to satire. At the same time, she presents a perfectly coherent and firm picture with which readers can agree or disagree as they wish.

The art world is one of a toughness to make an Al Capone hesitate to join in its commercial transactions – transactions to which piquancy is given by the fact that beauty and scholarship play a part. Finer feelings need not disturb the agents who put through a smart deal in steel or rubber. With pictures by Giorgione or Leonardo delicate factors inevitably lie – even though totally hidden – beneath the surface.

In his early days Berenson drew his income chiefly from building up the famous picture collection of Mrs Isabella Stewart Gardner, whose house, Fenway Court, is now a public gallery in Boston. Latterly, he was adviser to the late Lord Duveen, whose activities in relation to pictures were, of course, primarily commercial.

That Berenson liked – and was remarkably good at – driving a bargain is not to be doubted. It is clear from this book that he had no distaste for power for its own sake, particularly in the form of doing a good bit of business. At the same time he was deeply, indeed utterly, immersed in painting, most of all Italian painting. Inevitably there were times when these two sides of his life came into sharp and painful collision.

In one of the letters quoted in this book, Mr Roger Hinks (then of the British Museum, now head of the British Council in Paris), refers to Florence as 'that paradise of prigs'. Certainly there are moments when the reader feels that life at I Tatti may have been almost too much of a good thing. What with the royalty, the art experts, the love affairs, and being considered a bore if you spoke less than four languages, the strain on the less-well-equipped visitor must often have been considerable.

Of Berenson's early married life with Logan Pearsall Smith's sister (whom he removed from her husband). Mrs Sprigge sagely comments:

> In a curious way, with all their dislike of Bloomsbury and its ways – the guests sitting on the floor, the earnest discussions about ultimate matters, the break-up of a good few of the circle's marriages – the Berenson marriage seems to have had some typically pre-Bloomsbury characteristics.

In short, there was always something of a conflict in the Berenson home between high thinking and intellectual exclusiveness, on the one hand, and the sordid necessity of having to make a lot of money and the enjoyment of fairly cold-blooded social relationships, on the other. Berenson seems to have felt this conflict all his life. Even when the necessity for making money was really past, in spite of the unending stream of talent, beauty and wealth that passed through his house, he was somehow out of touch with life, and said, 'all my friends have let me down'.

If we turn to *The Passionate Sightseer*, extracts from his diaries between 1947 and 1956, we see Berenson speaking for himself. These are primarily notes of travels to Italy, Sicily and North Africa. The profuse illustrations are admirably arranged so that when a place or work of art is mentioned, the picture appears on the same page.

By no means all the diary is devoted to art. Berenson comments on many subjects. The odd mixture of sophistication and simplicity is attractive. No one was more direct, had less nonsense about him. He is the absolute antithesis of the type of art critic who presents his views in verbose, complicated form. There is, it is true, an individual manner of handling the English language (due probably to his close familiarity with other tongues), a strangeness of tone which sometimes gives his definitions a peculiar charm.

Witty, though never unserious, Berenson could not laugh at himself, says Mrs Sprigge. In some way, with all his grasp, he was too severely imprisoned in his own ego. Perhaps that is the key to what was lacking in a personality otherwise so immensely gifted.

As a critic he looked back to Pater – now remembered less often than he should be – as the man from whom his own standpoint ultimately derived. What Berenson's final position will be cannot yet be said. There can be no doubt that he left a mark on the whole approach to pictures. He was also one of the great figures of the social life of our time.

However, he is but six months dead, and the reassessment of some of his attributions in the catalogue of the recent exhibition of Italian painting at Burlington House already provides food for ironical reflection on the briefness of authority in this life.

Berenson: A Biography, 1960
Sylvia Sprigge, Allen & Unwin. *Daily Telegraph*

The Passionate Sightseer: From the Diaries 1917–1956,
Bernard Berenson, Thames and Hudson.

II

Bernard Berenson was seventy-seven when the United States entered the war. He had lived most of his life in Florence and refused to be repatriated to his own country, although, as an American citizen, a Jew, and an anti Fascist, he was in great peril.

However, Ciano gave some sort of undertaking that Berenson would be left unmolested. Although the danger naturally became more acute when hostilities were reaching their anarchic close, he managed to survive.

During that period of complete withdrawal from the world, Berenson devoted himself to reading. This book is a record of what came his way during 1942, and what he thought about the volumes that passed through his hands.

Two things strike one on closing *One Year's Reading for Fun*: the first, that it is never boring; the second, that its judgements are perhaps not so brilliant as the writer himself may have supposed. Berenson possessed an extraordinary accumulation of gifts. Apart from his skill in the sphere of painting, he could speak several languages fluently; he wrote with distinction; he had immense energy. At the same time, he lacked that lightness of touch that is required to speak authoritatively of imaginative literature.

The fact was that one side of Berenson was deeply concerned with the pursuit of power. This can be seen in Mrs Sylvia Sprigge's recent biography. It is made abundantly clear here by his comments on Plato and Hitler, and on the many books he read on political history.

John Walker, director of the United States National Gallery of Art, who contributes an Introduction and copious notes to this book, says:

> I am amazed at the impartiality and objectivity of his judgements. Much as he loathes Hitler, for example, he points out the astuteness running through *Mein Kampf*; and, much as he loves Plato, he criticizes Socrates for his tendency to turn conversation into chess-play dialectics.

Naturally, Hitler's anti-Semitism alone would have put anything but strong opposition out of the question for Berenson; but it is permissible to wonder whether he did not feel a strong pull towards authoritarianism. There is something more than mere objectivity, one feels, where Hitler is concerned.

Berenson made no secret of this love of power. He writes:

> Indeed, it is a problem that has preoccupied me since my youth – how to tame publicity of every sort, and make it an instrument for good only.

But who is to say what is 'for good'?

There is an odd entry for 18 January:

> By the way, I have looked over the list of Reclam publications and discovered that Heine and all other Jewish authors have been omitted – all except Spinoza. Presumably, like Shakespeare and Rembrandt, he has been assimilated and Aryanized.

But why should Shakespeare be 'Aryanized' and surely Rembrandt's Jewish birth is far from established? Had some process of self-identification with these great men taken place in Berenson's mind?

Conversely, on 30 November, Berenson writes: 'Shall we Anglo-Saxons do better after this war if we win it?' This seems having things both ways. It is, of course, clear that to take the judgements expressed in this diary too seriously, after blaming Berenson himself for lacking lightness of touch, must be avoided.

He seems rather unexpectedly impressed – perhaps through American patriotism – by the stories of Stephen Crane. Matthew Arnold's verse he praises above 'Tennyson's brainless jingle, or Browning's quasi-Arab ejaculations'. 'I seem unable to understand Russian humour,' he writes, 'whether Gogol or Dostoevski or Leskov.' On the other hand, when he speaks of Gogol, later one finds the shrewd comment: 'In the intellectual and spiritual sense, the Russians were the first nationalists in Europe.' Berenson also admired Gogol's views on art.

After some rather banal remarks on Dickens in general, he has lively comments to make on *Our Mutual Friend* – 'the first Dickens I ever succeeded in following to the end'. Berenson says that the characters in this novel are wooden and show no development, except for Bella, 'who, by the way, strikes one as far more American than British'. He goes on to speculate whether the novel was not written 'under strong influence of Eugène Sue, Hugo and others. For one thing the plot is so elaborate and "*policier*" . . . the intriguing, reciprocally hating married people, strike me as far more French than English.'

This is a very interesting criticism: especially in the light of a thought that has often occurred to me – no doubt to others, too – that Proust's Verdurins owed something to Dickens's Veneerings.

One of the best aspects of Berenson's writing is that there is never any affectation about it. If he thinks something absurd, he says so:

> A thing which is different from another does not have to become different from that which is already different; it must have become different from that which is already different; it must have become different from that which has become so; it will have to be different from that which will be so; but from that which is becoming different, it cannot have become, nor can it be going to be, nor can it already be different; it must become different and that is all.
>
> The above is not from Gertrude Stein, but is taken from among similar passages in the 'Parmenides', which some thinkers rank as Plato's masterpiece. I confess it has made me dizzy . . .

A mild protest must be registered with Mr Walker (and Berenson) for describing Sir Osbert Sitwell as 'Bloomsbury', even though Sir Osbert may have attended parties sometimes in that district. The Sitwells, if we are going to speak collectively, surely represent, aesthetically speaking, something very different from the former Bloomsbury Group; if not, indeed, the precise converse.

One Year's Reading for Fun,
Bernard Berenson,
Weidenfeld & Nicolson.

1960
Daily Telegraph

RENE GIMPEL

These diaries run from 1918 to 1939 and are written by a picture dealer, who was also the son of a picture dealer. René Gimpel was born in 1881, of a Jewish Alsatian family. He died in 1944 in a German concentration camp, where he appears to have behaved with great courage and self-sacrifice.

Gimpel's journal covers the period which saw art dealing change from a minor, on the whole national, form of commerce to a vast international industry involving millions of pounds. These were also the years when the experiments of the Modern movement earlier in the century suddenly found acceptance.

It should be said right away that to go through page after page on the subject of pictures sales, prices, dubious attributions, the imbecility of buyers (surpassed only by that of the lawyers concerned with the court cases that arose from some of the deals) requires a fairly strong stomach on the part of the reader.

On the other hand, those prepared to accept the arts primarily as a commodity will find much here that is of interest. Gimpel moved in the innermost circle of the big dealers. Lord Duveen – of whose probity he makes no effort to conceal an unfavourable opinion – was Gimpel's brother-in-law. His own deepest detestation was for Berenson.

As an observer of what went on around him, Gimpel is capable, straightforward and intelligent without too much subtlety. This approach sometimes turns out to possess a greater vividness than that of a more literary, more practised writer, for example, in relation to Proust. Gimpel first met Proust when they were both staying at the Grand Hotel, Cabourg (model for Balbec) in 1907. They wrote to each other occasionally. Gimpel conveys very well how Proust's mixture of eccentricity, of dedicated method in studying his material and of almost total withdrawal from ordinary life struck an intelligent acquaintance of a rather different world.

Many painters are described, though it should be borne in mind that a painter's demeanour to a dealer is a special one. Gimpel interviewed the dying Renoir, and he provides additional material for portraits of Monet, Degas, Braque and Forain, the last of whom was a great friend.

On the whole, where the better-known painters are concerned, what is said merely expands what has already been written about these dominant personalities. On the other hand, there are interesting references to figures less well known, like the American artist Mary Cassatt.

Marie Laurencin, particularly, appears as charming and comic as her own paintings – one of those beings who exist solely in their own world, and about whom endless stories are told. They are perhaps to be avoided in deeper emotional contacts (poor Apollinaire was singed in this case) but are enjoyable to read about.

> She [Marie Laurencin] loves princes and takes up their defence. She lunched with the King and Queen of the Belgians, but was disillusioned with them on learning that Belgium was so small . . .
>
> She has securities, but doesn't understand about stocks and shares. She has Suez shares bought at 10,000 which rose to 25,000, but have recently dropped to 20,000. Armand [Gimpel's nephew and Marie Laurencin's confidant] told her so and she replied: 'These are fabrications of the newspapers.'

When an acquaintance was awarded the *Légion d'honneur* she commented: 'I don't want the *Légion d'honneur* – oh, yes, I'd love it if it were pink, but red is vulgar.' When Lady Cunard was displeased by a horse introduced into a picture she had commissioned, Marie Laurencin painted her on a camel; though unfortunately this portrait appears not to have survived.

Gimpel's own taste in pictures was decided. He did not mind putting his money on doubtful starters among contemporary painters, sometimes, one would say, on a definitely wrong horse. He devotes some pages here to his conviction that the National Gallery's eighteenth-century *Girl with a Kitten* (presented by Duveen in 1921 and a very popular postcard item) is a clumsy fake.

The translation of *Diary of an Art Dealer* is American and includes horrors like 'mustache' (moustache) and 'burglarized'. Lord d'Abernon, the former ambassador and art patron, occurs as 'Lord Aberdeen'. It should be added that the Prince of Wales (later Duke of Windsor) was – perhaps wisely – never appointed 'curator' of the National Gallery.

These solecisms are no doubt no the fault of the author, but, when he records an American lady as denying that Whistler was essentially an American painter, and saying, 'when he painted the portrait of Lord Riversdale, now in the National Gallery, he painted a work as English as the portrait of his mother is American', we can only feel that everyone had got in rather a muddle. 'Lord Riversdale' is obviously Lord Ribblesdale, but the portrait in question is by Sargent.

The Diaries are excellently illustrated.

Diary of an Art Dealer,
René Gimpel,
translated by John Rosenberg, Hodder.

1966
Daily Telegraph

PABLO PICASSO

I

The name of Picasso immediately invokes a sense of conflict. Some go scarlet with rage at the thought of this exponent of 'modern art' who is at the same time the most financially successful painter of the age; others turn white with equal passion at the imbecility of persons unable to keep up with march of time, or unwilling to recognise such evident genius. Even *avant-garde* opinion is divided. Picasso has been described as a burden on the development of contemporary painting, while many of those who most admire his work pick and choose with discrimination among what he has to offer.

Mr Roland Penrose's excellent biography is just what is needed. Mr Penrose, himself a painter of distinction, can speak with authority of various technical matters that must be explained. He has also accumulated into something less than four hundred pages an enormous amount of information about Picasso and his background. Just at the beginning the book is a shade diffuse, but soon it finds a cruising speed well adapted to the mixture of narrative combined with explanation that is required by the subject. Over two hundred examples of Picasso's work are reproduced in miniature at the end of the volume, an invaluable form of reference.

Picasso was born in Málaga in 1881. He came of an old family called Ruiz, various past members of which distinguished themselves in the Church and the diplomatic service. He adopted his mother's surname, a common Spanish practice, perhaps suggested particularly in his own case as a more effective and uncommon name for a painter. There is reason to suppose that the Picassos were of Italian origin some generations back, coming from the neighbourhood of Genoa, but the painter's blood can be regarded as truly Andalusian.

Picasso's father was also a painter, though not a very successful one. He held a post in the School of Fine Arts and was a curator of a provincial museum. The importance of this fact was that Picasso himself was immediately recognised by his father as that exceedingly rare phenomenon, a child prodigy in the graphic arts. At the age of eight he was producing extraordinarily skilful and attractive oil paintings (one of which is reproduced), while the diploma drawing (also reproduced) by which he passed at the age of fourteen into the art school at Barcelona is an astonishing performance for a boy of that age: not only on account of the facility of the drawing but also for the strength conveyed of his personality.

Picasso was about twenty when he went to Paris and set to work on the sequence of paintings of harlequins and acrobats known as the Blue Period. He was very poor and suffered considerable hardships. By the time he was twenty-five he had already made some name for himself, and in 1906, more than half a century ago, he embarked upon work which was just as 'difficult to understand' as anything he has done since.

It is, of course, impossible to suggest briefly what Picasso was 'after', but most of those who decry him do not themselves bother to give a moment's thought to the complex nature of reality, especially visual reality. For example, in camouflage used for military purposes, if you want a building to look like a group of trees you do not paint a lot of trees on it; you paint certain zigzags and other shapes that give the required effect.

The fact that 'Cubism' and 'Abstract Art' have in fact triumphed is not to be seen so much in pictures hung on walls but in interior decorating, advertising and commercial design. It is probably true to say that there is scarcely a shop window in Regent Street that does not owe something to Picasso and the other Cubists.

However, this is not to deny that Picasso produces much that is hard to swallow. It would be difficult to name one of his Academic detractors who could themselves execute an academic drawing as dextrous as, say, the portrait of Max Jacob (1915), drawn somewhat in the manner of Ingres. And yet . . . and yet . . . there is something about all this dexterity, all this interest in the Fourth Dimension and exploration of the subconscious, that leaves us still at times unsatisfied.

Does his membership of the Communist Party show up in Picasso some basic inconsistency, some inner conflict, never truly resolved? Here is the richest artist in the world (about to move into the Château de Vauvenarques), his pictures banned in Communist countries, who yet remains a Party member. Would not this paradox in itself make a very suitable subject for one of the many 'autobiographical' canvases, perhaps in the manner of *Guernica* or *The Dream and Lie of Franco*, from Picasso's own brush?

Picasso: His Life and Work, 1958
Roland Penrose, Gollancz. *Punch*

II

Pablo Picasso has, biographically speaking, moved into an area somewhat beyond his status merely as a famous painter. It would be perfectly reasonable to regard Braque and Matisse – though perhaps less ubiquitously inventive – as his equals simply in the sphere of painting, even to prefer their work as more classical.

On the other hand, Picasso is 'news'. He is a familiar name, perhaps even a familiar face, to thousands of people who have probably never heard of Braque or Matisse.

It is no chance whim that made Picasso himself, as recorded in this book, anxious to meet Charlie Chaplin. The great painter rightly judged that he had in some degree the same world appeal as the great comedian.

Accordingly, feelings that delicacy has been outraged by the publication of an account of Picasso by a lady who lived with him for a decade, and had two children by him, sink into the background, largely because he has become such a public figure. In any case, Fernande Olivier, an earlier love, has already published her own brief, astringent account of what it was like to be Picasso's mistress. No doubt others will follow.

On this particular score there does not seem much to worry about. Picasso is obviously well able to look after himself, though Françoise Gilot's book does reveal unexpected areas of sensitiveness to criticism. On the other hand, objection can be raised to the side of the story elaborated by Carlton Lake.

Mr Lake assures us that Françoise Gilot has 'total recall'. She is (the illustrations show) a talented painter and, when Picasso first met her, was a young woman used to a world in which writing and painting were normal activities. Accordingly, the narrative would surely have been preferable unprocessed for the popular American market. Mr Lake, an art critic and editor of a *Dictionary of Modern Painters*, imparts to the book the glossy surface of a middlebrow novel. Picasso becomes intermittently a quaint old folksy artist person, when from time to time the Gilot material runs thin.

Let me make it clear that these criticisms are not in the least directed against writing in an American manner, as such. On the contrary, American English has a vigour and directness that make it an admirable vehicle in the right hands. It might have been that here. What is objectionable is that a great part of the book is represented as Picasso's direct speech and placed in inverted commas.

In the first place, unless some sort of immediate recording had taken place, it would be impossible to reproduce page after page of conversation accurately. Secondly, dialogue is one of the most fundamental indications of character. Mr Lake has no talent whatever for making all this talk come alive, much less sound like the *obiter dicta* of the world's most famous painter.

'It doesn't make sense, the way you act', 'Etching is a lot of fun if you get deep enough into it', 'My, you've developed quite a head for business, haven't you?', 'I guess you don't like it here' are alleged Picasso remarks taken at random; and, perhaps best of all (to the poet Aragon), 'Well, well, I'll bet you also like lace panties and silk stockings. Are you decadent!'

Fastidious Americans must find this sort of thing no less trying – even more trying – than we do here. Having registered a protest (and pointed out that Delacroix's twice-mentioned picture is *Women of Algiers*, not *The Woman of Algiers*) it is possible to sit back and enjoy some of the interesting information the book also imparts.

Mlle Gilot first met Picasso in 1943, during the German occupation of France, when she was twenty-one. It was in a restaurant, and she was sitting with friends, one of whom knew him. The account of how she went to live with this man forty years older than herself, although sometimes a trifle disingenuous, has also its vivid moments. One of the best is the description of going to see Picasso in the morning at his studio, where he was holding court. The atmosphere of the Picasso cult, stiflingly boring, yet necessary to the object of this adoration, is well conveyed.

Mlle Gilot herself had troubles at home. Her father (whom one takes to be reasonably well off, though this is never specifically stated) was very devoted to his only child, but in a dominating, brutal way that entailed a lot of riding and sailing, and did not preclude knocking his daughter downstairs in a family quarrel.

Finally she went to live with her maternal grandmother, who seems to have supported her. The uncomfortable relationship with her father offers almost too obvious a psychological explanation of the need for an older man that found expression in her union with Picasso.

All descriptions of married life, or its unofficial equivalent, are to be taken with the grain of salt. There is nothing here specially surprising in the picture that emerges. It is not a very sympathetic one, but, in the circumstances, that was hardly to be expected.

Françoise Gilot gives a convincing account of how it came about that Picasso joined the Communist Party. Communist antics where painting is concerned were at their most ludicrous soon afterwards, but somehow Picasso's membership survived, in spite of comic incidents.

One of the strange aspects of Picasso's behaviour this book reveals is his taste for owning houses – even châteaux – which he will live in for a time, then abandon, leaving them full of his own and other artists' paintings, letters, books, rows of scarcely worn suits. In order to tease him through this whim, an anti-Communist public authority proceeded against him under the law enacting that accommodation must be fully used, owing to housing shortage.

Picasso is, of course, as potentially rich as any man could be. This does not appear to have prevented much of his life with Françoise Gilot being lived in a fairly inconvenient and unluxurious manner. One suspects that a good deal about the subject of money has been omitted from this book.

We are, for example, told that Picasso's Russian wife, Olga Khoklova, wrote to him almost every day, letters full of money matters; while the technique of selling his own pictures is one of Picasso's great preoccupations.

This is just what one would expect, the mystique of money playing a much greater part than its actual use. Some of the comments attributed to Picasso about painting are also of considerable interest, but they have to be sorted out from what is, to a serious reader, a good deal of pretty intractable material.

Life With Picasso, 1965
François Gilot and Carlton Lake, Nelson. *Daily Telegraph*

III

In spite of the silly catchpenny title *Picasso & Co.*, given, in translation (American and a trifle uninspired), to Brassaï's *Conversations avec Picasso*, this is a most interesting and entertaining book.

In 1932, Brassaï, a Romanian subject from Transylvania, was commissioned to take photographs of Picasso's work for the famous art magazine *Minotaure.* This resulted in fifteen years of close co-operation and friendship between them, including the disagreeable period of the German occupation of Paris.

Brassaï is himself a painter of considerable talent – as drawings reproduced in the book show – who turned to photography. His literary gifts are also notable. He jotted down conversations immediately after they had taken place, working them into a book with excellent illustrations, thirty years later.

The great advantage Brassaï possesses as Picasso's Boswell is that he has no axe to grind. Admiring and respectful, without being in the least fulsome or obsequious, he does not attempt to hide Picasso's less attractive traits, though never emphasising these in a spiteful manner. It is all calm, dry, seen on friendly, but absolutely equal, terms.

Inevitably, *Picasso & Co.* will be compared with Françoise Gillot's *Life with Picasso.* In fairness to the latter, its not particularly alluring picture of Picasso remains recognisable. The qualities that make Brassai's book immeasurably better as a serious record than Mme Gillot's are the author's intelligence, depth and humour, against which Picasso's own character is reflected. *Picasso & Co.* is less pretentious, far more convincing, especially where Picasso's views about art are chronicled.

In this connection, one statement made by Picasso seems of first importance:

> But success is an important thing! It has often been said that an artist should work for himself for the love of art, and scorn success. It's a false idea. An artist needs success. Not only in order to live, but primarily so that he can realise his work. Even a rich painter should know success.
>
> Few people understand much about art, and not everyone is sensitive to painting. The majority judge a work of art in relation to its success. So why leave success to 'successful painters'? Each generation has them. But where is it written that success must always go to those who flatter public taste?
>
> For myself I want to prove that success can be obtained without compromise, even in opposition to all of the prevailing doctrines. Do you want me to tell you something? It is the success of my youth that has become my protective wall. The Blue Period, the Rose Period – they were the screens that sheltered me . . .

All kinds of implications are contained in this speech, among other things, Picasso's gargantuan 'self-love' – using the phrase not necessarily as depreciatory – which dominates the book from the highest aesthetic level down to a refusal to do more than lend – rather than give – half a dozen drawing pins.

One of Brassaï's most illuminating comments is his comparison of Picasso's world position with that of Goethe. Starting from the visitors waiting for an interview, often for hours at a time, in the ante-room of the great man's court, Brassaï develops the parallel. 'Universal renown', he says, 'exercises the same attraction and produces the same phenomena.'

If one wanted an example of Brassaï's deliberately muted humour, this Goethe/Picasso comparison could not be bettered.

> Paradoxical as it may seem at first, the more I think about it the greater number of affinities I find, in their characters, their natures, their loves, their lives. Great visionaries – but with eyes opened wide to the world around them – and a constant sense of curiosity and astonishment . . .
>
> An early celebrity juvenile presumption; authority, and ascendancy over those who surround them . . . *The Sorrows of Werther*, the Blue Period – romanticism, then romanticism overcome, denied . . . the thirst to learn – an innate sense of mimicry; to put oneself in the skin of others; to grasp at all forms of existence. A stomach and digestive system of cast iron.

Even in physical appearance there seems to have been something in common, for Schopenhauer was struck by the manner in which the eyes of Goethe, like Picasso's, seemed enormous not because of their real size, but on account of the way they opened wide, uncovering a rim of white, seeming to throw off sparks. Brassaï amusingly adds that Gertrude Stein and Charlotte von Stein might be also in their respective ways equated.

In addition, there is in the case of both Goethe and Picasso a certain sense that something, at some stage, went a little wrong – something more than the inevitable imperfections of all great men. Their very internationalism and universal acceptance, apart from anything else, seems to have bred a kind of narrowness, almost of 'provincialism'.

No doubt that is a very inadequate way of describing one of the various impressions produced by this book. All the same, it is perhaps worth recording. The reverse, the easy, quick intelligence so hard to convey in any biographical work is also glimpsed here from time to time.

For example, the Stone Age is mentioned, and Picasso makes a point, obvious enough when one comes to think of it, but never, so far as I know, previously emphasised:

> What is it that lasts, when buried in the earth? Stone, bronze, ivory, bone, sometimes pottery . . . Never objects made of wood, the fabrics, the hides. And that completely falsifies our ideas about the first men. I don't think I am mistaken in believing that the most beautiful objects of the Stone Age were made of hide, fabric, and especially of wood. The Stone Age should be called the Age of Wood. Among the Negro statues of Africa, how many are there in stone, in bone, or in ivory? Perhaps one in a thousand.

This may be a commonplace to archaeologists. To the layman it is a good point. At rather another angle, a friend telephones and says: 'Is that you, Pablo? This is van Gogh.' Picasso at once replies: 'Yes, but which one? Vincent or Theo?'

After the war was over, Picasso and Brassaï did not see each other for fourteen years. Their next meeting provides an epilogue, which, unlike many such additions to a book of this sort, rounds matters off very well.

Picasso, full of beans at eighty, receives Brassaï with more affection than he has shown to some of his other old friends who have tried to make contact with him in his comparative retirement.

He says – and one does not for a moment believe that he is speaking hypocritically – that he would not wish his worst enemy the discomforts of his fame. At that very moment, the two of them are probably being watched through telescopes. Nevertheless, burdensome as fame may be, the telescope Brassaï himself provides is well worth using on Picasso.

Picasso & Co., 1967
Brassaï, *Daily Telegraph*
translated by Francis Price,
Thames and Hudson.

IV

As the richest, the most popular, perhaps the most naturally talented painter the world has ever known moves into his tenth decade, these three books offer an excellent field for examination of what Picasso has done to achieve his unique position.

In some ways the first publication on the list, the painting book – coloured reproductions of Picasso pictures one side, their outlines in black on the opposite page, to be tinted by the possessor – is not the least significant, in its comment on Picasso's position in the contemporary scene; in a sense, too, on his own painting. Has this ever been done before? Perhaps it has. Yet one cannot quite imagine a copybook called *Paint with Titian*, *Paint with Rubens*, *Paint with Goya*, *Paint with Renoir*, even, if it comes to that, *Paint with Braque*. There is no reason why not. Painting books based on the great masters, past and present, might well provide an excellent exercise. Somehow the personality of Picasso seems peculiarly adapted to an experiment of this kind. The pictures chosen, for copying their colour, range between 1917 and 1962; the earliest, the Chinese Conjuror's costume for the Théâtre des Champs-Elyseés; the latest, *Woman Wearing a Hat*, now in the Picasso Museum, Barcelona. Of the former, one risks the irreverent opinion that Bakst might have done a more amusing job for what was required.

Jean Leymarie's book covers the whole field of Picasso's work. It is especially useful for following the incessant changes that have taken place in – not to say haunted – the artist's career. The whole story is laid out up to date. Before considering this panorama, chronology suggests investigation of Juan-Eduardo Cirlot's *Picasso: Birth of a Genius*, chiefly concerned with the painter's early work, on the whole more or less naturalistic. M. Cirlot's book (with an Introduction by the director of the Barcelona Art Museums) is largely based on paintings and drawings, come to light fairly recently, from the collections of the artist's family.

Here we are confronted immediately with the astonishing ability to draw displayed by Picasso as a child. Musical prodigies of an early age are comparatively common; in painting, or writing, rare. One has only to think of the crudity of the schoolboy drawings of Beardsley (with whose work Picasso, as a young man, appears to have been familiar) to appreciate the power and sophistication of what Picasso himself was doing at fourteen or fifteen years of age. The Hercules, the bullfighters, the doves (signed 'Pablo Ruiz', their subject to endure throughout the history of Picassian imagery), all executed at the age of nine, could not point more clearly to a professional painter's career.

By the age of fifteen Picasso was painting with complete mastery in the academic manner of the epoch. The *Self-portrait* of this period is interesting, not only on account of its facility and adroit naturalistic comment – it could well be by, say, Jacques-Emile Blanche – but also for the maturity of the features portrayed, which might belong to a man of twenty-five. Of this same period, *The First Communion* presents an absolutely straight academic 'subject' picture, almost insistently uninteresting in design. In the following year (1897), comes the slightly more adventurously composed *Science and Charity*, a doctor at the bedside of a patient (resembling Virginia Woolf), beside whom a nun, holding a child, offers a cup. It would easily have been the Picture of the Year at Burlington House.

One cannot help wondering, too, whether this pair of canvases were not, as academic offerings, made deliberately flatfooted, Picasso's tongue fairly well into his cheek, because contemporaneous with them are several marvellous drawings of the artist's sister, Lola, which show the influence of Degas, and Steinlen. In these naturalistic drawings, is there already a hint of Cubism? In any case, we are now approaching deeper waters. The pages that follow in M. Cirlot's book take the breath away, both in their originality, and, at the same time, their willingness to borrow, capacity for pastiche: Goya to van Gogh, Corot to Lautrec; Rembrandt to Greco. It is impossible not to pause for a moment to consider whether this power to master any, and every, style is not a terrible burden for a painter to bear.

Picasso: The Artist of the Century is naturally rather less extensive for studying the youthful work, for the whole course of the Painter's life takes a tremendous gallop over the fences – some of these obstacles of the utmost height and complication for jumping – which lead down to the present day, when, in his ninety-second year, Picasso shows not the smallest sign of faltering. A generalisation, that might perhaps cover the later days, is that the work settles down to a fairly consistent, if also fairly acid, frivolity. This is appropriate to the autumn of a great man's age, work less brutal in feeling, on the whole, than that produced, for instance, in the 1940s and 1950s.

M. Leymarie has interesting remarks to make about Harlequin, 'with whom Picasso complaisantly identified himself in his early days'. I think the translator may have got this wrong. Surely he means 'complacent' (self-satisfied), rather than 'complaisant' (obliging, polite). Anyway the cockedhatted figure, in ink and watercolour, seated against a pink background in 1905, very obviously the painter himself in a sad and disgruntled mood, becomes in due course Picasso's son, Harlequin, running through various avatars, until he reaches the 'enigmatic and blustering' figure of 1969, who brandishes a club.

These volumes make one reflect a lot on Picasso's life and art. When one considers the naively sentimental boyhood pictures, like *The First Communion* and *Science and Charity* – even if they were deliberately naive and sentimental – and the equally sentimental – though sophisticated – groups of the Pink and Blue periods, one cannot help wondering whether violent experiment was not vital for Picasso, to avoid becoming trapped in personal emotions less profound than his actual skill as a painter. A parallel might possibly be drawn with Joyce, fleeing from his earlier naturalism in order to save himself from artificialities and elaborations of the late nineteenth century, which clung to him in 'plain writing'. This may be seen in *Portrait of the Artist*, where (among much of the author's best work) occur pomposities of phrasing that nothing short of *Ulysses* would cure. In somewhat the same manner (on a vastly larger scale), did Picasso turn to Cubism, Africa, all the experiments that followed, to control an innate sentimentality and romanticism, which, to some extent, break out again years later in the Minotaur drawings and clownlike painter with his chocolate-box beauty of a model?

M. Leymarie's book includes a great many of Picasso's own apophthegms regarding painting. These gnomic sayings – which, torn from their context, perhaps also lose by translation – are rather a mixed bag, though on the whole less pretentious and more intelligible than some of the other painters quoted. Painters, on the whole, are probably better away from too explicitly expressed theory. For example:

> How can you expect an outsider to experience my picture as I have experienced it? A picture comes to me from far away. Who can say from how far away I have divined it, glimpsed it, made it, and yet the next day I cannot myself see what I have done. How can anyone penetrate into my dreams, my instincts, my desires, my thoughts, which have taken a long time to work themselves out and come to light? Above all, can anyone grasp what I have added to all that, perhaps involuntarily? [1935]

But, of course. So what? Whoever supposed anything else? To a greater or lesser degree, this is true of all art, and all artists, in whatever medium they operate. If all the knotty questions mentioned by Picasso had to be settled before any picture was to appreciated – anyway admired – why bother to look at a Piero di Cosimo, or a Brueghel, or a Blake, or indeed any painter? We don't really know what Constable felt before a hayfield, or Gainsborough before a fashionable beauty, or the artist of the Villa of the Mysteries at Pompeii about Isis. The best you can say is that to make a statement of that sort reveals something of Picasso's own personality.

What we come back to, as we turn the pages of these books, is that Picasso, in the course of his life, has, in truth, produced something for everybody. It is almost impossible to imagine anyone, who liked pictures at all, not finding at least one work by Picasso to his taste. Beginning with the genre pictures, mentioned earlier, the depressed acrobats, every known variety of naturalistic drawing, all forms of Cubism, a few of Surrealism, portraits of almost every kind, caricatures, personal images, which (as Picasso himself states above) defy analysis.

Among this galaxy, I should like to say a word for the outline drawings of friends in the art world, mostly done during the First World War and soon after. Bordering on caricature, while stopping just short of that, formidably resembling the sitter (one feels certain), they include Apollinaire, Stravinsky, Satie, Diaghilev, Derain, and several others. They seem to embody one of this great artist's happier, less tortured phases, where he, so to speak, holds out a hand to the other Arts, almost in the manner of a humorous Ingres.

Paint with Picasso.
A Painting and Colouring Book,
created by Françoise Mesuré,
Angus & Robertson.

Picasso: The Artist of the Century,
Jean Leymarie, Macmillan.

Picasso: Birth of a Genius,
Juan-Eduardo Cirlot, Paul Elek.

1973
Encounter

DADA & SURREALISM

I

Considering the difficulties involved, these two books give excellent accounts of their respective subjects. They show the difference between the two movements – which were, I confess, rather confused in my own mind – and plot their rise and decline. The personalities concerned are described and each volume is instructively illustrated.

Dada and Surrealism both came to birth during the First World War. They owed their immediate origins to pre-war Futurism, but can be traced back in various forms to the nineteenth century, for example, in certain of the Symbolist poets, and the works of the painter Odilon Redon.

Above all, Alfred Jarry (1873–1907) is at the root of much that they stood for; indeed, both Dada and Surrealism, in their different ways, might be described as 'playing Old Jarry with the arts'. In the more distant past, the paintings of Brueghel and Bosch display indoubted surrealistic, if not dadaistic, qualities.

Hans Richter, painter and film-maker, who has written *Dada: Art and Anti-Art*, was in Zurich in 1916 when the Romanian Tristan Tzara founded the Dada movement. Mr Richter admits the name itself is of uncertain origin. In Romanian 'da, da' means 'yes, yes'; the implication being an affirmative view of life against a background of café chatter, but the word is also French for a hobby-horse and is said to have been come upon by chance in a dictionary. Various other explanations are offered.

Dada denounced art in all forms, but found itself under the inevitable imputation of being itself a form of art. At the same time, even though the nihilistic though talented Picabia would produce attractive collages in feathers or matches, the fact remained that Dada had no programme, and was against all programmes. Explosion and destruction were to produce a new way of looking at things. Art was to become an adventure of liberated humanity.

Surrealism, on the other hand, was intended to be not merely an approach to the arts but a whole way of life, 'in the absence of all control exerted by reason'. The name first appeared in 1917, a year later than Dada, which it resembles in possessing more than one claimant as inventor. On the whole Guillaume Apollinaire seems to have given first expression to the word. The essential traditionalism of Apollinaire's work perhaps makes it reasonable for others to consider themselves Surrealism's founding fathers in its more exotic manifestations.

Patrick Waldberg, poet and for a time member of the movement, points out in *Surrealism* that the term has come to have two separate meanings. In the orthodox sense, there are hard and fast implications laid down by those who practise the Surrealist creed. On the other hand, its name – unlike Dada – has passed into current use, often meaning little more than 'bizarre'.

Dada was essentially revolutionary, therefore – in its own day – tending in general towards the Left politically. Surrealism specifically associated itself with Communism. This seems a surprising choice. Certainly no one found it more so than the official Communist Party, which was not slow to express disapproval for this – one would have thought – totally un-Marxian approach to existence.

The movement was directed at the start by Louis Aragon, André Breton and Philippe Soupault, but, as M. R. Waldberg points out, Valéry, Gide, Larbaud, Romains and other 'traditional' writers were to be found in the early issues of the primitive Surrealists' paper.

Soupault was excluded from the movement in 1929, Aragon left to become a card-holding member of the Communist Party in 1932, Breton remains the supreme incarnation of orthodox Surrealism. In 1935 he lost his position on the Congrès Mondial des Ecrivains pour la Défence de la Culture for boxing the ears of the Soviet author Ilya Ehrenburg for speaking lightly of Surrealists.

One is interested to learn that Breton – of whom there is here an engaging portrait at the age of eighteen months, from which the birth of Surrealism might already have been predicted – was brought up on the illustrations of Arthur Rackham.

Surrealism, although it has spread all over the world – in 1945 it caused a change of government in Haiti – is, on the whole, a Paris-born movement. Not so Dada, in which Zurich, Berlin, Hanover, Cologne and New York all played an important part.

It is noticeable that neither movement, in its younger, more vigorous days, had anything to be called a following in this country. There was, it is true, a Surrealist exhibition in London in 1936, and in the previous year David Gascoyne produced an admirable *Short Survey of Surrealism.* Roland Penrose is a distinguished English surrealist painter. Yet, even allowing for these and a few other aspects, Surrealism never really took a hold on Great Britain – Dada still less.

It is permissible to wonder whether this lack of early immunisation is not expressing itself today. Not only the arts (as demonstrated in the recently published collection *Private View*) but also the fashionable 'satire' and desire for a break with the past, without any particular taste for the future, seem to suggest something of the sort. In its more general aspects, one would say Surrealist painting and sculpture (in the widest sense of those terms) have, on the whole, stood up better than Surrealist writing.

Dada: Art and Anti-Art, 1966
Hans Richter, Thames and Hudson. *Daily Telegraph*

Surrealism,
Patrick Waldberg, Thames and Hudson.

II

Art criticism is apt to be unintelligible enough at the best of times. To make it comprehensible where Dada and Surrealism are concerned is an achievement. William S. Rubin brings this off with flying colours; one might almost say with literally flying colours. His *Dada and Surrealist Art* is clear, instructive, scholarly, by no means without humour.

Mr Rubin, who is curator of painting and sculpture at the New York Museum of Modern Art, threads his way through the daunting jungle of ideas, contradictions and quarrels that encompass these two movements, presenting them as they now stand historically. Dada appeared in Zurich during the 1914–1918 war. The nucleus, founded by Tristan Tzara and others, was therefore not Paris-based, nor French in tone. It was largely Central European, with aspects that owed something to Italian Futurism. Dada was anti-everything – anti-art as much as anything else.

Surrealism, Paris-based, but also only to a limited degree French in the artists it produced, derives from Dada. Equally revolutionary in orientation, and theoretically 'anti-art', it accepted painting as a 'lamentable expediment', more especially to express in a graphic form what Surrealism added to Dada, a preoccupation with the unconscious mind and its working. Tzara wrote in 1918:

> Honour, Country, Morality, Family, Art, Religion, Liberty, Fraternity had once answered to human needs. But nothing [remains] of them but skeletons. . . . There is a great negative work of destruction to be accomplished. We must sweep and clean.

That was written over fifty years ago. It sounds only too familiar today, still produced as the latest thing. The difference, alas, is that the Dadaists were, many of them, men of talent and wit, while the contemporary dons and 'sociologists', who echo them, as a rule have very modest claims to the former quality. None to the latter.

Surrealism systematised Dada. Although no less determined to reject inherent aesthetic values, above all the autonomy of 'pure painting', its elite could not altogether get away from the painful fact that there is no denying some people draw and paint 'better' than others. The Surrealists' employment of the subconscious, their deliberate association in painting, sculpture and writing, of normally dissociated objects, enabled the movement to absorb many of its own built-in contradictions and absurdities. These sometimes created in themselves surrealist 'happenings'.

One of the whimsicalities – one might even say intellectually damaging false steps – of the Surrealist movement was specifically to support Communism. This shows a strain of real obtuseness, as, of course, nothing was more opposed to 'Socialist Realism', and the whole bag of tricks of 'Marxist Art'.

However, its very absurdity gave this aspect of Surrealism a certain authenticity. Another amusing example may be quoted. In the Chronology of Surrealism here provided, it is noted that in 1926 the Surrealists kicked up a row at Constant Lambert's ballet *Romeo and Juliette,* because they thought the surrealist painters Miró and Ernst (both later returned to the fold) should not collaborate with Diaghilev. I remember Lambert telling me that this was reported in some papers as a disturbance made by 'Royalists'; an admirable example of practical Surrealism.

When Surrealism is looked into in larger terms, it can be found to have a long history in the past. Examples are illustrated here of painters like the sixteenth-century Larmessin; and nineteenth-century Redon or Klinger, to whom the Englishman Dadd might have been added, and many more.

In fact Surrealism is just one additional example of a recurring feature in all the arts, the war over fantasy. 'Pure painting' had never so much triumphed as with the Impressionists – even the Post-Impressionists were to some extent moving away – and a strong reaction from the pedantry, for example, of art criticism like Roger Fry's, was bound to come. Freud and the psychoanalytical way of looking at things provided a convenient lever. It is related of Miró that he said of the Cubists: 'I will break their guitar.'

Miró himself was one of the most distinguished of the Surrealist group, and Sir Roland Penrose's detailed study of him is recommended. The Spanish regime had the good sense to appreciate the value of this great Catalan artist, who has recently (1969) executed a mural (illustrated in Sir Roland's book) for Barcelona airport.

Mr Rubin considers the major Surrealist artists individually; Duchamp, Picabia, Man Ray (who used Samuel Beckett's title *End Game* in 1946), Arp, Ernst, Schwitters, Chirico, Miró, Masson, Tanguy, Magritte, Dalí (with due reservations), Giacometti, Picasso. Picasso was a marginal Surrealist case, and it is arguable that the connection was not mutually advantageous.

The Surrealists produced some splendid artists, who still stimulate the imagination. One cannot quite share Mr Rubin's comparative enthusiasm for Surrealism in exile, nor the more or less Surrealist New American painting; at least a lot of it. Surrealism is over. We can, with an appropriately Surrealist gesture, hang our Arps on a weeping willow tree and recall the triumphs of yesteryear.

Dada and Surrealist Art,
William S. Rubin,
Thames and Hudson.

Miró,
Roland Penrose,
Thames and Hudson.

1970
Daily Telegraph

MAN RAY

If there were no other reason for recommending Man Ray's autobiography, the book is like a breath of fresh air in its presentation of the arts as something to be lived with and enjoyed, rather than one of several available branches of moral and social improvement which all good citizens should study.

'It would be a great help [he says] if the word "serious" could be eliminated from the vocabulary. It must have been invented by critics not too sure of themselves condemning all of the most exciting and profound works that have been produced through the ages.'

Apart from that, the author's story is one of considerable interest both as an account of the adventures of an individual, and as a piece of necessary and comparatively unknown background to the history of the Modern movement in painting, which began to take shape in the first decade of this century.

Man Ray is probably best known in this country as a photographer, but he began his career as a painter, and, since the last war, it is painting that has again chiefly occupied him. Some of the results may be seen in his current show in London.

Self Portrait is not overloaded with dates, but from exterior evidence one may guess that Mr Ray was born in 1890, in not particularly affluent circumstances. Brought up in Brooklyn, New York, he looks in a photograph alarmingly knowing at the age of five, wearing a black velvet suit and lace collar. This mature appearance does not seem to have belied the fact.

He tried various jobs as a young man, but always came back to his interest in painting. This, in itself, may not have been particularly unusual, but what does seem very extraordinary is that his enthusiasm, without, so far as one can see, the smallest intellectual encouragement, should have taken a specifically 'modern' form in rather drab American surroundings. It is remarkable that this new approach should have flowered in so many utterly different places at the same moment. Of course it can be shown that the roots go deep in the history of art, but even so the suddenness and luxuriance of the harvest is notable.

For example, among the illustrations of this book is a portrait of the author's first wife, Donna, dated 1913, when Mr Ray was about twenty-three, which is completely assured in its 'modernistic' approach. Incidentally, the account of the break-up of this marriage is told with cool and effective force.

Paris was the inevitable goal. Man Ray arrived there on 14 July, 1921. Although his initial lack of French led him to suppose that *Hôtel Meublé* was the actual name of the place he first inhabited, he moved immediately into the heart of the Dada circle, founded by Tristan Tzara.

From this point Mr Ray became an integral part of that remarkable Paris renaissance of the 1920s. He lived with the famous model Kiki, and it was at this stage that his work became chiefly associated with photography.

There are a great many amusing anecdotes that stem from photographing people. The account of Paul Poiret, founder of the famous fashion house and talented amateur cook, is interesting and tragic; Mr Ray's visit to the country house of Comtesse Greffuhle (on whom Proust to some extent based the Duchesse de Guermantes) picturesque and comic. There are vignettes of most of the well-known people of the period who played some part in the art world.

When the war came in 1939, Mr Ray left France for America, not without an adventurous time doing so. Now he is back in Paris again.

The narrative style of the book is well kept up, and there are plenty of stimulating thoughts on life, for example, 'a creator only needs one enthusiast to justify him'. There is perhaps rather a tendency to suggest that amatory relationships are easier to handle than most people find them. All the same, this means that you can get on with the story, and are not held up with the author's emotional troubles.

In short, Man Ray's book is full of points for those who like the period. But to publish it without an index was worse than a crime; it was a blunder. Even a phoney one would have made a nostalgic Dada gesture.

Self Portrait,
Man Ray, Deutsch.

1963
Daily Telegraph

RENE MAGRITTE

This is an excellent account of the work of a painter who, although classed as a Surrealist, has always stood to some extent apart from the Surrealist movement. Suzi Gablik, herself a painter, tackles a lot of complicated material in a clear and businesslike manner. Her study brings Magritte into perspective – using the metaphor without forgetting Magritte's own painting – the bowler-hatted, overcoated figure emerging at times with startling clearness from the mist, then disappearing again, or duplicating and re-duplicating himself.

Miss Gablik bases her study on the extreme intellectuality of Magritte's painting, his philosophic approach, rather than the paint-on-canvas attitude of other schools. This preference seems to some extent illustrated by the painter's own inclination to use of the ordinary rooms of the house, the boudoir or kitchen, as the scene of his work, rather than allocating a special studio for painting.

René Magritte (1898–1967) disliked contemplating his own past, or anyone else's, so little is recorded of his early life in Belgium. This does not matter greatly, though one would have liked, at least, to know the profession of his father. Miss Gablik does, however, point out that Magritte comes under the sign of Scorpio, which is not at all a surprise, that touch of asperity in such astrological 'natives' certainly emerging in the pictures.

Magritte went to Paris, where, before he was thirty, he was moving in the world of Breton and Eluard. Although not specially politically minded, he was from time to time associated, like the rest of the Surrealists, with Communism, of which the best one can say is the Communist persecution of artists, writers and intellectuals generally was less well known in those days.

Examples are given in Miss Gablik's book of early pictures by Magritte, when he was more or less under the influence of Cubism, a school in which the illustrations here show him never to have been at ease. What concerned him in due course was the 'mystery of the image', the actual impact made on the viewer by the picture, which can be effected in no other way than the visual. The 'poetic meaning' of the object was what the artist aimed at providing, but this was something that could not be put into words, especially as words themselves often lacked meaning, or conveyed wrong impressions.

This preoccupation with words is a great feature of Magritte's form of attack. To illustrate the independence of words from meaning, Miss Gablik instances the name of the chief of a certain African tribe, 'who was called Oxford University Press'. Clearly these words were not interchangeable with their more commonplace use, and confusion would undoubtedly arise if the well-known publishing firm occasionally described itself as 'Headman of the Borioboola-Gha', or whatever the tribe and its ruler's specific designation.

Magritte tended to work over a comparatively small range of subjects, for example his *Lost Jocky* sequence, and it was up to anyone who looked at the pictures to decide what they meant. This did not imply that Magritte painted anything that came into his head. On the contrary, he took an enormous amount of trouble, tried out all sorts of experiments, before the subject was finally decided upon. There is perhaps a slight disparity of thought in this very careful decision, then complete abandonment of allowing that the picture had a special 'meaning'.

One of the landmarks in Magritte's painting life was his introduction to the work of Chirico, himself a figure set apart from the other Surrealists. Chirico, when contact was made, was perfectly polite, but obviously not immensely enthusiastic about the younger painter's work. Oddly enough this situation was to some extent reproduced by Magritte himself, in due course, in relation to the Pop Art of today, certain sides of which more or less derive from him.

Magritte found 'Pop' an easy way out, a sugared version of Dada, and it is hard not to agree with him, if most of what one sees on exhibition is anything to judge by. Magritte was equally unattracted by abstract painting. Like Sickert, he felt that every picture should tell a story, even if a philosophic one; the function of painting was 'to make poetry visible, and not to reduce the world to its numerous materialistic aspects'.

During the German occupation of Belgium, Magritte produced quite a different line of painting, which might be described as satirical Renoirs. These in due course greatly upset the French, and when they were followed up by burlesques of the Fauves the rage of Paris was unbounded. This was an enjoyable, and appropriately Surrealist, gesture; the French being very fond of ragging other people, but not at all keen on being ragged themselves. It might be added that the Belgians are particularly proficient at ragging the French.

In spite of his dislike for talking about his own work Magritte puts the case very well in one of his writings quoted by Miss Gablik:

> The other day someone asked me what the relationship was between my life and my art. I couldn't really think of any, except that life obliges me to do something, so I paint. But I am not concerned with 'pure' poetry nor with 'pure' painting. It is rather pointless to put one's hopes

> in a dogmatic point of view since it is the power of enchantment which matters.

Finally, it is impossible not to be struck by the professionalism of Magritte's painting, in whatever form. Some of his last pictures executed a short time before his death strike one as among the best.

Magritte,
Suzi Gablik,
Thames and Hudson.

1971
Apollo

MAX ERNST

Max Ernst was born in 1891, the son of a schoolmaster who had chosen to teach in a school for the deaf and dumb. The father was also an amateur painter, so, as ever, one finds unusual origins in those themselves unusual. However, Ernst's painting was in due course more than his father could put up with, and the son left his parents' home for ever. One recalls the Ernst picture *Young People Trampling Their Mother under Foot.*

John Russell, not only a critic deeply concerned with the artist's work, but also a friend who has enjoyed the advantage of long talks with him about it, has produced a lively narrative that touches – just as Ernst's pictures do – on all sorts of subjects, some of them only indirectly connected with the matter in hand. That is the way to do it – so to speak, to engulf Ernst in the manner he himself engulfs the people who look at his pictures.

One begins by being astonished by the contemporary nature of the 'abstracts' Ernst was producing as far back as 1906. Apart from their merits as paintings, they could be put on show today without giving the smallest clue to suggest they had not been painted during the last few months. From this flying start the painter's career was interrupted by the First World War.

When he emerged from the army he was a key figure in Cologne-Dada. Then he moved to Paris, where he was associated with the Surrealists. Mr Russell seems a trifle apologetic about Ernst's connexions with the Surrealists, somewhat soft-pedalling their support of Communism, though in fact he tells us that Ernst himself has always been more attracted by Nietzsche's approach to things than by Marx's.

The Second World War caused havoc to Ernst. After unpleasant and dangerous experiences, he managed to get to America in 1941. There he remained for eight years, taking a great fancy to things Red Indian, which there have on the whole been few to love and even fewer praise, so far as artists are concerned, if one excepts some attractive eighteenth- or early-nineteenth-century prints of Redskins.

> Max Ernst [writes Mr Russell] was used to working against the grain of society, and in his youth had gloried in it. But only for a brief moment had he really worked against the grain of European painting. He had

> been against 'beauty', against 'composition', against coherence of style, and against the sensuous use of oil paint at a time when these attitudes had an exemplary value and were part of a campaign to re-define the basis of art. But in 1953 those attitudes were a thing of the past, and there was no ideological basis to preserve them.

We are conscious of some relief at being told this. Those who are 'against' beauty and composition are, critically speaking, as difficult to commend as to blame. In fact, one feels that a mastery of form and colour is just what Ernst possesses. For instance, a picture like *Anthropomorphic Figure*, dating from 1929, might be judged, one would think, just as if it were an eighteenth-century Venetian canvas, which the head (looking like a tricorne hat) makes it somewhat resemble. We recall, of course, similar diatribes against beauty by Degas and other artists irritated by critics of an earlier vintage.

Ernst has always been drawn to sculpture and African influences are here very apparent. It is interesting to note some affinity between Ernst's *The King Playing [chess] with the Queen*, and Henry Moore's huge group called simply *The King and the Queen.*

The collages demonstrate very clearly Ernst's essentially intellectual approach, his lyrical humour and touch – more perhaps than a touch – of sado-masochism. Up to a point, of course, if supplied with appropriate illustrations to get to work on, it is not difficult with some imaginative gift, to produce good collage results. Even so, Ernst's have to be admitted to be not only pioneering but masterly. One would specially mention *Plus légère que l'atmosphère, puissante et isolée; Perturbation, ma soeur, la Femme 100 têtes.*

Indications that the life of a painter like Ernst is forced into the pattern of his art abound throughout the book. One of the best examples was provided when he was in the Army during the 1914–18 war. At first Ernst was a gunner, and an officer, whose name deserves to be preserved, Lieutenant Wohltat, turned out to be familiar with his work. It was arranged that the painter should only mark maps for an hour or two, then get on with his painting. That was naturally too good to last long. Ernst was sent backwards and forwards, from Western to Eastern front, then posted to an (apparently dismounted) detachment of the Death's Head Hussars. The combination of appropriateness and inappropriateness, like the components of many of Ernst's own canvases, almost passes belief.

However, in addition to this, the year being 1918, there existed a suspicion that the regular officers of this famous regiment were to be preserved to assist the post-war cadre, and that only the temporary ones, like Ernst, were to be sent into the dangers of the line. If that were true, one must greatly regret that no Ernst picture was produced called *The Life's Head Hussars.*

Even then, para-military experiences were not at an end. As if the cavalry theme was to be repeated endlessly throughout his life, Ernst, hard up in Paris in 1922, took a job as a film extra in a version of *The Three Musketeers*. After surviving a gallop over a field sown with firecrackers, he was dismissed (one hopes after court-martial) for removing his wig during a take.

Mr Russell describes all these adventures and many more, greatly adding to the enjoyment of the purely aesthetic side of the volume. Sometimes one may join issue with him over statements like '*La Nausée*, *L'Etranger* and *Murphy* were as destructive of established values as anything that the surrealists had thought up, and their authors were taking over the role played in the 1930s by the "great writers of officialdom" ' – or agree in perhaps a rather different context from his own. One also a little regrets use of the Americanism 'high-ranking' in place of senior' officer, for which a stand should be made. However, these criticisms are only to be excused by their dissociative characteristics in tune with the subject. We have been given very good value, if only for the mention of the German legend, here recalled of 'the Musicians of the city of Bremen whose music was so out of tune as to make an intending thief turn back in terror'.

Max Ernst: Life and Work, 1968
John Russell, *Apollo*
Thames and Hudson.

THE EUSTON ROAD SCHOOL

Writing in 1950 about a show of the Camden Town Group held at Lefevre Gallery, Wyndham Lewis said:

> As a nation, the English are naturalists. Impressionism is a kind of painting suited to their temperament. In 1911 there was the Camden Town Group; then about thirty years later I entered a small Gallery off Piccadilly and really believed myself at first among French impressionist pictures . . . This was the Euston Road Group . . . let me say at once that if a Camden Town team were matched against a Euston Road team it would be a pretty near thing. Of course if there were half a dozen good Sickerts and good Gilmans they would win. But with the team on show at the Lefevre it would be a walk-over for the Euston Roaders.

One might add, in favour of the Camden Town Group, certainly Spencer Gore and perhaps Charles Ginner, but this is an interesting view from an artist and critic who admittedly did not himself care for naturalism.

Bruce Laughton, who is head of the Department of Art at Queen's University, Canada, has produced an extremely full, lively, well-illustrated account of the Euston Roaders, whose initial phase was in 1937, when they decided to 'start again'.

Strictly speaking the original members of the school were Victor Pasmore, William Coldstream and Claude Rogers, with Graham Bell more or less behind the scenes. Of course many other painters, some appreciably younger, were later to have the label attached to them, several of these, like Rodrigo Moynihan and Lawrence Gowing, possessing characteristics very different from the founding fathers.

Graham Bell, whose family was based in South Africa if not exactly South African, also wrote. He has left an extremely vivid account of getting to know Pasmore and Coldstream, when he was living a very penurious life with his wife in Regent Square, Bloomsbury. The slight atmosphere of bleakness which hangs over the early work of the group was exemplified most by Bell, who was violently Left, somewhat Tolstoyan, at times given over to religiosity. Nevertheless, when war came in 1939, he at once saw his duty as in the Services, and was killed during a training flight with the RAF.

Old Bloomsbury was not wholly well disposed to these young painters, who could be critical of Duncan Grant and Vanessa Bell at times, but the Anreps were friends. The group was also associated with W. H. Auden, Coldstream painting a portrait of the poet and the poet's mother.

In 1937, the movement known as Mass Observation made various experiments of a supposedly 'sociological' kind, one of which was to attempt to discover what 'the public', in what was romantically described as 'Worktown', really liked in the way of pictures. Bolton was chosen as prototype of this concept, and four artists were invited to paint pictures of the town. Two of these, William Coldstream and Graham Bell, were chosen as of the 'Realistic School'; a third, Michael Wickham, was described as 'an impressionist, vivid, Gauguin sort of stuff'; the fourth, Julian Trevelyan, 'a leading exponent of the Surrealist School'; the last a group naturally not at all sympathetic to the Euston Roaders, although in earlier days some had strayed in that direction; and were later to be interested again in abstraction.

Quite unexpectedly the Bolton public decided they liked the Surrealist collages much the best, when the pictures were taken round pubs and barbers' shops. They were at least far the most jolly.

Pasmore, comparatively recently, gave a very clear definition of the Group's objective, which is quoted here, in which he says that 'it was his [William Coldstream's] militant initiative which gave the School both its lead and its unique character'. Pasmore adds that he regards his own major contributions as *The Thames at Chiswick* and *The Studio of Ingres*, both attractive canvases even in reproduction.

Claude Rogers's picture *Young Women and Children in the Broad Walk, Regent's Park*, painted in 1938, composed of drawings and small oil-sketches made on the spot, and photographs taken by someone else, seems to possess psychic overtones, because one of the women in the foreground is Sonia Brownell (later wife of George Orwell), who was not yet working on *Horizon*, while Cyril Connolly, who was not yet living near Regent's Park, appears to be approaching through the trees.

The Euston Road School, 1986
Bruce Laughton, Soho Press. *Daily Telegraph*

CONTEMPORARY ART

Perhaps one should begin by describing the format and scope of this impressive volume. It is some 11 × 13.5 in., with nearly three hundred pages, all of which contain illustrations, many of the pictures being in colour. Eighty-one painters and sculptors are examined, almost all *avant-garde*, but straddling a gap of about forty years between the oldest and the youngest here considered. Mr Bryan Robertson, director of the Whitechapel Art Gallery, and Mr John Russell, art critic of the *Sunday Times*, provide descriptive paragraphs about the various personages mentioned in the book – which include some art historians, patrons and dealers – while Lord Snowdon has photographed the lot, a Herculean task.

At least a couple of pages are devoted to each of them, and, however well versed the reader may be in the current condition of painting and sculpture in this country, it is impossible not to feel, after going through the book, that it offers something new and unusual, something that stimulates even if it does not always satisfy in every respect. It is, of course, inevitable that a kind of vast illustrated catalogue-cum-Who's-Who of contemporary British art should do this, if only because one inevitably thinks some of the artists exceedingly 'good', a few of them pretty 'bad'.

In this respect, the editors obviously cannot pick and choose in the way the reader can. They cannot say that we have got to put in so-and-so because he has some sort of name, though personally we find his work totally unsympathetic. Accordingly, there is a slight air of everyone being equally talented, which is not only far from the case, but also draws attention to the comparative disparity of aim that is one of the attractions of the collection.

John Russell deals with this problem by adopting quite frankly the tone of an 'ad-man'. Perhaps the most wearing thing about 'ad-men' is that much of what they say is often true. When Russell assures us, over and over again, that we've never had it so good, it is no use trying to deny that there is a lot in what he says. Bryan Robertson, less obviously insistent, is in his own way almost equally determined in his salesmanship. In the end you feel that if you do not wholly agree with the one, you will fall into the hands of the other. It is simply a question of compounding for a canvas that will take up no more than one whole wall of the house, or a piece of sculpture that will just go through the front-door without the necessity of any actual structural alteration to get it in. Sometimes Russell and Robertson engage in dialogues; the former, roughly speaking, defending the individual patron; the latter tending to put forward the case for governmental assistance.

Meanwhile, Snowdon is photographing the lot, almost too ingeniously. In fact it is the liveliness of the photography that makes one wonder whether it is really a good thing for artists to be treated in this way at all, or, alternatively, whether the *avant-garde* have become the academicians of our day. To make a political parallel, the characteristic fashionable objection to Socialism in the nineteenth century was that it was revolutionary, something that would bring upheaval and confusion. The same characteristic objection in our own day is that Socialism is something that brings a too great standardization. If we turn to the arts in a similar manner, the nineteenth and early twentieth centuries regarded the Modern movement as 'Bolshevism' in the aesthetic sphere, yet has it not today become a sort of conformism as dangerous as any academic?

Turning the pages of *Private View*, which admittedly excludes (with not a few certainly 'modern' artists) all those in general associated with the Royal Academy, it is hard not to feel that something of the sort has happened. The very praise, however well deserved, has now developed a certain academic ring. We are told, for example:

> Graham Sutherland's obsessions . . . have one unifying characteristic: a total lack of sentimentality. The sardonic visage of Somerset Maugham, the puckish countenance of Lord Beaverbrook . . . all are rendered in the same wry, concrete spirit.

But surely it could be argued that to depict Mr Maugham as 'sardonic', Beaverbrook as 'puckish' is, in itself, 'sentimental'. There may be nothing against that, but the epithets immediately recall academic criticism of the past.

Having made this tentative criticism about Robertson's approach, one must add how much sympathy one feels with his detestation of the idea of attempting to turn an art school into a kind of university. What unutterable rubbish that people should try to thrust a lot of literature and philosophy down their students' throats while they are learning to draw or sculpt! Indeed, here we do not feel Robertson has gone nearly far enough. Why, for example, should artists need 'Panofsky or Sartre at certain phases of their lives'? I cannot in the least see why either writer should be a 'must' in the graphic arts.

Russell, also, does not seem free of some of this desire to impose literature on drawing and sculpture, but he does give a good definition of the three sorts of teacher an art school is likely to get, if lucky. These are: first, the man who is a painter of real stature; second, one so concentrated on his own development that students can derive something from him – I suppose by his sheer dominating egotism; three, the man who tries to keep himself out as an aesthetic influence, but has a real desire and ability to give help. Russell also makes the good point that Tonks was an appropriate teacher for Matthew Smith because Smith hated him so much. This is the crux of the matter. How is everyone to go on being revolutionary when revolution is now what everyone wants and encourages?

One feels of so much of the work reproduced here that it is all right, so far as it goes, but, *mutates mutandis*, most of it could have been included in the minor detail of almost any Old Master's canvases. It is often as if a tremendous lot of fuss is being made about one specimen of the *hors d'oeuvres*, or slice from the cheeseboard, while no effort is made to supply a complete meal – certainly not one of the nine-course ones of former times.

However, even if it is possible to carp and feel resistance to the suggestion that artists must from now on exist in a world of large-scale advertising, there is no denying that artists of the Paris School were not backward in promoting their own particular form of ballyhoo, with Picasso leading the pack. Perhaps that is going to happen here, though we cannot help suspecting that one of these days not so far off there will be a reaction in favour of relatively naturalistic drawing.

In this last connexion, Snowdon's methods are worth noting. Although perfectly aware of the photographic experiments of the last thirty or forty years, he is not, in fact, extravagantly 'experimental'. Possibly that is why his photography dominates the book. Could it be true that these photographs indicate the way that painting and sculpture may go, too?

Setting *Private View* at its lowest, it is a volume that will be of unfailing interest in ten, twenty, fifty, a hundred years' time. The mere record of these eighty-one names is a coming-out-in-the-open on the part of two professionals which cannot fail to be of future interest. Will our great-grandchildren turn over these pages with roars of laughter or with hushed respect?

Private View,
Bryan Robertson, John Russell
and Lord Snowdon, Nelson.

1964
Apollo

DAVID HOCKNEY

It is perhaps a bit severe to be biographised while you are still alive – in fact just turned fifty – but apart from that Peter Webb's book is well researched, clear and excellently illustrated, both as regards the subject's paintings and his career to date.

David Hockney (b. 1937) comes from a strict Methodist, teetotal, non-smoking, vegetarian, nuclear-disarmament, upper-working-class family (with a touch of alcoholism in the background) in Bradford. He was educated at Bradford Grammar School, an excellent establishment, which produced the painter William Rothenstein, the poet Humbert Wolfe and Sir Arthur Colefax, husband of the redoubtable hostess of that name, to mention only a few of its alumni.

Hockney's gifts as an artist appeared young, the collage of himself produced at the age of sixteen or seventeen – a risky alternative to a school essay – as amusing now as the day it was done. It is interesting that, while one thinks of Hockney particularly in connection with the happy juxtaposition of bright colours, his first 'serious' painting (his father) is a typification of Euston Roadish sobriety in tones.

Hockney himself says that at the age of twelve he came across George Herbert's lines (no doubt in the hymn 'Teach me, my God and King')

> A man may look on glass,
> On it may stay his eye;
> Or if he pleaseth, through it pass,
> And then the heaven espy.

Reflections in looking-glass and water have always fascinated him pictorially; the Lewis Carroll element probably not forgotten.

Hockney's intelligence, wit, facility, extrovert personality, passion for publicity and domicile in California ever threaten a descent into kitsch, even if this Sword of Damocles never quite comes down to slay. The safeguards are probably exceedingly hard work, and a common sense that caused Hockney to protest against some of the 'modernist' rubbish acquired by the Tate. In the same way he does not mind being called sentimental or illustrational, regarding those aspects as having a place in painting.

This is not to suggest that Hockney is in the least unresponsive to Modernism; indeed his devotion to Picasso (at least in the most recent of Hockney's work shown here) might seem an old love perhaps now better consigned to fragrant memory. Again, it must be added that Hockney's naturalistic period invoked Piero della Francesca, sometimes with a touch of Fra Angelico, in contemporary setting, rather than any modernist.

So far as portraits are concerned Hockney likes to paint (more often draw) persons he knows, always resisting commissions to portray celebrities, though he has executed a few of these. He has also illustrated Grimms' *Fairy Tales* (1969) and the poems (translated from their modern Greek) of Cavafy (1966).

These has been a good deal of the theatrical décor (Stravinsky's *The Rake's Progress*, *The Magic Flute*, etc.) at which Hockney appears to be adept, all this followed by a photographic period during which he attempted a kind of Cubism in photography, examples of which are given here. Diametrically different opinions of this experiment are held by those concerned with photographic art.

Turning to the life, one cannot help being reminded of the concluding two lines of the clerihew (composed, I rather think, by Aleister Crowley) about the cinquecento Italian painter Giovanni Antonio Bazzi:

> They called him Sodoma,
> Which was not a misnomer.

Hockney's homosexuality is a very much emphasised aspect of his work as an artist, both in general subjects and in portraits of young men with whom he has been involved.

Mr Webb says, no doubt with truth, that Hockney is not on the whole promiscuous, indeed in certain respects more of a voyeur than an active participant. Even so, it is not always easy to identify all these young men as individuals as they flit through the pages, and they have a certain resemblance to each other even in the drawings.

One of the oddest episodes recounted in this biography is the film made of Hockney over an extended period, some of it real life, some of it fiction, which recounted the breakdown of a love affair. Hockney is described as being very upset by the result. The threat to hurt feelings might be thought nothing to the danger posed to the subject's personal identity by exposing it in this stylised manner.

Mr Webb draws attention to Hockney's taste for drawing his male models bottom-upwards, comparing this with Boucher's well-known picture of the young lady, briefly Louis XV's mistress, called 'Mademoiselle O'Murphy'. The picture is reproduced here. She is certainly often given this apparently Irish surname, but in his *Memoirs* Casanova (who does not claim to have seduced her) relates a circumstantial account of her being Flemish, called Morphi, O-Morphi being added by himself as a Greek pun.

Portrait of David Hockney, 1988
Peter Webb, Chatto. *Daily Telegraph*

KITSCH

The origins of the word 'kitsch' are obscure. My own impressions of first hearing the term suggest that what most people then stigmatised as 'chi-chi' was called 'kitsch' by those few familiar with Isherwood's Berlin. The epithet would be applied, for example, to decoration of a flat in which there seemed too many domes of Victorian wax-fruit, or pictures constructed out of beads and matchboxes.

After studying this book, I see that that was too narrow a definition, indeed hardly a correct one. Kitsch implies a pretentious vulgarity equally applicable to writing and music, even politics and religion.

On the other hand, to take in all 'bad taste', as one way and another do the contributors to *Kitsch*, is not only to devalue a useful label, but also to get extremely muddled in passing aesthetic judgements. In fact many of the essays here – some of which go back as far as 1933 – are pompous and confused in thought, themselves perfect examples of intellectual kitsch in action. Much more is to be learnt from the illustrations, which have often a gruesomeness all their own.

If, as the authors imply, almost all advertising is to be included as kitsch, and if tourism, for the very fact of what it is, comes in for wholesale condemnation, it is hard to know where kitsch is going to stop. It might certainly be postulated that the whole modern world is kitsch, but in that case another word must be devised for the more outrageous forms of it. In spite of what is alleged here about kitsch being a 'modern' invention, one would have thought the classical world – Pompeii, for example – full of kitsch, and Ancient Egypt, too.

I cannot for the life of me see why people should not buy alabaster models of the Leaning Tower of Pisa, even a beer mug shaped like Bismarck's head, if they so desire. Indeed such acquisitions suggest a certain simplicity of heart. On the other hand the chess set 'From as low as $5.95! Meticulously fashioned after the classic sculpture of Rome', or the photograph of Mr Salvador Dalí expressing 'the themes of death and love', come well within more reasonable terms of kitsch reference.

If we stick to moral and intellectual vulgarity, forgetting for the moment about garden gnomes and *Mona Lisa*s on packets of cheese, some interesting points emerge. A whole essay is devoted to religious, more specifically Christian, kitsch, though here again one would look to the papers and television, especially from time to time the latter, for really splendid examples, rather than the naivety of Sacred Hearts and Pope John XXIII framed in seashells.

Politics is naturally a rich field, particularly Fascism and National Socialism. Here again a plea must be put in for moderation in what is included. Obviously Hitler, on a picture postcard, as a knight in armour is an admirable example. On the other hand, Hitler making himself agreeable to a little girl is doing no more than any politician would do – the traditional MP kissing the traditional baby, hardly worthy to be included as kitsch.

A remarkable omission is the inexhaustible mine offered by Communism. There is one illustration, it is true, of a high-relief sculpture in an unnamed Russian museum, and Moscow University is mentioned as a good example of architectural kitsch, but, compared with the very similar Fascist field, an opportunity has been missed.

For example, at Odessa stands a statue, erected in memory of the mutineers of the battleship *Potemkin*. The sculptor's Rodinesque technique certainly suggests that it depicts the famous incident in Eisenstein's film of the same name, when the sailors are executed standing behind the tarpaulin. Apart from the obviously kitsch nature of the sculptural treatment, the fact that the incident – as Eisenstein himself states in his *Memoirs* – was entirely imaginary, surely makes this group enormously eligible for inclusion? Indispensable, too, one would have thought, Che Guevara in his beret.

A touch of eroticism is not out of place in kitsch, and the authors assign a section to pornokitsch, as opposed to run-of-the-mill pornography. The film – photography generally – is a fruitful medium, but it is rightly pointed out in one of the essays that Stroheim – whose films might be taxed with being kitsch because of certain erotic and sadistic elements – in fact rose above any such imputation by the irony and power of his directing.

Some unexpected views are expressed by several contributors, for instance that 'The inhabitant of any of the world's large cities – London, Tokyo, Paris, New York – is more likely to find himself "at home" in any one of them, than in the rural parts of his own country', or that 'Napoleon was a man of exquisite taste'. Most of the essays are translated from other languages. Some gems occur. What on earth did Pascal actually say when he is quoted as commenting: 'Naturally every man thinks he is a slater or whatever', and 'Pascal . . . speaks far more rarely of slaters and soldiers'?

Kitsch: An Anthology of Bad Taste, Gilo Dorfles and Others, Studio Vista. — 1970, *Daily Telegraph*

GERALD REITLINGER

During the war I was sent on an army course at Cambridge. While there, I was sought out by Andrew Gow, a don at Trinity College. He entertained me in his rooms, we went on walks together. I had first encountered him as an assistant master at Eton, where he taught me Greek. He had not struck me as particularly inspiring, but then, for a distinguished Greek scholar, I don't expect teaching schoolboys was an inspiring occupation.

Now, in Cambridge, I discovered a different aspect of his character. He showed me his collection of drawings. He, too, liked Degas. I had never dreamed Gow had these interests. He was also a connoisseur of wine. When checking the obituary of another Eton master, C. M. Wells, he found it ended with the words: 'He was an authority on Claret, Burgundy and Port.' Gow drew a line through the word 'Burgundy'. Both drawings and knowledge of wine were assembled on the stipend of an academic. Gow was, in the best sense, an amateur.

In the eighteenth century, the word 'connoisseur' undoubtedly carried with it a feeling of the cultivated amateur; even today that is perhaps one's first thought. Closer examination overturns this estimate. Bernard Berenson, for example, wrote in his diary in old age:

> . . . so my appetite now is ever so much more for Antique sculpture than for any other phase of European art. Except for the greatest and most rustic, homely painters – wild asparagus – I care less and less for the 'Old Masters'. I really prefer the French of the so-called impressionistic period, or even from David to the death of Degas. Minor Trecento painters, merely artisans, bore me, unless indeed I take them as handicraft. I still keep asking how much of Italian paintings would affect me if I were not interested in attributing and dating them. Little, I fear.

Berenson was certainly a connoisseur, but his is the voice of the professional – a man who has earned a living (not too bad a one) from pictures, even if love of pictures was the initial emotion. The diary illustrates how this led to more worldly considerations.

Both Gow and Berenson lived into their nineties. Is there some preservative in connoisseurship? What are its roots? Perhaps there is a element of compulsion, taste that must be expressed to the point of obsession. Then, certainly, there is the thought of making money in an agreeable way, while at the same time exercising an aesthetic gift. Some degree of breakdown in ordinary human relations could also have something to do with it.

If the last might be regarded as at all applicable as a classification, I would tentatively put forward my friend the late Gerald Reitlinger, a far more farouche figure than Gow or Berenson. One of his characteristics, which puts him into a definite category of connoisseur, is that his connoisseurship was scarcely at all recognised in his lifetime.

He was born in 1900 and named Gerald Roberts Reitlinger, the South African war still in progress, Field Marshal Lord Roberts the hero of the hour. Perhaps the middle name dowered Reitlinger with a certain affection for objects of the Victorian age, though that was chiefly manifested in his house by immensely elaborate Second Empire furniture. He was, however, a great frequenter of sale-rooms.

If people have heard of Reitlinger at all, they probably know him from some dozen books he wrote, notably *The Final Solution* (1953), an account of the Hitlerian extermination of the Jews, or several volumes called *The Economics of Taste* (1961–70), an amusing (if at times less than pedantically accurate) observation of the ups and downs of the art market.

He was also a professional painter. (His pictures were shown earlier this year at the Bowmoore Gallery, London.) His friends were never very enthusiastic about his painting, but had to admit that a canvas of his was accepted by the Biennale one year, where, they had also to agree, it was bought by an unknown Continental patron.

This unwillingness to allow him much talent was perhaps to some extent due to his being decidedly richer than the world in which he normally moved. It would also be true to say that Reitlinger did not get on with people easily. He was extraordinarily contradictory, while at the same time having a considerable exotic knowledge of an erratic kind. He also quite often got hold of the wrong end of the stick. I remember someone once saying that he would have been easier to accommodate as a friend if it had been possible to introduce him as 'Baron' or even 'Doctor'. In person he was a tall, shambling figure, untidy almost to the point of grubbiness, with thick spectacles, a habit of shaking his head slowly from side to side like a metronome when pondering any matter.

When I first met Gerald Reitlinger, in 1927 or '28, he shared a large house in South Kensington with his brother (also a collector), who was a good deal older. There was in the house already a number of Oriental pots. Reitlinger moved soon after this to a spacious studio of his own in Glebe Place, Chelsea. He was known, however, chiefly for his houses in the country where – although his reputation was not one of unrestrained generosity – he did a lot of entertaining.

The first of these residences was an attractive cottage, Thornsdale, on the edge of the Romney Marsh, romantic and isolated. He then moved to Woodgate House, a characteristic redbrick Sussex farmhouse of indefinite date on to which a Regency or early Victorian stucco façade had been added. Along the entablature of this, Reitlinger set a row of urns. It was the ownership of Woodgate which earned him among his friends the sobriquet of The Squire.

The discomfort of Reitlinger's houses became legendary. The food was always indifferent, and he was expert in the discovery of undrinkable vintages. Having said that, I must also emphasise that most of the friends who stayed with him had a great deal of casual fun of one kind and another.

I have made no attempt to gloss over Reitlinger's farouche side in order to show that he fits in with the potential category of connoisseurship as a kind of escape from human relations. We will now glance at the interior of the house.

On the right-hand side of the front door was the drawing room. The pictures were changed from time to time, sold or swapped with those in the London studio, but so far as I can remember they included a very dark Sickert (the lightest colour was brown), an Eve Kirk (some town in the south of France, Cassis or Villefranche perhaps), a John Frederick Lewis (of the kind one associates with Sir Brinsley Ford's great-grandmother's portraits by that artist), perhaps couple of naked ladies.

There were also, varying their location, two much odder pictures. One was a supposed Cranach of Luther and Melancthon, heads and shoulders of the two reformers. The other, also oblong in shape, painted almost in the manner of an inn sign, showed two groups of figures. That on the left was an eighteenth-century couple (slightly like a debased version of Gainsborough's *Mr and Mrs Andrews*) contemplating a much older couple hobbling off towards the right, wearing the clothes the eighteenth century imagined the seventeenth century had worn. Beneath ran the stanza:

> My Father and my Mother, who go stooping to your grave,
> Pray tell me in this world what good may I expect to have?
> My Son, the good you may expect is all forlorn,
> Men do not gather grapes from off a thorn.

This pessimistic view of life was greatly to Reitlinger's taste, and the last line of the verse became a catch-phrase among his friends.

One the left of the front door was a really excellent art library. In the visitor's chief bedroom upstairs hung a flower piece, a mixed bunch in a china pot by Christopher Wood; a bedroom interior by Paul Nash; a drawing or watercolour by Bernard Meninsky. There was no looking-glass over the washbasin, so that Constant Lambert, a fairly frequent guest, used to complain that one had to shave in the reflection of the Meninsky.

Also on the first floor was a room with a Russian billiard table surrounded by shelves behind glass which screened the Oriental vessels – these always steadily increasing in number. Once when my wife and I were staying at Woodgate, a fellow guest was Leigh Ashton, then director of the Victoria & Albert Museum. He was shown the Oriental pots. 'The pots are all right,' he said. 'Very nice. But some bloody fool has put modern varnish all over them.' The culprit had, of course, been Reitlinger himself. My impression is that he said nothing at the time. On one's later visits, however, he always had an Oriental pot under his arm from which he was scraping varnish. My wife named this process 'desharding'.

Reitlinger's gallows-humour, indicated by the words of the couple stooping to their grave, included, just before the war, playing on his gramophone a record of the 'Horst Wessel Lied', the Nazi rally song. This opens with a burst of hoarse commands for dipping the standards in salute. Reitlinger (who had fluent German) would join in.

Gerald Reitlinger's end was in its way typical and tragic. On a winter evening in 1978, the chimney of his sitting room at Woodgate – which I take to be the former drawing room – caught fire. I do not doubt that, like all his domestic administration, the chimney had not been swept for decades. Somehow the conflagation was extinguished, as it turned out only momentarily. With the obstinacy that only those who knew him will appreciate, Reitlinger lit the fire again. During the night the house was more or less burnt down.

Reitlinger thought that his lifework, the collection of Oriental ceramics, had been destroyed. He was approaching eighty, and died of shock a short time later. He was mistaken. Only a few of the less valuable Japanese items were lost. The collection had been willed to the Ashmolean Museum, Oxford, which had its representatives soon on the spot to do the work of rescue.

David Piper, the museum's then director, told me Reitlinger's was one of the finest collections of its kind ever brought together – at a rough estimate worth nearer two million than one. That was a dozen years ago. It was Gerald Reitlinger's last macabre joke. He is remembered as one of the Ashmolean's greatest benefactors. He should not be forgotten as a man.

1990
Sotheby's Magazine Preview

PART THREE

A Reference for Mellors

A REFERENCE FOR MELLORS

A long, low house in brown stone. Wragby Hall looked much as one had been led to expect. It was set among trees from which the rain still dripped forlornly on to tangled undergrowth. The oaks stood silent and tired, like old, worn-out seekers after pleasure, unable to keep up in this grimy, mechanised world of ours. The weather was sultry, and from where Tevershall pit-bank was burning, a scent of coal-dust and sulphur charged the atmosphere; while lowering macintosh-coloured clouds gave warning that another heavy downpour might at any moment take place. Away beyond the park at the far end of the drive a hooter gave three short blasts, and there came the noise of shunting trucks, the whistle of colliery locomotives, and the voices of men, bitter and discontented; loud, rasping voices raised in conflict. Ashes had been thrown down in front of the entrance to the house to fill the cavities of the gravel in which pools of brackish water had accumulated. He rang an iron bell and waited, trying to remove from one eye a small piece of grit, blown downwind from the furnaces. After some minutes the door was opened by a good-looking, middle-aged woman, dressed in black.

'Lady Chatterley?'

She smiled slowly, sphinxlike.

'Her Ladyship is expecting you.'

She took the hat and overcoat.

'Her Ladyship is in her own sitting-room. She said I was to show you straight up.'

Some concealed implication of enquiry seemed to rest in those rather defiant grey eyes. No doubt it was a little uncommon for a guest to be given access to that intimate, inviolate apartment; or some hint such as this was at least conveyed by her look, a questioning of the favoured stranger's credentials, it might be. Turning on her heel, she led the way up the main staircase, and along a passage hung with stark oil paintings and then up more stairs. On one of the landings, the door of a lumber-room was ajar and behind a pile of hat-boxes, suitcases, vestry chests, rosewood cradles, and engravings from Landseer's works, was the glimpse of a contraption which seemed at first sight an unusual form of mowing-machine, but declared itself almost immediately as Sir Clifford

Chatterley's wheelchair. It was rusty and covered with dust; and piled high with riding-boots and old golf clubs. Clearly it had lain unused for years.

'Sir Clifford won't be back for some weeks?'

'He's in London, sir. He often has to go there now on business.'

'He has become an important figure in coal.'

'He has indeed, sir.'

'I suppose he is – perfectly all right now.'

'Oh yes, sir. Absolutely.'

She laughed quietly to herself as if this was a rather foolish question to have asked, and she knew the answer all right. She was a thickset, healthy-looking woman, speaking with a broad Derbyshire burr, with keen eyes and a strong supple body, like a tigress, moving through some dark, thick undergrowth.

'Oh yes. Sir Clifford is absolutely all right now.'

She gave another of those secretive, excludatory laughs as she opened a door on the third floor and showed him into a small room decorated in pink and yellow distemper, upon the walls of which hung huge German reproductions of paintings by Renoir and Cézanne. He had the impression of entering a bright, up-to-date schoolroom where lessons are enjoyed.

Constance Chatterley was standing by the window, looking down on to the park. She turned slowly, and held out her hand with a movement that carried with it a challenge of hidden energies; fair, blue-eyed, with some occasional freckles. A faint fragrance of Coty's Woodviolet was wafted across the room.

'So you found your way here in spite of the rain.'

The other woman paused at the door.

'Will you have tea here or in the drawing-room, m'Lady?'

'In the drawing-room, Mrs Bolton.'

'At five o'clock or earlier, m'Lady?'

'I will ring when we are ready for it.'

'Very good, m'Lady.'

Lingering, almost rebelling, Mrs Bolton left the room hesitantly, as if unwilling to submit to this assertion of a subtler will than her own. Lady Chatterley was certainly handsome. Not in a too demure or dull way. On the contrary she had put on plenty of lipstick, and her clothes looked almost over-smart for the country. At the same time she gave an impression of a person at ease with herself and her surroundings, a person not easily embarrassed. This was a relief because it might be necessary to make enquiries that would sound – in the ordinary way – inquisitive. She held out a box of gold-tipped cigarettes.

'Do sit down,' she said. 'You wanted to see me about a reference?'

Best to go straight to the point. There was nothing to be gained by beating about the bush; especially with someone so unaffected.

'A friend of mine is looking for a suitable man for a post in one of the national game-preserves of the Dominions. He has had an applicant who seems to be the right type and who gave your name as a reference. Hearing that I was staying with neighbours of yours, my friend suggested that you wouldn't mind if I came over, and had a talk about this man.'

'But of course.'

'There were certain points my friend wanted to make sure about before he engages anyone. It is quite an important position, you know, and – coming under the Government – you will appreciate that one has to make the fullest enquiries. The man is a former employee of your husband's I understand. Mellors. I take it he gave your name as he knew Sir Clifford was away from home.'

For a moment she frowned, as if at a loss.

'Mellors?'

'Mellors,' I said. 'Oliver Mellors. A gamekeeper.'

'Mellors? It was Parkin. Wasn't it Parkin? Or was it Mellors? I dimly recall the name Parkin, and yet Mellors is familiar, too. Anyway, I remember the man you mean, I'm sure. I am so glad he is in the way of getting a good job. He never seemed somehow very happy here. But such a nice man.'

'My friend says he appears to be an excellent type. I believe he had a commission in India during the war.'

'Yes, a quartermaster, I think, or do they call it the Army Service Corps? Clifford told me, but I forget. Clifford says he always laughs when he thinks of Mellors handing out stores. You'd have had to have been a real old soldier to have got by Mellors, Clifford always says.'

'That sounds promising. He will be able to deal with the clerical side.'

'Oh yes, Mellors started in an office – but I think he liked to remember his army days. He always saluted if one came across him in the grounds.'

'I suppose he has the usual formal requirements – honest, sober, hard-working, an early riser – I mean he won't be too much of an old soldier?'

'Honest to a fault. An absolutely reliable man. Sober too – and didn't at all mind getting up early. I believe as a matter of fact he had rather a weak head.'

She pouted archly.

'Was there some trouble? Tipsy at the tenants' dance or something of the sort.'

'Really I have only the vaguest reason for saying he had a weak head. Perhaps I shouldn't have mentioned it. Only after he left us, my father happened to run into Mellors in the street in London. They had seen a good deal of each other because Papa has a passion for the rough shooting around here.'

'Your father is Sir Malcolm Reid, RA, of course.'

'Like most artists he is a bit of an eccentric. He took Mellors to a sort of Bohemian club he belongs to in Soho and gave him lunch. Papa always likes to do himself well – and he said that by the end of the meal poor Mellors got rather red in the face and kept on telling the same story over and over again about how when he was in the army in India he would have been a captain if it hadn't been for the dark gods.'

'I suppose the Indians had been getting on his nerves.'

'Visits to temples or something, I expect. Perhaps he had seen queer oriental carvings – I myself have been shown some that might easily upset a highly strung person. Anyway it was all rather a shame to my mind – but Papa is quite shameless where it's a question of having too many liqueurs after luncheon.'

'This was obviously a most exceptional occasion. But he is a hard worker – Mellors?'

'As far as he goes, he is a very hard worker. Of course, you realise that he is not a strong man. I remember in the days when my husband used a wheelchair, the engine that drove the chair went wrong. Mellors tried to push it as if it were a Bath chair, and got quite breathless, poor fellow. That breathlessness was really why Clifford's father had arranged for him to have the job in the first place.'

'So he dates back to your father-in-law's time?'

'Oh, he was quite an old retainer.'

'And knew his job well?'

'There was not a great deal to do, you see, as we couldn't afford big parties – just an occasional old friend like Mr Michaelis, the novelist, for a night or two. In fact Clifford always said it was a terrible piece of extravagance employing a gamekeeper at all these days, but he went on because he thought it would give Mellors time to himself for reading and so on.'

'Why reading?'

'Mellors was quite a highbrow in his way. He was a scholarship boy at Sheffield Grammar School and always had the air of having come down in the world a bit. We wanted to do anything we could for him.'

'His father was a local blacksmith, wasn't he?'

'Oh, surely not! A schoolmaster, I think. On second thoughts, I believe he did shoe horses for a time – to demonstrate the dignity of manual labour. Mellors had a lot of those rather William Morris-y ideas too, you know.'

'But I understand that he described himself as of "mining stock"?'

'His grandfather – or possibly his great-grandfather – had something to do with the mine – surface work of some sort. It's quite true. Mellors was very proud of being "mining stock" – all the more because he himself was a bit of a highbrow. In fact I believe he even had something published in the *New Statesman* once – a little piece of verse, or his impressions, or something of the sort.'

'I had no idea . . .'

'He had quite a small library of books in the cottage he lived in here – we might have gone to see it if it hadn't begun to rain so hard, it's rather snug. There were books about the causes of earthquakes, and electrons, and curious Indian customs – the "dark gods", perhaps – and Karl Marx, Freud, every sort of thing.'

'He sounds an out-of-the-way fellow.'

'Oh, Mellors was a real character. And then he loved dressing up. That was why he always wore a sort of green velveteen uniform and gaiters. Clifford made rather a fuss about the expense of getting it for him, but in the end he gave in, and Mellors got his way – as he usually did in things he had set his heart on.'

'He must have looked quite picturesque.'

'He did say to me once that he thought men ought to wear close red trousers and little short white jackets – but really we had to draw the line there. Unfortunately, the Chatterley livery is a rather sombre affair of black and drab so there was nothing much to be done for him in that direction. However, I think he was fairly happy with his green velveteens.'

There was a pause. Lady Chatterley looked out again towards the park, as if trying to recall more information about Mellors that might be of assistance to his new employers. Now the rain was coming down in sheets, thudding like artillery against the window panes.

'There was another . . . rather delicate question.'

'Yes?'

'A considerable female staff is employed on certain clerical and other duties connected with the scientific observation of the habits of the animals within the preserve in question. Mellors, I am sure, could be trusted not . . . not to make a fool of himself . . . Only there was a rumour about some sort of a scandal in connection with his wife – that is only why I ask. No doubt gossip and much exaggerated.'

'I am sure it was. That was certainly our impression here. I should say he was entirely trustworthy – unless some quite unusual circumstances were to arise.'

'Excellent.'

'In fact your question would make our housekeeper, Mrs Bolton – who let you in – laugh a great deal.'

'She had a poor opinion of Mellors?'

'I'm afraid she used to laugh about him sometimes.'

'Then we need to go no further into the matter of his wife?'

'I don't think the trouble about Mrs Mellors was to be taken too seriously – although, of course, there was a certain amount of talk in the village at the time. The Mellorses had all sorts of what were then thought to be rather "advanced" ideas. For example, he always used to refer to her by her maiden name as "Bertha Coutts".'

'No relation to the banking family?'

'If so, very distant. There were endless – and I believe rather unnecessarily public – discussions as to whether or not, for example, it was better for husband and wife to have separate rooms, whether companionate marriage was a prudent preliminary; how large families should be; and if it was desirable for a married couple to spend a certain time apart from one another in the course of the year.'

'She was rather a highbrow, too?'

'She had lived in Birmingham. I think moved in circles on the outskirts of the Repertory Theatre.'

'One can understand that all this was not wholly appreciated in the neighbourhood.'

'It was during one of Mellors's temporary separations from his wife that he returned to his situation with us.'

'You say "temporary" – did he go back to his wife, then?'

'In the end they decided in favour of a divorce – but without any hard feelings on either side.'

'Were there any children?'

'A little girl. Mrs Mellors held rather decided views as to how her daughter should be brought up, and was very anxious that no early harm should be done by frustration. I understand there were signs of – well – a bit of a father fixation. Besides Mrs Mellors was conscientiously opposed to blood sports, which created difficulties vis-à-vis her husband's profession.'

'There would be no question of Mrs Mellors wanting to accompany him if he took up this post?'

'On the contrary. During their periods apart Mrs Mellors found herself increasingly influenced by the personality of one of the colliers at Stack's Gate – a prominent figure in local Chapel circles. They used to discuss social and economic questions with others in the village interested in such matters. In the end they married.'

'So Mellors is entirely without encumbrances.'

'It is a long time since I have seen him – but this talk of ours has made me remember a lot of things about him. When he finally parted company with his wife there was some vague question of his getting married again – to someone younger than himself and in rather a different walk of life.'

'Indeed.'

'It would not, I think, have been particularly suitable!'

'A local girl?'

'I believe . . . It was after he left us. They used to meet in London.'

'Did anything come of it?'

'Very sensibly, the understanding was broken off by mutual consent.'

'No doubt all for the best.'

'After that, Mellors let it be known that he very definitely intended to remain single. He was quite happy, he used to say, with his wild flowers and his animals – and the wonderful imitations he used to give – when he had an audience – of the local dialect, in the origins of which he was keenly interested.'

'Why did he actually leave your service, finally?'

Lady Chatterley considered for a moment.

'Temperament,' she said at last. 'It was a question of temperament. And, after all, most of us want a change at times. I suppose Mellors was like the rest of the world and enjoyed a little variety at intervals. He used to say, "There are black days coming for all of us and for everybody." In some ways he was a very moody man. An unusually moody man.'

There was another pause.

'I am really most grateful to you. I think you have told me quite enough to assure me that he would fill the vacancy admirably – that is, if his health holds up.'

'That is the question,' she said very quietly. 'If his health holds up.'

She swung her feet on to the sofa, and lay back, stretching towards an ashtray to extinguish the stub of her cigarette. One of her suede slippers fell to the ground. She did not bother to recapture it. Outside the rain had ceased and a dull sun showed through the heavy cloudbanks. Below the window the hazelbrake was misted with green, and under it the dark counterpane of dog's mercury edged the velvet of the sward. Still the breeze bore on its wings the scent of tar, and all the time came the thud, thud, thud of industrial afternoon in the Midlands; while the gentle perfume of Coty's Woodviolet was more than ever apparent above the insistent incense of the undying furnaces.

INDEX